CW00507442

IN THE BEGINNING
- the Manchester origins of Rolls-Royce

Michael H Evans

HISTORICAL SERIES No 4

Originally published in 1984 by the
Rolls-Royce Heritage Trust
PO Box 31, Derby, England DE24 8BJ

Extensively rewritten second edition 2004
© 2004 Michael H Evans

ISBN : 1 872922 27 9

The Historical Series is published as a joint initiative by the
Rolls-Royce Heritage Trust and the Rolls-Royce Enthusiasts' Club.

Cover picture:
The illustration on the cover is taken from an oil painting by Ray Tootall, GAvA, entitled *An Historic Meeting*. The original was created specially for an art exhibition in Derby in 1983 which marked the 75th anniversary of the move of Rolls-Royce from Manchester to Derby. The exhibition was inspired by Peter Ward and mounted jointly by the Guild of Aviation Artists and the Derby Branch of the Rolls-Royce Heritage Trust: following the exhibition in Derby City Art Gallery the latter acquired the painting.

The painting depicts the meeting of Rolls and Royce on 4 May 1904 in the Carriage Court of the Midland Hotel in Manchester. Performing the introduction is Henry Edmunds; the car is one of the prototype Royce two-cylinders. The Carriage Court remains and is now the main pedestrian entrance to the hotel, but its original purpose is still revealed by shadows on its two archways of the words 'in' and 'out'. The author worked with the artist to try to get the Royce car right in every detail but feels a sense of guilt in that he failed to recognise that the car present on the day must have been the second Royce, as the first had not yet returned from the Sideslip Trials by the date of the meeting: it did so three days later.

As originally painted, the car was the first Royce – dark green and bearing the registration number N-MR-6. The artist has kindly changed his work to reflect the fact that the car shown was the second Royce. It had almost identical coachwork but in crimson rather than dark green and it had borrowed the number originally used on the first: N-414.

A final error would seem to be that Edmunds ensured that Rolls and Royce took lunch before they got absorbed by the detail of the car – so they had already met.

Printed in 2004 by **océ** Printing for Professionals.

Océ Document Services, Bristol.

CONTENTS

FOREWORD

Alec Harvey-Bailey's foreword to the first book by Michael Evans on the early days of the Company noted the painstaking research and detailed cross-checking which had gone into the work. This is even more apparent in this new book, where Mike has discovered many new sources and facts, not the least of which is that the first factory was not at Cooke Street as we had previously believed.

Mike presents a very detailed study of the early days of Rolls-Royce from the viewpoint of the founders, the work people, the products and the developing structure of the Company.

His attention to detail is quite extraordinary even to the early lime wood block road construction used in London. I can confirm that these blocks were still in use in 1953 when I experienced the dreaded 'sideslip' and parted company with my motorcycle, incidentally almost in front of the Rolls family home in Knightsbridge, though I didn't know that at the time.

The profound contribution that Michael Evans has made to preserving the heritage and recording the history of this great company is further enhanced by this book.

Sir Ralph Robins
Rolls-Royce plc

February 2004

AUTHOR'S PREFACE

When the Rolls-Royce Heritage Trust was launched through the pages of *Rolls-Royce News* in the autumn of 1981 it had only one achievement to its credit. That was the small exhibition mounted in the Marble Hall at Nightingale Road in Derby in March of that year to mark the Company's seventy-fifth anniversary. More needed to be done – and quickly – to attempt to establish benchmarks of professionalism which placed the Trust alongside local branches of the Royal Aeronautical Society and The Institution of Mechanical Engineers. A lecture programme was an obvious ingredient, but it was important that the series be of a high standard. Alec Harvey-Bailey volunteered his services, supported as he was in everything in life by his wife, Joan. The question, though, was what would be suitable subjects.

It took little discussion to agree that many years had passed since Harold Nockolds' *Magic of a Name* had been readily available. A broad background lecture covering motor cars and aero engines would, therefore, serve a real purpose in educating employees new to the heritage interest. Alec and Joan pitched into this and produced a stunning lecture entitled *Rolls-Royce – the formative years, 1906 to 1939*. The book followed: the Trust had decided to publish a series of historical volumes to bring its researches within reach of the wider public. David Birch and Peter Kirk came up with a formula and Peter saw volume one, *the formative years*, through to fruition. It was a worthy beginning.

Beyond that, Alec chose as a second lecture a subject very dear to him: the Merlin. Those in the know on Rolls-Royce achievements – Bill Morton among them – always rated two of extreme importance, yet immense difficulty in the telling. The first was the saga of the 40/50 hp Silver Ghost and the latter the Merlin engine. As Alec said, it transformed Rolls-Royce from its interwar status of a brilliant sprat in the ocean of technology into a world contender in aeropropulsion.

Alec had been in charge of defect investigation on the Merlin in the war and retained not only vivid memories of the time but an incredible memory of Mark numbers, incidents and mods. He had begun to set all this down by recording it on tape years earlier while he was Managing Director of the Arab British Engine Company in Egypt. The tapes were sent to me and became part of the secretarial workload of my Manufacturing HQ Personnel & Industrial Relations department. So, much material was to hand. The great genius Alec brought to his lecture was in making the Merlin family and its marks and mods understandable to those who had not lived with the engine through its lifetime. Alec's first book is now out of print. It has been superseded by Peter Pugh's three masterful volume *Magic of a Name*. His second volume, however, *The Merlin in perspective – the combat years*, has been the worldwide Trust bestseller, already having appeared in four editions and several reprints.

The lecture programme was further extended when my offer to speak on the origins of Rolls-Royce was taken up. This had been a special interest to me for over twenty years by then, and it soon became clear that the information I had pulled together was more than enough for a single talk. I set myself the task, therefore, of delivering two: the first became this volume, covering Henry Royce, his upbringing, early experiences, and the growth of his business in Manchester from 1884 until the slump after the turn of the century which saw him turn to cars. It covers the first Royce cars, the meeting with the Hon Charles Rolls and the launch of the Rolls-Royce motorcar range. The second, yet to appear in book form, was entitled *The formation of Rolls-Royce Limited – and the move to Derby*. It covered C S Rolls & Company established in 1902 and something more on the successes of the early Rolls-Royce cars in events such as the 1905 and 1906 Tourist Trophy races. In particular, it showed how Rolls-Royce Limited came to be registered in March 1906, how C S Rolls & Co was later absorbed into it and how the first share flotation in December 1906 almost resulted in a premature end to Rolls-Royce. It told of the search for a new home and the choice of Derby and of the saga of the move. Lastly, it covered the launch of the 40/50 hp Silver Ghost, which consolidated the reputation of the Rolls-Royce as *"the best car in the world"* by the time the Company was little more than a year old.

When I originally began to seek information on the Cooke Street factory in Hulme I had no intention of writing a book. I had been inspired, as had many others, to take an interest in the history of Rolls-Royce by my tutor when a graduate apprentice with Rolls-Royce in Derby – C W 'Bill' Morton. When I joined the Company in 1959 Bill was writing his book, *A History of Rolls-Royce Motor Cars 1903-1907*, as well as restoring the one remaining three-cylinder 15 hp Rolls-Royce. Bill concentrated very much on the early cars in his book and never attempted to understand the Cooke Street factory. He introduced me to the dwindling band of old Cooke Street employees – Ben Pope, George Clegg, Tom Broome, 'Little' Jimmy Chadwick, Ernie Wooler and Tommy Nadin – and curiosity led me to ask them independently what they remembered of Cooke Street. They drew plans and annotated them with details of activities, people and machinery. In the main, these aligned well with each other, but the complexity of the Cooke Street premises left many uncertainties and inconsistencies. Small additional snippets could be drawn from things A G Elliott recalled being told, years later, by Henry Royce and more from what he had told Maurice Olley, with whom I corresponded.

A first real breakthrough came some twenty years later when Derek Gration, then Insurance Manager of Rolls-Royce Limited, discovered in his files the old insurance folders and correspondence on Cooke Street. The folders contained contemporary plans of the factory and correspondence relating to the testing of petrol engines in the open stable yard in Blake Street. Until then we had not known where the engines were tested. Then A G 'Tom' Bowling, Rolls-Royce Director of Product Assurance, found in his inherited desk a photograph of the first engine on test. It was on the basis of this information that the book was published in 1984. Bill Morton was gracious in his commenting that he had not thought it possible to understand Cooke Street: he said I had made sense of a "*rabbit warren*".

Twenty years on, it is time to launch this second edition to honour the centenary of the meeting of Rolls and Royce. What amazes me is just how far off the mark I was over certain aspects of the early days in Hulme, how we now seem to have the answer to the way in which Royce's early products were marketed, how much more we now know about the background to the meeting and how complex the histories of the Royce prototype cars really was. Three tenacious and gifted researchers have made the difference, and I refer to them in 'Acknowledgements'. My narrative has, as a result of their generosity, come a whole lot better focused to recording fact. My purpose has not been to create the definitive work on the period but on the factory, and to be a source of reference on the other works which these three fellow-researchers in particular have produced and which, collectively, allow us to understand the events of a hundred and more years ago with surprising clarity.

Michael H Evans
January 2004

ACKNOWLEDGEMENTS

In my preface I have already acknowledged the inspiration I received from Bill Morton, the value of the memories of the old Cooke Street employees I was privileged to know, and the importance of the Cooke Street insurance folders found in the files of the Insurance Department by Derek Gration. In addition, Tom Bowling is recorded as having found the photograph of Royce's first petrol engine on test.

When I first published the book I recorded gratitude for the help and encouragement I had received also from:

- Peter J Waszak MSc, who helped me understand the Great Northern Railway's activities in Peterborough.

- Graham Grocock, then Company Secretary of Herbert Morris of Loughborough, which took over Royce Limited in the 1930s, and his colleagues Arthur Hack and Ralph Smalley. They gave me help on matters relating to Royce Ltd from 1899 to that time and provided original evidence on the Pritchett and Gold electric car motor as well as on the first Royce petrol engine.

- Miss Jean M Ayton, Archivist of the City of Manchester, and David Taylor, the Manchester Local History Librarian who went to great lengths conducting research for me, which contributed to the accuracy of the narrative.

- Paul Tritton for allowing me freedom to extract from the work he had done by then on Henry Edmunds, the 'godfather' of Rolls-Royce, and on Sir Henry's various residences.

- Lt Col Eric Barrass OBE for lending then unpublished material from the collections of the Sir Henry Royce Memorial Foundation.

- Bill Boldison, Assistant Company Secretary of Rolls-Royce Limited, who dug deep to try to find answers to my questions relating to Henry Royce's and the Hon Charles Rolls's earlier companies.

- Richard Haigh, then Chief Librarian of Rolls-Royce but now Chief Executive of the Rolls-Royce Heritage Trust and my successor as Head of Corporate Heritage for Rolls-Royce plc, and his Technical Librarian Anne Barker. They had carried out research for me into Royce's early work covering Leeds, Liverpool and Manchester.

- Mick Watts of the Rolls-Royce Architects Department, as it then was, for redrawing the Insurance Department factory plans of Cooke Street to make them more legible, and for producing the drawings reconstructing the factory from the plans and remaining photographs.

- John Powner, then manager of the Photographic Services Department at Rolls-Royce in Derby, and his staff – notably Geoff Shaw, Andy Siddons and Dorothy Goodwin for copying original documents and photographs.

- Donald Bastow CEng, late of Henry Royce's personal design staff, for identifying the employer for whom Henry Royce worked in Leeds.

Lastly, I thanked Miss Jill Kenderdine for generating the script on her word processor. Recently I recalled that event with her. Now Mrs Jill Archer, she was on the point of leaving Rolls-Royce and her HR management post for a new life in Australia with her husband. Looking back I realise now that I should have recorded thanks to Mr Harry Myers of the Manchester solicitors Linder, Myers and Pariser who, when I met him in February 1965, was working on behalf of Levisons when the Cooke Street factory was on the point of being demolished. He was able to give me much of the history of occupancy of the Cooke Street and Blake Street area. I should also have thanked Lamar H Gilbert, a Trust member in Atlanta, Ga, for permission to publish Henry Royce's signature in the early French book of motor car design. Finally, it was remiss of me to fail to thank Beryl Neish (née Royce) for a great deal of patience in helping me understand the Royce family.

Since going to print in 1984 much has come to light. Rod Weaver of the Trust's Coventry Branch was able to add substance to the account given to Sir Max Pemberton by Mr Yarrow, with whose father Royce lodged while with the Great Northern Railway, of the conversion of locomotives during Royce's time there. His letter forms an appendix to this second edition. Mrs Jean Gray has been in contact with us, whose great great grandfather was George Yarrow with whom Royce lodged and whose great great uncle, Havelock Yarrow, had spoken with Sir Max, author of *The life of Sir Henry Royce*. The 1881 Census brings even more focus to the Yarrow family, as it does to our understanding of why Royce went to Leeds when he had to leave the GNR: he went to live with his sister and mother.

Bill Boldison deserves my heartfelt thanks for the way in which he pursued my assumption that there must have been a paper company called Rolls-Royce Distributing from 1904 until Rolls-Royce Limited and Rolls-Royce Distributing Limited were registered on 15 and 16 March 1906. He may not have found the direct answer but he did find a legal agreement dated 23 December 1904 between Royce Ltd and the Hon C S Rolls. Yes: the original agreement between the two parties covering the manufacture and distribution of Rolls-Royce cars. It is reproduced in part as an appendix.

My greatest thanks, however, must go to:

- Tom Clarke, who has done so much to research the Manchester era of Royce, for his permission to draw on his work. Key among his findings is the fact that Royce and Claremont did not set up in 1884 at Cooke Street but in Blake Street. His research into Royce's original business partner, brother-in-law-to-be and first Chairman of Rolls-Royce, produced the key work of reference *Ernest Claremont – a Manchester life with Rolls-Royce and W T Glover & Co.* Additionally, he wrote the first section of John Fasal and Bryan Goodman's massive treatise entitled *The Edwardian Rolls-Royce.* His contribution *Before the 40/50 hp: 1903-1907* finally makes sense of the registration number and coachwork swaps between the three Royce cars and catalogues every pre-Ghost car, including the V-8s. Lastly, he has done much detailed research into the origin of the Rolls-Royce radiator badge.

- Paul Tritton, whose original work on articles for the *Rolls-Royce Motors Journal* led him to undertake research the equal of a Doctorate thesis on Henry Edmunds, and to publish both *The Godfather of Rolls-Royce – the life and times of Henry Edmunds MICE, MIEE, Science and Technology's Forgotten Pioneer* and *John Montagu of Beaulieu, Motoring Pioneer and Prophet.*

- Michael Forrest, whose discovery of a photograph of his great grandfather, Thomas Searle, posed with early electrical products, led him to research which – beyond all doubt – showed Searle to have been the first salesman of Henry Royce's products in the pioneering years between 1884 and 1894. Again, help from Manchester in the form of David Taylor made this possible. Michael most generously allowed me to incorporate these findings and to reproduce the all-important photograph which portrays the earliest known products of Royce's original company.

In finality, I wish to record my deepest thanks to Julie Wood of the Corporate Heritage Office who has given such a stalwart support over many years. She was able to transcribe this manuscript as she has developed a facility I do not invariably possess – an ability to read my own writing! And she transcribed it on top of all her many day-to-day duties: a truly heroic effort!

Michael H Evans
January 2004

IN THE BEGINNING

CHAPTER ONE

Introduction

Rolls-Royce was registered as a limited liability company on 15 March 1906 (Fig 1). Seventy-five years later, a small exhibition in Derby marked a milestone anniversary of that event (Fig 2): the exhibition itself heralding the advent of the Rolls-Royce Heritage Trust.

Cooke Street (Figs 3 and 4), Hulme, Manchester, was the first registered office of Rolls-Royce Limited, for it was there that the early motor cars with their distinctive radiators were created. The simple facts of the story are well known. Henry Royce built three prototype motor cars of two cylinders, some two litres and ten horsepower (Fig 5) in the Cooke Street factory, then of Royce Limited, in 1904. These were brought to the attention of the Hon Charles Stewart Rolls who, through his Mayfair-based C S Rolls & Company, was selling the best cars available to fellow members of the nobility and gentry (Fig 6). Rolls was introduced to Royce over lunch at the Midland Hotel, Manchester, in May 1904 and that meeting led to an agreement between the two concerns. Under this agreement, which was put into effect almost immediately yet which was not formally concluded until 23 December 1904, Royce Limited built a range of motor car chassis which were sold – initially complete with coachwork – by C S Rolls & Co in London (Fig 7). The cars all bore the name Rolls-Royce, yet a year and a half was to elapse before the Rolls-Royce Company came into being.

Henry Royce, or Fred as he was known in his earlier years to the few in that formal era close enough to address him as anything other than 'mister', had already been in business in the Cooke Street and neighbouring Blake Street area with his partner, Ernest Claremont, since 1884. In this book I attempt to lay before the reader such facts as are known concerning the whole era of his endeavours in Manchester. In my first version I felt forced to comment that preparing the text had proved at times more a matter of industrial archaeology than a study of the written record. An enormous amount of work has been done on the subject since by myself and, more particularly, fellow researchers whose generosity in allowing me free access to their work has ensured a clarity of focus on the era unattainable in 1982.

In order to arrive at an understanding of the events which motivated Henry Royce to set up in business as F H Royce & Company in 1884 it is necessary to look back even further in time. It is relevant that one should examine the circumstances of both his childhood and his formative years, for it will be seen that, while the circumstances which surrounded his life were acts of fate, his response could never be described as unmeasured. As Frank Shaw, Chairman of the Sir Henry Royce Memorial Foundation, has remarked, every adversity was surmounted by him, and turned to positive effect. It was a trait which was to define the very core of what Rolls-Royce has come to represent.

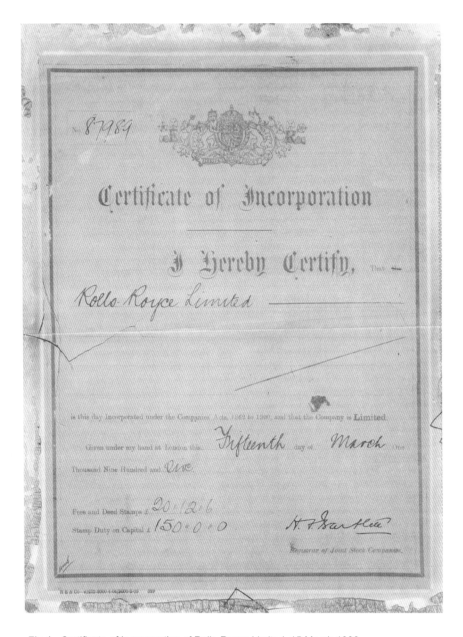

Fig 1: Certificate of Incorporation of Rolls-Royce Limited, 15 March 1906.

Fig 2: Small exhibition marking the seventy-fifth anniversary of Rolls-Royce Limited in the Marble Hall, Rolls-Royce Main Works, Nightingale Road, Derby. In the photograph, left to right, are Bill Wright, General Secretary of the Rolls-Royce Heritage Trust; Frank Turner, then Rolls-Royce Manufacturing Director, Derby; the author; Gordon Watson, then Head of the Illustrations Department; Peter Kirk, founder member of the Trust; Roy Heathcote, then Rolls-Royce Director of Engineering, Derby, and Company Director of Design; and Peter Little, a further founder member of the Trust.

Fig 3: The frontage of No 1A and 3 Cooke Street, Hulme, Manchester, photographed – it is believed – in the 1930s.

Fig 4: A further view of No 1A and 3 Cooke Street, again probably photographed in the1930s. The three-storey building housed a drawing office on its top floor, which was designed with double-hipped roof and glass roof lights for that purpose. Its gable, however, was triangular on the architect's proposal yet truncated as built. Doubtless Royce would have insisted on this to save brickwork which would have served no useful purpose.   *(Manchester City Libraries)*

Fig 5: Royce's first prototype two-cylinder 10 hp car outside No 1A Cooke Street. The brass plates show this to be the registered office of Royce Limited.

Fig 6: The Hon C S Rolls demonstrating a Panhard to a potential lady client: believed to be Miss Wilsden.

18

C. S. ROLLS & CO.

ROLLS-ROYCE CARS.

10 h.p. R.R. TONNEAU.
Two cylinders.

With Barker body   ..   ..   ..   **£395.**

10 h.p. R.R. PARK PHAETON
With disappearing back seat, leather hood, patent leather wings, and glass front   ..   **£436.**

30 h.p. SIX-CYLINDER ROLLS-ROYCE CAR.
With Barker side-entrance tonneau   ..   **£890.**
With Barker six-seated limousine   ..   **£1,000.**

15 h.p. R.R. LANDAULET.
Three cylinders

With Barker side-entrance tonneau   ..   **£500.**
Barker single landaulet   ..   ..   ..   **£550.**

20 h.p. R.R. PHAETON de LUXE.
Four cylinders.

With Barker side-entrance tonneau   ..   **£650.**
Phaeton de Luxe ..   ..   **£695.**
Extra for Brougham top with extension   **£60.**

Telephone
2328, Gerrard

C. S. ROLLS & CO.,

Telephone
104 and 1692, Kens.

28, BROOK ST., BOND ST., W.   LILLIE HALL, EARL'S COURT, S.W.

Fig 7: The first advertisement for Rolls-Royce cars placed by C S Rolls & Company. The showroom at 28 Brook Street was first rented by Rolls from H J Mulliner in October 1903, having previously been a De Dion Bouton showroom. However, 14/15 Conduit Street became C S Rolls & Company's principal showroom when it was rented in January 1905. This advertisement must date no later than the early days of January 1905. Brook Street was dispensed with before May 1906.

19

CHAPTER TWO

Royce's childhood

Frederick Henry Royce was born on 27 March 1863, the same year as another Henry who was later to make a great contribution to motor car engineering, Henry Ford. Henry Royce was the youngest of the five children of James Royce and his wife Mary, whose maiden name was King, the daughter of a large-scale farmer from Luffenham. James had grown up in farming but, after marrying in 1852, had become a miller, renting a mill at Castor in Northamptonshire. There, four of their five children were born: Emily in 1853 - she later emigrated to America, Fanny Elizabeth in 1854 – she married William Martin Gerrard, moving to Leeds where he worked, Mary Anne in 1856, and James Allan in 1857. Mary Anne married Frederick Willison, and their descendants today are Henry's nearest surviving relatives.

In 1858 James and his family moved a mile or so across the River Nene to a mill at Alwalton in Huntingdonshire. The mill – or two mills according to Sir Max Pemberton's *Life of Sir Henry Royce* – one corn, the other bone – were the property of the Ecclesiastical Commissioners and rent was paid to the Dean and Chapter of Peterborough. It was at Alwalton that Frederick Henry was born, the youngest of the family by more than five years and, in that same year, his father was forced to mortgage his lease to a London flour company due to failure in business.

The Royces were a long established family of substantial millers and farmers in the Rutland area, and they were not averse to adventure or travel. One first-hand account that survives covers the journeying of members of the Royce family long before Henry was born. It entailed travel by stagecoach from the eastern counties to see a relative near Alderley Edge in Cheshire, then on to Manchester where the train was taken to Liverpool. From there, a paddle steamer conveyed them to the Clyde. Loch Lomond was reached then crossed by boat for the walk over to Loch Katrine, where they were rowed along the loch by a team of sturdy highlanders. They continued by horse and trap to Oban where they recorded, surprisingly, seeing the farming of ostriches! It is easy to forget that travel in the western highlands was far from easy then. Many of the roads simply did not exist until the Navy created hard-surfaced tracks in the Second World War.

Henry's own grandfather, Henry William Royce (Fig 8), had this wanderlust. He was a successful miller and farmer at South Luffenham (Fig 9) and an account of one of his journeys has been provided by A R Traylen of the Rutland Local History Society.

In February of 1843 a highway robbery was committed between Ketton and Tinwell on Mr Henry Royce, miller of South Luffenham, (Sir Henry Royce's grandfather), as he was returning from Stamford market. On his arriving at a bend in the road overhung with trees he met three men coming towards Stamford, one of whom sprang out and caught hold of Mr Royce's horse's head with both hands. A violent blow was then given to him on his own head, and after a desperate struggle he was unhorsed. One of them continued beating him, and two of them held his arms, whilst the other robbed him of a brown canvas purse, containing over £4 and an American coin, along with a silver watch with three gold seals. The villains made off as Mr Ingram, corn merchant of Uppingham, rode up. He quickly raised the alarm and the Chief Constable of Stamford sent police in to all quarters of the town. They were soon found, two men hiding at the back of St Martins, Mr Royce's watch being found on one of them. The third man was caught later and they were brought before the Rev Henry Atlay at Casterton, where they were fully committed by him to Oakham Castle for trial at the Assizes.

The fate of the assailants is not given, but one suspects a long sea voyage more likely than a few hours' community service.

Henry William Royce married three times, his wives being Elizabeth, Mary and Mahala (née Lane). James Royce was the second of four children by Elizabeth: Henry William junior – born 1829, James – born 1832, Sam, and Allan – who was born in 1835. I am unaware of any children by Mary, but Mahala bore him John Charles, Annie, Arthur, Henry (not Frederick Henry), Mary Cooper and Thomas Cooper Royce.

In 1826 two of Henry William Royce's cousins, William and George Cooper, emigrated to Toronto in Canada. William died after being scratched by a bear kept captive for the entertainment of customers in his pub, whereafter George bought the 400-acre plot they had planned to acquire jointly. Later, George married his brother's widow: they had no children, so Henry Royce's uncle Allan joined them. He grew up with them and eventually became George's manager and heir. Timber from the plot was felled and sold off to help finance the establishment of a farm. It prospered.

Some years later, certainly well before 1870, and possibly as early as 1866, Henry William Royce was invited to join his cousin in Toronto. Never one it seems to do anything by halves, he took his third wife, Mahala, and most of his offspring by both Elizabeth and Mahala with him, leaving England's shores for a new life in Canada. Only two of his family stayed behind – James Royce, whose business at Alwalton was by then failing, and his half brother, John Charles Royce, who preferred to stay in England. It is from Henry William Royce's great granddaughter, Beryl Neish (née Royce), that we can learn so much of Henry Royce's family tree (Fig 10). Beryl's husband, Ian, has been a long-term colleague and friend at Rolls-Royce and, since we retired, in the Rolls-Royce Heritage Trust.

The emigration of Henry William Royce and his family might seem to have little relevance to the story of Rolls-Royce. Not so: Frederick Henry Royce's cousin, James Charles Royce, was a professional engineer and when the former became seriously ill in 1911, Claude Johnson, General Managing Director of Rolls-Royce, attempted to entice James to work in Derby. The Hon C S Rolls had been killed in a flying accident a year earlier and Henry was perilously ill. To Johnson, the prospect of losing both founders of the Company, then a mere five years old, was unthinkable. As we know, Henry Royce did recover and, some time later, he enquired of his cousin what he had intended doing, had he come to England. Diplomacy avoided the real answer.

Later, during the First World War, James Royce did become the engineer of Rolls-Royce for the USA and Canada (Fig 11) and, in that role, was heavily involved in the campaign to get the US Government to make the Rolls-Royce Eagle aero engine in quantity under licence. But the connection does not end there. In the 1990s the General Secretary of the Rolls-Royce Heritage Trust, Stan Todd, had to relinquish the role when he was posted from Derby to Toronto to become President and Chief Executive Officer of the then Rolls-Royce Industries Canada Inc, an organisation since combined with Rolls-Royce Inc in the United States. Rolls-Royce Industries Canada was responsible for a wide portfolio of companies in Canada and Mexico, some of which had grown from aero engine activities during and immediately after the Second World War and some of which came to Rolls-Royce as a result of acquiring Northern Engineering Industries Ltd in 1989. Among the latter was Ferranti-Packard, the pioneers in Canadian electrical manufacturing. In March 1995 Stan sent me the newly published monograph on the company[1] , and in it one reads

The early years of Ferranti's business in Canada illustrate that achievement in one area often leads to other opportunities. The Canadian branch of the Royce family played a leading role in the development of the West Toronto Junction area. The Royce brothers – Allan, George and James – started the Davenport Electric Railway and Light Company Limited in 1890 to encourage settlement in the newly incorporated West Toronto Junction area. Their experience with electrical technology prompted the Ferranti family to ask the Royces to be their agents in Canada.

All three were sons of Allan Royce, youngest brother of Henry's father James – the man who had been brought up by George Cooper in Toronto. One wonders whether there was any contact of substance between the Toronto Royces and their struggling cousin Henry in the early days of F H Royce & Co, or in the

[1] *Ferranti-Packard, Pioneers in Canadian Electrical Manufacturing* by Norman R Ball and John N Vardalus, published by McGill-Queen's University Press, Montreal and Kingston, 1994, ISBN 0-7735-0983-6.

prosperous era of F H Royce & Co Ltd. Or do the parallels simply indicate a shared entrepreneurialism among members of the Royce family? Of particular interest in the Ferranti-Packard book is a photograph (Fig 12) showing uncle Allan, aunt Sarah Jane, née Gilbert, with all Henry's cousins. But let us return to the childhood of the young Frederick Henry Royce.

Being so much the youngest of the five children Fred enjoyed little in the way of companionship. Perhaps this hindered his development. L F Ramsey, writing under the heading *A terror for work* after Sir Henry died, recorded that he was late to walk and late to speak, claiming he did not utter his first word until he was four. As a very small child he had to help the family by earning a few pence. Even before he was four he learned what solitude really felt like when he was employed to scare birds from the fields on the Alwalton side of the Nene near Chesterton. The return for his efforts amounted to 6d (2½p) per week. This is known because years later he returned to those fields to reflect. The story also remains of the infant Fred falling into the millrace and of his being rescued from a premature end. Additionally, Ramsey recorded that Royce had remembered being carried into the roundhouse of the mill to see the wheels go round. He returned once to Alwalton to try to acquire the lease on the mill, but he found it only had three years to run and dropped the idea. The mill was later knocked down and the stone used to build a mill at Castor nearby. Almost all traces of it had disappeared long before he died (Figs 13 and 15). All that remains of the house in which he spent his first few years is a single chimney pot (Fig 14).

James Royce (Fig 16) failed in his milling business. Henry Royce's biographer, Sir Max Pemberton[2] described James Royce as an "*unstable miller*", as "*bustling, hearty, florid but wholly unreliable*". It would seem that his father, Henry William Royce, gave him no help, a logical explanation perhaps being that he was already in Canada. I used to wonder whether he might have been a little too fond of the bottle. That does not seem to have been the case, for it came to light that he suffered from Hodgkin's Disease, which has certain affinities to leukaemia. Henry, incidentally, described his father as unsteady but clever, remarking that he lacked the determination to apply himself single-mindedly to a task.

When the business failed, the family was forced to split up. Mrs Royce (Fig 17) and the three girls were taken into lodgings for a while in the village by a Mrs Clarke. James Royce took his sons to London where he sought work at the London Steam Flour Company Limited in Southwark, which had only just been established, as a technical expert in steam power. This seems a little odd. Some sources claim he was ahead of his time in installing steam power but Henry Royce that he failed because he had not done so. It would seem that James's father installed steam at South Luffenham. He had mortgaged his lease on the mill to this concern. Henry at that time, 1867, was a mere four years old.

---

[2] *The Life of Sir Henry Royce* by Sir Max Pemberton, published by Selwyn & Blount, 1933 or 1934.

Henry was only nine years old when his father died in a public poor house in Greenwich, in July 1872, from his disease at the age of only 41. By then, Henry had had only one year at school, the Croydon British School. Between the age of nine and fourteen he had to survive on the best conditions his mother, aided by an aunt at Fletton, could make for him. She worked as a housekeeper with a number of families and then as a nurse to a wealthy man by the name of Pott in Tunbridge Wells. Despite her efforts, Henry was to remark many years later that in one lodging "*my food for the day was often two thick slices of bread soaked in milk*". And that was in spite of his own efforts to supplement his mother's income. He sold newspapers for W H Smith and Son at Clapham Junction or Clapton – there is some doubt which – and Bishopsgate Stations for a year at the age of ten in 1873 and 1874.

1875 saw Henry at school again between the ages of eleven and twelve but by the following year his schooling was at an end. Circumstances led him to work as a telegraph boy in Mayfair, delivering telegrams in the years 1876 to 1878. In his 'in memoriam', *A terror for work*, Ramsey quoted him as saying:

> "*I had no regular wages …… They believed in payment by results in the Post Office in those days. Telegrams cost only sixpence, as you know, and the boy who delivered them got a halfpenny, irrespective of distance. If you dawdled over the deliveries, you didn't get much in a day.*"

One of those strange coincidences is that Charles Rolls was born in Mayfair in 1877, on 27 August to be exact, at 35 Hill Street. It is, therefore, not beyond the bounds of possibility that the young Henry might have delivered a telegram to Henry Allan and Georgiana Rolls (Fig 18) congratulating them on the arrival of his future business partner. This is pure conjecture, but it is possible and it might indeed have happened.

Fig 8: Henry William Royce, Sir Henry's grandfather – a strong personality.

(Mrs Beryl Neish, née Royce)

Fig 9: Luffenham Mill, home of Henry William Royce, in its later days as a railway hotel around 1910. *(Rutland Local History Society)*

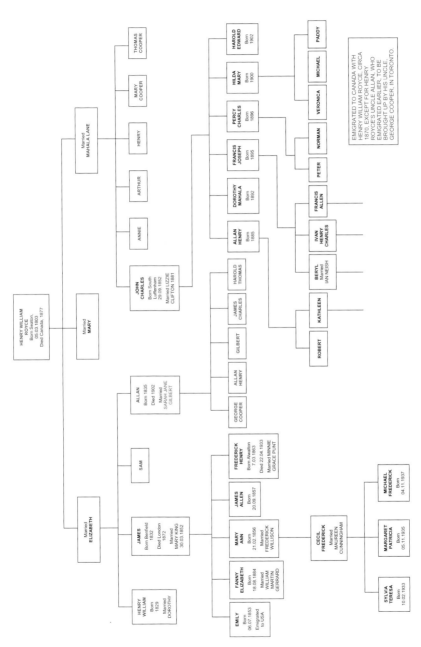

Fig 10: The Royce family tree – emphasising members of the family who emigrated to Canada.

CARD DRIVEN BY OUR OWN STAFF ARE AT OWNERS RISK.

FIRE.- ROLLS ROYCE Lᵗᴰ DO NOT ACCEPT LIABILITY FOR ANY INJURY WHICH MAY BE CAUSED BY FIRE TO ANY PROPERTY ENTRUSTED TO THEM FOR ANY PURPOSE

Fig 11: Letterhead of Henry Royce's cousin, James Royce: engineer for the USA and Canada.

Fig 12: Henry Royce's Canadian aunt, uncle and cousins in 1901. Back row: Lt Col Gilbert Royce, Harold Royce, Allan H Royce. Front row: Col George Cooper Royce, Allan Royce (uncle), Mrs Allan Royce (aunt – née Sarah Jane Gilbert), James Cooper Royce (the engineer). *(National Library of Canada, NL18171)*

28

Fig 13: Site of Henry Royce's childhood home on the left side of the lane down to the mill at Alwalton. All that remains is a chimney pot.

Fig 14: The only remnant of Henry Royce's family home at Alwalton: a chimney pot.
(Sir Henry Royce Memorial Foundation)

Fig 15: The surviving arch of the millrace at Alwalton, in all probability the one in which the young Fred Royce nearly drowned. Frank Shaw, Chairman of the SHRMF, whose father had worked at Cooke Street, points to the culvert. The photograph was taken on 14 September 1991 when Frank unveiled a plaque in memory of Sir Henry Royce in the village nearby. It shows, left to right, the author – Chairman of the RRHT, Byrnece and Frank Turner – then a Vice President of the RRHT, and Flora and Frank Shaw.

Fig 16: James Royce, Sir Henry's father, with his sister Emily.

Fig 17: Sir Henry's mother, Mary (née King), whom he cared for from around 1890 until she died in 1904.

Fig 18: The Hon C S Rolls with his parents, Lord and Lady Llangattock, who are seen on the left of the basket. Rolls is about to make an ascent from Monmouth gas works near his family seat, The Hendre.

CHAPTER THREE

His formative years

1877 presented Henry Royce with a great opportunity. Through the generosity of the aunt at Fletton, who found the necessary £20 annual premium, he became an apprentice with the Great Northern Railway at Peterborough (Fig 19) in September of that year. The aunt in question is believed to have been from his mother's side of the family – possibly Mrs Betsy King, who was born in Empingham in 1842. In her later years she lived in Lincoln. In the earlier edition of this work I mistakenly referred to Royce having been a Premium Apprentice. Indeed a premium was paid; and £20 was a considerable sum in 1877 (well over £2,000 now), but he was an Indentured Apprentice engaged to gain skilled status as a fitter on completion of his term. Premium Apprentices were the sons of the wealthy. At Rolls-Royce they were to continue in parallel with Trade Apprentices until about 1938 when they were succeeded by Engineering Apprentices. The difference was significant, not least in terms of social status, but more fundamentally in that a Premium Apprentice trained to become a mechanical engineer: the Trade Apprentice to become a skilled worker, whether on lathe, milling machine, fitting or what. In his autobiography[3], W O Bentley rather neatly summed up the difference, writing of the takeover of his bankrupt company by Rolls-Royce in 1931:

> *It seemed inconceivable that Rolls-Royce should want to employ me. What could they do with me? They had their own design staff, and it seemed to me that I would be as embarrassing as a prisoner of war after the armistice signing. I simply couldn't imagine what they might have in mind when I was asked to call at their London head office for an interview with Sir Henry Royce.*
>
> *It might be called an exploratory interview, I suppose, and I have often wondered what was its purpose. The opening was not propitious.*
>
> *"I believe you're a commercial man, Mr Bentley?"*
>
> *"Well, not really", I said. "Primarily, I suppose I'm more of a technical specialist".*
>
> *"You're not an engineer, then, are you?" Royce asked in some surprise.*
>
> *I didn't know quite how to answer this without appearing vain. And then I remembered from thirty years back.*
>
> *"Yes, I suppose you could call me that. I think you were a boy in the GN running sheds at Peterborough a bit before I was a premium apprentice at Doncaster".*

---

[3] *W .O. The autobiography of W O Bentley,* published by Hutchinson & Company, 1958.

This was accepted with a nod, and I heard no more on the subject. Instead I was offered a job ......

There is a double swipe in this because, not only was WO's apprenticeship much the higher in social and technical ranking, but Doncaster was the Mecca of the Great Northern Railway and the 'New England' works at Peterborough (Fig 20) its satellite.

When Sir Max Pemberton wrote *The life of Sir Henry Royce* he recorded that Royce had lodged with a Mr Yarrow and his family. Mr Yarrow's son had recalled the era:

"I remember being sent early in the year 1878", he said, *"to the village of Fletton to bring Fred – as we always called him – from his aunt's house to my father's house in Peterborough. He was to come and board with us and to go as an apprentice to the locomotive works of the GNR, then, as far as the locomotive department went, under the charge of Mr Frederick Rouse. I understood that the aunt had paid the sum of £20 to get the boy into the works which were, as you may know, secondary to the head shops at Doncaster.*

He was a very earnest lad at that time, some six years younger than myself, as interested as he could be in all that concerned the great machinery in Mr Rouse's charge. I suppose it was here that he saw for the first time the use of machines on a large scale and apprehended the task that lay before him in learning to play a part in the use of them. One of our first jobs at that time was the conversion of some of Mr Stirling's 'eight-foot' coupled 4-4-0s into single-wheelers. The truth was that we could not get the connecting rods to stand up against the coupled fours, and they what we call 'bowed'. Fred may have remembered this in later years when he came to deal with metals, in which, they tell me, he was a wonderful expert. He may have recollected that if the proper steel had been forthcoming there would have been no necessity to alter Mr Stirling's engines, for the connecting rods would have stood up against the big wheels and we should have had better traction. You won't have forgotten how difficult it was to start up one of those 'single-wheelers'. I've seen one take two or three minutes on a slippery day to get out of Peterborough sheds, and Gooch, the great engineer, had the same trouble with his broad-gauge 'eight-footers', as you may remember. But we didn't know enough about metals at that time, and so we had to convert them.

Fred himself was one of those who worked on that job, and in the course of time he began to make himself quite a good mechanic, though I would not say that he was over-quick at the mastery of tools. He learned by degrees, but what he learned he learned thoroughly.

Once, I remember, he and I with another mechanic were sent out to rescue a broken-down locomotive, and I think it was through some of Fred's suggestions that we got her back again after two hours' hard labour. Instead of receiving any thanks, we were abused by the foreman as though we had been pickpockets, and I do not think Fred ever forgot that unjust dressing-down.

He was a very quiet lad at that time, and rarely went out at night. You couldn't keep him away from books. Although he had had hardly any schooling, he managed to teach himself quite a lot about electricity and algebra, and something also about foreign languages. I believe he had a book about French, and he studied that with the others. But electricity was the thing that interested him most. Not very much was known generally about electric currents in those days, and everything was in a primitive stage, batteries and generators particularly, although electric light was beginning to be heard of, and some of the companies, I believe, were actually using arc lamps for the illumination of their goods sidings, the GWR at Paddington being among the number.

My father, I should let you know, had quite a nice little workshop out in our back garden at Peterborough. He had a six-inch lathe there and a carpenter's bench, a shaping machine and grindstone, and it was always his idea to do for himself every bit of work that had to be done about the house. He was a clever workman, and he was very much interested in Fred's first endeavours to use the tools. I think it was the instruction he received with us that made him a master of the lathe and taught him a lot about fitting and filing. When he left the works he was a very capable mechanic, and Mr Rouse had come to think highly of him; in fact he carried away testimonials which should have got him employment anywhere.

You ask me if his mother ever came down to see him when he was at my father's house. I cannot recollect that she ever did so, and from what I hear of her then being a housekeeper to some distant family it is very possible that she could not get there. His sister Emily did come, however, and she, they tell me, is still living in America. As for his mother, my father had at that time the idea that she was dead, but, of course, we have learnt since that this is not so. His father, however, had died in London some four or five years previously. That much I did know, though in what circumstances he died I never heard.

How I came to lose sight of Fred was simple enough. I was ordered away to Glasgow, and when I got back home again after more than a year's absence they told me that the aunt at Fletton could not provide any more money and that the boy had been forced to leave the works. I never heard of him again, though when he got his 'honour' I did write to him and remind him of the old days. He had too many letters, I expect, to answer mine, but there were a good many people in Peterborough pleased enough at what had happened to him ......"

Strangely, when I put this account to the National Railway Museum at York they were in disagreement with the majority of its content. They were even of the belief that Royce had served with the Midland Railway in Derby. They claimed that Patrick Stirling built no 4-4-0s and that this was, in any case, a rare wheel arrangement, anywhere as early as 1877. None of Stirling's eight-foot single drivers was created by reconstructing a coupled locomotive and they had never heard of Frederick Rouse.

Before exploring this response in some detail, let us return to the matter of the Yarrow family. The Rolls-Royce Heritage Trust head office was delighted to welcome as visitors Alan and Jean Gray from near Plymouth in October 1997. A friend near Derby had heard Jean's story of her connection with the Yarrows with whom Fred Royce had lodged, and put her in contact with us. Jean was later to become a good friend of Donald Pepper, previous Vice Chairman of Rolls-Royce, but that is another story. What she had to tell us was well summated in a letter she wrote to me at the time:

14 October 1997

Dear Mr Evans

Alan and I had a most enjoyable time with you last week. It is exciting and humbling to think that my great great grandfather George Yarrow would, aged about 67 yrs, have taught the talented young Henry Royce his own skills on the lathe in his workshop. His son, Havelock, was obviously the one recalling his memories to Sir Max Pemberton for his book on Royce. ....

Jean Gray

She enclosed further details which, when added to those revealed when the 1881 census was released, give us a much more complete picture.

George Yarrow and his wife lived at Stone Lane, Peterborough. He is recorded as head of the household and then aged 71, which is entirely consistent with Jean Gray's letter. He had been born in Cowbridge near Hexham, Northumberland, on 9 April 1810 and we know from Jean that he died on 7 February 1886. The census records him as an Engine Fitter (Ry) which suggests he was still working. His wife, Sarah, came from Parton in Cumberland and was, in 1881, aged 67. She died in 1887. Another occupant of the house was Havelock J Yarrow, their son. Born on 5 March 1858, and then aged 23, he was the youngest of their ten children. Interestingly, he was born in Doncaster, home to the GNR's main workshops and, like his father, was recorded as an Engine Fitter (Ry). One has to assume (Ry) indicated railway. A last occupant was not a member of family but a lodger, Edwin R Carter, aged 18. He had been born in Bristol and, again, was an Engine Fitter. We now know from another source – touched upon later – that 'Fred' Royce lodged with the Yarrow's not from early in 1878 as Havelock's recall indicated: he may have fetched him from Fletton early in 1878, but he had joined the household earlier – in September 1877, in fact. And the aunt's inability to keep paying forced 'Fred' to leave the New England and the Yarrow family in November 1880 with his apprenticeship incomplete. It would seem, therefore, that Edwin Carter moved in as 'Fred' moved out. To complete the picture from Jean Gray's researches, Havelock Yarrow married Elizabeth Priscilla Wood and they had one daughter, 'Barty'. Havelock died in Peterborough in January 1941 having lost his wife in August 1937. 'Barty' died unmarried at Heacham near King's Lynn in 1982, having lived for years at Hunstanton.

Let us now return to the response I received from the National Railway Museum. I had to start from the premise that Havelock Yarrow's recall might have suffered a little with the passage of the years between the 1870s and his talking to Sir Max Pemberton around 1933, but that the validity of its basic substance remained beyond question.

The New England Works were the GNR's second most important engineering centre, and I remain grateful to the National Railway Museum for pointing me to the expert on the history of the site, Peter J Waszak. From him I learned that it had remained an important railway centre until its decline in the 1950s and ultimate closure on 30 September 1968. Its end was almost coincident with the end of the age of steam. Donald Bastow had also confirmed the existence of Frederick Rouse as a member of the Institution of Mechanical Engineers, although at the time of first writing this book his role at GNR Peterborough was not known.

When a book is published, a flood of correspondence can follow which brings with it gems of information the author wished he had possessed at the time of writing. I have seen this happen with sufficient frequency to be known to express the view that definitive editions are always second or even later editions. In the case of this volume, a letter from Rodney Weaver of the Rolls-Royce Heritage Trust Coventry Branch was a 'classic'. Written in February 1990, its contents were such as to warrant its reproduction in full as an appendix to this volume. In it Rodney identified the importance of the Peterborough Works in the early days of the GNR as a major traffic and operating centre. He stated that, although Peterborough did not actually build new locomotives, it was at the time Fred Royce went there effectively the second locomotive works of the GNR undertaking intermediate and general overhauls and conversions. On the subject of Frederick Rouse, Rodney pointed out that he was District Locomotive Superintendent at Peterborough by the mid 1890s and that, as Peterborough provided the locomotives for most of the principal expresses into and out of London's King's Cross station, he was in effect – if not in reality – in overall control of the southern end of the line. He reported directly to Patrick Stirling, the legendary Locomotive Superintendent of the GNR.

So this identified Frederick Rouse: Havelock Yarrow had been completely correct in his memory of him, but what of his recall of the 4-4-0s and their conversion to single wheelers? Here I quote from Rodney's letter:

Shortly before his retirement, Archibald Sturrock – Stirling's predecessor – ordered six large 2-2-2 locomotives, three from John Fowler and Company of Leeds and three from the newly formed Yorkshire Engine Company of Sheffield. The latter were in fact the very first order received by Yorkshire Engine and carried works number 1-3; coincidentally (?) Alfred Sacré, a partner in the new firm, was a former GNR man from Peterborough. These were among the largest and most powerful express locomotives of their time and while under construction they were altered to 2-4-0s to improve adhesion.

Unfortunately, this introduced coupling rods no less than 9 ft 7 in long, by far the longest so far used on a British express locomotive, and in an age only just beginning to appreciate (and indeed afford) the benefits of steel they were too long. Bent or thrown rods were a common problem in those days but these big 2-4-0s were worse than most. Despite rapid advances in metallurgy and the widespread adoption of steel for motionwork, it would be another thirty-one years before anyone used coupling rods of that length again.

Patrick Stirling had a horror of thrown or broken coupling rods; as a young man he had seen the result of a broken rod piercing the side of the firebox. Right to the end of his days (he died in office on 11 November 1895 at the age of 75) the fastest GNR expresses were hauled exclusively by 4-2-2 or 2-2-2 locomotives. It was hardly surprising, therefore, that between 1873 and 1878 the six troublesome 2-4-0s were rebuilt as 2-2-2s.

Having been designed as such, the conversion was relatively simple. They were fitted with standard Stirling boilers in 1885-89 and withdrawn between 1898 and 1902.

Rodney recalls that the six locomotives in question were as follows:

GNR number	Maker's number	Delivered new	Converted at Peterborough from 2-4-0 to 2-2-2
264	John Fowler 747	November 1866	October 1878
265	John Fowler 748	November 1866	November 1875
266	John Fowler 749	December 1866	December 1873
267	Yorkshire Engine 1	December 1866	February 1873
268	Yorkshire Engine 2	January 1867	March 1878
269	Yorkshire Engine 3	February 1867	March 1875

And as we know that Royce was at GNR from September 1877 to November 1880 we can see that Havelock Yarrow's recall was almost correct. Royce must have worked on the Yorkshire Engine Company built 268 and then on the John Fowler built 264. The two statements attributed to Yarrow that were incorrect, as the National Railway Museum pointed out, were firstly the reference to 4-4-0s: they were 2-4-0s. And secondly that the engines were not designed by Stirling. They were, in fact, ordered by his predecessor, Archibald Sturrock. The errors might have been in Havelock Yarrow's memory or in Sir Max Pemberton's recording.

Rodney concludes his letter:

> *In later years, Royce seems to have had a horror of overloaded crank pins, this being the reason he would never entertain a radial engine. Might this be in part attributable to his earliest contact with the realities of rotating and reciprocating masses?*

A fair point, but I suspect bending loads as much as bearing overloads were the problem with the 2-4-0s. The experience may have had more relevance to Henry Royce's innate understanding of connecting rod designs than to his real concerns over the loads on the single crank pins of radial aero engines such as the highly successful Bristol Jupiter.

Royce showed himself slow to learn the use of tools, as Havelock Yarrow recalled, and much of his early ability was acquired from George Yarrow's tuition in his garden shed. In my earliest days at Rolls-Royce I recalled reading that the proprietor of a chemist's shop in Wem in Shropshire possessed a series of brass model wheelbarrows made by Royce in that shed and I set out to find what might have happened to them. The chemist, it transpired, had long since died and the solicitors who had dealt with his estate had no knowledge of the wheelbarrows. Their interest was kindled by my recall, however, and they kindly wrote to all beneficiaries of the will. There was a positive response: the three wheelbarrows survived, and the owner allowed me to have them photographed (Fig 21).

When not at the works or in the garden shed, Royce once more sold newspapers and studied. As Havelock Yarrow recalled, he taught himself what he could about electricity and algebra, and he also took an interest in French. Electricity, however, was what interested him most. Things like batteries, generators and electric lighting were all very new. Years later Royce himself was to recall the era to Claude Johnson, stating that he *"acquired some skill as a mechanic but lacked technical, commercial and clerical experience"*.

The formal learning experience came to an end, as we have noted, when the aunt's money ran out in November 1880. Many an account of Royce's life has referred to the age being one in which jobs were scarce, despite the excellent testimonial he carried from the GNR, and to his walking many fruitless miles in search of work. I repeated the story in the original script for this book, but we now know more. It was indeed a time of recession and many of the big companies were laying people off, but the release of the 1881 census has explained exactly why he should have headed for Leeds. The 1881 Census was searched for this information by the sister of Michael Willison: both are descended from Henry Royce's sister, Mary Ann Royce. Listed under 12 Ingleby Street, Wortley in Bramley, Yorkshire, as head of the household was William Martin Gerrard, a 25-year old born at Kirkstall, Leeds, in 1855. He is described as an Oil Extractor Wool: nothing remarkable in that. But then we come to his wife, Fanny Elizabeth Gerrard, aged 26, born at Empingham in Rutland – Henry Royce's middle sister. And the other two occupants of the house: Mary Royce, widow, aged 52, born at Empingham, Rutland, and listed as mother-in-law, and Frederick Henry Royce, unmarried, aged 18, born at Alwalton, Huntingdon and listed as brother-in-law. His occupation is listed as Machine Fitter.

After no more than weeks he found a job in Leeds with a firm of machine tool makers who were fulfilling a contract for the Italian arsenal. He referred back to those times in later years with a hint of bitterness as the wage was 11/- per week (about £65 now) for a 54-hour week. For some time he worked 6.00am till 10.00pm and all through Friday nights. Why he should have been so minded is not immediately obvious for 54 hours was still the basic week when the early Rolls-Royce cars were built. Furthermore, he frequently worked his team from normal start on Friday morning till lunchtime on Saturday without a stop and was even known to fetch employees out of the pubs around Cooke Street on Saturday lunchtimes to return and get a job complete ready for Monday. His skilled men received of the order of 30/- to 35/- (36/- in 1906) a week and it was not unknown for this to be handed over with the comment "*You don't deserve it*".

Until shortly before this volume first appeared we did not know for whom he worked in Leeds although I suspected it was for Greenwood & Batley. Few companies have employee records going back that far and the working hours and wage were of little help as they were pretty well standard in Leeds at that time. However, Richard Haigh made enquiries that indicated the names of two concerns which are believed to have had contracts for the Italian arsenal around 1880. These were Greenwood & Batley, and Fairbairn Lawson. Later, the former was acquired by the latter, although it continued to trade under its own name until it went bankrupt in 1980. Greenwood & Batley made some of the most accurate service rifle ammunition that our Armed Forces ever had. I well recall using .303 ammunition head-stamped GB56 (Greenwood & Batley, manufactured 1956) at Bisley. Donald Bastow then established that employees of Greenwood & Batley many years ago shared a belief that Royce had once been an employee.

Just before publication of this book in its original form Donald Bastow telephoned me one morning. On the previous day he had visited the Institution of Mechanical Engineers to hear the Presidential Address. Not being until the evening he had spent the afternoon with Mr S G Morrison, Librarian of the Institution.

Mr Morrison showed Don a most interesting document – the Proposal of Membership in respect of Frederick Henry Royce dated 11 October 1897. This document contains a brief curriculum vitae of Royce's career, and I quote

Served premium apprenticeship to Great Northern Railway (Loco Dept) Peterborough from Sept 1877 to Nov 1880, Greenwood & Batley Leeds 1880 to 1881, Electric Lighting & Power Generating Co afterwards named the Maxim Weston Co 1881 to 1882. Transferred to Lancashire Maxim Weston Co 1882 to 1884. Partner in F H Royce & Co 1884 to 1894, Managing Director in F H Royce & Co Ltd 4 June 1894 to present date.

One of the three supporting signatures to this application was that of F Rouse (Fig 22).

So Greenwood & Batley was proven. What more do we know of the concern? In 2000 Peter Baines, General Secretary of the Rolls-Royce Enthusiasts' Club, told me that the company had been founded in 1856 and had ceased trading in 1980. At first most of their work was in the design and manufacture of machine tools for making small arms and ammunition, but they moved on to making electrical generation equipment. By 1890 the site covered 11 acres with 6.5 million square feet of workshops, 1600 employees, its own power station and a branch line from the Great Northern Railway. The site was known as the Albion Works.

Fig 19: Frederick Henry Royce when an apprentice with the Great Northern Railway at the 'New England', Peterborough. In his application for membership of the Institution of Mechanical Engineers a member of his staff wrote, *Served Premium apprenticeship to Great Northern Railway (Loco Dept), Peterboro' from Sept 1877 to Nov 1880.* W O Bentley, himself a Premium Apprentice with the Great Northern Railway at Doncaster, claimed Royce was only a 'boy' apprentice.

Fig 20: The 'New England' workshops of the Great Northern Railway in Peterborough. The Great Northern built all its new locomotives at their Doncaster works, but looked to its other works to conduct much of its locomotive overhaul work. At the time Henry Royce was there, the 'New England' was effectively the GNR's second locomotive works.

Fig 21: The model brass wheelbarrows made by Henry Royce in George Yarrow's garden shed while he was at the 'New England'.

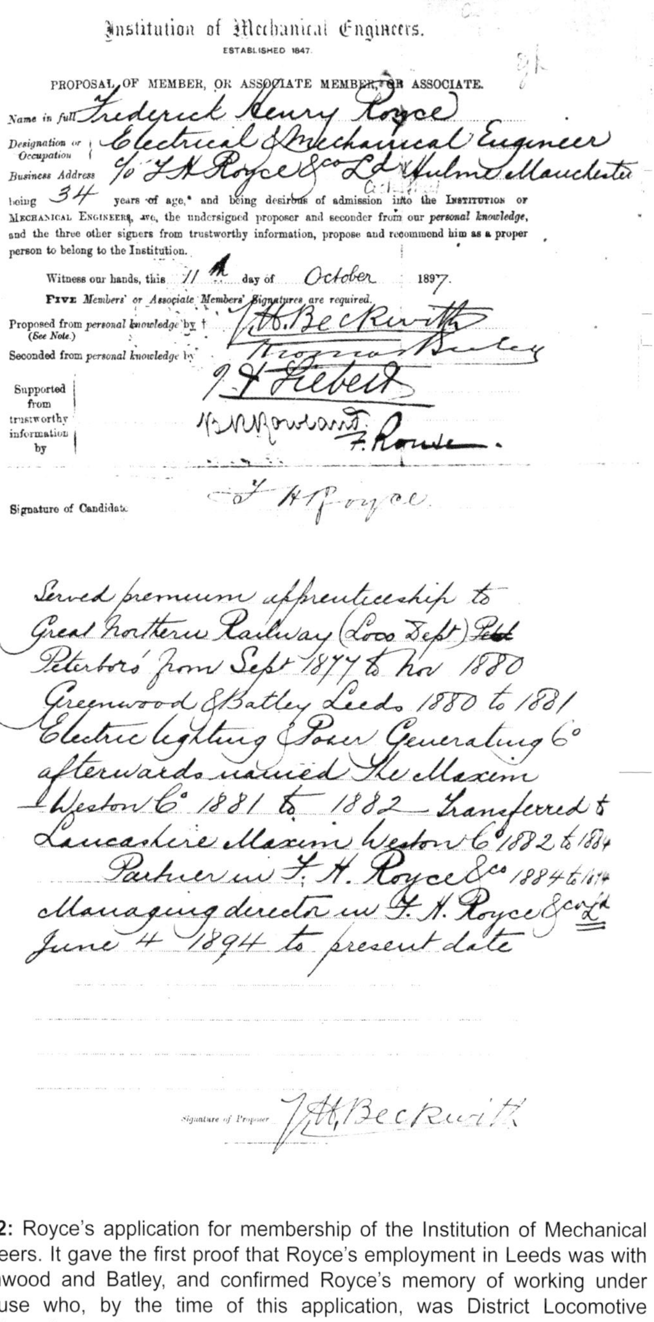

PROPOSAL OF MEMBER, OR ASSOCIATE MEMBER, OR ASSOCIATE.

Name in full *Frederick Henry Royce*

Designation or Occupation *Electrical & Mechanical Engineer*

Business Address *℅ F.H. Royce & Co Ld Hulme Manchester*

being *34* years of age,* and being desirous of admission into the INSTITUTION OF MECHANICAL ENGINEERS, we, the undersigned proposer and seconder from our *personal knowledge*, and the three other signers from trustworthy information, propose and recommend him as a proper person to belong to the Institution.

Witness our hands, this *11th* day of *October* 1897.

FIVE Members' or Associate Members' Signatures are required.

Proposed from personal knowledge by † (See Note.) *J.H. Beckwith*

Seconded from personal knowledge by *Thomas Barley*

Supported from trustworthy information by *J. F. Hebert* *H.N. Rowlands* *F. Rouse*

Signature of Candidate. *F.H. Royce*

*Served premium apprenticeship to
Great Northern Railway (Loco Dept)
Peterboro' from Sept 1877 to Nov 1880
Greenwood & Batley Leeds 1880 to 1881
Electric lighting & Power Generating Co
afterwards named The Maxim
Weston Co 1881 to 1882 — Transferred to
Lancashire Maxim Weston Co 1882 to 1884
Partner in F. H. Royce & Co 1884 to 1894
Managing director in F. H. Royce & Co Ltd
June 4 1894 to present date*

Signature of Proposer *J.H. Beckwith*

Fig 22: Royce's application for membership of the Institution of Mechanical Engineers. It gave the first proof that Royce's employment in Leeds was with Greenwood and Batley, and confirmed Royce's memory of working under F Rouse who, by the time of this application, was District Locomotive Superintendent at Peterborough.

CHAPTER FOUR

Early experience in electric lighting

Royce did not stay long at Greenwood & Batley – from the end of 1880 to some time in 1881: less than a year. There may have been domestic reasons for his moving on, but one would think that leaving his sister and mother for the uncertainties of London was more likely driven by an ambition to rise above his lot. He was not fully time-served as a fitter, and so could not expect a skilled man's wage. Where he was, there were constraints from which he could not break free.

We have already noted from Havelock Yarrow's account that young Fred studied electricity, and he must have known of the fact that arc lamps were being used by railways to illuminate goods sidings. Havelock remarked on this, citing the GWR at Paddington as an example. Then there was the likely contact with electrical work at Leeds. Electricity was a new subject which clearly fascinated Royce. It is almost certain that the entrepreneur in him saw it as a growth industry, unfettered by issues such as 'time-served' and as yet unpopulated by large companies or the need for heavy investment as a precursor to being competitive. It was new enough to succeed in, with few constraints.

In 1881 Royce moved to London where he joined the Electric Lighting & Power Generating Company. Initially he lodged in the Old Kent Road but he moved subsequently to Kentish Town. After he joined, the company acquired rights to the patents of Hiram S Maxim on incandescent lamps and to those of Edward Weston on arc lamps. On doing so, they changed the company name to the Maxim-Weston Company in June 1882. Maxim, like Weston, was an American, although he lived in England, and a great innovator. Apart from his work with electricity he developed the wax capsule automatic fire extinguisher rose and the highly successful Maxim machine gun. He experimented with both recoil and gas-operated designs and has been described by military historians as the 'real father of the machine gun'. It was apparently his total dissatisfaction with the way in which his patents were being used by the Maxim-Weston Company that led him to devote his energies to machine guns. The legend remains of the Maxim being demonstrated to a group of Chinese Army officers by shooting trees down, and of their observation that axes would be cheaper! The Maxim was developed and manufactured by Vickers – a company eventually to end its days by being absorbed by Rolls-Royce – as the standard medium machine gun of the British Army through two World Wars. It became the standard armament fitted to Rolls-Royce 40/50 hp 'Silver Ghost' armoured cars once sufficient were available (Fig 23). Early examples were given old Maxims. Hiram Maxim was also a pioneer in aviation. He built a steam-powered aircraft in 1894 (Figs 24 and 25) some ten years before the Wright brothers succeeded in achieving their epic first powered flight on 17 December 1903. It hardly needs adding that Maxim never attained powered flight. A final oddity was that Maxim designed and built one of Blackpool's first fairground rides. It remains in daily use.

The phenomenon of static electricity had long been appreciated, not simply through thunderstorms but also through substances which, when dry and subjected to friction, would attract other materials. Amber, which had been prized for jewellery since Bronze Age times, was one such and its name in Greek was Elektron. Hence the name electricity. Studies of current electricity were much more recent. They followed the invention by Count Alessandro Volta of the battery, or Voltaic Cell as it was known, in 1799. Sir Humphry Davy – remembered as a parallel inventor with George Stephenson, of railway engine fame, as originators of the miner's safety lamp – had demonstrated electrically-induced luminescence to the Royal Institution in 1802 and, in the same year, the electric arc as well. He *'astounded the scientific world'* by linking 2000 Voltaic Cells and passing the current from them between the tips of two charcoal electrodes: a dazzling blue-white light resulted. He had even suggested the possibility of incandescent lighting, using carbon or platinum filaments. A few arc lights were subsequently used, notably in lighthouses, but each light required its own dynamo to generate sufficient current. Development of the dynamo was the key to the expansion of the nineteenth century electrical engineering industry.

The principle on which the dynamo works is that of electromagnetic induction, and this was not understood until Davy's old assistant, Michael Faraday, discovered electromagnetic induction in the 1820s. It was the key to the subsequent development of the dynamo. Small dynamos were made soon after that, but it was not until 1867 that the dynamo began to represent a commercial proposition. In that year, a number of inventors hit upon the idea of using an electromagnetic field energised by the dynamo itself. By the late 1870s dynamos employing this principle were being manufactured, notably the Siemens and the Gramme. These were able to generate sufficient power to allow several lights to be run from a single machine, and at a low enough cost to make electric lighting and power viable propositions. Gramme dynamos were made in the UK at Chelmsford in Essex from 1879 on by Colonel R E B Crompton: he was credited with being the first person in Britain to install electric lighting in his own home.

The first demonstration of a multiple lamp system in England was made by Paul Jablochkoff, a Russian army officer, at the West India Docks in London in June 1877. The first single arc lamps had appeared in Paris in 1841 and the first seen in London was at Hungerford Bridge over a two-week period of demonstration in 1849. Whilst Jablochkoff's 'candles', as he called them, were not truly successful they did create an impression. Among those who witnessed the demonstration was Henry Edmunds (Fig 26), a young man of 21 from Halifax. His name will recur as the story unfolds. Soon after this Charles F Brush of Cleveland, Ohio, developed a successful system. Edmunds was a party to its introduction into this country.

In December 1879 the Anglo-American Electric Light Company was formed with Edmunds as its Chief Engineer. It subsequently became the Brush Electrical Engineering Company and the story of commercial arc lighting was thus begun.

In the following year Edison in the States and Joseph Swan in Newcastle upon Tyne, working independently, produced practical incandescent lamps. Others, notably St George Lane-Fox in this country and Hiram Maxim and William Sawyer in the USA, were working on such lamps but Edison and Swan collaborated on sewing up the patents. Two years later, in 1883, they amalgamated to form Ediswan. The early commercial success of the Swan lamp can be attributed to the marketing efforts of his friend, Henry Edmunds. Incandescent lamps offered a direct alternative to gas lighting, output being about 16 candlepower (1/100th of an average arc light's power). They were cleaner and cooler than gas lamps and emitted no smell.

The advent of the arc lamp led to a boom in the electrical engineering industry over the years 1880 to 1882, and in particular 1882. As early as 1879 arc lighting was being exhibited in many of Britain's major towns and cities. There were many companies engaged in this field, some formed simply to exploit the patent rights to a lighting system or its components. Some manufactured. Some simply sold imported plant and some offered to install electrical systems and sell the light thereby produced, usually on a contract basis. Arc lighting installations were often limited to as few as a dozen lamps. When incandescent lighting was invented, many of these companies also bought patents from the inventors of successful lamps. If one system proved unsuccessful, they tried another.

Many of the lighting systems used at that time were based on foreign patents; the company concerned having acquired the UK rights. The company would then arrange a demonstration as a preliminary to securing a contract to light some conspicuous place. 1880-1882 saw municipalities and other bodies keen to try out this novel form of illumination.

The success of the boom depended heavily on the assumption that the cost of electric lighting would be no more than gas. The pioneer companies of that period launched their ventures on the expectation of being able to achieve that goal. Pilot schemes were frequently tendered below cost on the assumption that economies would result from the larger scale of the subsequent permanent installations. Their assumption proved over-optimistic and all the companies found themselves losing money. 1883 proved a disastrous year. Taking Brush as an example, sales for

1881	£80,000
1882	£200,000
1883	£35,000

Many of the companies did little better and liquidations were common in 1884. Those that survived did, however, enjoy a steady increase in the sale of lighting plant in the years that followed.

Another factor worked against these pioneer companies. Electric lighting became a commercial proposition at the very time when Parliament was experimenting with various methods of regulating the public utilities, and the municipal trading movement was then coming to the fore. The system of granting limited period franchises had its precedent in the Tramways Act of 1870. Trams then were horse-drawn, of course. The Act, strangely, gave the towns the power to own the trams, but no authority to run them. All they could do was pass by-laws, which regulated the operations of private owners. Then in 1882 Huddersfield Corporation met a snag. They could find no private company willing to operate trams to their policy. Parliamentary powers were in consequence given to corporations under which they could run their own tramway system, provided no private company was forthcoming with a 'reasonable offer'. The powers were more restrictive than they appeared for it was not until about 1896 that leave was freely granted to corporations and the tram boom began. Nonetheless the big towns had begun to buy up waterworks and gasworks after the 1870 Act.

Parliament reacted quickly to the advent of electric lighting. A Select Committee was formed in 1879 and while it did not propose early legislation, the boom from 1880 onwards led to the Electric Lighting Act of 1882. Its pattern followed the Tramway Act and called for Provisional Orders or Licences to be issued through the Board of Trade. Licences were highly restrictive, giving rights for a mere seven years. More commonly used were the Provisional Orders, which had a 21-year life. Under the Act, local authorities had precedence over private companies in applications and the right, at the end of 21 years, to compulsorily buy out a private company at its plant value.

Although these terms were seen to have restricted the growth of electricity supply too much, with the result that the period was extended to 42 years and 'plant value' changed to 'fair market price', in 1888, the damage had been done. Private capital had been frightened off by this early attempt at something akin to nationalisation. There was not to be another boom of investment in electrical methods until the mid 1890s.

So Royce got in on the ground floor of a completely new and rapidly growing industry in its boom year, 1881. Royce became a tester at a wage of 22/- per week with his new employer and, as witness the embryo state of the electrical engineering industry, was able to describe himself with some validity as an electrician. While he lodged in Kentish Town he continued his studies in the evenings, making good use of the opportunity to overcome the deficiencies he had noted in his education at the close of his apprenticeship days with GNR. He attended evening classes held by Professor William E Ayrton at the City & Guilds Institute in Finsbury, and other lectures at the Polytechnic. His progress was rapid, for, late in 1882, the

Maxim-Weston Company posted him to a subsidiary in Liverpool. There, at the age of 19, he became First, or Chief, Electrician of the Lancashire Maxim-Weston Electric Company Limited. The job was not to last long, for apart from the two factors already described as contributory to the disasters of 1883, there was a third in the case of the company for which Royce worked.

Among the competing concerns it was an extreme example of those which bought patent rights. They had bought the patents to the French Lontin arc lamps. These they used to illuminate a section of the City of London. The contract for this job was tendered at £3,000. It lost them £4,000. So they bought the patents on an American arc lighting system evolved by the pioneer Edward Weston and, as they had no incandescent lamp, they bought the patents of Maxim. By March 1883 the company had spent £114,000 on patents as compared with £2,000 on plant and £21,000 on stocks and work-in-progress. Maxim visited the company on his return from the Paris Exposition in 1881 to investigate the way in which his patents were being used. His autobiography records the event as follows:

> *I have never seen anything like it in my life. The place was unspeakably dirty, everything was so out of order that we were tripping over copper wires everywhere; the windows were so thick with dust that they admitted little light and the few men at work were burning gas out of the open end of the pipe without a burner. In walking about the place, I saw a high-priced Brown & Sharps milling machine. It was smothered with dirt and appeared to be in a very dilapidated condition. The roof was leaking and the machinery had been rained on and was slightly rusty in places.*

Only four or five men worked in the factory at the time and, interestingly, one of those Maxim may have seen might have been Royce. When Maxim volunteered his services he was offered a guinea a year. Not surprisingly this company had lost £32,000 by May 1884 and in 1888 it was finally liquidated when the auditors discovered that the assets were valued at £42,000 against a true value of £25,000. With an economic structure such as this, there was no way in which Royce could have made any significant success out of his posting to Liverpool. But what is known of his work there?

Early references to the Lancashire Maxim-Weston Electric Company Limited lie in the pages of Sir Max Pemberton's book. He recorded that the object of the company was to light a number of streets and the theatres of Liverpool, and also a conversation that Henry Royce had with him concerning the venture: *"I used to wait in my office in as critical state of suspense as those people in the house who were looking for the death of the villain or the salvation of the heroine. Would the whole place be plunged into darkness? From time to time, I sent a small boy round to see if the lights were still burning. Happily the tale of casualties was slight, and in the main we managed to lighten their darkness. But it was the devil of a business."* We now know through Tom Clarke's researches that the Liverpool subsidiary resulted from the London concern having successfully provided lighting to the Prince of Wales theatre there.

The Lancashire Maxim-Weston Electric Company Limited was established in October 1882 at Peter's Lane, Liverpool. Its aim was to dominate electrification schemes in the north-west, and the new company was offered to outside shareholders. It was chaired by Thomas Whitworth and directors included Admiral Sir Edward Inglefield, who had previously chaired the parent company, and Hugh Watt, a local Liverpool businessman, who had been managing director of the parent company. The name Inglefield is interesting. Admiral Inglefield, it appears, married a member of the family of Colonel R E B Crompton and changed the family name to Crompton Inglefield. He built a beautifully situated home, 'Flower Lillies', at Windley, north of Derby. The nearby village hall at Turnditch was opened by a member of the family and bears the name Crompton Inglefield. One of Rolls-Royce's greatest aero engineers lives immediately adjacent to 'Flower Lillies' and another just opposite Turnditch village hall. The Admiral is, however, probably most widely known as the inventor of the Inglefield Clip used to attach flags to the lanyards on flagpoles.

When I originally wrote this book, a member of Richard Haigh's library staff at Rolls-Royce, Anne Barker, succeeded in putting some substance to the existence of this company in the form of transcripts from the minutes of the City's Watch Committee and the printed Council Proceedings. From the latter, dated 30 October 1883, can be seen (Fig 27) that it was resolved *That the Tender of the Lancashire Maxim-Weston Electric Company Limited, to provide, fix and maintain twenty 1,600 candle arc-light lamps in Castle Street, Lord Street, Church Street, Parker Street, Clayton Square and Elliot Street, from dusk until midnight, and ten 1,600 candle arc-light lamps from midnight to sunrise, at 4d per lamp per hour, for 12 months, be accepted'.*

From the Council Minutes one learns that on the 25 March following, under the heading *Electric Lighting* (Fig 28), *'The Engineer begs to report that the Lancashire Maxim Weston Electric Light Company have made the terms of their Contract for the Experimental Electric Lighting in the Streets specified therein. The continuous lighting commenced on the 24th instant.'* Under the company's manager, Mr S A Thomson, Royce had clearly succeeded in his technical task of lighting the streets as well as the theatres, but for how long?

Two short months later one reads (Fig 29) *'Read notice from the Liquidators of the Lancashire Maxim-Weston Electric Company Limited stating that from and after the 24th instant (May) the Company will cease to light the streets at present being lit by their Weston System of Electric Light'.*

'Also read the following report of the Engineer – Electric Lighting Lord Street, Church Street by the Maxim-Weston Electric Light Company. The Engineer begs to report with reference to the letter from the Maxim-Weston Electric Light Company

51

as to the terminating of their Contract with the Corporation that he proposed giving requisite Notice to the Gas Company to refix the lamps in the lanterns and he requests the instructions of the Company under their Contract to remove their fittings etc'.

Tom Clarke has researched the collapse of the Liverpool company and I can do no better than to quote him:

15,000 shares were allotted but from the start the company was under-capitalised at £8,000 and this was exacerbated when James T Dadson and Gustavus P Harding did not pay for the shares they had contracted to buy. The limited work the company undertook from early 1883 included a private house and several schemes in Liverpool, which the users rented from the electrical concern. These rentals were insufficient although a rental contract in Manchester had it seems been worthwhile. Steamships and mines were also targeted for contracts. In the journal 'The Electrician' for 27 January 1883 (p262-3) reference was made to work done in Manchester under the control of Royce's boss, Whitworth. This is the earliest record of work Royce did in the city he was soon to move to although, sadly, the journal did not name the company or building(s) involved. In 1884 the Lancashire company chairman described their successful warehouse electrifications in Manchester as 'simply beautiful' and 'they had lit up some magnificent warehouses'.

By the end of 1883 the situation was becoming parlous although Royce was unaware, too busy attending to theatre lighting and existing rental contracts.

The parent company now proposed to buy out the insolvent subsidiary with a one-for-one share offer. This was a better deal than selling off the equipment, for which there was no market in view of bad publicity surrounding some electrification schemes. The offer was accepted on May 16 1884. Meanwhile Royce had been encouraged by colleagues at the Lancashire company to think about setting up on his own. This probably indicates that the parent company could not find work for all its former employees, either in Liverpool or back in London. In May 1884 the Maxim-Weston Co, as successor to the insolvent Lancashire company, began fresh negotiations with Liverpool City Council for new lighting schemes. The town clerk 'expressed himself very favourably with respect to ... the electrician and engineer'. In spite of his commendation Royce could not wait, unpaid, for contracts not yet agreed. Aged 21 he left Liverpool shortly after and began his precarious existence in Manchester.

We might wonder if Tom's analysis is not perhaps slightly negative in its conclusion. Royce had benefitted greatly from first-hand experience of the electrical lighting industry. He must have appreciated the technicalities, the pitfalls and the opportunities it involved, and, at the same time – for all the shortcomings of his formal education – he had become an accomplished mechanic if not an engineer and, by the standards of the day, an accomplished electrical engineer. The Royce family had, for generations, made a success of their chosen fields of endeavour. They had never been afraid of 'pastures new', as their record of both travel and emigration shows. The qualities necessary for success in life seem to have been inherent in the family, with the singular exception of Henry's father, and his illness may have been the major contributor to that.

When one considers the privations of Henry's early childhood his very survival indicated his mettle and he certainly learned the hard way what it took to earn money. On the educational front he never missed a relevant opportunity, and his obsession with hard work can have come from nowhere but within. 1884 must have been a watershed. Should he stay and take his chances with a company that sought to rise from the ashes of failure, or should the company's plight be the signal for a fresh start? There was a final factor which must have influenced him. He had reached the age of 21 – then the age of majority – and was free for the first time to consider setting up a business of his own. If he again took employment he had only testimonials to rely on. He had no professional qualifications and was not a member of any of the engineering institutions. Such factors would tend to constrain the salary he might command. Having become accustomed to living frugally and something in his nature preferring the making of his own decisions to being told what to do, he elected to 'go it alone'. He knew that the electrical manufacturing industry was young and as yet did not require much in the way of resources to make a toehold start. He also had one last characteristic that almost made this inevitable – a self-assurance that amounted almost to arrogance.

Fig 23: Rolls-Royce 40/50 hp 'Silver Ghost' armoured cars with Maxim's (Vickers) machine guns. The concept of the armoured car was that of the Royal Naval Air Service, here seen on exercise in 1915. *
(*Courtesy Patrick Coyne*)

Fig 24: Sir Hiram Maxim's aeroplane. It predated the Wright brothers first flight by nine years – but, of course, unlike the Wright machine, it never successfully flew.

Fig 25: Sir Hiram Maxim demonstrating the light weight of his steam aero engine. Unlike the Wright's gasoline engine, Maxim's required burners and boiler too.

55

Fig 26: Henry Edmunds at the age of 24. *(Paul Tritton)*

WATCH.

The proceedings of the Watch Committee (to 23rd October, inclusive) having been read,

Resolved—

That the Tender of the Lancashire Maxim-Weston Electric Company, Limited, to provide, fix, and maintain twenty 1,600 candle arc-light lamps in Castle Street, Lord Street, Church Street, Parker Street, Clayton Square, and Elliot Street, from dusk until midnight, and ten 1,600 candle arc-light lamps from midnight to sunrise, at 4d. per lamp per hour, for 12 months, be accepted.

[NOTE.—Copies of the Reports of the City Engineer will be bound with the printed Council Minutes for 1882-83.]

Fig 27: Extract from the printed Council Proceedings of the City of Liverpool dated 30 October 1883. *(Liverpool City Libraries)*

Fig 28: Extract from the minute book of the City of Liverpool's Watch Committee reporting its meeting on 25 March 1884. *(Liverpool City Libraries)*

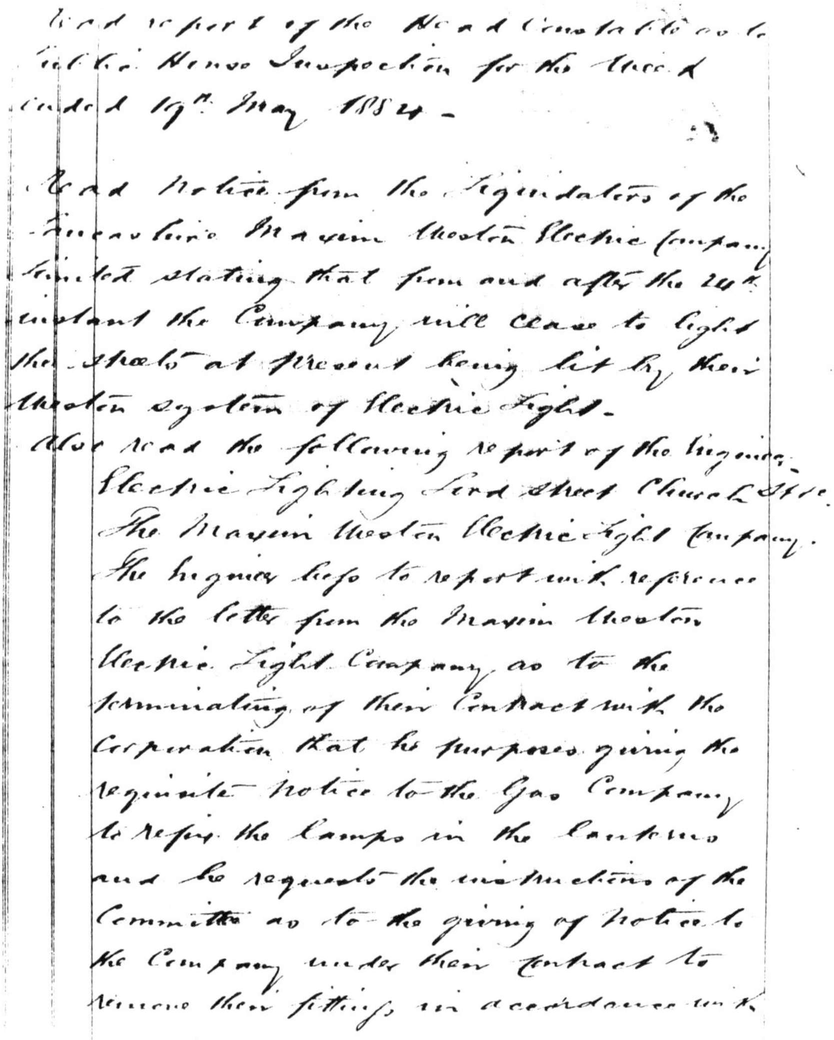

Read report of the Head Constable as to Public House Inspection for the week ended 19th May 1884 –

Read Notice from the Liquidators of the Incandescent Maxim Weston Electric Company Limited stating that from and after the 24th instant the Company will cease to light the streets at present being lit by their Weston system of Electric Light.

Also read the following report of the Engineer. Electric Lighting Lord Street Church Street. The Maxim Weston Electric Light Company. The Engineer begs to report with reference to the letter from the Maxim Weston Electric Light Company as to the terminating of their Contract with the Corporation that he purposes giving the requisite notice to the Gas Company to refix the lamps in the lanterns and he requests the instructions of the Committee as to the giving of notice to the Company under their Contract to remove their fittings in accordance with

Fig 29: A further extract from the minute book of the Liverpool Watch Committee reporting a meeting in late May 1884. *(Liverpool City Libraries)*

58

CHAPTER FIVE

F H Royce & Company

Why, if Royce had decided to set up on his own, did he recall years later, *"I was induced to found …… a small company in my own name"*? Induced by circumstances? Persuaded by his superiors that he should make it on his own rather than risk going down with a sinking ship? A clue comes from recollections late in life that the idea of working on his own account first came to him in 1883 when people he knew and worked with offered him electrical work if he branched out. Perhaps, though, it was simply a self-effacing way of alluding to the initiative he had taken. The Victorians had a real enthusiasm for writing about engineering and artistic achievement yet a great reluctance to couple this with any for profit and the acquisition of wealth. One has only to read Samuel Smiles *Lives of the Engineers* to recognise this trait. We shall never know, and it remains possible that he did feel forced by circumstances. However, leave he did – not immediately on reaching the age of 21 nor in the crucial month of May when the company was taken over. It seems he left not long afterwards.

It is on record as fact that Royce established F H Royce & Company in Manchester in the latter part of 1884. Furthermore, the story that has come down to us is that he did so with Ernest Alexander Claremont and that they set up at Cooke Street in Hulme, as electrical and mechanical engineers. Recent detailed examination of surviving records has shown that neither the address nor the involvement from the outset of Claremont was correct. This whole era has been most admirably researched and is covered by *Ernest Claremont – a Manchester life with Rolls-Royce and W T Glover & Co,* written and published by Tom C Clarke. But first, why Manchester? Why not Liverpool?

There are no firm answers but there are pointers. The quote from Tom Clarke's writings in the previous chapter alludes to the Lancashire Maxim-Weston Electric Company doing work in Manchester. Reported in *The Electrician* early in 1883 there is mention of the Managing Director, Whitworth, but not of Royce. As the company's young Chief Electrician he will inevitably have been involved in the lighting of the warehouses mentioned. Indeed, in later years Royce alluded to working in Manchester while with the Liverpool company. The warehouses mentioned, incidentally, were probably associated with the railways: the Manchester Ship Canal still lay a decade ahead in time.

Manchester was a thriving industrial centre embracing engineering, the cotton mills and commerce, and it was on the 'up'. Many of its engineering companies were small – rather like the 'little mesters' of the knife-making industry of Sheffield. Royce must have been able to assess opportunities for starting up there and he must have developed contacts, as he would in Liverpool. One senses that either might have appealed as fertile ground to set up a small backstreet company more than London, which Royce also knew, or perhaps Leeds – and Manchester, unlike Liverpool, had not witnessed a failure in attempting to move from gas lighting to the use of electricity. We don't know – but these are likely considerations which might have been taken into account. So where did he start, what was Claremont's part in the enterprise, and what did they make? Our understanding of the latter has moved on, since the first edition of this book, thanks to the work of Michael Forrest, and of the former through the painstaking work of Tom Clarke. Both, incidentally, share with the author in being past employees of Rolls-Royce.

Perhaps the first question to ask is what part Claremont had in the founding of F H Royce & Company. There has always been the oddity that the two got together as partners, a relationship reflected in Royce's application for membership of the Institution of Mechanical Engineers, in 1884, yet that the Company's name did not include Claremont's. Legend further records that Royce had £20 in savings and that Claremont lent £50. I believe this can be relied upon because the fastidious John De Looze, called upon by Ernest Hives to record the earliest days before his retirement after fifty years service, in 1943, set the combined capital at £75.

Sir Max Pemberton's *The life of Sir Henry Royce* includes a hint that Claremont's £50 may have been borrowed from his father and this is supported by other sources. The money could, if only a loan and not an investment, have been key to the Company only bearing Royce's name rather than those of both. The other possibility is that Claremont's joining Royce, while it was in 1884, may not have happened until the Company had already been set up. Days or weeks might have separated the two events. If Royce did leave Liverpool shortly after the May takeover then this has to be matched against Claremont's own statement that he worked in London for Cordner, Allen & Co of Wandsworth *'until the end of 1884'*. Add to this Royce's words *'I was induced to found ...... a small company in my own name'* and there seems to be a logic: Claremont joined F H Royce & Co at some time in the first half-year or so of its existence.

Before turning to what they made, and where, we should pause to ascertain more about Ernest Claremont. He was to be a part of Royce's life and work as partner in F H Royce & Co, as Joint Managing Director of F H Royce & Company Limited, Chairman of Royce Limited and the first Chairman of Rolls-Royce Limited until his failing health led him to resign in 1921: he died in the following year.

Ernest Alexander Claremont was the son of a surgeon, Claude Clarke Claremont, and his wife, Emma (née Hill). One of ten children, he was born just before Henry Royce on 3 February in the same year, 1863, at 1 Thorney Place, Oakley Square, Camden, London. One brother, Albert William Claremont (1857-1934) was also to feature greatly in Rolls-Royce history for he was to become senior partner in the solicitors Claremont Haynes of London. The practice provided legal services to Royce and Rolls-Royce from its inception for three-quarters of the century. The family was gifted, several becoming doctors and one a lapidarist in London. The only 'disappointment' was Theodore, who married his mother's housemaid, for which act he became an outcast.

Oddly, Ernest Claremont always celebrated two birthdays. His father had his birth certificate, registered on 16 March, dated for 3 March. His record of baptism, however, gave the date 3 February – as did the family Bible. His mother claimed his birth date to have been 3 February and, as Ernest Claremont remarked, she ought to have known. It was a great excuse in later years to give himself birthday presents on both occasions.

Ernest Claremont was educated privately and attended University College, London, although he did not graduate. Had he done, so he would have included his qualification along with his MIEE (Member of the Institution of Electrical Engineers) and MIME (Member of the Institution of Mechanical Engineers) – professional memberships which, in 1899, exactly paralleled those of Henry Royce. In fact, he spent only the years 1879 to 1881 there, reading pure maths, physics, mechanical drawing and, again something in common with his future business partner, French. His second year was part-time only, for by then he was serving a (presumably premium) apprenticeship with the Anglo-American Brush Electric Light Corporation Limited in London. This concern, as we have noted, had been registered on 24 March 1880 to take over the Anglo-American Light Company, which in turn had been incorporated to acquire rights to the patents of Charles F Brush on 12 December 1879. Ten years later the former combined with other concerns to create the Brush Electrical Engineering Company Limited. We do not know whether Claremont worked on lamps at the company's Belvedere Road plant or dynamos at the works in Borough Road, Lambeth. What we do know is that, again in common with Royce, he did not complete the apprenticeship. The reasons were different, however … he fell out with a foreman. He then worked with the nearby Cordner, Allen & Company in Wandsworth.

While at Brush he almost certainly met Henry Edmunds, who until shortly before had been the company's engineer, and who continued in part-time service of the company promoting its electrical equipment. As the narrative will later reveal, Edmunds was to play a role which earned him the cachet 'the Godfather of Rolls-Royce'.

As to how Royce and Claremont met, we have no facts, yet this is highly likely to have happened while Royce was with the Electric Lighting and Power Generating Company, renamed Maxim-Weston Electrical Company, at Bankside on the Thames in 1881 or 1882 before the posting to Liverpool. Paul Tritton (*The Godfather of Rolls-Royce,* 1993) suggests that the meeting might well have happened at one of Professor William Ayrton's evening classes at the Finsbury Institute; Claremont did not live far from there, or at one of the Professor's other demonstrations in London. It is even possible that, through such meetings, both came to the attention of Henry Edmunds at this early date.

Before moving on to what they made, and where, let us briefly turn to Ernest's brother, Albert William (1857-1934). He was admitted as a solicitor in 1879 and began a practice from his own home at 81 Camden Road, later moving to the High Street in Camden Town. Early in the 1880s he met Joseph Haynes who had been in practice since 1840 as a junior partner in Carlton, Haynes & Company and they set up Haynes & Claremont in 1888 at Marlborough Chambers, 49 Pall Mall, London. Sadly, Joseph Haynes drowned in an accident before their first year was out. Some years later, in 1899 – by which time the practice had moved to 4 Bloomsbury Square, London – Albert Claremont restyled it Claremont Haynes & Company. When I remembered them they were at Vernon House in Sicilian Avenue off Southampton Row, to which they had moved around 1907. Albert Claremont's concern handled the flotation of F H Royce & Co when it became a limited liability concern in 1894, the 1899 share flotation which was accompanied by the change from F H Royce & Company Limited to Royce Limited, and – jointly with another practice – the first public share flotation of Rolls-Royce Limited. They continued as the Company's solicitors into the late 1960s dealing, among other issues, with all senior executive salaries and the personal affairs of Henry Royce. These included his will and the distribution of portions of his estate for research into the common cold. Albert Claremont was one of only two mourners at Royce's funeral at Golders Green. The other partner, Tyldesley, married Royce's nurse, Ethel Aubin, after his death in 1933, although the union did not last long: Nurse Aubin became aware that he had non-heterosexual tendencies, but not before he had spent a significant part of her inheritance from Royce. A final point of interest concerns Albert Claremont's remarkable wife, Ethel. During the First World War she launched an anti-war campaign, believing that only women could stop wars. They formed the vision of a Society of Nations which transpired to be a parallel initiative to that of H G Wells who envisaged a League. They merged to form the League of Nations Society, forerunner of the United Nations societies of today.

We have digressed, so let us return to F H Royce & Company. It has become firmly embedded in history that Royce started at Cooke Street and from that came the assumption that this was at 1A. That was the best information available when the first edition of this book was written. If 'Cooke Street' is taken as generic – a recognisable road off the Stretford Road and its environs – then that might be a fair description, but Tom Clarke found no reference to Royce in the records of Cooke Street in the mid 1880s. What he did find came as a surprise. *Slater's Directory* for 1888 lists *'Royce, F H & Co (manufacturers and fitters of electric bells and speaking tubes. Estimates free for every description of repairs &c &c. Sample fittings for inspection at the Works) Blake Street, Hulme'*. There is no mention of Cooke Street until January 1889, by when the directory listed the Company with leased premises at 3 Cooke Street as well as in Blake Street. The Poor Rate records take us further in showing that F H Royce & Company moved into workshops at No 1 and a house at No 3 Cooke Street on 3 December 1888.

Returning to the matter of Blake Street, he found that most of it was filled with stables and cabinetmakers' workshops at the time. The earliest listing of Royce came from the Poor Rate records. It dates to 1885 and refers to premises shared with W Sargeant, the £17 rate being a single charge on the two of them. Sargeant may have been William Sargeant, who is listed in contemporary directories, but there is no evidence to indicate that there was any business relationship between them. The 1887 directory was useful in noting that F H Royce & Company occupied premises on the west (Cooke Street) side of Blake Street. Such was the method of recording that one can ascertain that it was somewhere between a Temperance Hall and one George Benson, close to a solitary house and next to stables.

In June 1888, the Poor Rate records describe the location of F H Royce & Company as by then being virtually at the end of Blake Street and covering three workshops on one account. They were shared with George Benson, an organ builder. Royce had by then extended to include a storeroom between two stables and a tiny workshop. No wonder, if the first four years in Blake Street involved so much movement, that it was simplified for us to Cooke Street, which remained a constant from late in 1888 until 1910. Tom Clarke compared the 1888 rate list for Blake Street's occupants with the Ordnance Survey map of 1891 and was able to identify where F H Royce & Company's first and subsequent premises must have been (Figs 30 and 31).

Having established where F H Royce & Company must have operated in its early days, the next questions are what did they make and how did the partners survive? Precisely how they built up the new business was never recorded. One had to rely on Royce's reminiscences and those of early employees, given years later to friends and acquaintances. When these were all put together a hazy picture emerged. However, since writing the first edition of this book, a great deal more information has come to light.

Initially, the partners manufactured arc lamps and filaments and lamp holders for incandescent bulbs. Although not clear from written records, the filaments must have been for lamp bulbs of their own manufacture. Ted Foulds, previously of the Rolls-Royce Derby 'Experi' Department, related his mother's recall from old Cooke Street employees that memories remained years later of broken glass everywhere. Swan's first successful bulb – his second design with a carbon filament – had been in production since 1879 and there were others. Furthermore, the man behind the commercial success of the Swan lamp had been Henry Edmunds. Lamp bulbs were not listed in the 1889 directory, but this may have indicated that they were only made thereafter for Ediswan. Clear evidence exists from 1894 that they had a licence from Ediswan, but we do not know how long the licence had been held: Ediswan had been formed in 1883 by Edison in the US and Swan in the UK joining forces. These very early days were not easy. 1884 was a disastrous year for the infant electrical industry, and the capital Royce and Claremont brought to the enterprise dictated a humble beginning. Recalling the period years later to the

News Chronicle, Henry Royce said, *"For many years I worked hard to keep the Company going through its very difficult days of pioneering, personally working on Saturday afternoons when men did not wish to work, and I remember many times our position was so precarious that it seemed hopeless to continue. Then, owing to the great demand for the lighting dynamos we made for cotton mills, ships and other lighting plants, we enjoyed a period of prosperity"*. One suspects he was referring to the period after 1888 and, more likely, that from shortly before the early 1890s until the turn of the century as the era of prosperity.

Initially, it seems, there were just Royce and Claremont. Claremont was small and dapper, and later became an officer in the Yeomanry (Fig 32). He prided himself on his military bearing and fitness, which he took great pains to maintain. Tennis and later polo helped keep him fit, but more unusually, once he could afford it, he employed the services of a professional wrestling partner. A martinet, he had a nasty habit of trying to catch people out, and he was a poor loser. He was, nonetheless, to become widely respected for his fair-mindedness.

In the early days, however, life was more frugal. Most of the £70 went on tools and equipment, leaving little money for food. The partners lived in a room over the works at Blake Street and they ate and slept in the same room. Sandwiches frequently had to suffice and such cooking as was done was performed in an enamelling oven, a distinctly unwise process, especially if they were using lead glaze. Claremont himself was to attribute the digestion problems he and Royce suffered in later years to their early period. Their only diversion was a wild card game called Grab, which – the way they played it – embodied elements of all-in wrestling. These games frequently finished with the partners rolling about on the floor fighting in their overalls. These days the HR profession might label that as corporate team building.

Circumstances did improve and at some time between 1884 and 1886 – sources vary – Royce took lodgings with John and Eliza Pollard at 24 Talbot Street, Moss Side. It is likely that Claremont did so too, for they were both at that address in 1888. As business improved, both partners were able to better themselves in terms of housing as we shall find.

In the course of time a number of girls were employed to assist in routine manufacturing operations. Non-routine work, one memory recalled, included the repair of sewing machines. Not surprisingly, really, for the domestic sewing machine was one of the great boons to the working Victorian household. They came from many manufacturers, until Singer cornered most of the patents and virtually created a monopoly, and were not of consistently competent design or manufacturing quality. F H Royce & Company had established themselves as 'electrical and mechanical engineers', and repairing sewing machines fell neatly into their spectrum of competence. One of Singer's sons – they were named after the places they were born – was Paris Singer. His name would gain relevance in the early days of motoring. Claude Johnson would work for him briefly before joining

C S Rolls & Company in 1902, and Paris Singer became closely associated with the Rolls-Royce car.

Royce's first commercially successful product was a simple electric bell set for household use. It sold well, being greeted by the owners of the large mansions, so common in Victorian times, as a great novelty. Such houses, it should be remembered, contained a number of maids who could be summoned to any room at the pull of a bell rope. These ropes or cables ran from something akin to a lavatory plug in each room to a series of clapper bells, which were usually mounted in the kitchen. My late mother's house still contained the vestiges of such a system. Royce's bell, with its pushbuttons and wires, appealed to the Victorians' sense of scientific wonder. The bell sets John De Looze recorded as having sold for seven shillings and sixpence. He further stated that they comprised a bell, a push, wire and a Leclanché cell.

Demand for the bells came in a steady stream and, small though the profits were, they kept the creditors at bay. Royce became obsessed with his work and nothing would drag him away from the factory. Often he worked all night and on several occasions he was found, his head resting on his arms, asleep at his workbench. Furthermore, he worked Saturday afternoons and evenings to ensure that orders for lamp holders and bell sets were fulfilled.

Throughout his life Royce was very careful to avoid infringing patents – even German ones during the course of the First World War. It is fair to assume, therefore, that the earliest products were of Royce's own design and that they were novel, at least in as far as achieving their objective without trespassing on existing patents. Royce would have had excellent opportunities whilst employed in London and Liverpool to obtain a thorough knowledge of the patents surrounding the infant electrical industry.

Commenting on these early days Royce was later to say, *"In dynamo work, in spite of insufficient ordinary and technical education, I managed to conceive the importance of sparkless commutation, the superiority of the drum-wound armature for continuous current dynamos and (the company) became famous for continuous current dynamos which had sparkless commutation in the days before carbon brushes. While at Liverpool from 1882 to 1883, I conceived the value of the three-wire system of conductor in efficiency and economy of distribution of electricity, and also, afterwards, the scheme of maintaining a constant potential at a distant point. Both of these I successfully applied. In the early days I discovered and demonstrated the cause of broken wires in dynamos through the deflection of the shafts by weight and magnetism"*. Carbon brushes, incidentally, began to replace copper in 1888 and 1889.

Royce was not the only one, however, to see the value of the three-wire system. Edison paid particular attention to developing it in 1882.

As confidence in their business increased, the partners took on more employees. Perhaps the best account of these early days is that which Bill Morton gleaned[4].

---

[4] *A history of Rolls-Royce Motor Cars 1903-1907* by C W Morton, published by G T Foulis, 1964.

It came from his first supervisor when he joined Rolls-Royce in 1924 as an apprentice in No 1 Shop at Nightingale Road. 'Old Tom' Jones told Bill how he became the ninth employee of F H Royce & Co. He was given a vice at which to work as a journeyman right next to Royce's. On the other side of the room six girls worked at a large table assembling filaments into lamp sockets and putting switches and bell sets together. Royce made the drawings, the small assembly jigs and the awkward parts. Claremont, Tom believed, sought the orders. He also kept the books, ordered the materials Royce required and paid for them. He paid the wages and bills, sent out the invoices and collected the money. In fact, he did everything but make parts, as far as Tom knew, and – despite his liking for being well dressed – he did not mind getting his hands dirty when the need arose. The year to which 'Old Tom' referred is not recorded, but it would be reasonable to assume that 'Old Tom' was recruited once the business had turned the corner. Bell sets are mentioned, and the fact that 'Old Tom' made no mention to Bill of a move from Blake Street to Cooke Street would suggest that the move had already taken place. This would put the date at no earlier than the end of 1888. Jimmy Chadwick also told me that Royce's first turner was the father of one of his friends at Cooke Street, Jimmy Whiteley, but he could not give a date for that.

Royce would not countenance an office in these early days. He just had a small table and chair in a corner of the workshop, which served as his main base for sketching when he was not making parts. The practice continued well into the 1890s once the business had begun to blossom and, as a consequence, Claremont and other staff – together with secretaries and typists – all had to work together in one room.

Dynamos were an early addition to the product range, although electric motors were not to follow for some years. The reason for this was that electricity was employed in the early days mainly for illumination rather than a source of motive power. Product designs and modifications (the latter, known as 'mods', were to become a fundamental element of Rolls-Royce from the day it was founded) flowed from Royce's blue pencil. Claremont later recalled that one dared not wear a boiled shirt for fear his partner would sketch a dynamo on it.

When I wrote this book originally we had no sharp focus on the nature of the products of F H Royce & Company, and no knowledge of how they were sold. There was the assumption that Claremont did that. The small scale of the business almost placed it on a par with the local butcher or baker if not, perhaps more relevantly, the candlestick maker. Markets would either have been larger electrical manufacturers and dealers or distinctly local – perhaps even door-to-door. We knew the bell sets were the first truly successful products commercially, and possibly it was for this reason, namely that the sale was direct to the customer. Having its own Leclanché cell, the bell set was self-contained and did not require a household to have any other electrical equipment. All that was needed was access to a service which would recharge the accumulator. I recall as a child in wartime London that one or two neighbours still had radios powered by accumulators and there was a local shop that would recharge them. One set of accumulators would be in use while the other set was away being recharged.

At this point in the narrative we should turn to the researches of Michael Forrest[5]. His remarkable story begins with a large box of photographs which came into his possession some years ago. Among them all, one stood out (Fig 33) portraying a gentleman with an array of basic electrical apparatus dating to the period when electricity first came to intrigue the minds of the Victorians – the 1880s. The man portrayed was Thomas Weston Searle, who was known as an electrical engineer in Leicester in 1903. It occurred to Michael that in the pioneer days the electrical practitioners would have added up to a small number in total, and that Searle might have known of Henry Royce.

Michael's local Leicestershire records office could shed no light on Searle, so he thought to try the Manchester Local Studies Unit. His enquiry led to his speaking to David Taylor, who had been of immense help to me over the original version of this book. He was equally helpful to Michael, exceeding by far all that he dared hope in not only establishing the presence of Searle in Manchester but also researching all his addresses there. They were all clustered around the Cooke Street and Blake Street area over the crucial period 1886 to 1894. Michael plotted all Fred (as he was known at the time) Royce's addresses over the period and this showed them all to be within about a half-mile radius of his business premises. He did the same for Thomas Searle – and got a matching answer. All were among the Victorian terrace houses of Moss Side, Hulme and Old Trafford. When Royce and probably Claremont lodged at 24 Talbot Street, Searle was a mere one hundred yards away in Hulton Street.

The proximity of Searle to the premises of F H Royce & Company and, more so, to its founders' residences suggests far more than coincidence. We should accept Michael's conclusion that Searle was the agent who sold the Company's products. We should also accept that the photograph is the only clear evidence so far of what these were. Sadly, the professional photographer sought to focus on Searle at the expense of the product range, and Michael adds that the picture shows signs of having been cut down to fit a frame: he wonders what further products originally showed on the left-hand side.

Census returns and trade directories describe Thomas Searle variously as 'electrician', 'manager', 'electrical engineer' or 'traveller'. The latter was the term used for salesmen who today might fall into the category of commercial traveller. The products appear to be mounted on portable display stands and central to the main stand is an electric bell, together with a variety of push-button and pull-cord switches, in the latter case with handles similar to those used on mechanical bells or in Victorian toilets. Above is an indicator box in the windows of which movement let the maid or butler know which room was summoning attendance as the bell

---

[5] For his full account, readers should refer to Issue 215 of the *Rolls-Royce Enthusiasts' Club Bulletin* or Number 59 of the Rolls-Royce Heritage Trust Derby & Hucknall Branch magazine, *Archive*.

rang. The door below the bell set possibly conceals a Leclanché cell, for it must be assumed that the units were demonstrated audio-visually. A further smaller display panel is largely hidden by Searle himself. I do not believe there can be any doubt that these were the products of F H Royce & Company. It is tantalising to note that the proof almost certainly lay in the wording of the cards resting on the top of each display panel …… but they have so far proved indecipherable, even with computer enhancement. Michael writes that no-one has ever admitted seeing a Royce bell set. That is true, and the famous chime makers V&E Friedland of Manchester joined with me back in the early 1960s in trying to prime a number of 'scouts' to look out for them. On the other hand, there appears to be one in the photograph of the Cooke Street fitting shop (Fig 125). There are two sizes of electric bell in the Searle photograph and the one in the factory looks bigger still. Electric bells were often of this shape, but one cannot believe Royce would have bought something he could make for himself. So, if we are right, we now have a first image of the product which proved the breakthrough for Royce and Claremont.

Two further items remain – one visible on the tabletop and the other in Searle's right hand. That on the table, in the form of a small glass dome mounted on a plinth, appears to include a semi-circular vertical scale, with a pointer just beyond the vertical. In his analysis, Michael suggests that this might have been an earth field inclinometer (a vertical rather than horizontal compass). It would have registered any other nearby magnetic field. On the other hand, it is known, as Michael notes, that 'registering instruments' were among Royce's early products – galvanometers first and later voltmeters and ammeters. A galvanometer indicates the flow of electricity without measuring either its potential in volts or current in amps. All cells and batteries give direct current (DC) as did many early mains generating stations. AC followed later. If the instrument shown was a galvanometer, it would make sense for its 'rest' position to be at centre scale, movement to either side indicating both the presence of an electric current and the direction of its flow.

Finally, Searle is holding in his hand what appears to be a small dynamo or electric motor. It could have performed as both. Here I quote from Michael's writings:

It appears to have a horseshoe electro-magnet, with many turns of cotton-covered wire on the upper half. Three terminals suggest a field, armature and common winding. At the left-hand end is a grooved pulley. Plates bolted underneath are bent up each end to form the open bearings common to early electrical machines. Brushes could be either housed in the disc and box on the left, or in the indiscernible collection of pieces at the far end. It is probably the first Royce rotating machine, and everything stemmed from that.

Certainly, one might suspect that the star product – that most likely to touch the Victorian sense of scientific wonder – would be the one Searle might show most prominently. It could have been wired to a Leclanché cell to perform as a motor or to the galvanometer to show that it could generate a current in one direction if turned one way and in the opposite direction if turned the other.

Searle disappeared from Manchester in 1894, whereafter his health deteriorated rapidly. He died in Ripon in 1908. I do not see the date of 1894 as a coincidence. My view is that Searle sold the majority, if not all, of the electrical products of F H Royce & Company throughout most of its period of existence. 'Old Tom' Jones recall that Claremont *"sought the orders"* was probably right – but the assumption that he handled the sales would be wrong. That never sat well with me. Claremont was an administrator of real competence but never seemed to be the type who would have succeeded in selling. Michael's researches give us the answer: Claremont sold to Searle and Searle, as a freelance, found his customers. It is possible that W Sargeant did likewise but we do not know. Such arrangements can work well. They did originally between Rolls and Royce and between Selwyn Francis Edge and Montague Napier – but, as history has shown, the latter became a disaster. Napier's profits as manufacturer fell over the years, while Edge's as salesman increased. A 'bust up' became inevitable. In the case of Rolls and Royce, it is recorded that Arthur H Briggs suggested the combining of manufacturing and marketing to form a Rolls-Royce company very early in the relationship. One now has to ask; did experiences from 1884 to 1894 help convince Royce and Claremont of the wisdom of the suggestion?

If one looks at the first decade of trading, Royce products gradually moved from the simple local or domestic lights, through the pivotal bell sets into dynamos, then later into electric motors, and finally cranes. The latter were industrial products with potential countrywide markets. In fact, they ultimately sold internationally. The success of the bell sets triggered a fundamental change in the product-market relationship. John De Looze (Fig 34) was recruited in 1893 to prepare for the flotation of the company as F H Royce & Company Limited in the following year, and it would seem inevitable that Claremont and De Looze had to rethink the process of marketing. They established branch offices and agents. The business had outgrown Thomas Searle and he became a victim of his own success. One can only wonder why he was not recruited to help manage the new structure: perhaps he simply felt his forte was in selling, not managing. Whatever the reason, the flotation spelled the end of his relationship with the Cooke Street factory; yet for that event – and all that followed – we owe an enduring debt of gratitude to him, and his endeavours in those early years.

A final point? Michael Forrest's box of photographs were family heirlooms and Thomas Weston Searle was his great-grandfather. Born in 1843, he had been a salesman in both London and Bristol before moving to Manchester. It is not known what he sold, or how he came to move to Manchester and become associated with Royce. Michael's grandmother was the fourth of Searle's seven children and she was almost ten when the family lived virtually back-to-back with Royce in Hulton Street and Talbot Street respectively. Michael adds that his grandmother was an accomplished name-dropper with a love of Rolls-Royce cars, yet she never mentioned a Royce connection to him. He felt forced to conclude that she never made the mental connection between the twenty-something year old bachelor, Fred Royce, and the illustrious Rolls-Royce Company. So there is not a single item of solid proof that Searle was Royce's first sales outlet, even though that seems beyond all doubt to have been the case.

The change in the Company's fortunes (or lack of them) started with the bell set. That kept the creditors at bay. But then, as Royce later recalled, the manufacturing of dynamos led to a period of prosperity. We do not have a clear chronology for these events, but I have suggested that 'Old Tom's memories made no reference to a move to Cooke Street. He must have been the first – or among the first – to join after the move early in December 1888. A further clue as to when fortunes began to change came from Ralph Smalley when I visited him at Herbert Morris, the crane makers in Loughborough: Morris' had acquired Royce Limited, the direct descendant of F H Royce & Company, in the 1930s. Ralph Smalley showed me that the first formally recorded drawing dated to 1887, and that suggests the inception of more formal disciplines, a possible precursor to the move and expansion which followed. Equally of interest, in going through the Royce archive, Tom Clarke found that Royce's book of rough calculations for 1877 included significant coverage of dynamos. He also found that it was the year in which Royce lodged his first patent – the bayonet cap lamp socket – in October 1877. We have not tracked the patent to see whether this was a variant of the basic bayonet concept or whether Royce was the originator of the bayonet. Most other countries adopted the screw fitting. Years later 'Little' Jimmy Chadwick told me that electricians claimed they would go out of business if they used them, because they never went wrong (Fig 35).

Another possible indicator lies in the fact that Claremont married in 1889 and that shortly before, in 1888, the two bachelors left their lodgings at 24 Talbot Street, Moss Side. Claremont married Edith Punt, it transpires, not as had so long been supposed in the same year as Royce married her sister, Minnie Grace Punt, but much earlier – on 19 January 1889. Edith was married from 147 Euston Road, London, at the nearby New St Pancras Church. The young couple took up residence at 246 Moss Lane East, Moss Side, an address to which Claremont had already moved and from the outset they were able to afford a young servant, Mary Walton. In parallel, Royce took up a house at 13 Milton Terrace, Stamford Street, Old Trafford, but he did not remain there for long. At some time in 1889 he moved to 45 Barton Street, Moss Side, a residence which – like Milton Terrace – has since been demolished. There he was able to have his mother, Mary, join him and he engaged a young maid, Patricia Brady, to undertake the domestic chores. None of these events would have been possible until fortunes had begun to turn. That process had begun for the electrical engineering industry as a whole, and the trend was poised to continue through the last decade of the century. It was to be a golden age for the industry (Fig 36) and Royce was well placed to capitalise on it.

We have noted that the previous belief that Royce and Claremont married the Punt sisters in the same year, 1893, was incorrect. Royce must have met his wife-to-be, Minnie Grace Punt, through his partner's wife. Minnie Grace was born in 1867, making her three years younger than Edith Claremont, and she had been a governess in Scotland. At the time of her marriage she was living at 20 Grosvenor Gardens, Willesden, London. Their marriage took place on 16 March 1893 at the nearby Parish Church of St Andrew, Willesden (Fig 37) whereupon they began their married life at 'Eastbourne', No 2 Holland Road (now Zetland Road), Chorlton-cum-Hardy (Fig 38). Perhaps wisely he found his mother a home of her own close at hand, rarely failing to visit her on his way home to bed. Frequently his visits to Albert Terrace, 21 Warwick Road, Chorlton-cum-Hardy were late at night and he would find her sitting up in bed, propped up with pillows, knitting to keep herself awake until he came. The old lady knitted him endless pairs of socks, many of which he was unable to wear. She finally died in 1904 and was buried at the District Council Cemetery in Knutsford. At much the same time as the newly married couple set up home, the Claremonts moved to a newly built home nearby on Cavendish Road (now Corkland Road), Chorlton-cum-Hardy. They named it *Electron*. It was then on the edge of open country – but that is no longer the case.

Before moving on to the flotation of the Company let us look a little more closely at the Punt family. Edith and Minnie were the daughters of Alfred Punt, a London-based licensed victualler. The girls had a sister, Florence, and a brother, Walter. We did not know until Tom Clarke found out in recent years that there were two more brothers – Ernest and Fred. Ernest had a printing business at 55 Jewin Street, London EC and did work for Royce and Claremont from the early 1890s for many years. Whilst we knew of Ernest Punt, the printer, his relationship to the girls did not become clear until this discovery.

Walter Punt was a civil engineer and he emigrated to South Africa when he was about twenty. There he met and married Helena da Fonseta, the daughter of Tovares da Fonseta, the Portuguese Consul in East Africa – previously in Madrid. Walter met Helena at parties thrown by her father, which were attended by such notables as Cecil Rhodes, Paul Kruger, Barny Barnato (whose family fortunes later kept Bentley on the road), Starr Jameson, Sir J B Robinson and Sir Alfred Beit. The couple married and had two children – Violet Helena Punt (1887-1988) and Errol Walter Punt (1889-1967). Sadly, Helena died as a result of an accident shortly after Errol was born. In due course, Walter remarried and the children were sent to England to be cared for by their grandmother.

Granny Punt used to visit Manchester frequently with the two children but both were spirited and there came a time when she could no longer cope. This was in 1895 or 1896 when Errol went to live with the Claremonts and Violet with the

Royces. When Granny died, the Royces adopted Violet, but Errol suffered a less happy existence. Edith Claremont was later recalled by Errol's son, Patrick, as a rather Victorian figure with little sense of humour, no warmth and somewhat unsocial. Violet's daughter, Mary, recalled her as prudish and easily shocked yet not without a sense of fun. Either way, as Tom Clarke records in *Ernest Claremont*, she shared with her sister Minnie a horror of the physical side of life including illness and the thought of becoming pregnant. Claremont, who was as enthusiastic about pastimes as work, enjoyed the social life. Edith he could find exasperating so he sought his pleasures and needs elsewhere, often being absent from home. Royce was to show more loyalty to Minnie, yet in the end Claude Johnson had to engineer their separation in 1912 to overcome a similar frustration.

As we shall see, the Royces and Claremonts moved to Knutsford in 1898 and from then on Errol spent more time with them than with the Claremonts.

Violet lived with Aunt Minnie long after the 1912 separation and ultimately married, becoming Mrs Maynard. She lived at Bexhill on Sea, as did so many ex-Rolls-Royce people, including the Hon C S Rolls' secretary, Florence Caswell, and ex-Cooke Street Tommy Nadin, with both of whom I used to correspond in the 1960s. Violet's nephew, Patrick Punt, described her to me when she celebrated her hundredth birthday on 18 July 1987 as a grand lady with a remarkable memory for her age. She still, correctly, recalled the third prototype Royce car, registered N-MR-7, as 'Mister Seven'.

Errol's life did not run smoothly and it seems Royce gave him a hard time. Whether this was *'he who thou lovest most thou chastiseth most'* or a case, as happens at times even with sons of great men, that they were expected to start at the bottom as their fathers had done, we can no longer find out. Errol was still living with the Royces when they moved to Quarndon in Derby, but he served throughout the First World War and remained in France thereafter, working for the Rolls-Royce agents, Franco Britannic Autos, in Paris. When war broke out in 1939 he was living at 226 Boulevard Raspail with his first wife. His son, Patrick, relates that he escaped in 1940 by the skin of his teeth, in just what he stood up in plus a small haversack. He returned to Derby to work under Alec Harvey-Bailey, who had got to know him when they both liaised with the French coachbuilders, and ran Photographic for a decade. He lived on Mansfield Road near Chester Green, Derby, and died in 1967. I visit his grave from time-to-time at nearby Breadsall Church. But let us return to the fortunes of the business and the flotation of F H Royce & Company Limited.

Fig 30: Aerial photograph showing the Cooke Street factory taken in 1926. Arrows 1 intersect on Cooke Street factory and Arrows 2 on Royce's original Blake Street workshop. *(Courtesy Manchester Central Library - Manchester Archives & Local Studies)*

73

Fig 31: Tom Clark's identification of the movements of FH Royce & Co in Blake Street between 1884 and 1888, based on the 1891 Ordnance Survey map.

74

Opposite page: the 1891 Ordnance Survey map of the Blake Street area. Some street names have been added to help the reader. Street numbers have also been added parallel to the buildings. Numbers within the premises refer to the notes below.

1-2	Cellar and workshop next to or under the Conservative Club.
3-4	Clubrooms and cellar.
5-8	Nos 35-29 houses.
9	Stable.
10	Workshop.
11	Stables and yards. From this point up the buildings were taken for Royce by 1894.
12-15	Large workshop and stables. The two oddly shaped stables were later rented by Royce and were used to disassemble the Decauville and test the Royces.
16-17	Workshops in this area.
18-20	Stables in this area.
21-26	Workshops, slaughterhouse, stables and storeroom in this area. The long area with the diagonal lines was a covered way. Royce's later storeroom was near here. This square became the 1895 crane extension.
27	No 2A stables and workshops, 14 units. This whole area became Royce's by 1893 and in 1894 new buildings replaced those abutting the works. At the bottom the diagonal lines show the covered entry. In 1931 it became Parkinson's works.
28	Royce's later small workshop around here.
29	No 2 workshop.
30	No 2 house.
31-33	Believed nos 4-6 stables, workshops. This was Royce's original location in 1884, later adding 26 and 28 above.
34	No 8, believed location of later temperance house.
35	1 and 1A Cooke Street occupied by Royce in December 1888.
36	3 Cooke Street occupied in December 1888 showing the original house and the large rear extension.
37	The area used for the post 1899 'garage'.
38	An area which always remained empty.
39	No 5 caretaker Schofield's house. No 7 next door was also Royce's.
40	A shed and yard on the Oswald St corner used later by Royce.

Fig 32: Ernest Claremont as a lieutenant in the 4th Volunteer Battalion, the Manchester Regiment in Scarlet Undress – before November 1901.

(Melnotte photograph, courtesy of John V C Claremont)

Fig 33: Thomas Weston Searle, beyond all doubt responsible for the sales of F H Royce & Co's original range of products, many of which are to be seen.

(Courtesy of Michael Forrest)

Fig 34: John De Looze joined F H Royce & Company in 1893, became Company Secretary of F H Royce & Co Ltd in 1894, of Royce Ltd in 1899 and of Rolls-Royce Limited in March 1906. When he retired in 1943 he had served for fifty years.

ROYCE,

LAMP HOLDERS.

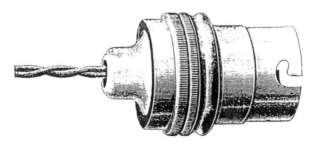

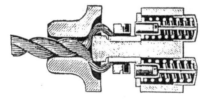

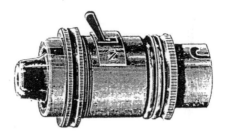

(ROYCE PATENTS.)

Fig 35: Royce's patent bayonet socket for lamp bulbs.

Works, Manchester.

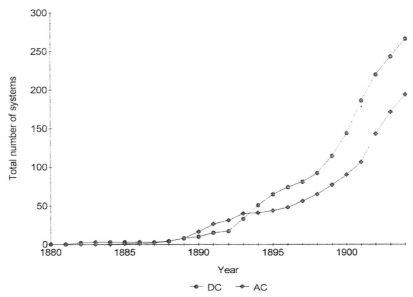

Fig 36: Growth in the numbers of electricity supply systems in Great Britain in the late nineteenth century. *(From 'The Electrician', January 1905)*

Fig 37: A 1980s photograph of the Church of St Andrew, Willesden, in which Henry Royce was married to Minnie Grace Punt on 16 March1893.
(Paul Tritton)

Fig 38: 'Eastbourne', Holland Road (now Zetland Road), Chorlton-cum-Hardy, to which Royce moved when he married in 1893. 'Eastbourne' is the right-hand of this pair of houses.

(Courtesy of Roger Varney)

CHAPTER SIX

F H Royce & Company Limited

By 1893 the partners judged that they were poised for a period of significant expansion. To meet this it would be necessary to raise capital to extend their premises and to pay for additional machinery, extra labour and materials. In consequence, they initiated processes which would lead to the re-launch of F H Royce & Company as a limited liability concern owned by shareholders. To that end, they recruited John De Looze (*D*) to become Company Secretary. Then in March 1894 they had their business valued as a 'going concern'. That valuation still exists in the Trust's possession and it gives the first accurate picture of the size of the business (Figs 39 and 40).

From it (Fig 41) one can see that they had a

Turning and fitting shop
Monitor shop – that is a Capstan Lathe shop
Lamp storeroom
Brass finishing room
Storeroom
Boiler house, packing shop and yard
Pattern room
Dynamo room
Girls' workroom
Cookhouse
Instrument room
General office
Private office
Showroom
Staircase and entrance

and plant at the Manchester Ship Canal contract.

The value of the business, excluding premises which were rented, work-in-progress and finished products, at 31 March was £2,721-18s- 4d, a very considerable sum at that time. Among other plant the inventory included no less than 53 machine tools of which 30 were lathes, 7 drilling machines and 5 milling machines or planers. From the detail of the inventory, it is reasonable to assume that the workforce in total numbered about 100 or perhaps marginally more.

Two points of interest arise from the valuation. The first, a minor one, was that Royce had at last succumbed to the need for a private office, although he shared this, when in it, with Claremont and their secretary. The second is the allusion to the Manchester Ship Canal contract. The inventory of equipment listed against this contract is compatible with that required by electricians to wire a large building. Indeed, the Manchester Port Authority confirms that the Company installed electric lighting in the docks and warehouses. At some later stage they also installed cranes (Fig 42). The inventory is so detailed that it lists *one Royce Advertisement Sign'* as being out with the tools on the contract and records that the main entrance door at Cooke Street was provided with a push-button for a bell upstairs. While telephones were used for external communication, speaking tubes served to connect the office to the stores. Such devices were among the product portfolio.

The Manchester Ship Canal was begun in 1887, the first sod being cut on 11 November. It was completed in January 1894, according to the Port Authority, and inaugurated on 21 May. What, one might therefore ask, was Royce's equipment still doing there when the valuation was completed on 31 March? Do electricians ever fall behind schedule? The Ship Canal was to bring great prosperity to Manchester, making it perhaps the greatest engineering city in the world for a time, and Royce benefited from that fact. He had installed arc lighting on 'many miles' of the waterfront and in the warehouses. The size of the contract helped trigger a change in gear for Cooke Street.

Lighting was not the Company's only involvement in the Ship Canal. George Clegg told me they took on general engineering work as well. He remembered worm and screw gears to operate lock gates. Measurement and interchangeability were still infant sciences then, having got little further than nuts and bolts and small arms for the military. Royce nonetheless succeeded in producing an accurate fit. He cut a worm drive longer than was required. A portion was parted off, given teeth and hardened, thus forming the milling cutter with which the mating gearwheel was cut. Olley was told similar tales by Royce of how he had made wormwheels. Unfortunately, while George's recall of the worm gears was correct, R Howells, Port Engineer of the Manchester Ship Canal Company told me in 1990 exactly how the lock gates were operated, and the mechanisms did not come from Cooke Street. That said, Olley recalled Royce telling him of electric motors he did supply to the Ship Canal and of problems he had experienced over C2R losses. Even when the early cars were built, equipment such as micrometers, vernier callipers and bore gauges was rare. Royce's instructions, which hung in the shops, exhorted the workforce to *'work to a model'* (Fig 43). Using callipers and a delicate sense of feel they machined the parts to duplicate the master component. This was standard practice on the railways: my father used callipers with the Cambrian Railways at their Oswestry sheds in the 1920s.

Comparing this inventory and its value with the total investment of £70 or £75 just under a decade before and, more significantly, with a workforce of Royce and Claremont plus six girls and 'Old Tom' Jones at the very end of 1888 or later – more likely 1889 – and we begin to appreciate the enormity of the expansion achieved in the early 1890s.

A prospectus was issued to launch the new company, and F H Royce & Company Limited was registered on 20 June 1894. Claremont and De Looze had the sense of occasion to record the event by framing the first cheque from the new company's first chequebook (Fig 44). They did the same on 15 March 1906 with the first cheque in the name of the new Rolls-Royce company.

First to subscribe were Royce and Claremont with 5349 shares each. Claremont's brother took one, as did De Looze. More significant as shareholders were the Punt sisters, Minnie with 1131, Edith with 1101 and Florence with one. Claremont's friend, the engineer James P Whitehead, who then lived in the same street as Royce at 26 Holland Road (now Zetland Road), Chorlton-cum-Hardy, became the holder of a large number of shares. He later became a Director. Tom Clarke found in his researches that Royce and Claremont were paid for F H Royce & Company wholly in shares. They received £500 for goodwill, £9340 for stock and work-in-progress and £2674 for debt surplus. This is difficult to reconcile with the valuation unless one was based on cost and the other on market value. Oddly, he found, this excluded the licence they had obtained in July 1893 to make and sell Edison and Swan United Electric Light Company incandescent electric lamp holders. Royce became the new company's Managing Director and Claremont its Chairman.

The study of the products of Royce and Claremont is a tantalising process. So far, no single product of the original F H Royce & Company has come to light, and neither has any catalogue: perhaps not surprising if sales seem to have been in the hands of Thomas Searle rather than the company. Once F H Royce & Company Limited had been launched that changed. A number of artefacts remain – dynamos, electric motors and switchgear, and there are a small number of catalogues. Once one comes to the later change to Royce Limited in 1899 there is a profusion of artefacts – notably cranes, and many remain in daily use.

The early period from 1884, as we have noted, saw the partners struggling to establish themselves and during the period up to the launch of the bell sets products would seem to have been simple. Between about 1889 and 1894, however, there was a step change into dynamos, registering instruments and other more sophisticated products.

The years 1889 and 1892 saw the real beginnings of electric power generating stations. Prior to that only London had seen much in the way of development and then only because there were wealthy sections of the community willing to pay over the odds for the novelty of electric light. The cost of electricity in the early 1880s was about 9d or 10d per kWh. By 1900 it had fallen to about 2d. Even so, it was not until 1911, with the advent of the drawn tungsten filament, that electric lighting became undisputedly cheaper than gas in this country, for the advent of the incandescent gas mantle had maintained its competitive position. From 1892 onwards power generator stations began to spread into the provinces. The Duke of Devonshire installed electric lighting, using a water turbine to drive the generator, at Chatsworth in that year: sadly it was not of Cooke Street provenance! Manchester and Derby were among the first towns to establish facilities in 1893. By 1895 the industry was well established and, around 1900, there was a major boom in investment as the size of stations began to grow. Some were AC but many still DC. My parents' house in London in the 1940s was supplied with DC by the local power station and two-pin plugs were used without any earth safety.

Then, with the potential the Cooke Street site offered, came the opportunity to move into cranes, and this happened soon after the 1894 flotation provided the capital for rebuilding programmes. It might be that the failure to transfer the Ediswan licence was because the partners put light bulbs behind them as they followed the often seen trend into increasingly technical product fields. The earliest known catalogue of F H Royce & Company Limited was found by Tom Clarke in the Manchester Museum of Science & Industry in 1998. Several pages of it are reproduced (Figs 45 and 46) and it will be seen that the Company was still making incandescent lamp sockets and ceiling roses, even if it no longer made lamp bulbs. Another potential confusion will meet the eye: products were referred to as 'Royce', even though they were marked as F H Royce & Company Limited.

Later came the launch of Royce Limited but that event seemed, as we shall see, to have more to do with capacity to manufacture existing products than with changes to the product portfolio. There are many cases when one finds the only thing which differentiates an F H Royce & Company Limited product from one of Royce Limited is the labelling.

The Ship Canal contract marked a start point to the business becoming involved in site contract work. This was to become increasingly important, and necessary, as the Company's markets expanded, particularly on the industrial side. When Royce started making cranes, the Company undertook to install them on the customer's premises (Fig 47). The same was true of other products and Royce undertook complete contracts, as Rolls-Royce was to do in later years on the Industrial and Marine side. Where necessary, Royce procured specialist units such as water turbines from other companies to drive his dynamos.

In addition to arc lamps and dynamos, which were now produced in increasing variety, he added electric motors (Fig 48) and a wide range of switchgear. Then came the electric crane (Fig 49), a product that was to become legendary for its longevity and reliability. In due course, they were exported as far afield as Australia, South Africa, India and Argentina. The Japanese Imperial Navy had one in their dockyard at Kobe (Figs 50 and 51). When Royce's agents subsequently visited the yard to see if the crane was performing satisfactorily they found that the Japanese had paid it the ultimate compliment. There were two cranes and the copy even had a Royce nameplate.

Among those with whom I correspond is Ray Millington of Round Corner, New South Wales, Australia, and he is an expert on Royce cranes. He was able to tell me that by January 1905 the Ship Canal Company of Manchester had acquired nine. More to the point, he sent me the illustration and caption from the catalogue (Figs 50 and 51) which showed just how easy it was to produce a copy from the detail supplied.

The story has often been told of Royce's concern when he saw that the jerking movements of cranes employed in foundries caused molten metal to slop from the ladles they were carrying. He told Tommy Nadin that he suffered from nightmares of slipping ladles. To overcome the problem he designed and incorporated centrifugal braking control to ensure progressive acceleration and deceleration (Fig 52). The cranes were produced in a large variety of capacities and spans yet examination of them shows that there were many common parts. Whilst many parts were unique to an individual crane, others came from a virtual Meccano set of standard components. So varied were the cranes, however, that Graham Grocock of Herbert Morris told me that no two were ever the same (except in Japan).

Controllers were also added to the product range when trams began to be electrified in 1895. Initially horse-drawn when they appeared in 1870, steam or cable power preceded the electric motor from the late 1880s.

Quite apart from what he made, Royce also worked with others. Among them was Hans Renold when he developed roller chains for 'safety bicycles'. It was over that experience that Royce learned that one had, at that time, to go to Germany or Belgium or perhaps America for accurate press work.

It is now appropriate that we examine what happened at Cooke Street. In the first edition of this book I got so much wrong. None of us had suspected from the memories that had come down to us that the Company had started at Blake Street. Much guessing was employed in tracking the development of Cooke Street from 1894 on, but we can now be much more accurate on that and, again, thanks to Tom Clarke's meticulous researches.

To begin at the beginning we must go back further and turn to information I gleaned much earlier yet did not incorporate originally. It was in 1965 that the whole area around Cooke Street was demolished and with it disappeared a record of a proud era and a proud people. We shall come to the demolition in due course, but that was not all I found out. At the time – February 1965 – the Manchester solicitors, Linder Myers and Pariser, were acting on behalf of a client, Levisons, the pottery wholesaler then vacating the old Cooke Street factory. One of the partners, Harry Myers, was exceedingly kind and patient in showing me papers and plans covering the precise area. His first record dated to 1852 when one Lawrence McKenna bought land (Fig 53) at the top of Blake Street and built a number of houses, workshops and a stable for rental. He borrowed £600 from a widow, Elizabeth Lloyd, to achieve this and the deeds are in the names of Oswald Milne, E C Milne and Lawrence McKenna. Ground rent was £33-14-0 per annum.

Some years later, in 1863, the land subsequently occupied by Royce between Cooke Street and the western edge of Blake Street (Fig 54) was acquired by Oswald Milne, E C Milne and George Shorland. Ground rent was £36-11-3 per annum.

Then, in 1865, the earlier plot referred to was sold by one Robert Turner to George Shorland. It then comprised houses, joiners' workshops, stables and a slaughterhouse. Ground rent for the two parcels of land amounted to Royce and Claremont's total capital in 1884: there is no way when one thinks that they could have started on either parcel of land.

With the passage of time, the Cooke Street building had been extended by its then owners, the George Shorland Trust. This happened in April 1881 and July 1884. To the end of their period of occupation, F H Royce & Company, F H Royce & Company Limited, Royce Limited and Rolls-Royce Limited rented the premises and, in fact, the last to leave Cooke Street, as we shall see, did so in 1910 within months of the termination of the lease from what had then become Shorland & Ball estate[6].

Having moved to the business premises at 1A and house at 3 Cooke Street on 3 December 1888, the new location gave Royce and Claremont adequate space, for several years, as the property extended eastwards as far as Blake Street. By 1893, however, expansion began to press. Even before the flotation, a planning application was lodged in the December by the George Shorland Trust. It sought to demolish and redevelop the buildings which occupied the area enclosed by the houses on Cooke Street and the edge of Blake Street – but not the large shop directly behind 1A. The application was approved in May 1894 and its architect was Hartley Hacking of Manchester. Perhaps one should add that this was the *'rabbit warren'* that Bill Morton could never understand.

In October 1895 a second extension was approved. Although the plans are missing, there can be no doubt that this was the large shop (most of which comprises area A in Fig 53). It was clearly designed for the manufacture of cranes. Its steel stanchions incorporated carrier brackets (Fig 174) for crane rails and the balcony to one side of the shop suggests it was designed to give access to the crane mechanisms. Until this building was completed no large span overhead travelling crane could have been built. It is likely, though, that smaller swinging arm cranes were already being sold before completion of this shop in 1896.

The third extension entailed the replacement of the house at number 3 Cooke Street with a three-storey building. Its middle floor extended available office space, and above it was a purpose-built drawing office with two north-facing glass roof lights. The application for this work was approved on 22 June 1898. It was again designed by Hacking (Fig 54) and was completed in May 1899. Interestingly, the upper part of the wall as designed was an ornamental feature. If one compares this with photographs of the building (Figs 3 and 4) one can see that Royce must have involved himself. The aforementioned feature was deleted, as it served no useful purpose. This was a fundamental principle of his engineering, although it did not necessarily apply to his domestic residences.

---

[6] The last lease on the Cooke Street premises was signed on 13 August 1896 and covered the 14-year period from 24 June 1896 to June 1910. It begins, *"We William Burrow Shorland of the City of Manchester, Estate Agent, and William Ball of Torquay, Gentleman"*, and is signed by both at G Shorland Ball, Solicitor, 11 King Street West, Manchester. The annual rent was £565.00.

A fourth, and final, extension made use of the residue of the strip of land on which the house had stood at number 3, and of the unoccupied land beside it. It included staff time clocks, and possibly served as a cloakroom. Its date is not known but is likely to have dated to shortly after the three-storey building.

The later 1890s were clearly a highly successful period for the partners. Normally a frugal man as a result of his many years of hardship, Royce nevertheless felt sufficiently confident in his business to indulge in a little personal luxury. He decided to build a house for himself and his wife, for their adopted niece Violet and, increasingly by that time, for their nephew Errol (Fig 55). This he did in the most fashionable road in Knutsford, Legh Road. This road had been under development by the artistic yet eccentric local businessman Richard Harding Watt – mainly in Italianate fashion in a development of the 'arts and crafts' style. Royce did not follow the trend.

When I wrote this book originally the suggestion was that Royce might have engaged Alfred Waterhouse, the architect of Manchester's pseudo-Gothic Town Hall, to design Brae Cottage (Fig 56). It now seems that this was not so. The work, Tom Clarke found, was that of the Manchester architect and surveyor Paul Ogden (1856-1940). Ogden's name was to reappear in 1907 when he was asked to prepare a report on the suitability of the land at Nightingale Road in Derby for the new Rolls-Royce works. His report survives and shows that he recommended that it was not suitable. It was ignored and, Rolls-Royce being unable to afford the professional charges of an architect, Royce was left to design the whole factory! In the design of Brae Cottage, Royce uncharacteristically allowed himself a little ostentation for the initials of Frederick Henry and Minnie Grace Royce were incorporated into one of the gables, together with the date, 1898 (Fig 57). It seems likely that Claremont's move to Legh Road happened before Royce's. He lived in a palatial semi-detached house called Endsleigh at the time. It had been built in 1875, although not as part of the later Italianate development, and it boasted seven bedrooms. Gossip remained half a century later of Edith's nagging and of Claremont's final departure to seek a more peaceful existence living in the works of W T Glover. Royce's mother, Mary, did not move to Knutsford. She spent her last few years living at 3 Ivy Grove, Chapman Street, Hulme, where he could keep an eye on her. She died in 1904 and was buried, as we have noted, in Knutsford. Other members of Royce's team lived a little more humbly, although John De Looze was proud enough of his home at Parkfield Road, New Moston, to photograph it (Fig 58).

To return to the fortunes of the business, by October 1897 orders in hand were worth £6000. By the following March the figure had risen to £9000. When the order book rose to £20,000 in February 1899 good business was having to be turned away. Major expansion of manufacturing facilities was needed and that had already been planned.

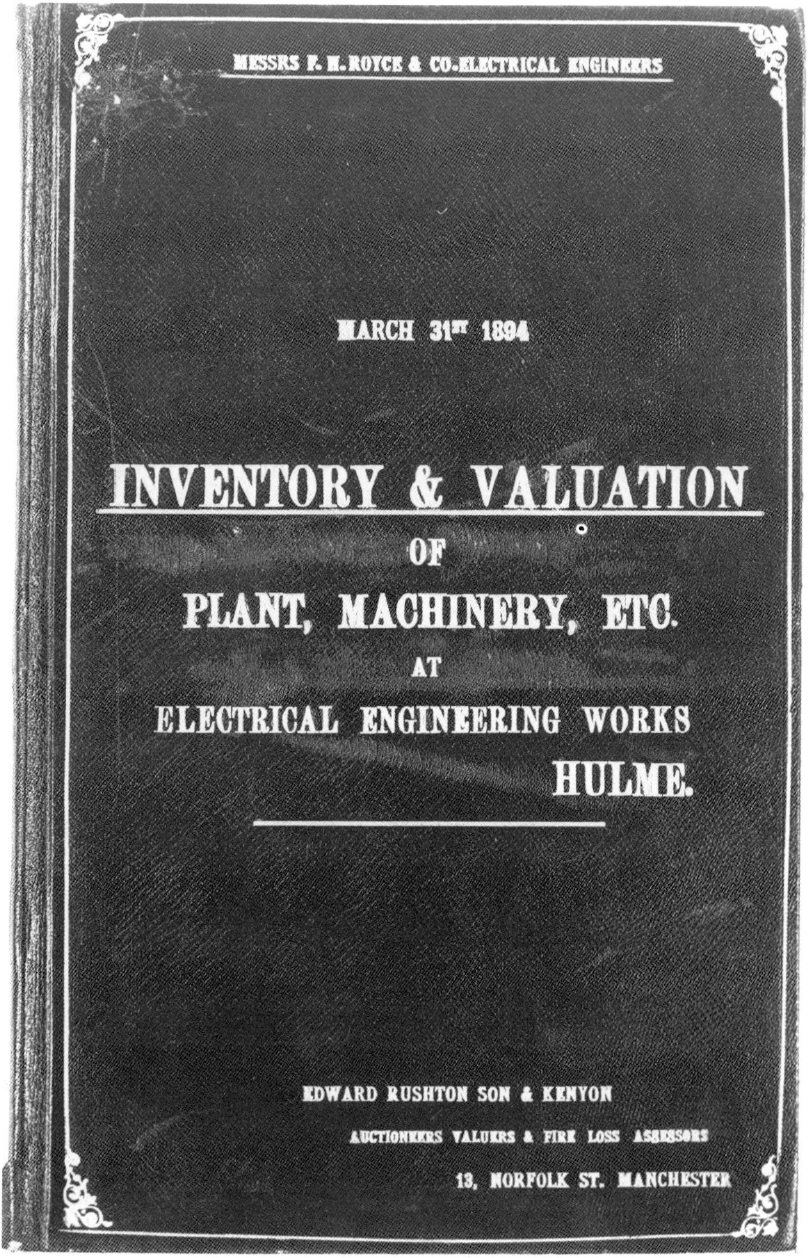

MESSRS F. H. ROYCE & CO. ELECTRICAL ENGINEERS

MARCH 31ST 1894

INVENTORY & VALUATION

OF

PLANT, MACHINERY, ETC.

AT

ELECTRICAL ENGINEERING WORKS

HULME.

EDWARD RUSHTON SON & KENYON

AUCTIONEERS VALUERS & FIRE LOSS ASSESSORS

13, NORFOLK ST. MANCHESTER

Fig 39: The valuation of F H Royce & Co carried out in 1894.

Fig 52: Crane mechanisms incorporated brakes and other devices to ensure smooth acceleration and deceleration in all directions of movement.

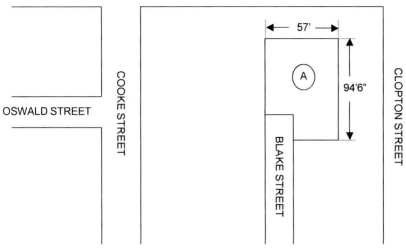

RUTLAND STREET

1852

OSWALD STREET

COOKE STREET

BLAKE STREET

CLOPTON STREET

57'

A

94'6"

A - 1348 square yards   Rent £33-14-0
Land bought by Lawrence McKenna,
owned by Oswald Milne, E C Milne and Lawrence McKenna

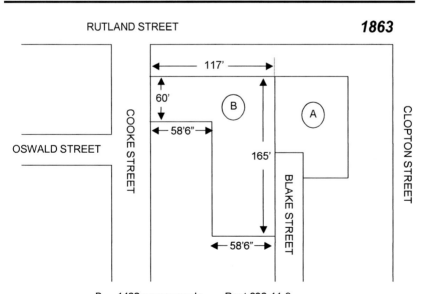

RUTLAND STREET

1863

OSWALD STREET

COOKE STREET

BLAKE STREET

CLOPTON STREET

117'

60'

58'6"

B

A

165'

58'6"

B - 1462 square yards   Rent £36-11-3
Land owned by Oswald Milne, E C Milne and George Shorland

Fig 53: Blake Street premises in 1852. Cooke Street and Blake Street premises in 1863.

101

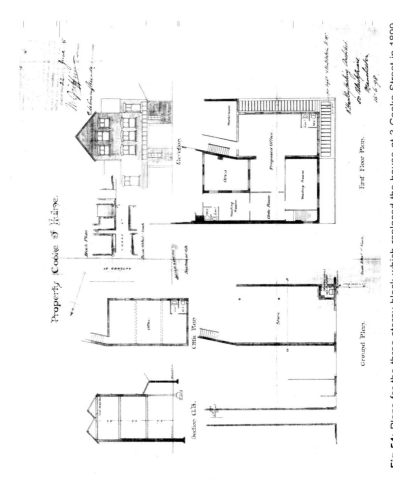

Fig 54: Plans for the three-storey block which replaced the house at 3 Cooke Street in 1899. The gable was not built to Hacking's design as it would have used more bricks to no purpose.

Fig 55: Henry Royce aged 33 with his adopted niece, Violet Punt, and nephew, Errol Punt.

Fig 56: Brae Cottage, Legh Road, Knutsford, which Henry and Minnie Royce had built for themselves in 1898 – a visible testimony to the success of his unrelenting endeavours over the previous fourteen years.

Fig 57: The gable of Brae Cottage showing the plaque with the initials of Frederick Henry and Minnie Grace Royce, and the date 1898.

Fig 58: The road in which John De Looze lived, Parkfield Road, New Moston: he was a keen photographer, and this came from his album.

CHAPTER SEVEN

Royce Limited

The turn of the century saw investment in electrical manufacturing at its peak. It seemed the right time to expand, so a prospectus was issued in March 1899 (Fig 59) seeking £30,000 in new share capital: £20,000 of this was to be earmarked for additional Works and £10,000 for the general requirements of the business. The prospectus gave a number of interesting figures. One was that the net value of assets (exclusive of goodwill) was then £20,664-13-0, which compares impressively with the figure in the 1894 valuation, namely £2,721-18-4. Another was that total issued capital was £21,580, most of which was in Ordinary Shares of £1 and the remainder in Deferred Shares of the same value.

The prospectus included a brief history of the business to that date. It records that the business started in 1884 as *'F H Royce & Co, Electrical and Mechanical Engineers, and manufacturers of Dynamos, Motors and Kindred Articles'*. I always wondered where *Magic of a Name*[7] found that appellation and the description would not have been correct initially because Royce did not make dynamos or motors in 1884. The history continued, stating that this business had been acquired in 1894 by F H Royce & Co Ltd, Electrical & Mechanical Engineers, and that by 1899 authorised share capital amounted to £30,500. The intent was to virtually double this number. Directors at the time were F H Royce, MIEE, MIME and E A Claremont, MIEE, MIME – joint managing directors – and James P Whitehead. An Extraordinary General Meeting of F H Royce & Co Ltd was held on 28 September to approve the restructuring and a further one on 16 October to confirm that the company should be wound up voluntarily with Royce and Claremont as liquidators. The effective date of the liquidation was to be that day, 16 October. The flotation was successful, and saw the Company change its name once more – to Royce Limited. Claremont became Chairman of Royce Ltd and remained so until his death in 1922. His brother Albert, of Claremont Haynes, succeeded him and when he died, his colleague, George Henry Richards Tildesley, succeeded him. Tildesley later married Royce's nurse, Ethel Aubin. That was in 1935 – but they separated in 1937.

The new Trafford Park Industrial Estate was chosen as the location for the new factory. The estate, claimed to be the first in Europe, had been begun in 1895 on Sir Humphrey de Trafford's parkland alongside the Manchester Ship Canal[8]. Land was acquired there on 8 June 1901 and Royce undertook much of the design work on the new factory himself. Building work commenced on 4 July and was carried out by William, J B and W H Southern. The new Royce factory was situated opposite to the new factory being built by W T Glover, the cable makers whose products

---

[7] *Magic of a Name* by Harold Nockolds, published by G T Foulis, 1938-1961

Royce had used for some time. The choice of site was almost certainly for this reason.

Walter Twiss Glover had made cables since 1868 at Salford and one wonders whether Royce already knew him in his Liverpool days. However, the particular significance of the firm was that Glover and the ubiquitous Henry Edmunds became partners in 1886 and it was under their joint leadership that the business had flourished. Glover died in 1893 and thereafter the man at the helm was Edmunds. Glovers went public in 1898, floating 200,000 £1 shares and, with the money raised, moved from Salford (Fig 60) to their new factory. They had signed a lease on a large plot of land in 1899: work was well under way by the early months of 1900 and they were among the first to move to the site in 1901. Another early occupant was the British Westinghouse Electrical & Manufacturing Company whose American plant engineer was the father of Sir Arthur Whitten Brown who flew the Atlantic with Alcock in 1919. Claremont, Chairman and Joint Managing Director of F H Royce & Co Ltd, became – additionally – a director on Edmunds' Board in 1899, and it appears that Edmunds, in turn, became a shareholder in Royce Ltd. The new Royce Ltd factory (Figs 61 and 62) was occupied around 1902, with the transference of the iron foundry (Fig 63) and crane manufacture (Fig 51) from Cooke Street.

The process of product development was, as has been noted, continuous and the events of 1899 served only to change the wording on the nameplate. Part of the range of goods offered in 1904 is illustrated in this book with the aid of two simple sales catalogues (Figs 64-67). These deal solely with dynamos (Fig 68), motors and starting switchgear. There were also the cranes and capstans and an endless variety of accumulators, domestic lighting switches, fuses and lamp sockets, ammeters, voltmeters and switchboards. John De Looze recorded that, among other products were 'electro magnetos' for the Hope-Jones organ manufactured at Birkenhead. I suspect De Looze meant electro magnets. These would allow an organ to be separated from its keyboards by distances which could not be accommodated by direct mechanical linkage. One wonders, did Royce develop these while sharing premises in his early days at Blake Street with an organ builder? It was quite amazing that such a small concern – then employing perhaps between 200 and, at most, 400 people – could market so many different products.

Additionally, they were tendering for contracts. Extracts from a file covering the installation of electric lighting at Penny Bridge Hall near Ulverston appear among the illustrations as an example of this work (Figs 69-74). The dynamo was powered by a water turbine which was procured from W Gunther & Sons of Oldham. Among the papers illustrated is a handwritten letter (Fig 75) with a

---

[8] By 1900 the Trafford Park Estate Company was developing 1200 acres of land on an island between the old Bridgewater Canal and the Manchester Ship Canal – Manchester United had their ground near to the W T Glover factory. A decade later the Ford Model T was assembled at Trafford Park, and in the Second World War the names of Ford and Rolls-Royce again had a significance at Trafford Park. Ford Motor Company built 30,428 Merlin aero engines there, employing over 17,000 people and turning out no fewer than 900 engines per month by the summer of 1943.

rather charming comment on the bottom to the effect that, the factory being shut for holidays, there was no-one to type it. As I rewrite this book, Philip Hall of the Sir Henry Royce Memorial Foundation has taken what remains of the installation at Penny Bridge Hall. I quote from *Foundation Corner* in the RREC Bulletin for September/October 2003:

ROYCE SWITCHBOARD

Last year, during a visit from his home in Bermuda, Club member Russell Southern happened to mention that he had two Royce Ltd voltmeters similar to the instruments on display in the Royce room. He explained that some years ago he removed these from a switchboard at Penny Bridge Hall, near Ulverston, because he thought that it would be a pity if they were not preserved. Royce Ltd had installed electric lighting at the Hall in the early 1900s, as is documented in Mike Evans' Heritage Series book, In the beginning.

We, of course, asked Russell if anything else remained of the installation; he said that he thought that the switchboard might still be there, possibly with one or two components still on it. However, it was in an outhouse and he had not ventured near it for many years as the floor had given way. Penny Bridge Hall is now owned by Russell's son, Mark, and Russell suggested that we contacted him.

At Mark's invitation, Philip Hall visited Penny Bridge, expecting to find perhaps nothing more than a decaying wooden panel. What greeted him was an absolute treasure: a large slate panel complete with instruments, circuit breakers, regulator switches, porcelain fuse boxes etc, and the maker's plate – Royce Ltd, Manchester (Fig 76). There were several other smaller slate panels containing switches and fuses, and a large quantity of electrical fittings. Among these are Royce lamp holders, bearing the stamp FHR & Co – Patent, confirming that the sprung contacts, which to this day are part of every bayonet cap lamp holder, are in fact a Royce invention.

Mark has most kindly agreed to place all this equipment on loan to the Foundation. We are in the process of cleaning it, prior to putting it on display.

As has been seen, the turn of the century saw Royce Ltd prepare for a period of increased prosperity. What in fact happened has not been unknown in more recent times. Recession set in just as the manufacturing capacity increased. The German home market collapsed in 1901 and in consequence Germany exported, often at very low prices, and especially to Britain. In Britain the expansion of the domestic electrical manufacturers was augmented by the big American companies like Westinghouse and the GE subsidiary BTH expanding their manufacturing bases here. And, to cap it all, not only did the established mechanical engineering firm Dick, Kerr and Company enter the electrical manufacturing field, but so did a newcomer – GEC.

The effects on profitability were disastrous, competition driving the price of electric motors, in particular, down sharply. As an instance, a Crompton 10 hp motor sold for £65 in 1901. By 1905, the price had been driven down to £30. The competition did have the effect that electrical power became economical for factory use, and by 1907 over half the electrical consumption was in factory power. But the electrical manufacturers were not to recover from the recession until the years immediately before the First World War.

Unlike many of his competitors, Royce refused to lower his standards, but he did make strenuous efforts to reduce the cost of manufacture, and thereby selling price, without sacrifice of quality (Fig 77).

The Lists will be OPEN on MONDAY, March 13th, at 10 o'clock a.m., and will be CLOSED on WEDNESDAY, March 15th, at 4 o'clock in the afternoon.

WILLIAMS DEACON AND MANCHESTER AND SALFORD BANK LIMITED are authorised, at their Head Office, Mosley Street, Manchester; Birchin Lane, London; or at any of their Branches, to receive applications for the undermentioned Preference Shares.

F. H. ROYCE & COMPANY LIMITED,

Electrical and Mechanical Engineers.

INCORPORATED UNDER THE COMPANIES ACTS 1862 to 1893.

SHARE CAPITAL - - £30,500;

Increased by Special Resolution in view of this Issue to £60,500.

DIVIDED INTO

6000 SIX PER CENT CUMULATIVE PREFERENCE SHARES OF £5 EACH - - - (Preferential as to Dividend and having priority on the return of Capital.)	£30,000
30,000 ORDINARY SHARES OF £1 EACH - - - - - - - - - -	30,000
500 DEFERRED SHARES OF £1 EACH - - - - - - - - - -	500
	£60,500

Of the above there had been issued up to 31st March 1898 20,754 Ordinary Shares of £1 each, and 500 Deferred Shares of £1 each. Since that date there has been issued 326 Ordinary Shares of £1 each. Total Capital issued - £21,580

The remaining Ordinary Shares will be issued as and when required for the further extension of the business.

Present Issue, 6000 Six per Cent Cumulative Preference Shares of £5 each.

PAYABLE: 10s. on Application; 15s. on Allotment;

The balance as required in Calls of not more than £1 at intervals of not less than two months.

It is proposed to pay the Preference Dividends half-yearly, on the 1st July and 1st January in each year, the first dividend being payable on the 1st July 1899. The dividend is payable on the amount for the time being paid up on the Shares.

There are no Debentures; and no Debentures, Debenture Stock, or other Mortgage, Charge, or Lien, having priority over the Preference Shares now offered, can be issued or created without the consent of a Resolution passed by two-thirds of the Preference Shareholders present or by proxy at a meeting called for the purpose.

RESERVE FUND.—The Articles provide that the Directors shall set aside in each year, for the purpose of forming a Reserve Fund, 10 per cent of the total profits remaining after the payment thereout of the Preference Dividend, until such Reserve Fund shall amount to £10,000, after which the Directors may add to the Reserve Fund such a sum in each year as in their discretion they shall think fit.

DIRECTORS:

F. H. ROYCE, M.I.E.E., M.I.M.E., Knutsford,
E. A. CLAREMONT, M.I.E.E., M.I.M.E., Knutsford, } *Managing Directors.*
JAMES P. WHITEHEAD, Engineer, "Redcot," Chorlton-cum-Hardy.

BANKERS:

WILLIAMS DEACON & MANCHESTER & SALFORD BANK LIMITED, Manchester.

SOLICITORS:

London: HAYNES & CLAREMONT, 4, Bloomsbury Square.
Manchester: HOCKIN, RABY & BECKTON, Mount Street.

BROKERS:

MEWBURN & BARKER, Pall Mall and Stock Exchange, Manchester, and Crossley Street, Halifax.

AUDITORS:

STOCKWELL & WILLIAMSON, Chartered Accountants, 52, Brown Street, Manchester.
Who have audited the Accounts of the business since 1890.

SECRETARY:

JOHN DELOOZE.

REGISTERED OFFICES:

COOKE STREET, HULME, MANCHESTER.

Fig 59: The prospectus issued in 1899 when F H Royce & Co Ltd were seeking capital to build the Trafford Park works. It also signalled the change in name to Royce Ltd. Haynes & Claremont – later Claremont Haynes – remained Rolls-Royce's solicitors until 1971. Note that Claremont and Royce were joint managing directors of F H Royce & Co Ltd.

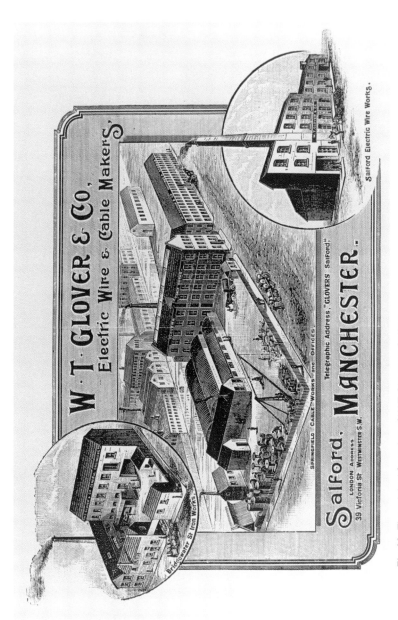

Fig 60: The original factories of W T Glover at Salford.

Fig 61: Aerial view of Trafford Park showing W T Glover's new factory on the far side of the road, and on the nearside the new Royce Ltd factory (arrows denote road). Beyond Glovers, on the left of the picture, is Manchester United's Old Trafford football ground.

Fig 62: A photograph showing the Trafford Park industrial estate. To the right is Royce Ltd. To the left W T Glover's factory.

Fig 63: The Royce Ltd iron foundry at Trafford Park. The crane will be one of their own.

Fig 64/67: Illustrations from two catalogues published by Royce Ltd shortly after the turn of the century.

"ROYCE"
CLASS F OPEN-TYPE TWO POLE
DYNAMOS AND MOTORS
(Patented)

For Belt or Rope Driving, fitted with Two Bearings.

Shunt or compound wound for various voltages.

CONTINUOUS CURRENT.

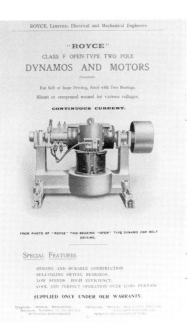

FROM PHOTO OF "ROYCE" TWO-BEARING "OPEN" TYPE DYNAMO FOR BELT DRIVING.

SPECIAL FEATURES.

STRONG AND DURABLE CONSTRUCTION.
SELF-OILING SWIVEL BEARINGS.
LOW SPEEDS. HIGH EFFICIENCY.
COOL AND PERFECT OPERATION OVER LONG PERIODS.

SUPPLIED ONLY UNDER OUR WARRANTY.

Telegrams "SWITCH," MANCHESTER.
Telephone NATIONAL 771, 1866 and 4832.
All Previous Lists Cancelled.

Cablegrams "SWITCH," MANCHESTER, ENGLAND.
A B C and Private Code Used.
subject to Alteration without Notice.

"ROYCE"
CLASS A OPEN TYPE
MULTIPOLAR DYNAMOS
(Patented)

For Direct Coupling, fitted with Long Bearing and ½-Coupling forged solid on shaft, and Shunt or Compound Wound for various Voltages.

CONTINUOUS CURRENT.

FROM PHOTO OF "ROYCE" OPEN TYPE MULTIPOLAR GENERATOR
FOR

DIRECT COUPLING TO ENGINE OR TURBINE.
SUITABLE FOR USE IN CENTRAL STATIONS. FOR TRANSMISSION OF POWER PLANTS, HAULAGE AND PUMPING PLANTS, &c., &c.

SPECIAL FEATURES.

STRONG AND DURABLE CONSTRUCTION.
SELF-OILING SWIVEL BEARING.
LOW SPEEDS. HIGH EFFICIENCY.
COOL AND PERFECT OPERATION OVER LONG PERIODS.

SUPPLIED ONLY UNDER OUR WARRANTY.

Telegrams "SWITCH," MANCHESTER.
Telephone NATIONAL 771, 1866, and 4832.
All Previous Lists Cancelled.

Cablegrams "SWITCH," MANCHESTER, ENGLAND.
A B C and Private Code Used.
subject to Alteration Without Notice.

"ROYCE"
CLASS C SEMI-ENCLOSED TYPE
MULTIPOLAR DYNAMOS
(Patented)

For Belt or Rope Driving, or for Direct Coupling to High-speed Engines, Turbines, &c.

Shunt, Series, or Compound Wound for various Voltages.

CONTINUOUS CURRENT.

FROM PHOTO OF "ROYCE" SEMI-ENCLOSED MULTIPOLAR DYNAMO FOR BELT DRIVING.

SUITABLE FOR BELT OR ROPE DRIVING, OR DIRECT COUPLING
TO ENGINE OR TURBINE.
ELECTRIC LIGHTING. TRANSMISSION OF POWER.
HAULAGE AND PUMPING PLANTS, &c., &c.

SPECIAL FEATURES.

STRONG AND DURABLE CONSTRUCTION.
SELF-OILING SWIVEL BEARINGS.
LOW SPEEDS. HIGH EFFICIENCY.
COOL AND PERFECT OPERATION OVER LONG PERIODS.

SUPPLIED ONLY UNDER OUR WARRANTY.

Telegrams "SWITCH," MANCHESTER.
Telephone NATIONAL 771, 1866, and 4832.
All Previous Lists Cancelled.

Cablegrams "SWITCH," MANCHESTER, ENGLAND.
A B C and Private Code Used.
subject to Alteration Without Notice.

"ROYCE"
CONTINUOUS CURRENT
ELECTRICAL MACHINERY.

ILLUSTRATION No. 8 FROM PHOTO OF "ROYCE" BALANCER, ARRANGED FOR WORKING
ON THREE-VOLTAGE SYSTEM.

ENQUIRIES ARE SOLICITED FOR ALL DESCRIPTIONS
OF ELECTRICAL MACHINERY, INCLUDING:—

SPECIAL GENERATORS OF ALL CLASSES.
LOW VOLTAGE GENERATORS FOR ELECTROLYTIC WORK.
PLATING DYNAMOS.
SPECIAL MOTORS FOR ALL DESCRIPTIONS OF MACHINE TOOL
DRIVING AND SIMILAR DUTIES.
MOTOR-GENERATORS. BALANCERS. BOOSTERS.
ROTARY CONVERTERS. ELECTRO-LOCOMOTIVES etc. etc.
SPECIAL GEARING FOR SPEED REDUCING.

SUPPLIED ONLY UNDER OUR WARRANTY.

Telegrams "SWITCH," MANCHESTER.
Telephone NATIONAL 771, 1866, and 4832.
All Previous Lists Cancelled.

Cablegrams "SWITCH," MANCHESTER, ENGLAND.
A B C and Private Code Used.
subject to Alteration Without Notice.

STARTING

SWITCHES.

ROYCE, LIMITED, MANCHESTER.

MOTOR STARTING AND REGULATING SWITCHES.

TYPE "A." (Overload and no Voltage Release.)

FROM PHOTO OF "A" TYPE SWITCH FOR STARTING ONLY.

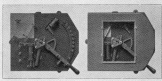

FROM PHOTO OF "A" TYPE SWITCH FOR STARTING AND REGULATING.

SPECIAL FEATURES.

AUTOMATICALLY SWITCHES OFF IF THE OPERATOR ATTEMPTS TO SWITCH ON
TOO QUICKLY; IF THE CURRENT EXCEEDS A GIVEN AMOUNT, OR IF THE
SUPPLY IS INTERRUPTED OR THE VOLTAGE IS GREATLY REDUCED.
IMPOSSIBLE TO SWITCH ON WITHOUT HAVING THE RESISTANCE IN CIRCUIT.
BREAKS THE CIRCUIT ON CARBON SPARKING CONTACTS.
ALL CONTACTS EASILY RENEWABLE.

SUPPLIED ONLY UNDER OUR WARRANTY.

(For Prices and particulars see following page.)

Telegrams: "SWITCH," MANCHESTER.   Cablegrams: "SWITCH," MANCHESTER, ENGLAND.
Telephone: NATIONAL 772 and 2962.   A B C and Private Code Card.
All Previous Lists Cancelled.   Subject to Alteration Without Notice.

MOTOR STARTING AND CONTROLLING SWITCHES.

TYPE "B." (Tram-car Controller Pattern.)

FROM PHOTO OF "B" TYPE CONTROLLER.

SPECIAL FEATURES.

COMPLETELY IRON-CLAD.   INCOMBUSTIBLE MOUNTINGS.
SPECIAL QUICK "MAKE" AND "BREAK."
ACTUATING HANDLE EFFECTUALLY INSULATED.
SEPARATE EXTERNAL RESISTANCES ON INCOMBUSTIBLE FRAMES.

ESPECIALLY SOUND AND SOLID CONSTRUCTION.

SUPPLIED ONLY UNDER OUR WARRANTY.

For Prices and particulars see following page.)

Telegrams: "SWITCH," MANCHESTER.   Cablegrams: "SWITCH," MANCHESTER, ENGLAND.
Telephone: NATIONAL 772 and 2962.   A B C and Private Code Card.
All Previous Lists Cancelled.   Subject to Alteration Without Notice.

RESISTANCE FRAMES.

TYPE "D."

FROM PHOTO OF No. 2 SIZE "D" TYPE RESISTANCE FRAME.

SPECIAL FEATURES.

INCOMBUSTIBLE METAL FRAMES.   SLATE MOUNTS.   RESISTANCE
COILS OF SPECIAL ALLOY.   LAMINATED BRUSH TO SWITCH.

SUPPLIED ONLY UNDER OUR WARRANTY.

(For Prices and particulars see following page.)

Telegrams: "SWITCH," MANCHESTER.   Cablegrams: "SWITCH," MANCHESTER, ENGLAND.
Telephone: NATIONAL 772 and 2962.   A B C and Private Code Card.
All Previous Lists Cancelled.   Subject to Alteration Without Notice.

Telegrams: "SWITCH," MANCHESTER.   A B C and Private Code Used.
Cablegrams: "SWITCH," MANCHESTER, ENGLAND.   Telephones : National 772, 2962, and 4651.

Established 1884.

ROYCE, Limited,

Electrical and Mechanical Engineers,

MANCHESTER.

Manufacturers of

DYNAMOS,
MOTORS,
ELECTRICAL CRANES,
HOISTS, CAPSTANS, Etc.,
ELECTRO-LOCOMOTIVES,
MOTOR STARTING and
CONTROLLING SWITCHES,

ARC LAMPS,
BALANCERS, BOOSTERS,
MOTOR GENERATORS,
RESISTANCE FRAMES,
SHUNT REGULATORS,
Etc., Etc.

Contractors for the Erection of

TRANSMISSION OF POWER
PLANTS,
ELECTRICAL TRACTION,
HAULAGE AND PUMPING
PLANTS,
ELECTRICAL CRANES,

HOISTS, CAPSTANS, Etc.,
ELECTRIC LIGHTING of
FACTORIES,
COLLIERIES,
HOTELS, SHIPS, Etc.

Fig 68: This illustration indicates how large some of the Royce Ltd dynamos were.

118

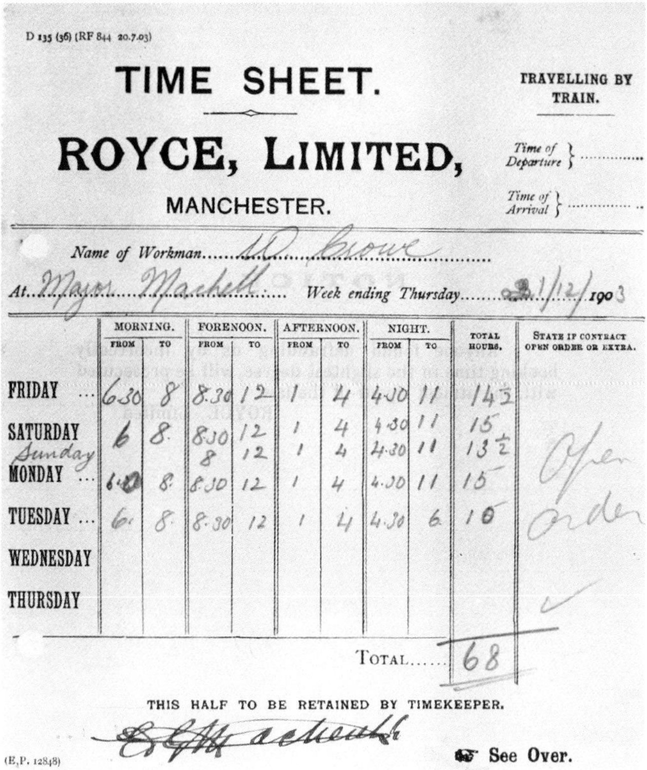

D 135 (36) (RF 844 20.7.03)

TIME SHEET.

TRAVELLING BY TRAIN.

Time of Departure } ....

Time of Arrival } ....

ROYCE, LIMITED,

MANCHESTER.

Name of Workman......W. Crowe......

At......Major Machell...... *Week ending Thursday*......31/12/1903

	MORNING. FROM	MORNING. TO	FORENOON. FROM	FORENOON. TO	AFTERNOON. FROM	AFTERNOON. TO	NIGHT. FROM	NIGHT. TO	TOTAL HOURS.	STATE IF CONTRACT OPEN ORDER OR EXTRA.
FRIDAY ...	6.30	8	8.30	12	1	4	4.30	11	14½	Open order
SATURDAY ...	6	8	8.30	12	1	4	4.30	11	15	
Sunday			8	12	1	4	4.30	11	13½	
MONDAY ...	6.30	8	8.30	12	1	4	4.30	11	15	
TUESDAY ...	6	8	8.30	12	1	4	4.30	6	10	
WEDNESDAY										
THURSDAY										

TOTAL...... 68

THIS HALF TO BE RETAINED BY TIMEKEEPER.

E. G. H. Machell

(E.P. 12848)

☞ See Over.

Fig 69: Timesheet from the file covering the installation of electric lighting at Penny Bridge Hall near Ulverston. Note the hours worked, and the time of year. Some years ago the generator house was bulldozed because it had become unsafe. Many remnants of the original system were recovered on loan by Philip Hall on behalf of the Sir Henry Royce Memorial Foundation in mid 2003.

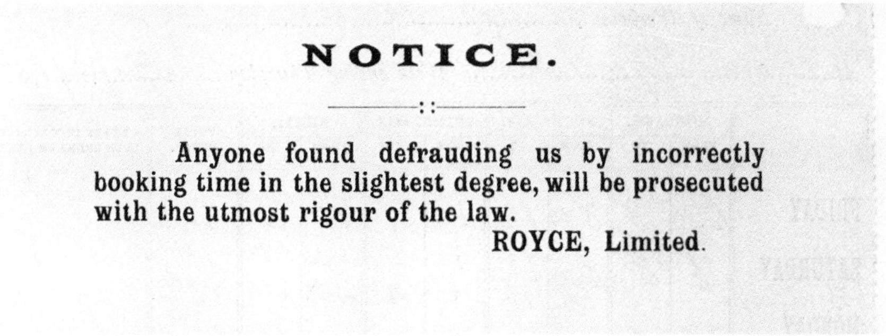

NOTICE.

Anyone found defrauding us by incorrectly booking time in the slightest degree, will be prosecuted with the utmost rigour of the law.

ROYCE, Limited.

Fig 70: Dire warning on the rear of the timesheet.

F.H. ROYCE, M.I.E.E. M.I.Mech.E.
E.A. CLAREMONT, M.I.E.E. M.I.Mech.E. } Managing Directors.
R.D. HULLEY, M.I.Mech.E. Director.

TELEPHONE NATIONAL 772.
NATIONAL 3562.

Telegrams,
SWITCH, MANCHESTER.
ROYCES, GLASGOW.
Cablegrams,
SWITCH, MANCHESTER, ENGLAND.

ESTABLISHED 1884.

FROM ROYCE, LIMITED.

CONTRACTORS TO H.M. GOVERNMENT

ON ADMIRALTY,
WAR OFFICE
AND
INDIA OFFICE
LISTS.

Patentees &
Sole Makers of the
ROYCE
2 POLE & MULTIPOLAR
DYNAMOS & MOTORS
OF ENCLOSED
AND OPEN TYPES.
ELECTRIC CRANES.
HOISTS, ETC.
Varied assortment of
MOTOR STARTING & CONTROLLING
SWITCHES.
ARC LAMPS IN GREAT VARIETY.
SWITCHES.
CUT OUTS, CEILING ROSES.
LAMP &
SHADE CARRIERS.
VOLTMETERS,
AMMETERS.
RESISTANCE FRAMES, &c.
COMPLETE INSTALLATIONS OF
ELECTRIC
LIGHTING,
TRANSMISSION OF POWER
TRACTION,
HAULAGE,
PUMPING,
VENTILATING. &c.

Electrical & Mechanical Engineers,
HEAD OFFICE AND WORKS,
(COOKE STREET.) HULME,
MANCHESTER, 28th Jan. 190 4
TO WHICH ADDRESS ALL COMMUNICATIONS SHOULD BE SENT

BRANCH WORKS, TRAFFORD PARK, MANCHESTER
GLASGOW OFFICE, I, PARTICK HILL ROAD, PARTICK, GLASGOW

In your reply please refer to c.I. 28/1.

Mr. Mackereth,
Penny Bridge Hall Estate,
Greenodd,
Nr. Ulverston.

Dear Sir,

In further reply to your telegram of to-day we are sending off a Wireman by the 6-50 train to-morrow morning, and he is bringing with him as much material as we think will be required for either a temporarily or permanently repair or break down. As he will have a pretty heavy load, will you kindly send Douglas to meet him at Greenodd Station where he should arrive at 10-39 a.m.

If it should be found absolutely necessary for the Writer to come, he can manage to get up to Greenodd for Saturday and Sunday by putting off other

(Contd.)

Fig 71: No mention is made of motor cars in the left-hand of the letterhead. Ulverston contract detail. Royce Limited, like its predecessor, had a tendency to use old paper stocks until the supply was exhausted, so one cannot automatically assume letterhead was current when used.

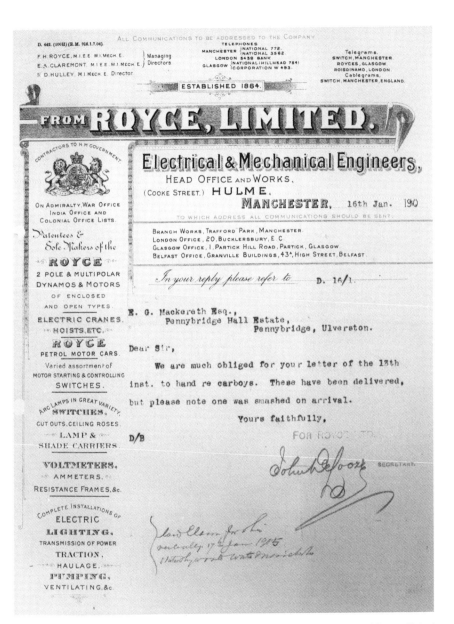

D. 442. (100H) (R.M. 916.1.7.04).

F.H.ROYCE, M.I.E.E. M.I.MECH.E.
E.A.CLAREMONT, M.I.E.E. M.I.MECH.E.
N.D.HULLEY, M.I.MECH.E. Director.

} Managing
Directors.

TELEPHONES.
MANCHESTER { NATIONAL 772.
            { NATIONAL 3562.
    LONDON 5438 BANK.
GLASGOW { NATIONAL(HILLHEAD 754)
        { CORPORATION W 493.

Telegrams.
SWITCH, MANCHESTER.
ROYCES, GLASGOW.
ROISDINAMO, LONDON.
Cablegrams.
SWITCH, MANCHESTER, ENGLAND.

ESTABLISHED 1884.

FROM ROYCE, LIMITED.

CONTRACTORS TO H.M GOVERNMENT

ON ADMIRALTY, WAR OFFICE
INDIA OFFICE AND
COLONIAL OFFICE LISTS.

Patentees &
Sole Makers of the
ROYCE
2 POLE & MULTIPOLAR
DYNAMOS & MOTORS
OF ENCLOSED
AND OPEN TYPES.
ELECTRIC CRANES.
HOISTS, ETC.
ROYCE
PETROL MOTOR CARS.
Varied assortment of
MOTOR STARTING & CONTROLLING
SWITCHES.
ARC LAMPS IN GREAT VARIETY.
SWITCHES.
CUT OUTS, CEILING ROSES.
LAMP &
SHADE CARRIERS.
VOLTMETERS.
AMMETERS.
RESISTANCE FRAMES, &c.
COMPLETE INSTALLATIONS OF
ELECTRIC
LIGHTING.
TRANSMISSION OF POWER
TRACTION.
HAULAGE.
PUMPING.
VENTILATING. &c.

Electrical & Mechanical Engineers,
HEAD OFFICE AND WORKS,
(COOKE STREET.) HULME.
MANCHESTER, 16th Jan. 190

TO WHICH ADDRESS ALL COMMUNICATIONS SHOULD BE SENT.

BRANCH WORKS, TRAFFORD PARK, MANCHESTER.
LONDON OFFICE, 20, BUCKLERSBURY, E.C.
GLASGOW OFFICE, I, PARTICK HILL ROAD, PARTICK, GLASGOW.
BELFAST OFFICE, GRANVILLE BUILDINGS, 43ᴬ, HIGH STREET, BELFAST.

In your reply please refer to   D. 16/1.

E. G. Mackereth Esq.,
    Pennybridge Hall Estate,
            Pennybridge, Ulverston.

Dear Sir,

    We are much obliged for your letter of the 13th
inst. to hand re carboys. These have been delivered,
but please note one was smashed on arrival.

            Yours faithfully,

D/B   FOR ROYCE LTD.

                            John Defoore
                                        SECRETARY.

Fig 72: A further document from the Ulverston contract file. Note the listing of Royce Petrol
Motor Cars on the left of the letterhead.

Fig 73: Yet another document from the Ulverston file. The letterhead now lists Rolls-Royce Petrol Motor Cars as products.

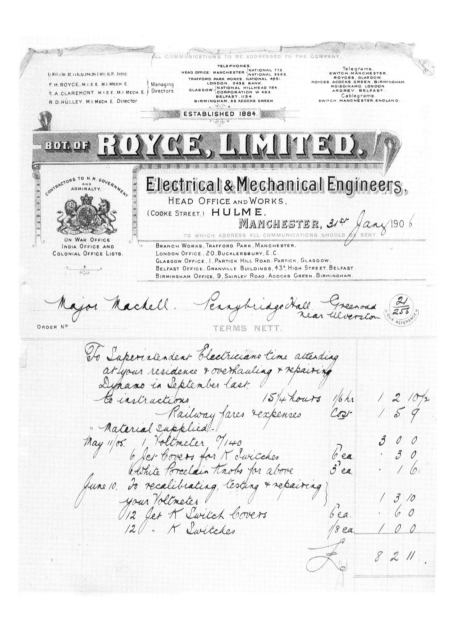

Fig 74: A further letterhead in use by Royce Ltd for invoicing specifically. This comes from the Ulverston file.

D 114

TELEPHONE (NATIONAL) 772.
(Do.)   (Do.)   3562.
TELEGRAMS "SWITCH, MANCHESTER."

ESTABLISHED 1884.

CONTRACTORS TO H. M. GOVERNMENT.

Works : Cooke Street, Hulme, Manchester.

From

F. H. ROYCE & Co., LTD., Manufacturing Electricians.

August 7th 189 1900

Major Machell,
    The Hall, Penny Bridge,
        Greenodd, near Ulverston.

Dear Sir

We are in receipt of your favor of the 6th inst and have pleasure in advising you that we are willing to extend the date of acceptance of our estimate F 502, July 23rd 1900 until the 21st inst.

We shall be glad to give you any further information in our power on hearing from you.

Awaiting your esteemed instructions

We are, yours faithfully,

FOR ROYCE LIMITED,

F. H. Casson,

Kindly excuse paper, our offices & works being closed for annual holidays. &c.

Fig 75: Handwritten letter of Royce Ltd apologising for the reply not being typed due to it being factory holiday closure. Note that old F H Royce & Co Ltd stationery was being used up, as witnessed by the rubber stamp 'For Royce Limited'.

124

Fig 76: The switchboard as recovered by Philip Hall of the SHRMF from Penny Bridge Hall in 2003.   *(Courtesy Sir Henry Royce Memorial Foundation)*

ROYCE, LIMITED.

Electrical & Mechanical Engineers.

CAUTION.

OUR wish in tendering for Electrical Work is to include everything occurring to us as likely to add to the reliability of the installation, and as we often find our competitors, on the contrary, deprive the installation of as many of the details as possible in order to reduce the cost, and so secure the order, we trust you will before ordering, be satisfied all are quoting on the same lines.

Owing to the inexperience of the public upon electrical matters, in consequence of the industry having been created comparatively recently it is an easy matter for unscrupulous contractors to under-cut us, by omitting important items, without attracting attention until the work is finished.

MANCHESTER.

Fig 77: Royce caution concerning reduction in quality.

CHAPTER EIGHT

Royce acquires a motor vehicle

Royce had worked with singular commitment to his company since 1884 and the rapid expansion through the later 1890s must have placed a continuous strain on him. That was inevitably added to by the planning of the new factory at Trafford Park and the move of crane work and the iron foundry to the new site. Additionally, the frustrations of his home life, which had led to his gardening at night by the light of bulbs on bamboo poles, on top of very long working days, must have taken their toll. The disappearance of much of the order book in such a short space of time effectively came as a final blow. His health began to suffer. Claremont recognised the problem, as did their doctor: Royce had been working too hard, and his natural propensity for doing so had been spurred on by the lack of the sort of relationships nature intended in the bedroom.

Claremont and the doctor, who was not as has been suggested Dr H Campbell Thomson[9] but more likely the local Knutsford general practitioner Dr Theodore Fennell, connived to get Royce out in the fresh air by purchasing primitive motor vehicles known as De Dion 'quads', and persuading him to do likewise. Tom Clarke believes these machines were purchased in 1901. No formal record of this exists but Maurice Olley wrote of the period when he and I corresponded in the 1960s. Writing on 26 April 1965 he commented, *"R[10] was a genius, and was distinctly paternal in his attitude. It was necessary to be young and mouldable, and to be greedy for instruction, to get along with R. Older and more experienced men eventually clashed. E was six months younger than I. A great part of our education occurred casually in anecdotes about the early days with Ernest Claremont in Manchester ... Then there was R's earliest entry into motoring. The three young men making runs at weekends in their three De Dion quads."* The period to which

---

[9] Dr Campbell Thomson became associated with Henry Royce and his problems around 1911 or 1912 and became the Company's first medical consultant. Claude Johnson had recognised that Royce was not the only person at risk through overwork, and instituted regular medical check-ups at Company expense for senior officials. He also organised what were effectively compulsory attendances from time-to-time at Derby Playhouse to ensure that senior officials at least took some breaks from work. Legend has it that he ensured Royce did not find out as he would have viewed the practice as frivolous. When I joined Rolls-Royce in 1959 a Dr Levin performed the same role. To this day, senior staff receive scheduled health checks, albeit largely by the in-house team of the Chief Medical Officer. The lessons of Royce's overworking were well learned.

[10] Until current times seniors in Rolls-Royce on sites which had always been part of the Company were known by their 'reference'. In the early days, for instance, Royce was known as *R*, Claremont as *EAC*, Rolls as *CSR* and Claude Johnson as *CJ*. A G Elliott *(E)* was at the time right-hand man to *R* wherever he was located as principal design assistant. After *R's* death in 1933 he rose to become the Company's Chief Engineer and ultimately its Deputy Chairman. Maurice Olley was *Oy* and made outstanding contributions to the ride and handling of motor cars in his later career with General Motors.

Maurice referred was his first experience of working with Royce at Le Canadel in the winter of 1913-1914. In other letters he told us more of the fun Royce and his friends had with their machines. They were more like two bicycles than a car. One started pedalling and this got the single-cylinder engine to fire. The brakes were inadequate due to oil leaking onto them and the carburettor was of the surface evaporation type, which was not remarkable for its response. The first modification that Royce carried out was not the quad but to his driveway (Fig 117) at Brae Cottage. He built a rockery at the end of it to arrest the progress of the machine in the event of a brake failure, and thereby prevent the embarrassment of descending the sloping lawn beyond, which terminated in a small copse. The rockery, incidentally, was still there when I last enquired.

Whether it was as a result of the quads that Royce first set his sights on building a motor car, or whether they were no more than a stage in that process, we shall never know. Other items of information do point towards that ultimate outcome. Shortly before writing the first edition of this book, Lamar H Gilbert, a Trust member in Atlanta, Georgia, USA wrote saying that he had bought a book in London in September 1984. Published in 1902 and entitled *The Automobile – its construction and management* (Fig 78), it was a translation of a French textbook on the subject by Gerard Lavergne. The point of interest was that the flyleaf bore the signature F H Royce and date alongside, September 1902. He wondered if this had indeed belonged to Henry Royce. There could be no doubt that the signature was genuine. The book had been found in the south of France, a fact consistent with its having been in the bookshelves of *Villa Mimosa* at Le Canadel when Royce died.

But the ruse – if ruse it was – of the De Dion quads was only a partial success because Royce ultimately collapsed as a result of the pressures on him. With difficulty, he was persuaded to take a holiday and for ten weeks he and Mrs Royce were away. They visited relations of Minnie's in Capetown (probably, although not recorded, her brother) and the peace of the long sea voyage refreshed Royce both physically and mentally. This is the conventional interpretation of the holiday, and doubtless true. But there are other potential deductions.

We know that the Royces returned late in 1902. Add to that the date in Lamar H Gilbert's book – September 1902 – and the fact that they were away for ten weeks, and one might conclude that the book was bought to occupy Royce's mind on the voyage. He may indeed have taken other books on the same subject. Whether so or not, the long voyages must have offered opportunity to review the situation in which Royce Limited found itself, and options for the future. Bearing in mind the dire situation the Company faced, it is unlikely that his first action on returning home was frivolous, yet he bought another motor car. Another factor emerged from the experience, and this was that Minnie Royce did not wish to repeat the experience of journeying outside the British Isles. Some years later Claremont and Johnson, Chairman and General Managing Director of Rolls-Royce Limited respectively, were to use this fact as the method of parting Henry Royce from Minnie. Johnson ensured that Royce fell for the village of Le Canadel, knowing that his wife would not follow. Additionally, they found Nurse Ethel Aubin to tend his needs. A long lost memo between Claremont and Johnson, according to Bill Morton, decreed that it was necessary to find a 'nurse', because Royce *"was not one to seek outside the house that which he could find within it"*. But we digress.

The car Royce bought was a two-cylinder Decauville, made by the railway locomotive constructors just outside Paris (Fig 79). The ten horsepower Decauville had been launched by the company in 1901 and had been introduced to England in March 1902. In Tom Clarke's view, it is possible that Royce actually bought his before the South African trip. He recently discovered among the papers of the late William J Crampton that Royce's Decauville was one of the first four imported. Crampton had taken delivery of one of the others. Fitted with an open tonneau body, and painted grey, one might assume that it was acquired as an instrument of family pleasure and a useful means of getting to and from work in the summer months. But there might be the alternative view, namely that Royce was moving towards the manufacture of motor cars.

Before proceeding to relate Royce's experiences with the Decauville it might be well to mention that Royce had already been involved in yet another car. Mention is made of his having done work on an electrically-propelled car for Pritchett and Gold in Sir Max Pemberton's biography of Royce (page 172). The mention is tantalisingly brief but at least it sufficed to spur Paul Tritton and the author on to a little more research. Paul found that Pritchett and Gold had their factory at Feltham in Middlesex and that the firm existed from around 1902 until somewhere between 1906 and 1910. It was well known for the manufacture of accumulators. It also made a few electric cars, which it sold under its own name, and petrol-driven cars, which it sold as the Meteor. The electric car was a two-seater open car with a sloping bonnet similar to a Renault.

More than one model of petrol car were made, the 14 hp in 1903 and 12 hp and 24-30 hp in 1904. All had four-cylinder engines and the 14 hp at least was equipped with a Blake engine. It is possible too that the others were not of their own manufacture. Similarly, it would seem, neither was their electric motor. They turned to Royce Ltd for this – perhaps understandable as Pritchett Brothers had been agents for Royce dynamos in the south of England since the late 1800s.

I visited Arthur Hack and Ralph Smalley at Herbert Morris', who took over Royce Ltd in 1932, and here Ralph Smalley was able to put substance to the brief allusion. In the Royce Ltd drawing register, page 192, is entered drawing 3255 (Fig 80) dated 18 November 1902. It is for an Auto-car Motor for Pritchett and Gold. Ralph Smalley did one better. He produced that general arrangement drawing (Fig 81). Whether this was the motor sold in the production car, of course, we cannot be certain. What it does indicate is a further association between Royce and the new form of transport, the car.

The arrival of Royce's Decauville was not an auspicious event. Bill Morton recorded, and Jimmy Chadwick confirmed to me, that Royce took a tram down to the Goods Station at London Road to collect it. The car refused to start, no matter what Royce did to it, and in finality he had to suffer the indignity of being pushed all the way to Cooke Street by four strong fellows, each duly tipped for his efforts. Arriving in this unceremonious manner, Royce locked the car up for the night in the stable yard in Blake Street. The following day the fault was remedied, but there were lessons yet to be learned. On the Sunday he ran out of petrol three miles from home.

THE AUTOMOBILE

ITS CONSTRUCTION AND MANAGEMENT

TRANSLATED FROM GÉRARD LAVERGNE'S
"MANUEL THÉORETIQUE ET PRATIQUE
DE L'AUTOMOBILE SUR ROUTE," WITH
ADDITIONS AND NEW ILLUSTRATIONS

REVISED AND EDITED BY PAUL N. HASLUCK
AUTHOR OF "LATHEWORK," "MILLING
MACHINES AND PROCESSES," ETC., EDITOR
OF "WORK" AND "BUILDING WORLD"

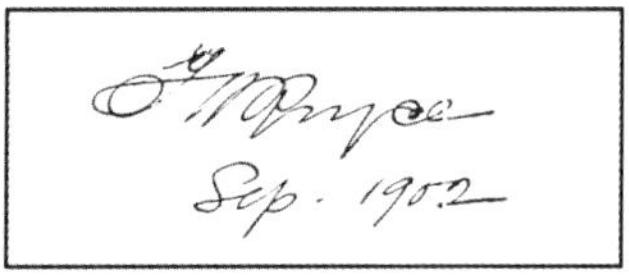

Fig 78: The French textbook on car design bought by Royce in September 1902 and, inset, his signature on the flyleaf.

Fig 79: A Decauville similar to that acquired by Henry Royce.

131

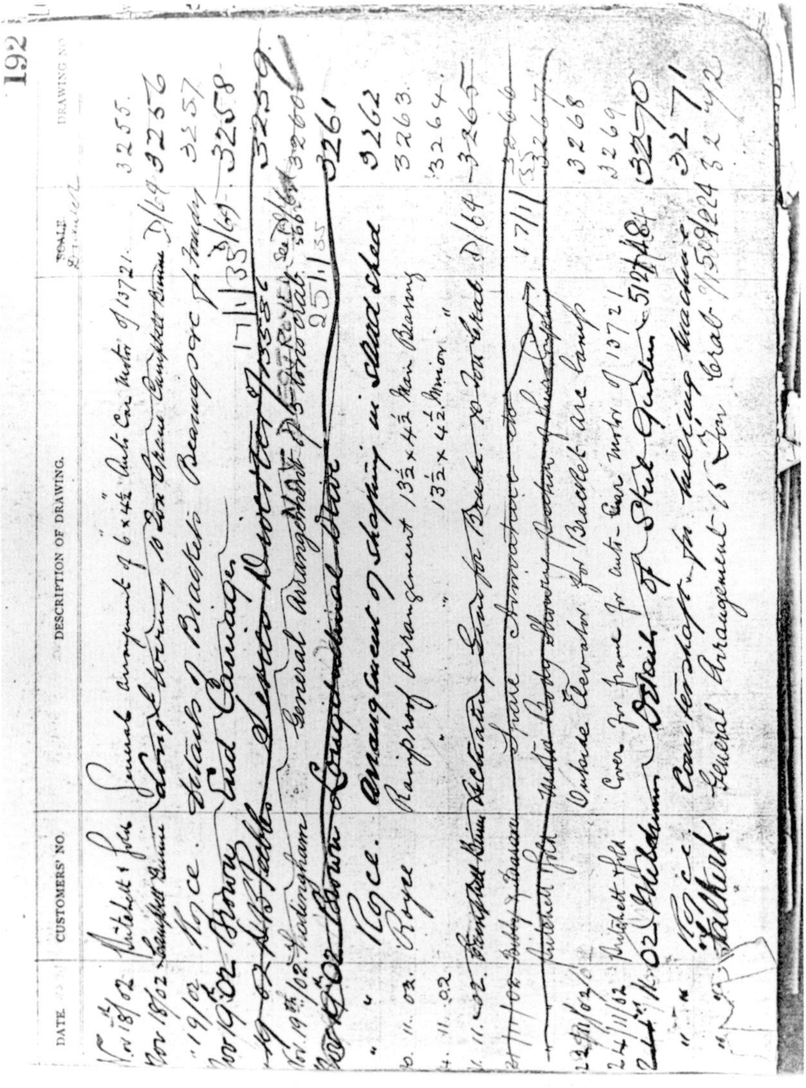

Fig 80: Royce Ltd drawing register page showing an entry for the motor designed for Pritchett and Gold late in 1902.
(Herbert Morris Limited)

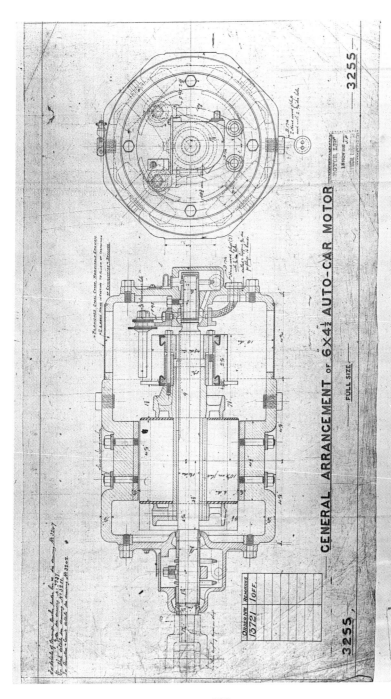

Fig 81: The Royce Ltd General Arrangement drawing for the Pritchett and Gold electric motor for car propulsion. *(Herbert Morris Limited)*

133

CHAPTER NINE

Royce builds a car of his own design

The choice of a Decauville was not without reason. France and Belgium rather than Germany led the way at the time. Writing thirty years later, Sir Max Pemberton[11] commented that the *"comparative excellence"* of cars such as the Panhard and De Dion saved the automobile movement in Britain from being strangled at birth. Royce (Fig 82) ran the car for a period so that he could become conversant with it and establish both its good points and its bad ones, and he recalled his experiences in later years to his young designers. In one of Maurice Olley's treasured letters to me, he wrote *'... And his purchase of the Decauville, because, while the Americans were still making 'horseless carriages', the French had the imagination to make something that was distinctly a 'motorcar'. Then the sad discovery that the French imagination did not extend to details, and the Decauville's flywheel was fixed to the crankshaft by a setscrew! His exasperation with the Decauville details made him decide to pull it apart in Cooke Street and put it together right'.*

Even before this had happened – and we will return to the matter shortly – Royce told his fellow directors that he proposed building three prototype cars to a broadly similar specification. Claremont (Fig 83) was utterly opposed to making motor cars. Precisely why is not on record but one can be pretty accurate in one's guesses. He was always an exceedingly cautious man and understood the dangers in taking a step too far in business. He was prudent and always felt a great responsibility to the shareholders, as well as in staying within a company's Articles of Association[12], and motor cars clearly did not in his view. It is interesting to note, however, that his abilities in management were recognised outside the Company. In 1899 he had become a Director of W T Glover & Company Limited, the cable makers, before its move from Salford. His remuneration was £500 pa – a tidy sum then – and this had risen to £1000 pa by 1902. A year later Henry Edmunds relinquished some of his day-to-day managerial responsibilities at Glovers, becoming Chairman, and at that stage Claremont was appointed Managing Director – a task in which he was to excel, albeit in the style of the martinet he was.

So, we had a situation in which the workload of Royce Limited had nose-dived, as it had for all other manufacturers in similar lines of business. By 1904 Royce cranes had to be offered at 25% discount. Claremont saw the situation as demanding the utmost prudence and frugality. He had done all he could to safeguard the health of his partner Fred, got him out in the fresh air with the ruse of the DeDion quads,

---

[11] *The Life of Sir Henry Royce* by Sir Max Pemberton, published by Selwyn & Blount, 1933 or 1934.
[12] In later years he opposed the entry of Rolls-Royce into aero engine manufacture despite that eventuality having been covered in the Memorandum of Association from the day Rolls-Royce Limited was registered on 15 March 1906.

sent him off on holiday to South Africa, and what had been the result? The commitment of precious and unaffordable resources to making – for whatever reason – three motor cars. It was, to quote a later era, a bridge too far. To Claremont, Royce had either lost his sense of responsibility or was taking the biggest risk in their twenty years together. He was initially so concerned that he advised the young apprentice Ernie Wooler to get out and join W T Glover.

R D Hulley[13], fellow Director and Works Manager of Royce Limited, was not interested either. He had problems enough with the existing raft of live part numbers and the complexity of scheduling against a falling workload. Morale and job uncertainties must have added to his problems. But, whatever Claremont and Hulley might have said, Royce followed his intent.

His first action was to set up a car drawing office. A J Adams was put in charge of the section as he had some experience of car work in America. A man called Shipley was placed under him, along with a junior assistant named Arnold, who was the son of a well-established Manchester coachbuilder. Sadly he died a year later at the age of 19 from an ear infection. His replacement was a young indentured premium apprentice named Ernie Wooler, who years later, among other things, was to become Mayor of Pompano Beach in Florida. But that is a story in itself.

Let us take a look inside the drawing office. The only picture we have of it came to light in 1979 when I was lent the family albums of the late John De Looze (Fig 84). It clearly shows the large drawing board on which Shipley (Shipham in Bill Morton's book) worked to Royce's instructions incorporating details into the General Arrangement drawings. Also in the office was George Tilghman Richards. The office of John De Looze and his staff lay beyond the glass partition. A J Adams left the Company in 1905 for the cycle maker Eclipse Machine Company when they started making cars. George Tilghman Richards later joined Marshall, working under their chief designer on cars, George W McKnight – brother of Clara McKnight, a typist at Royce's solicitors, Hockin, Raby & Beckton. Clara and Ernest Claremont had formed a relationship in 1899: she was to remain his mistress for the rest of his life.

On the works side Ernie Mills (Figs 85 and 86) was made foreman on the car job and he was given two young electrical apprentices to help him, G Eric Platford (*EP*) and Tommy S Haldenby (*Hy*). Both had joined Royce Limited in 1900. In later years Eric Platford was to become Chief Tester of Rolls-Royce on production, covering both cars and aero engines. Among the many tasks he accomplished was the installation and final testing of the Eagle engines in Alcock and Brown's Vimy before their first direct crossing of the Atlantic by air in June 1919; Alcock and Brown both came from Chorlton-cum-Hardy incidentally. His sudden death in

---

[13] Hulley joined Royce Limited from Crossley, a noted Manchester engineering firm that ultimately came to belong to Rolls-Royce plc in 1989 when Northern Engineering Industries, of which it was a constituent, was taken over. The author was subsequently party to the launch of major new Rolls-Royce diesel engines at the old Crossley plant which incorporated a development test bed for such large engines. The Trust holds title to a Crossley motor car held by a local museum still.

135

1938 shocked the whole workforce and the General Manager, Ernest Hives, decreed that no-one would ever bear the title Chief Tester again. In the late 1960s I served under his nephew, Walter Hewkin, who was Personnel & Administration Manager at the Rolls-Royce Flight Test Establishment at Hucknall. Haldenby too progressed through the organisation. At an early age he managed the Lillie Hall repair base in London inherited from C S Rolls & Company. He virtually began the Experimental Department and ultimately held overall responsibility for Plant and Equipment. The wartime expansion of Rolls-Royce to cope with demand for the Merlin and Griffon was led by him and one of his last jobs was to set up Rolls-Royce Canada in Montreal after the war. His son, Alan, when the original version of this book was published, was a partner in Partridge, Haldenby & Cawdron, the solicitors in Derby Market Place.

Early in this chain of events Royce sent for Ernie Wooler[14] one day in May. Morton recalls Wooler's memory of the event thus:-

One morning, soon after Mr Royce had arrived, George Bagnall, the shop general foreman, came up to me and said, "Mr Royce wants to see you up in the drawing office". His voice was ominous and I went quickly. Mr Royce gave me a severe dressing-down for casual 'visiting' and scribbling sketches on the draughtsmen's boards. He then said, "Now go along to the store room and get a typist's note pad!" I departed at the double, returned with the pad and offered it to Mr Royce. He waved it away and said, "You hold onto that and follow me".

They went down into the shops, where Royce told Mills to join them, and thence out across not Cooke Street as I had originally believed but Blake Street. We have since found written reference to what followed having taken place in the open stable yard on Blake Street – not in the pattern store, which Royce subsequently used as a garage for his car. Having got to the Decauville, which stood in the stable yard, Royce took off his jacket and rolled up his sleeves. He then set to work with Mills, stripping the car piece-by-piece. 'Little Ernie', as he was known, was told to sit on a box and sketch each part on his notepad as it was removed, and to add principal dimensions. The information contained in that pad served as a datum from which the design of the Royce cars was to emerge. This in itself was a tribute to the Decauville, which Royce must have judged to represent a fair state of the art. Indeed, he retained the Decauville until at least 1906. He had looked at other cars. H Massac Buist recorded in his *Rolls-Royce Memories* that, in 1903, Royce *'undertook repair and investigation work on various makes*

---

[14] Ernie Wooler was among those sent by Rolls-Royce to the USA in the First World War to try to establish Eagle engine manufacture there. He left the Company and, among other things, designed a motor car engine for one employer. In the Second World War, as Chief Engineer of the Bower Bearing Company, he arranged the supply of complete sets of Merlin ball and roller bearings to the UK. To the end of his life he made trips to Derby because he never lost his affection for Rolls-Royce.

of cars belonging to friends or acquaintances ... that he might gain some first-hand experience ...' Royce's own records indicated that he covered 11,000 miles in the years 1902 to 1905, and many of them must have been in this car. Royce took great care in the detailed engineering (Fig 87) of his cars and although many of their features and dimensions echoed the Decauville, there were many that differed. In common with the Decauville the car was to have a two-cylinder engine and a live propshaft and differential rather than chain drive. New were mechanically rather than atmospherically-operated inlet valves and an effective radiator in place of an elementary one and a large capacity water tank. Also new was the single gear lever. On the Decauville there were two to manipulate simultaneously – something of a party trick. Also, Royce did not like the steel-on-steel arrangement of the Decauville's main, big end and gearbox bearings. Weight was considered of paramount importance by Royce and hence his use of nickel steels. An outcome of this preoccupation was that Claremont referred, a little sarcastically, to the cars as the 'guinea an ounce job'. Some of the savings cannot have been too hard to achieve for the existing Decauville has its audible means of warning in the form of a bell, cast in bronze, and weighing in - it is said - excess of 40 lb[15].

As the drawings emerged, they were sent to the shops (Fig 88). The patterns, aluminium and bronze castings were made at Cooke Street. Iron castings, such as the cylinder block, were poured at Trafford Park. Mountford Bros of Manchester produced the forgings and, in due course, Marsdens the fabrications (Fig 89). The switches, coils and commutator were made by Billy Ellis in the instrument room next to the drawing office and it was there that Florrie Austin wound the ignition coils on a modified Singer sewing machine. Florrie was yet another of the team who was to serve many long and faithful years in Derby. Henry Wiggins were among other suppliers, their speciality being nickel steels. They were to remain a supplier of nickel-based alloys for turbine blades into the current era, under the brand name Nimonic.

The small team worked hard, their efforts frequently being sustained by Royce's enthusiasm or the razor-sharp edge of his tongue, depending on his mood (Fig 90). Mondays were the easy days for work started at 8.00am. On other days it was 6.30am. It was not the alarm clock that woke employees in the morning but the 'Tapper up'. The practice was to pay a sum weekly for a man to tour the neighbourhood on his bicycle tapping on bedroom windows at the appropriate hour, with the aid of a long pole. On arrival at the factory gate the first sight one saw was John De Looze. He watched every employee arrive with his eagle eye and woe betide anyone who crossed the threshold after the minute hand of the works clock had passed its deadline: the consequences remained equally onerous for years in Derby. Fridays were the worst for, as related earlier, they lasted until lunchtime on Saturday.

---

[15] For further details see *Henry Royce – mechanic* by Donald Bastow, RRHT Historical Series No 12.

In due course, the first engine was brought near to completion and preparations were made to test it. The first question was where should it be tested. The answer to this question was lost to history until early in 1981. Then, clearing out some very old files, Derek Gration, the Insurance Manager of Rolls-Royce, found the original insurance folders on the Cooke Street factory among his records. One document (Fig 91) shows, dated 9 September 1903, the proof of that location in the form of a letter from the Brokers. It states *'in the open stable yard adjacent to number 17 on the plan'*. And a week later one of the insurance companies that shared the risk added that it was in order to keep eight gallons of petrol in two-gallon tins in that yard (Fig 92).

This information would be of little help in itself had there not been another vital piece of information in the file, namely the first authentic and contemporary plan of the factory, dating to this precise period (Fig 93). Let it suffice at this stage to note the location of the stable yard, for the narrative will turn to the matter of a factory tour in due course.

As if it were not remarkable enough to have found these documents Tom Bowling, then Rolls-Royce Director of Product Assurance, had found a picture in the bottom of his desk in 1980 (Fig 94). It clearly shows the two-cylinder engine on test, linked to a Royce dynamo, in the stable yard. Also visible is one of the two-gallon cans. Strangely, the answer had virtually been in our hands for years, but we had failed to recognise it. Jimmy Chadwick had recalled the running of petrol engines to drive dynamos in the stable yard, as he put it, to generate electricity for the factory. It seems his observation was correct, but not his deduction: the engines had been on test. His recall is easily understood because the electricity generated was not wasted. It was used, at least on occasions, to drive the line shafting in the factory.

The momentous occasion of the test of the first Royce internal combustion engine took place on 16 September 1903. In charge was Eric Platford and he meticulously recorded his results in a logbook which, happily, has survived. The engine was given the number 15196 and time was booked to Order Number 17527. The log sheet contains a number of primitive observations which, with the passage of time, take on a charm of their own (Fig 95). He notes, for instance, that the water boiled at 212°F, a fact of which one could perhaps have warned him. And at the bottom *'2 gallons of petrol cost 2/2d'*. A lovely thought in itself and oh! that the powerful gas turbines of the current era could be tested on so little fuel. Lastly, he works out the cost of one BTU of energy as *'equals 2d nearly'* (two old pennies: less than one today). Testing is a lot more sophisticated than that today. But it does make a point that remains intrinsic to Rolls-Royce philosophy, namely that component testing is an important adjunct to the testing of the final product. Another interesting point is that a modified camshaft was installed and on test by the following morning, indicating what is now known as 'fast make capability'.

Performance testing continued under Royce's close personal supervision and the process of modification inevitably too. The log tells that it only took two days to get the fuel consumption down to 1.7d per BTU, and that with an increase in the cost of petrol to 2/4d per can.

By the spring of 1904 the first car was completed, its coachwork having been supplied by a little-known local concern in Hulme, that of John Roberts. Before relating the story of the first runs (Fig 96), however, one should pose a question. Why did Royce build these cars, a very expensive diversion, right in the middle of such a traumatic decline in the market for electrical equipment?

Many of the standard works on the Company's history have left that question open. They have suggested that Royce might have built them to prove to his own satisfaction that he could do a better job, or that he might have intended entering the field of motor car manufacture. The judgement of Bill Morton[16] supported the latter view most strongly and I have always been in agreement with him. Royce never dabbled where work was concerned. His decisions, both technical and commercial, were always clear and his commitment to following them through both courageous and total. He would not have diverted the considerable resources in time, men and money to a venture which did not aim to bring in a financial return. Bill and I long shared the view that, if he did deviate from form, he would have built one car. That he built three had always been tantamount to proof of his commercial intentions and witness of one of the most courageous objectives he ever set himself.

Early in 1982 Ernie Guthrie, then of the Rolls-Royce Derby Photographic Department, borrowed some old apprentice indentures to copy into the negative library. With them was a cover letter from Royce Ltd and it lists among the Company's products 'Royce petrol motor cars' (Fig 97). This notepaper, which Tom Clarke now believes was introduced in February 1904, was the evidence Bill and I had long sought to substantiate our views. Clearly, after the initial excursion into supplying car components to Pritchett and Gold, Royce had fixed his intent on selling cars and, apparently – like all his other products – direct to the customer by way of his own network of agents. The meeting with Rolls, therefore, led to a change in his marketing intent but not to the intent itself.

And what of his timing in terms of entry into motor car manufacture? By then legislation had long served to retard the growth of motoring in this country. Even before the invention of the internal combustion engine the application of steam to road vehicles had occasioned the Locomotives and Highways Act of 1865. It became known as the 'Red Flag Act', and required a minimum of three persons to drive a self-propelled vehicle. Whilst in motion one of the three had to precede the vehicle on foot by at least sixty yards. Furthermore, he had to carry a red flag *'constantly displayed'* by day and a red lantern at night. The driver was required to give way to all other traffic, which was empowered to demand that any self-propelled vehicle stop by the raising of a hand. The maximum speed permitted

[16] *A history of Rolls-Royce Motor Cars 1903-1907* by C W Morton, published by G T Foulis, 1964.

was four miles per hour in open country and only two miles per hour in towns and villages. Additionally, a licence fee of £10 was payable (perhaps £1,000 in today's money) for each county in which the vehicle was used. The Act effectively protected the interests of horse owners and maintained the monopoly of the railways in offering swift transportation.

In 1896 a further bill, placed before Parliament by Henry Chaplin, became law. Popularly known as the Emancipation Act[17], it dispensed with the requirement to have a man walk in front of a vehicle (the Red Flag requirement had been withdrawn in 1878) and raised the maximum speed to 14 miles per hour. Unfortunately, the Local Government Board immediately reduced this to 12. This made a difference – but not enough to encourage the development of a motor car industry in Britain. Continental countries were still much better positioned in that regard. Then, in June 1902, the pioneer motorist John Montagu secured a first reading in the House of Commons of his Motor Vehicles Registration Bill. This proposed to abolish the speed limit and place the responsibility for driving sensibly on the individual motorist. His proposal was that those who erred should be disciplined under an Act from the age of the horse – 1835 – which prohibited 'furious driving'. In exchange for this proposed freedom car owners would have to register their vehicles and carry number plates such that errant drivers might be identified.

John Montagu's Bill received many setbacks and he much criticism before, over a year later, it effectively became law as the Motor Car Act[18]. In essence the Government did not allow the Bill to go to second reading but, instead, introduced its own Motor Car Bill in July 1903. This offered what Montagu sought, so he dropped his Bill. In the event, the 'no speed limit' was pressured down to 25 miles per hour and, on final reading, a compromise between support for this figure and those who sought only 15 miles per hour resulted in a maximum of only 20. Furthermore, in addition to registration and the requirement to display number plates, drivers' licences were introduced. These were annual yet required no test. On 1 January 1904 this Bill passed into law as the Motor Car Act. It made all the difference to the emergence of a British motor car industry.

It might be of interest to note that the speed limit was finally abolished in 1931, when 30 miles per hour was also introduced for built-up areas. At the same time, driving tests were introduced and these had to be passed to obtain a driver's licence. It could be argued that, since the 1960s, Parliament has lost the plot with 70 mph on dual carriageways, a normal maximum of 60 mph on other roads, and 30 mph

---

[17] The Emancipation Act became law on 14 November 1896 and was celebrated by the Motor Car Club by a run from the Northumberland Hotel near London's Charing Cross station to the Metropole Hotel in Brighton. Among the many spectators was the young Claude Johnson, who followed the cars half way on a bicycle. The experience was to have a bearing on his future career. Since 1896 the London to Brighton Run has continued annually, the criterion being that participating vehicles should date to no later than 1904.

[18] Those interested in more detail should refer to *John Montagu of Beaulieu, 1866-1929, Motoring Pioneer and Prophet* by Paul Tritton, published by Golden Eagle/George Hart.

in built-up areas and the recent addition of 20 mph in heavily-populated areas plus intermediate 40 mph and 50 mph limits on trunk roads. Anyone driving on the A6 in Derbyshire is likely to comment that the biggest danger of an accident arises from the constant distraction of trying to spot the continuous changes in speed limit. Drivers feel they should concentrate on the road if they are to drive safely – not on a plethora of signs. A further comment of interest is that the majority of Rolls-Royce cars built after 1905 were capable of three times the maximum speed limit and the occasional example four times until the change in the law in the 1930s.

To return to the question of Royce's timing, we have to compare his apparent first interest in motor cars which, as we have seen, arose in 1901 or 1902 when he acquired his 'quad' and bought at least one textbook, with Montagu's Bill, which had seen its first reading in June 1902. We then must compare the Bill's becoming an Act on 1 January 1904 with the first run of Royce's first prototype motor car in April 1904.

A further point of interest is that the Society of Motor Manufacturers and Traders had been formed in 1902 and, by 1906, there were no less than 300 firms engaged in the motor industry in this country. The first petrol-driven London bus appeared in 1904 and the first London taxi was seen in 1906. Incidentally, the first design to meet the London taxi specification was the work of R W Harvey-Bailey before he joined Rolls-Royce. By 1909 London had 3,500 taxis. Statistics on the number of private cars registered in the UK reflect a similar pattern:

1904	8,400
1906	32,000
1909	48,000
1911	72,000
1913	105,000

Far from accident or coincidence, one is forced to deduce that the prototype cars were not the result of an irresponsible act: Royce had determined to get in on a new industry almost on day one. He had shown similar vision when he chose to enter the infant electrical engineering industry some twenty years earlier.

Let us now turn to the first run of the Royce car. The date was 1 April 1904, and the car had been made ready inside the factory. With the engine running, Royce boarded the car, engaged a gear, and moved towards the factory gates and into Blake Street beyond. As it did so, the workforce greeted the event with a cacophony of hammering. Bench tops, metal sheet, castings – anything to hand – was used as an anvil to raise a din in honour of the occasion[19]. Beyond the gates the car passed under the covered causeway and by the stable yard into the wider parts of Blake Street. Followed by Platford on the Decauville, Royce continued through to Stretford Road, the noise of the factory fading away as he gathered speed. In due course, the two cars returned. They had been to Knutsford and back, a distance of 15 miles each way, without event.

Despite the success of the run, however, the date was given for many years as 31 March. Cars were a good enough source of jokes in music halls then, particularly with comedians such as Dan Leno, without inviting an association with 1 April: April Fool's Day.

Some days later Royce took De Looze out in the car. The story has been told that the factory doors into Blake Street – or possibly the stable doors – incorporated a gate stop, which caught a coolant system drain cock, deftly removing it as the car passed. Examination of the way in which the car was built suggests that this was unlikely. The rest of the story, however, is not thereby thrown into doubt. For whatever reason, the engine overheated and, a few hundred yards from Blake Street, clouds of steam issued forth from under the bonnet. De Looze was a rather dour individual who normally kept his cool and was always respectful of Royce. On this occasion his composure deserted him. Legend has it that he panicked, being convinced that the engine was about to blow up, and demanded that Royce set him down immediately. Royce stopped the car, whereupon De Looze took the most energetic action he dared to put distance between himself and the car without totally abandoning his dignity. Taking refuge in his office, he decided there and then that motor cars were not for him. An early picture of the car (Fig 98) indicates that the experience had not been forgotten. The man at the wheel is A J Adams, head of the Drawing Office from 1903 to 1905. For whatever reason, Royce used to refer to him as *'The man who won the battle of Waterloo'*. De Looze sits beside him looking as if he would rather be anywhere else. But such incidents were rare, and as development miles were accumulated, the competence of the car's design began to show. Meanwhile, the second and third cars were coming nearer to completion.

---

[19] Such din-raising persisted into the current era on the occasion of the impending marriage of employees. Colleagues would make a collection and then conceal it. The bride or groom-to-be was then expected to search for the cache, and the nearer they got the louder the hammering became. Office staff used rulers on metal waste paper bins and the works often more substantial implements. My own secretary at Elton Road, Karen, was subjected to this, as well as being dressed up and paraded round the site, in the mid 1970s. A well-remembered instant dated to the 1930s when Carl Stapleton married: I knew him years later as a manager in the Process Department at Nightingale Road. Carl's collection was hidden among the roof trusses in an enamel 'potty' in which, employees recalled with pride, the first experiments had been carried out on the indium plating of lead bronze bearings for the Merlin aero engine.

Fig 82: Henry Royce in 1907. One of the rare photographs taken during his early life. This one was taken for publicity purposes following the successful 15,000-mile run by The Silver Ghost, 60551.

Fig 83: Ernest Alexander Claremont photographed in 1907. This picture too was used for publicity following the 15,000-mile run.

Fig 84: The Car Drawing Office at Cooke Street. This unique photograph came to light in the albums of the late John De Looze. See the plan reconstructing the first floor at Cooke Street as it was in 1904 (Fig 124).

Fig 85: Ernie Mills, appointed foreman on the new car work by Royce, became a key figure in the creation of the early cars, together with Adams and his team of designers and Platford and Haldenby on testing.

146

Fig 86: A caricature indicating the temperament of Royce.

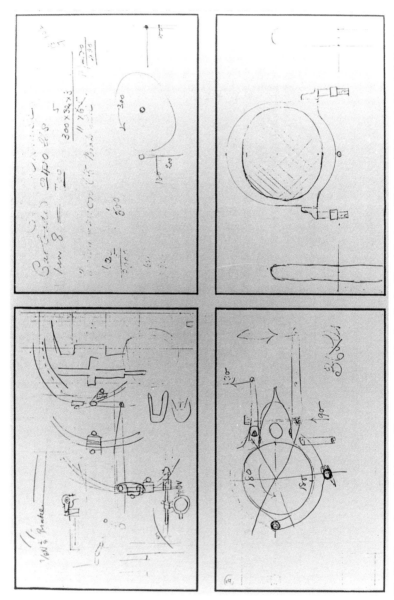

Fig 87: The early car sketches by Royce preserved by the Cooke Street designer Tilghman Richards in his sketchbook.
(Sir Henry Royce Memorial Foundation)

148

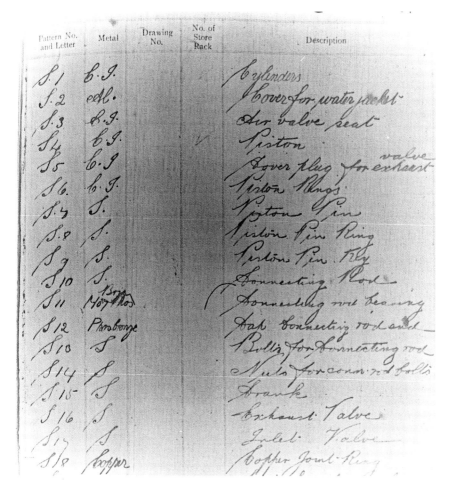

Pattern No. and Letter	Metal	Drawing No.	No. of Store Rack	Description
S.1	C.J.			Cylinders
S.2	cdl.			Cover for water jacket
S.3	C.J.			Air valve seat
S4	C.J			Piston
S5	C.J			Cover plug for exhaust valve
S6.	C.J.			Piston Rings
S.7	S.			Piston Pin
S.8	S.			Piston Pin Ring
S9	S.			Piston Pin Key
S10	S.			Connecting Rod
S11	Mot Rod			Connecting rod bearing
S12	Phosbronze			Cap Connecting rod end
S13	S			Bolts for connecting rod
S14	S			Nuts for conn. rod bolts
S15	S			Crank
S16	S			Exhaust Valve
S17	S			Inlet Valve
S18	Copper			Copper Joint Ring

Fig 88: Page from the Detail Pattern Register covering drawings for castings, forgings and machined components for the first two-cylinder 10 hp Royce prototype car.

(Herbert Morris Limited)

149

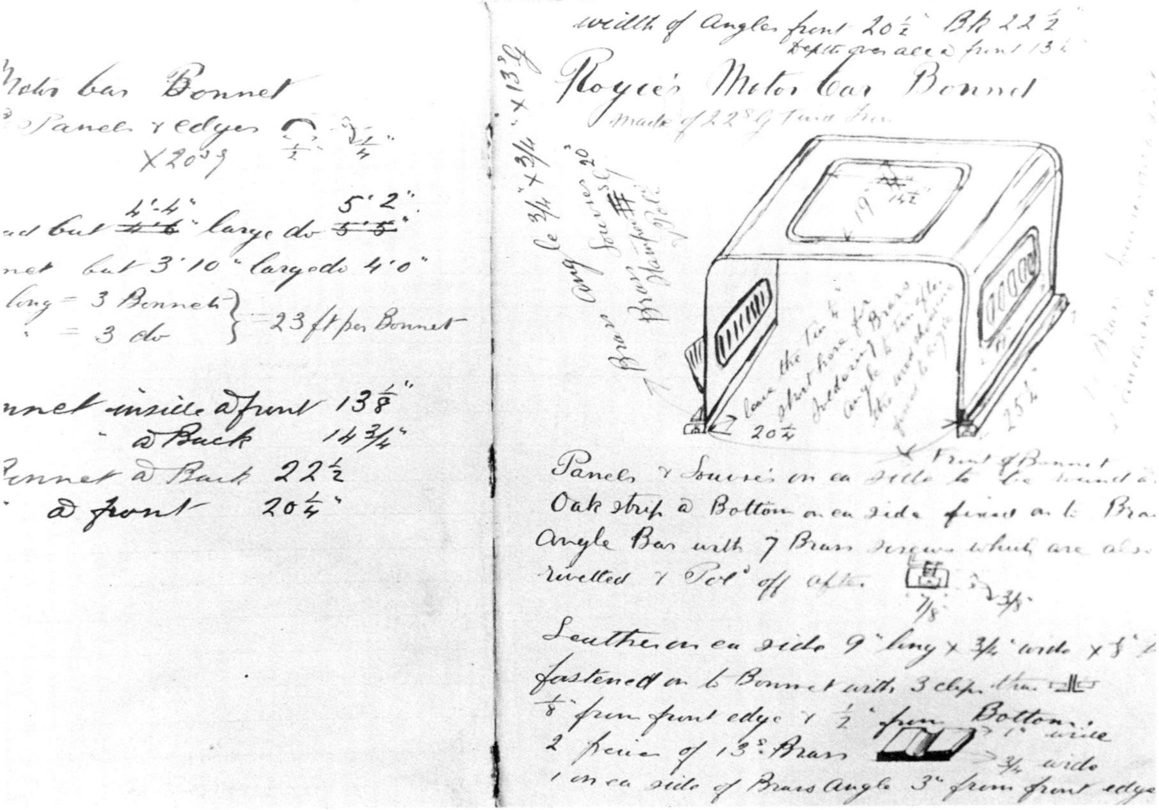

Fig 89: Details of the two-cylinder 10 hp bonnet recorded in the Marsden Day Book.
(Sir Henry Royce Memorial Foundation)

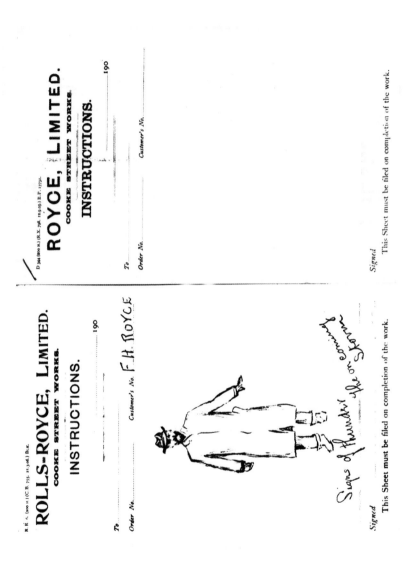

R R (1000 n) (C.B. 755 21.3.06.) B.t.

ROLLS-ROYCE, LIMITED.

COOKE STREET WORKS.

INSTRUCTIONS.

..................190

To ....

Order No. .... *Customer's No.* F. H. ROYCE

Signs of thunder the on Spaten

Signed

This **Sheet** must be filed on completion of the work.

D 344 (800 R.) (R.X. 798. 14.9.05.) E.P. 1773t.

ROYCE, LIMITED.

COOKE STREET WORKS.

INSTRUCTIONS.

..................190

To ....

Order No. .... *Customer's No.* ....

Signed

This Sheet must be filed on completion of the work.

Fig 90: Another caricature of Royce indicating the awe in which he was held. Side-by-side these two Instruction Sheets show how small the initial change was between Royce Ltd and Rolls-Royce Limited.

151

TELEPHONE Nº 1549.

BH/LE.

Wᵐ HEAP & SON, LIMITED.
BROKERS

78, King Street,

MANCHESTER, Sept: 9th 190 3

Messrs. Royce Ltd.,

Hulme.

FIRE, LIFE, ACCIDENT, EMPLOYERS'
LIABILITY, ENGINE & BOILER INSURANCE &c.

9 - SEP 1903

Dear Sirs,

   Herewith we have pleasure in handing you copy of a letter received from the Norwich Union Insurance Company agreeing to allow you to test Petrol Motor Engines in the Open Yard of your Stables in Blake Street.

    We may say that the fact of your doing this, in no way prejudices the various Insurances on your Cooke Street Works.

    Yours faithfully,

    Wm. HEAP & SON, LIMITED.

    DIRECTOR

Fig 91: The Insurance Broker's letter which confirms the location of the first petrol engine tests. Years earlier Ben Pope had told the author that petrol engines were used to drive a dynamo in the stable yard to generate additional electricity for the factory, a practice followed in Derby using 40/50 hp Silver Ghost engines in the 1920s. It seems BP had misunderstood: the engines were all tested there. The author had failed to recognise this.

D.

NORTH BRITISH & MERCANTILE INSURANCE C?Y
FIRE, ANNUITIES, LIFE.

ALL LETTERS TO BE
ADDRESSED TO
THE MANAGER.
Telegraphic Address,
"Norbrit" Manchester.
Telephone N° 540.

48 Brown Street

Manchester _____ Septr. 16th., 1903.

Messrs. W. Heap & Son Ltd.

MANCHESTER.

Dear Sirs,

Policy 4019020, Royce Limited.

I beg to acknowledge receipt of your favour
of yesterday, and note that above firm purpose keeping 8 gallons of
petrol (in 2 gallon metal drums) in an open yard belonging to the stables situate adjoining No.17 on plan of their Cooke Street Works, and
also that they intend to use about 2 gallons at a time for the purpose
of running engines to see that they are in proper working order, this
being done in the same yard.

Yours faithfully,

Manager.

Fig 92: The further letter approving the storage for use of eight gallons of petrol in two-gallon
cans in the open stable yard. The numbering shows on the plan reproduced as Figure 93.

153

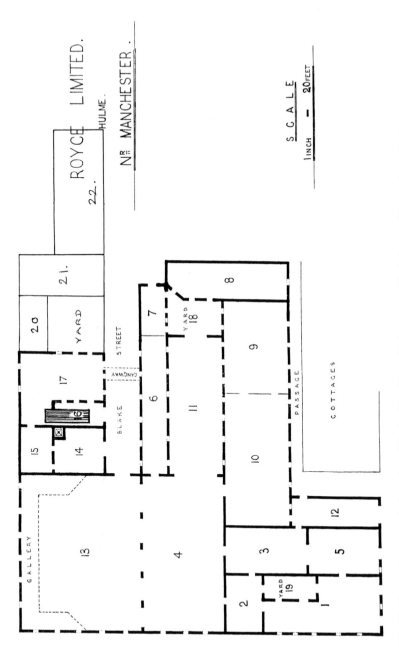

Fig 93: The contemporary factory plan of Cooke Street from the Insurance File (minor addition by the author).

Fig 94: First Royce two-cylinder 10 hp engine on test in the open stable yard. One of the two-gallon cans can be seen, as can the Royce Ltd dynamo absorbing the power output: the picture which had laid hidden in Tom Bowling's desk.

155

16-9-03   Test of Car °/15196

Volts.	Amps.	Revs.	Temp.	Time	Remarks.
			about 100°F	a.m. 9-45.	Started up 2. galls
110	30	640	132	10·30.	of Petrol
120	40	720	158	10·45	These readings are the
120	40	760	171	11·0	maximum load attainable
120	35	720	186	11.15	without smoking
120	40	760	198	11.30	2 gallons of petrol
120	43	770	209	11·45	weighs 14 lb 2 ozs.
120	·45	770	212(Boils)	12·0	
120	45.	770	212.	12·15	Attained 110 amp. hrs.
				12.30	Stopped down, no petrol
				2·10.	⎰ Started up. 4 gallons
110	18	670	209	2·30	⎱ of petrol
122	42	740	212	3·15	Water boils.
120	45	780	212.	3·45.	

Constant load as above
Until   5·30.

Remarks continued:
load very steady
Stopped down for
alteration to cams.

2 gallons of petrol each 2-2

2 " gives 110 amp hrs.

$\frac{110 \times 120}{1000}$ B+H

$\frac{110 \times 120}{1000} = 26$

1 BT that $= \frac{26 \times 1000}{100 \times 120}$

$= 2^d$ nearly.

Cost of.

Fig 95: Record of the first test on 16 September 1903 from the log kept by Platford and Haldenby. Note their observation that water boiled at 212°F and calculation that the cost of a unit of power '= *2d nearly*'.

Fig 96: A photograph of the first Royce car on the road.

ALL COMMUNICATIONS TO BE ADDRESSED TO THE COMPANY

TELEPHONES

MANCHESTER { NATIONAL 772.
{ NATIONAL 3562.
LONDON 5438 BANK
GLASGOW { NATIONAL (MILLHEAD 784)
{ CORPORATION W 493.

Telegrams,
SWITCH, MANCHESTER.
ROYCES, GLASGOW.
ROISDINAMO, LONDON.
Cablegrams,
SWITCH, MANCHESTER, ENGLAND.

ESTABLISHED 1884.

—FROM ROYCE, LIMITED.

CONTRACTORS TO H.M GOVERNMENT

ON ADMIRALTY, WAR OFFICE
INDIA OFFICE AND
COLONIAL OFFICE LISTS.

Patentees &
Sole Makers of the

ROYCE

2 POLE & MULTIPOLAR
DYNAMOS & MOTORS
OF ENCLOSED
AND OPEN TYPES.

ELECTRIC CRANES.
HOISTS, ETC.

ROYCE

PETROL MOTOR CARS.

Varied assortment of
MOTOR STARTING & CONTROLLING
SWITCHES.

ARC LAMPS IN GREAT VARIETY.
SWITCHES.

CUT OUTS. CEILING ROSES.
LAMP &
SHADE CARRIERS.

VOLTMETERS.
AMMETERS, &c.
RESISTANCE FRAMES, &c.

COMPLETE INSTALLATIONS OF
ELECTRIC
LIGHTING.
TRANSMISSION OF POWER
TRACTION,
HAULAGE,
PUMPING,
VENTILATING, &c.

Electrical & Mechanical Engineers,
HEAD OFFICE AND WORKS,
(COOKE STREET.) HULME.
MANCHESTER, 20th Jan. 1905. 196

TO WHICH ADDRESS ALL COMMUNICATIONS SHOULD BE SENT

BRANCH WORKS, TRAFFORD PARK, MANCHESTER.
LONDON OFFICE, 20, BUCKLERSBURY, E.C.
GLASGOW OFFICE, 1, PARTICK HILL ROAD, PARTICK, GLASGOW.
BELFAST OFFICE, GRANVILLE BUILDINGS, 43ᴬ, HIGH STREET, BELFAST.

In your reply please refer to   C.R. 20/1.

J. H. Dobson Esq.,
          Holme Rook,
                    Birch Lane, LONGSIGHT.

Dear Sir,

Further to your favor of the 12th instant,
enclosing the Apprenticeship Indenture of your son
John, we have very much pleasure in returning this
document, which you will notice has been suitably
endorsed by our Managing Director, Mr. Claremont, to
you herewith.

With regard to the matter of our retention
of your son upon the staff of our Installation Dept.,
we have pleasure in confirming the verbal arrangement
made with him by Mr. Claremont viz; that we should be
pleased to retain him upon approbation for a period
of six months from the date of the expiration of his

Fig 97: The actual piece of Royce Ltd paper which included Royce Petrol Motor Cars
among the Company's products and gave us the first indication that Royce intended
marketing cars for himself.

Fig 98: Adams and De Looze in the first Royce car, chassis 15196, outside 1A Cooke Street. Captioned 31 March 1904 it was probably taken rather later.

159

CHAPTER TEN

Henry Edmunds – the man who introduced Rolls to Royce

The pioneering days of electric lighting

The time was fast approaching when Cooke Street would be able to launch the Royce car on the market. Its emergence had already been heralded on company letterhead since February 1904 and the factory had been busy readying the first car for the road in the early months of the year. There is even some evidence that Royce was looking beyond the two-cylinder to a four-cylinder model[20], although this is inconclusive as the relevant drawing cannot be accurately dated.

Over the twenty years of their existence, Royce and Claremont's companies had progressively developed their marketing from door-to-door sales through Robert Searle – supplemented in all probability by sales to specialist suppliers – to international horizons. Their products found applications in a wide range of industries, both at home and abroad, and it is fair to assume that Royce intended tapping into these for prospective purchasers of his cars. He knew many successful businessmen who might like to enter the new age of motoring. As we know, that is not quite what happened: Henry Edmunds introduced the Hon Charles Stewart Rolls to Henry Royce in early May 1904, and the net result was that production motor cars built by Cooke Street became known by the name Rolls-Royce.

So who was Henry Edmunds? We have already noted his having witnessed the demonstration of Jablochkoff's 'candles' at London's East and West India Docks in June 1877, and his being appointed Chief Engineer of the Anglo American Electric Light Company on its formation in December 1879. We have noted that the Swan incandescent lamp owed its commercial success to Edmunds, and how Edmunds must have come across the young Ernest Claremont when the company above became Anglo American Brush Electric Light Corporation. We have also noted that Edmunds had joined Walter Twiss Glover in his Salford cable-making business in 1886, and that, when Glover died in 1893, Edmunds had become Chairman. Edmunds must have known Claremont to have invited him to join the W T Glover & Company Ltd board in 1899, and he clearly respected Claremont's abilities for he appointed Claremont the company's Managing Director in 1903.

In the annals of Rolls-Royce, Henry Edmunds remained little more than a shadowy figure for years – a man who happened to know the right people and turn up at the right time to earn himself the appellation 'the Godfather of Rolls-Royce'. Paul Tritton set out some years ago to find more, and his researches showed Edmunds to

---

[20] *The Edwardian Rolls-Royce by John Fasal and Bryan Goodman,* published by John Fasal – volume one, section one: Tom Clarke's contribution *Before the 40/50 hp, 1903-1907.*

have been an entrepreneur, a pioneer, an inventor and a scientist across the whole period of the evolution of electrical engineering[21]. An outline of what Paul found is appropriate to this narrative as a lead-up to the circumstances of the historic introduction he was to perform.

Henry Edmunds was born on 20 March 1853, almost exactly ten years before Henry Royce, at 2 Silver Street, Halifax, in Yorkshire. At the time, his father was an ironmonger, but he later became the owner of Edmunds and Hookway, engineers and iron merchants. In the early summer of 1877 Henry was given a ticket by an acquaintance, John Crossley, to witness the demonstration of Jablochkoff 'candles' at the East and West India docks in London. By then Britain's early lead in electrical lighting had passed to France, where Paul Jablochkoff had developed his multiple lamp arc-light system, using alternating current. The demonstration did not take place, due to a pump failure, but Edmunds returned two weeks later to witness a successful attempt. He had meanwhile managed to make a small arc lamp work himself.

At the demonstration he met Richard Sigismund Karl Werdermann, who invited him to lunch on the following day – Saturday 16 June – at the Palmerston Restaurant in Broad Street. At lunch Werdermann explained that he had bought Gramme's English and American patents and that he had built improved versions of the Gramme dynamo in Britain. He had demonstrated his arc lights at Charing Cross Hotel, experimented with electric furnaces, devised electric brakes for railway trains and invented a semi-incandescent lamp. Then came the request which might have led Edmunds to wonder *"Why me?"* Werdermann asked if he would journey to New York to sell his patent rights in America. The invitation was made on the assumption that Edmunds would pay his own expenses. Perhaps Werdermann could not afford the expense – or maybe the time. He was engrossed in work on his semi-incandescent bulb. In conversation it transpired that Werdermann and Jablochkoff had worked in parallel and that Werdermann regretted having sold his British patent rights to Jablochkoff. The inference was that he had not sold his American rights, and that these might have commercial value.

After the lunch, Edmunds returned to Halifax to tell his father. Despite parental concern, he sailed eight days later from Liverpool on the *Abyssinia*. In terms of Werdermann's hopes, the trip was a failure because rapid progress was being made in electrical engineering in America. Werdermann subsequently died at the age of 55 in September 1883, leaving a wife and four children destitute. Such was the integrity of his reputation, however, that an appeal was launched to help his family. From Edmunds' point of view, however, the trip was the beginning of a lifetime's journeying across the North Atlantic, pursuing both the technical and commercial advancement of science, and electrical engineering in particular.

---

[21] *The Godfather of Rolls-Royce. The life and times of Henry Edmunds, MICE, MIEE, Science and Technology's forgotten pioneer* by Paul Tritton, published by Academy Books in 1993.

On that first trip Edmunds found that Professor Farmer had already demonstrated arc lighting powered by dynamo in Philadelphia. So too had William Wallace, one of his first contacts there. And Edison was rumoured, having 'perfected the telephone' to be turning his energies to lighting. On the negative side, Professor Silvanus P Thomson had decreed that, *"Anyone who tries to invent an incandescent electric light is doomed to failure"*. In 1878, the richest man in America – J P Morgan – joined with W H Vanderbilt in forming the Edison Electric Light Company to provide Edison with $300,000 to finance his research: it was the forerunner of GE. Within a year Edison had patented firstly a platinum filament bulb and then a high vacuum bulb using a carbon filament. Edmunds was among experimenters in conjunction with Sellon and their work covered both incandescent and arc lights. In that same year, Farmer-Wallace dynamos imported to Britain through Edmunds failed due to insulation breakdown and, to honour their commitment, Wallace introduced Edmunds to Charles F Brush. Brush's work so impressed Edmunds that he wanted to become his agent for Britain – but he was a week too late. However, before returning from his first trip, he visited Hiram S Maxim in Bridgeport, Connecticut, and William E Sawyer – both competitors of Edison, as well as Edison himself.

On returning he caught up with Thomas J Montgomery, who held Charles Brush's patents, and as a result customers for the Farmer-Wallace dynamos received Brush replacements. Sellon then got the money together to acquire the British rights to the Brush patents and, in 1879, the Anglo-American Light Company Limited was founded. Montgomery, Sellon and Ladd were Directors and Edmunds Chief Engineer. One year later the company was reconstituted as the Anglo-American Brush Electric Light Corporation, with £800,000 share capital. The 14,000 sq ft Victoria Works were built at 112 Belvedere Road, Lambeth. It made and sold dynamos, lamps and carbons for lighting systems, it sold Brush patents overseas and leased lighting systems powered by central dynamos. Contracts were fulfilled with corporations, private firms, for public services and with individuals. In the first year alone they made sales of £350,000, which included lighting systems for HMS *Inflexible*, the Royal Arsenal at Woolwich, the Barrow Shipbuilding Company and the Great Western Railway. Shortly afterwards, the Victoria Works also became a power station – possibly London's first – but, before this happened, Edmunds had resigned. Not for the only time in his life, he had displayed courage and vision in establishing an enterprise, only to move on before benefiting from the rich rewards they subsequently generated. On this first occasion, he wanted to return to Halifax to be nearer to a young lady, Annie Wayman. She was the daughter of Thomas Wayman JP, previous Mayor of Halifax, and was to become Mrs Edmunds on 2 June 1880. Her death in childbirth less than a year later stunned Edmunds who, throughout his life, remained in contact with his father-in-law.

There were many independent experimenters, both in Britain and America, working on the development of a successful incandescent lamp. Among them were Maxim, Edmunds, Lane-Fox and, of course, Edison and Swan. Lane-Fox had developed a reasonably efficient lamp and, through John Sellon, it was introduced commercially in Britain by the Anglo American Brush Electric Light Corporation. Joseph Swan had been the first to experiment, even before Thomas Alvar Edison was born. Swan had begun his work in 1845 at the age of 17, but had ceased experimenting in 1860. Then, in 1877, he resumed work when Hermann Sprengel's highly efficient vacuum pump made possible the removal of most of the air from a bulb, thus delaying the oxidation of the element.

For nearly two years Edison and Swan ran neck-and-neck. Then, in 1880, Swan patented methods of removing residual gases from a bulb and for making better carbon elements, using cotton threads. In October of that year, Edison produced his first potentially commercial bulb at his Menlo Park laboratory: he had abandoned work on metallic filaments and, like Swan, was using carbon. Early in 1881 Swan put his bulb into commercial production at the Swan Electric Lamp Company factory in Northumberland. That event had been heralded at a lecture to the Newcastle-upon-Tyne 'Lit and Phil' on 20 October 1880. At the conclusion of his address, the 70 gas jets had been turned off and 20 Swan lamps switched on.

Edmunds did not attend this lecture, but he read about it in the *Leeds Mercury*. He sought a meeting with Swan, at which he asked to become his partner. This he achieved, albeit confined to foreign patents but he did become Swan's sales agent, although on commission – not salary. Shortly afterwards Captain John Fisher, RN – later to become the celebrated Admiral Lord Fisher – decided he wanted Swan lamps on the Navy's new vessel, HMS *Inflexible*, the greatest battleship of her day. The completion and commissioning of this ship was long-winded. Launched in April 1876, she did not enter service until October 1881. *Inflexible* had Brush arc lamps already for the masthead and bow lights. Fisher took command of the ship at Portsmouth in January 1881, but found himself at loggerheads with the Admiral Superintendent of the dockyard over every feature upon which he tried to insist. He described Rear Admiral the Hon Fitzgerald Foley as being *"prejudiced against all new-fangled notions"*. Foley even resisted Fisher's insistence on more water closets. When it came to Swan lamps, Edmunds had to demonstrate that a failed bulb would not ignite a tray of gun cotton sprinkled with black powder. This was Foley's test to ensure safety in the ship's powder magazines and, Edmunds' breaking of a bulb not causing it to ignite, the Admiral had to concede that *Inflexible* would have Swan lighting installed. In the same year Edmunds secured the selection of Swan lamps in Cunard's new steel-hulled *Servia* liner, the biggest ship built since Brunel's *Great Eastern*. The Inman Lines *City of Rome* followed.

All this was good business for Edmunds. He received a commission of 5/- per bulb from a selling price of 25/-. Edmunds felt this was too expensive and, at about the time Swan was helping Edmunds get through the loss of his wife, confided that the Swan lamp would not become a wide-scale commercial success unless they could be produced to sell at 5/- each.

The successful pioneers of incandescent lamps – Joseph Swan, Thomas Edison, St George Lane-Fox and Hiram Maxim all exhibited at the Paris Electrical Exposition which ran from 1 August until 15 November 1881. In all, there were 1767 exhibitors and in charge of the phenomenal show of Swan lamps was Edmunds. The patents war followed, in which Edison and Swan settled their differences out of court, merging to form the Edison and Swan Electric Light Company. 'Ediswan' rapidly monopolised production, suing Edmunds' old company, Anglo-American Brush Electric Light Corporation, which had to cease the manufacture of bulbs based on the Lane-Fox patents.

The successes of Paris were followed by an electrical exhibition at Crystal Palace in January 1882 and, while it was running, the Edison Electric Lighting Company opened the world's first central generating station for incandescent lighting at 57 Holborn Viaduct. It powered 2000 lamps in streets, shops, offices and the City's Temple Church. It was a peak year for electric lighting in Britain and, although Edison's company had monopolised the publicity (Edison had a flair for that!), the Anglo-American Brush Electric Light Corporation had really led the way. The future looked most promising, but it was at this stage that the Government became anxious to control new technologies. It imposed restrictions on the growth of the electric light industry. As with the earlier Red Flag Act, all the interference succeeded in doing was to lose such leadership as Britain possessed to its competitors overseas. We have already noted Royce's problem, having launched F H Royce & Company in what turned out to be the 'wilderness years', between the Electric Lighting Act of 1882 and its easement through the similarly entitled Act of 1888.

Although this period was bleak for those involved in electric lighting, the 1880s did see progress in other directions, especially once the potential for using electricity to power vehicles was recognised. Fresh opportunities were created for entrepreneurs to set up factories not just to make electric motors but, more particularly, ancillary equipment such as wires and cables, switches and connectors – and on an unprecedented scale. Edmunds himself became involved in the controversy over what type of locomotive should be used on London's first tube train – the City of London and Southwark Subway. In parallel, he was establishing a factory at Cleveland, Ohio, with Montgomery to get Swan lamps into production in the USA.

The Glover connection

Among those who entered the wire and cable production arena was Walter Twiss Glover. His Bridgewater Street Iron Works had been established in 1868 by the then 22-year old to make machinery for the cotton industry. He had also set up an agency for yarn and cloth traders, again in Salford. At some stage in the 1870s Glover had met a Nottingham man, George T James, who had invented machinery for making cotton braids and cords. One of these machines was adapted to put braid on dressmaker's hoops and onto the lead wires from which curlers were made. Glover saw the potential for using such machines to put silk or cotton onto electrical conductors so, in partnership, they set up another company on Bridgewater Street in Salford – the Salford Electric Wire Works.

Starting with about twenty men, the new company made cotton-covered and braided insulated copper wires. This soon escalated to making cables as well and, in 1880, Glover opened another factory – the Springfield Lane Cable Works. This made conductors insulated with up to three layers of rubber, and covered with waterproof tape and cotton braid. One of their first customers was Henry Edmunds. That was in 1881, when he was looking for a source of flexible insulated wires and cables with which to build the display of Swan lamps at the Paris Electrical Exposition. Glover came up with solutions better than Edmunds had in mind involving braided insulation which he offered in a range of colours and patterns. Edmunds was duly impressed, and the event marked the beginning of a long association.

Edmunds married again – to an American, Ellen Murray Howard, in Providence, Rhode Island, on 7 September 1882, but the couple did not settle there. They moved to London, where Edmunds became a consulting engineer. He seems to have parted company with Joseph Swan, John Sellon and his other associates of the early incandescent light era. Swan had then set up a factory at Ponders End in North London, where he was producing over 10,000 lamps per week. But, in a way, that was the story of Edmunds' life. Edmunds' initial consultancy office had been 2 Victoria Mansions, London SW, but by 1887 his address appeared as 10 Hatton Garden: this was also the London address of W T Glover & Company. He had become a director of the company a year earlier and invested significant sums in it in 1887 and 1889. For the next twenty-five years he helped shepherd its growth into one of the world's leading manufacturers of power and electric traction cables. In particular, he developed cables for use under ground, and held patents on the sheathing of cables with lead. He remained in London, but spent much of his time in the factories in Salford (Fig 60). By the time Edmunds joined Glover, Henry Royce had already been in business in Hulme for over a year, and would have been using small quantities of electric wire. As Glover's partner it was inevitable that Edmunds would sooner or later meet Claremont or Royce – if he had not already done so some years earlier in London. Of course, as a customer – if indeed F H Royce & Company then was – they were small beer. When Manchester celebrated Queen Victoria's fifty years on the throne in 1887, the Jubilee Exhibition put on the *"largest lighting scheme ever installed in Europe"*. It involved 500 Brush arc lamps fed by no less than ten tons of copper wiring supplied by Glovers.

Hatton Garden must have been an interesting place in the 1880s. Apart from Edmunds being at Glover's office at No 10, Hiram Maxim had set up at 57D. Disillusioned with the management of the Maxim-Weston Electric Company, he was concentrating on machine guns. And in the same building, at 57B, Sebastian

Ziana de Ferranti was making alternators, arc lamps and meters to his own designs. He was later to build London's first large-scale power station at Deptford.

Edmunds had other strings to his bow of less significance to electrical engineering. He was with Edison at Menlo Park on the day Edison first recorded the sound of the human voice, *"Mary had a little lamb"*, but missed out on becoming agent for the resulting 'Phonograph'. Instead he became involved with Bell and Tainter in the competing 'Graphophone'. Both were shown to the American public in 1888 and Edmunds brought the Graphophone to Europe in the summer of that year. He was subsequently responsible for the recording, by his colleague Sydney Morse, of the voice of Queen Victoria at Balmoral on 28 August 1888. Walter Glover briefly joined with Henry Edmunds in setting up an agency for the Graphophone, but by the end of 1889 they had sold their interests to the Graphophone Syndicate. This was largely occasioned by the sudden decline in Glover's health at that time. Edmunds felt it necessary to concentrate his efforts on W T Glover & Company, and did so for several years, running the business virtually single-handed. He had to abandon his earlier entrepreneurial involvement in inventions and patents, although they might have made him a very rich man. Walter Glover died in Northampton on 27 April 1893, but it was not until Godfrey B Samuelson joined Edmunds as a director in 1895 that he felt able to delegate, and rekindle a wider range of interests.

By 1898 Edmunds realised that Glovers needed to expand. The company was relaunched as W T Glover & Company Limited, with a capital of 200,000 £1 shares. Edmunds was Chairman and Managing Director and the board was augmented by the appointment of H P Holt and W P J Fawcus as directors. A year later Claremont joined them. These events were, of course, precursors to the company's move from Salford to their new factory on the Trafford Park Industrial Estate. The cable making industry was growing fast – so fast that Edmunds mounted a dinner party at Glover's London offices – then at 2 Queen Anne's Gate – for twenty of the industry's leaders on 10 January 1900. All agreed that they should work together for their mutual interest: it was the birth of the Cable Makers' Association.

The act of inviting Claremont to join his board, and of subsequently taking shares in Royce Limited – whether intended or not – must have ensured that Edmunds became well aware of the achievements of Henry Royce. Indeed, it would seem that Glovers had been the sole supplier of cable and wire to Cooke Street since the days of the Manchester Ship Canal's construction.

Edmunds and the motor car

Let us now turn to Henry Edmunds' interest in the early days of the motoring movement. A man who had shown such a passion for technological progress could hardly have failed to embrace the motor car. In 1896 the Light Locomotives Act, as already noted, raised the speed limit from 4 mph to 12 and, on 14 November, the Motor Car Club organised the historic Emancipation Run from London to

166

Brighton. Claude Johnson followed the event on his bicycle. Rolls had intended participating, but he had broken a back axle on the way south from Cambride. Edmunds too watched from a vantage point on Brixton Hill. He later recorded, *"It is almost impossible to describe that scene or to recall the feelings of those of us who saw it."* It was a beginning for him and, in May 1898, he went to Paris to buy his first motor vehicle – a De Dion Tricycle and trailer, with a single-cylinder air-cooled engine. It was trained back to Herne Hill and driven the rest of the way to the Edmunds' home in Streatham where, to quote from his subsequent writings, *'My gardener, William Goody, forsook his ancient trade and applied himself to the most recent, that is, motor driving; and he speedily became expert, as far as the mechanism of that time would allow.'*

In 1899 Edmunds bought his first proper motor car. This he chose at the Paris Motor Show, where he was drawn to a Daimler. He ordered it on the spot and then sent Goody to Paris to learn to drive and maintain it. When delivered, however, this German-built car proved less than satisfactory. It was sent to London but its faults were not easily resolved. On the basis of personal experiences related to him by the pioneer motorist Campbell Muir, Edmunds decided to buy a model like Muir's. This was a Daimler again, but Coventry-built. It was a two-cylinder 4 hp model with solid rubber tyres, tube ignition, chain drive and had tiller steering, and it was to serve the Edmunds family well over many miles and through many adventures. Motor cars did not as yet require number plates, so Edmunds and his wife, Ellen, named it 'Rhoda' to remind them of Rhode Island: they had earlier named their first home in London 'Rhodehurst' for the same reason. They entered Rhoda in the first great motoring event of the twentieth century, the One Thousand Miles Trial, organised by Claude Johnson, who by then was Secretary of the Automobile Club of Great Britain – later to become the Royal Automobile Club. The event had as its aims the popularisation of motoring, including building bridges with shire constabularies and magistrates. It was, of course, won by the Hon Charles Stewart Rolls.

Edmunds subsequently bought other cars, but let us dwell awhile on the origins of the Automobile Club and, more particularly, on how Edmunds and Rolls came to be acquainted. The Automobile Club of Great Britain and Ireland (later Limited, and incorporating the Self-Propelled Traffic Association) was formed by C Harrington-Moore and Frederick R Simms and held its first meeting on 10 August 1897 at 4 Whitehall Court, London SW. Moore had been Secretary and Simms a Vice President of the Motor Car Club, but both had resigned when the Club began to be used for the promotion of individual companies and interests rather than simply for the cause of motoring. There were some thirty people at the first meeting, at which it was agreed that the Club's constitution should be based on that of the Automobile Club de France. The Club was formally launched through a general meeting and luncheon on 8 December: it was attended by 120 persons. Among founder members was Charles Rolls. Claude Johnson was appointed full-time secretary on a salary of £5 per week, plus a commission of 10/- (50p) for every new member he enrolled. Edmunds was not among them. He did not acquire his first motor vehicle until May 1898, but he did join in 1899 and became an active member, supporting club events and, for a year, chairing the Club's touring section. By December 1900 he was a member of the Club's committee, fellow members including many of the leading lights in the establishment of motoring in Britain. Among them the minutes list:-

Roger Wallace QC	(Chairman)
The Hon Evelyn Ellis	(Vice Chairman)
Frederick R Simms	(Vice Chairman)
The Earl of Caernarvon	
The Hon C S Rolls	
Sir David L Salomons JP	
W Worby Beaumont	
Frank (Hedges) Butler	(Hon Treasurer)
Colonel R E B Crompton RE	
Henry Edmunds	
T W Staplee Firth	
Professor H S Hele-Shaw FRS	
Hiram S Maxim	
The Hon John Scott Montagu MP	
C Harrington-Moore	(Hon Secretary to the Committee)
Alexander Siemens	
Paris Eugene Singer	
E Shrapnel Smith	
The Secretary (Claude Johnson)	(ex officio)

There were many more, but the above serve to show how many leaders in other fields such as electricity were also among the leading automobilists of their era. The Club, incidentally, had grown to 750 members by then. The Club newsletter, *Automobile Club Notes & Notices*, recorded shortly afterwards, on Wednesday 2 January 1901, *'A member of the Club committee is included in the list of New Year's Honours. Mr Hiram S Maxim has become Sir Hiram S Maxim, Knight Bachelor.'*

Another contribution Edmunds made to the Club was the gift of the Automobile Club Hill Climbing Trophy. It was more widely known as the Henry Edmunds Hill Climbing Trophy, and was delivered to the Club, then rehoused at 119 Piccadilly, in December 1902. The trophy had been designed by Gustav Gerschner in Vienna and was cast in bronze. Gerschner was a celebrated sculptor and the trophy represented a driver and his mechanic earnestly focussed in the act of getting their rather rakish car to some distant point as quickly as possible.

The trophy was first put up for competition in 1903, the year in which Britain was to host the Gordon Bennett Cup motor races – forerunner of the Grand Prix in a way. Selwyn Francis Edge had been the winner in the previous year when the race was run from Paris to Innsbruck and it was his success that brought the cup to Britain in 1903. There was a problem, however – the British mainland speed limit – and, as John Montagu's proposed removal of the speed limit would not be addressed by Parliament in time, he introduced a Bill at Westminster (which still governed Ireland) which allowed the race to be held on a course near Dublin. It is not part of this story, but it is held that 'British Racing Green' actually owed its origin to marking Ireland's part in the Gordon Bennett race.

Following the race on 2 July 1903 – which was won by Germany – a fortnight of motoring trials and tours took place in Ireland. As part of the speed trial for the Graphic Trophy, which took part around Castlewellan in County Down, the Henry Edmunds Trophy was contested over a section of hill near Clough. It had gradients of up to one-in-nine. The winner was Edmunds' friend, Campbell Muir, closely followed by Charles Rolls[22]. In subsequent years the trophy was put up for competition until the outbreak of war in 1914. Its last winner was Kenelm Lee Guinness of KLG sparking plug fame, and then it went missing for three-quarters of a century.

1900 must have been a busy year for Edmunds with the move of W T Glover & Company Limited from Salford to Trafford Park looming. His mind was also active on inventions: during the year he made eight patent applications for electrical inventions and one for self-propelled vehicles. There were to be more of the latter, as motoring and the mechanics of cars began to absorb an increasing amount of his attention. He found time to participate in the One Thousand Mile Trial, supported by the faithful Goody. During the Trial he must have developed his relationship with Rolls, for a week later Edmunds was among pioneer motorists invited to dine at the Rolls' family's London house, South Lodge, Knightsbridge, by his father, Lord Llangattock: His Lordship had joined the Automobile Club at the beginning of the year.

Edmunds recalled the occasion, and a particular incident after dinner when the assembled company had retired to an adjacent room for cigars and cigarettes. The butler had entered and informed Lord Llangattock that he had an important message. Both retired for a moment, whereafter His Lordship returned to announce the relief of Mafeking. Edmunds recalled that he had great difficulty getting home to Streatham afterwards due to crowds out in the streets. His account concluded, *'That was one of the most vivid recollections left to me by my association with Mr Rolls in those early days'*. Forty-five years later, the author, as a young boy, experienced similar jubilation on VJ night in London when the Second World War finally ended. For the first time since 1939, the streetlights – and what remained

[22] *The Godfather of Rolls-Royce. The life and times of Henry Edmunds, MICE, MIEE, Science and Technology's forgotten pioneer* by Paul Tritton, published by Academy Books in 1993.

of other lighting – were switched on. He was walked for miles through jubilant London crowds until the early hours of the morning, tended by young neighbours. He did not know it at the time, but his route took him right past the Rolls home, South Lodge, at which Charles' sister, Lady Shelley-Rolls, was still living. Final comments on the year 1900 for Edmunds: he became involved in lead mining in Derbyshire, forming the Ashover Fluor Spar Company, to obtain supplies for the sheathing of cables. He also engaged the services of A W Claremont as his personal solicitor.

After the One Thousand Mile Trial, Edmunds ordered his second 'proper' motor car, a new Parisian Daimler of 10 hp. It had all the latest additions, including roller bearings, a new Estcourt cooling system, electric ignition, Falconnet compound pneumatic tyres and a steering wheel in place of a tiller. Its delivery was due on 3 August such that the family could set out from Streatham for a holiday touring Scotland. Its late arrival did not deter Edmunds: he sent Goody and all their luggage to Leamington Spa and arranged to take delivery of the car, which the family named 'Antrona', there. The two cars bore the family, and Goody, as far as Douglas, with many excursions, and as far back as York, where news of business problems brought about a premature end to the journey. Edmunds approached long distance driving with the same enthusiasm as he had shown for his adventures in America.

Inevitably, further cars followed. Oddly, in the period which now interests us – 1904/1905 – he seems to have purchased two. One the family named 'Tulsilla' to reflect their residence, 71 Upper Tulse Hill, Streatham. It was, by that date, of course, registered and bore the number A 875, and has been identified from photographs as a 1904 Daimler. The other was named 'Antronette', bore the registration A 3558 and was a 1905 De Dion Bouton – although, whether a 15 hp or 24 hp is not known. Both employed pneumatic tyres.

Edmunds and the Hon C S Rolls

It is at this point that we can turn to the relationship in matters of motoring which had grown between the Hon Charles Stewart Rolls and Henry Edmunds. Rolls' commitment to furthering the motoring cause had extended to an active role in their sale and repair[23]: he needed income beyond the £500 a year he received from his father to finance his expensive involvements in motoring and ballooning so, in 1902, he established C S Rolls & Company. From an early date he based his operations at Lillie Hall, in Seagrave Road, Fulham – an old roller skating rink. In due course, he added showrooms at 28 Brook Street, Mayfair, which he rented from H J Mulliner from October 1903 until May 1906, and then at Conduit Street as well. Lillie Hall survived with Rolls-Royce Motor Cars Ltd, as did 14/15 Conduit Street, into the era after this book was first published but, under Vickers plc ownership, both were dispensed with. Lillie Hall was demolished in June 1991.

[23] *Rolls of Rolls-Royce by Lord Montagu of Beaulieu,* published by Cassell in 1966.

Rolls sold and repaired high quality cars which, as the inevitable result of the constraints of British law, were in the main of Continental origin. At first he dealt exclusively in Panhard cars. Later he added agencies for the New Orleans, which was initially a Belgian Vivinus built under licence in Twickenham, and for the Minerva, which was also of Belgian origin. He trained drivers and supplied them, hired out chauffeur-driven cars and, occasionally, even hired on a self-drive basis to friends. For such work only Panhards were used. He sold accessories, offered facilities for charging batteries in electric cars and took on insurance repair work. As the business consolidated, he established a department to advise on the equipping of private garages, or 'motor houses' as they were then known. He even launched hire purchase terms on new Panhards.

Rolls was not satisfied, however. He felt the Panhard was beginning to lose its pre-eminence. Conservatism had begun to set in, and the factory at Avenue d'Ivry had begun to lose its design initiative: he had inadvertently launched C S Rolls & Company on a waning star. In reality, he had created a distributor and servicing organisation without a credible quality product to sell. Rolls, as were so many of his associates, was a patriot, and the efforts of John Montagu to raise the speed limit offered the glimmer of hope that something might emerge which was British and the equal of the creations from across the Channel.

Trying to bring Rolls and Royce together

It is at this point in the narrative that we turn to Henry Edmunds' own account of his life, written years later – based on a mixture of diaries, letterbooks and his recall – in the Apprentices' Magazine of Mavor and Coulson. Under the title *Reminiscences of a Pioneer*, his writings appeared in editions over the period 1919 to 1924. Despite frustrating omissions, they include the vital source of reference to what we know of the meeting of Rolls and Royce. In Part XIV, he wrote:-

Mr Rolls was one of the most active pioneers of modern locomotion. He began as a cyclist; and when motoring was introduced, he took part in many contests in different parts of Europe; and in most cases carried off the prize. He was an enthusiastic aviator and may be said to have been one of those who pioneered the art of flying in aeroplanes. When I first met him, at the inception of the infant Automobile Club, which has grown to be such an important body, he was more or less identified with the Panhard car. One day he said to me, "I wish you would give me any information you may get hold of relating to improvements in the building of motor cars. I have some ideas of my own which I would like to follow out; and there may be opportunities for doing so".

Having joined Edmunds' board at W T Glover, it was inevitable that Claremont would talk of events at Cooke Street, especially once Edmunds had become a shareholder in Royce Ltd. It may even have been that Claremont's concern and frustration over his partner's launching a motor car at such an unpropitious time – as he saw it – led him to seek reassurances from his motoring chairman. Edmunds' narrative continued:-

> *Mr Claremont informed me that Royce Ltd was specializing in electric crane work but Mr F H Royce had been building a motor car according to his own ideas which he wished me to see.*

This indicates, as does all the circumstantial evidence, that Edmunds visited Cooke Street and took a first-hand interest in Royce's creation.

> *This was in the spring of 1904. I told Mr Rolls about this car, and he said he would like to have an opportunity of meeting Mr Royce and trying it for himself.*
>
> *I have looked up my letter books and have found some interesting information. On the 26th of March, 1904, I wrote to Messrs Royce & Co at Manchester, and among other things, I went on, as follows:-*

> *"I saw Mr Rolls yesterday, after telephoning to you: and he said it would be much more convenient if you could see him in London, as he is so very much occupied; and, further, that several other houses are now in negotiation with him, wishing to do the whole or part of his work. What he is looking for is a good high-class quality of car to replace the Panhard; preferably of three or four cylinders. He has some personal dislike of two-cylinder cars. I will do all I can to bring about this arrangement with Mr Rolls; for I think your car deserves well; and ought to take its place when it is once recognised by the public on its merits."*

On the same date I wrote a letter to Mr Rolls saying:-

"My dear Rolls – I have pleasure in enclosing you photographs and specification of the Royce car, which I think you will agree with me looks very promising. I have written them asking if they can make an early appointment to meet you in London; and also whether they can arrange to send up a car for your inspection and trial. The point that impressed me most, however, is this. The people have worked out their designs in their own office, and knowing as I do, the skill of Mr Royce as a practical mechanical engineer, I feel one is very safe in taking up any work his firm may produce.

Trusting this matter may lead to business to our mutual interest in the future, believe me,
Yours faithfully
(Sgd) HENRY EDMUNDS"

Many photographs were taken of the chassis in complete form, of the second engine, gearbox, axle and at piece part level by Royce Ltd's highly competent photographer, Miss Irwin (or Unwin). How many Edmunds (Fig 99) sent to Rolls (Fig 100) we do not know, but they are likely to have included those reproduced herein (Figs 101-105). Royce wrote up the specification, personally (Appendix II) and entitled it *The Engineer's Car*. The description actually differs in certain respects from the build specification of the first Royce car: it originally had a French Longuemare carburettor whereas Royce describes his extra air valve type *'fitted with an automatic valve for preventing the mixture becoming too rich when the suction in the carburettor is great'*. This followed later. Similarly, the rear hand brakes were described as *'of the internal double-acting type having metal-to-metal surfaces, and are formed by expanding a band of metal within a drum which forms part of the driving wheel hub'*. The first arrangement came nearer to the brakes he had used on cranes – a drum with an external contracting band brake, and this arrangement tended to be more difficult to control in that it had a tendency to wrap itself up tightly and cause over-braking. The internal expanding type was easier to control and was introduced as an early modification.

There has been some debate over whether this description is a later modification of the document Royce wrote for Rolls, or the original. We have no answer to that, but can surmise. What purpose would an updated specification have served after the original had been sent? That is not easy to answer. The alternative is that Royce wrote the specification, not to describe the first prototype, but to describe the intent he had in mind as the first car was about to take to the road. I tend to subscribe to the latter view, not least because the whole team at Cooke Street seem to have sensed that they were making history, as is evidenced by the little things that were squirrelled away and survived. In preserving the specification, surely someone would have held onto the original rather than a later version.

For all this effort, Rolls did not bite. He had already conveyed the message that he was busy, had other irons in the fire and – perhaps Mohammed and the mountain – that a meeting in London would be much more convenient. He also had a dislike of two-cylinder cars, as Edmunds had told Royce: understandable in that the firing order gave two pulses – then a pause – then two pulses – and then a pause again. It was not even. The three was far better as it fired at 120° rather than 180° angles, and the four, although it fired at 180° intervals, filled in the pauses. Rolls was right.

The other side of the equation was Royce. He was fully occupied in getting the first Royce chassis, 15196, completed and out on road test, and the second, 15881, was not far behind. The engine for the latter was on test from 23 March 1904 and, some days later on 7 April, was ready for fitting to the second chassis. He would have been reluctant to break off work to journey to London – not necessarily because he had failed to see the advantage of selling through C S Rolls & Co – but because he would have been totally focussed on ensuring that his first car worked. One of Royce's great strengths was that he always led from the front, but it was also his great weakness. He found it hard to delegate the leadership of a project.

So there was an impasse. But Edmunds was determined: he had already told Royce, *"I will do all I can to bring about this arrangement with Mr Rolls ...,"* and he was a man of his word.

Fig 99: A splendid portrait photograph of Henry Edmunds taken some years before he introduced Rolls to Royce. *(Courtesy Dr Michael Pritchard)*

Fig 100: The Hon Charles Stewart Rolls MA in his office.

Fig 101: Royce's second petrol engine with Longuemare carburettor: a photograph taken to send to Rolls. This engine survives at the Manchester Museum of Science & Industry.

176

Fig 102: One of the photographs almost certainly among those sent by Edmunds to Rolls with the objective of tempting him to Manchester. The photographs at Cooke Street were taken by Miss Irwin (or Unwin) and are generally of an excellent standard. This one of the first Royce before completion was taken in the open stable yard.

Fig 103: A further photograph taken at the same point in the stable yard.

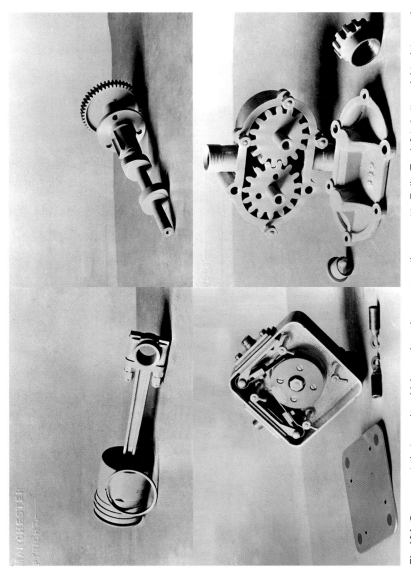

Fig 104: Component photographs which may have been among those sent to Rolls. Top left to bottom right: piston and connecting rod, camshaft, ignition distributor and water circulation pump.

179

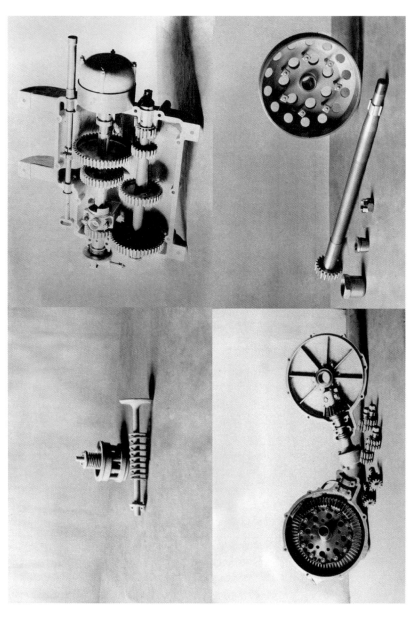

Fig 105: Component photographs which may well have been among those sent to Rolls. Top left to bottom right: exhaust valve and, beyond it, inlet valve in its cage, gearbox, rear axle differential and half shaft with the original contracting brake.

CHAPTER ELEVEN

Rolls and Royce meet

Sideslip

Edmunds had good reason to want to help Royce. For a start he was a shareholder in Royce Limited, and his long years in the electrical engineering industry must have made him almost uniquely able to judge that the recession was more serious than a mere perturbation. Diversification was a potential answer and, although few industrialists would yet have shared the vision, Edmunds was clear in his mind that cars were going to become big business. His next move in drawing Rolls and Royce together had begun to take focus within days either before or, more likely, just after writing the letters reproduced in Chapter Ten to Rolls and Royce on Saturday 26 March 1904.

To understand how Edmunds came to dangle a further carrot in front of Rolls we have to make another major excursion from the mainstream of events. Quite apart from its suspected relevance in bringing about the meeting, it will illustrate once again how tight knit the circle of leading players was in the early days of motoring.

Prior to the 1920s most cars had only rear wheel brakes and, in fact, Rolls-Royce was a little late when four-wheel brakes were first introduced on the 40/50 hp 'Silver Ghost' in November 1923. It was inevitable that what rally drivers now call a handbrake turn was frequently the inadvertent outcome of applying the brakes. Tyres then were of the high pressure variety, with little tread pattern and an even smaller area of contact with the road. Add to that the fact that much of London's road system was created from pinewood blocks covered in pitch[24] and then wet days when the pitch was lubricated with rain water and horse droppings (some 600 tons a day in London at the turn of the century) and one sees that the motorist was driving on a skid pan. 'Sideslip', as it was known, was a major hazard, not unknown even to Rolls. It happened to him one day while demonstrating an early Panhard car to a prospective lady customer. He was driving towards the circus end of Tottenham Court Road when a policeman on point duty put up his hand to stop the traffic. Rolls jammed on his transmission brake and, on the wet surface, the car turned 180°: Rolls caught the slide, and immediately continued back the way he had come, observing casually, *"You see these cars are so handy you can turn them on a sixpence"*.

---

[24] The pine blocks were laid much as a brick pathway is laid today. Many of these surfaces remained until after the Second World War when the blocks were sold in London as firewood. I recall that, split into kindling, they burned well but, as complete blocks, they burned unpredictably and created a lot of tar smoke.

On 26 November 1902 *The Car Illustrated* had heralded a trial of anti-skid devices. Alfred Harmsworth, later to become firstly Sir Alfred and then Lord Northcliffe[25], had donated £100 towards a prize fund. Every member of the Automobile Club was asked to contribute at least one guinea (21/-, or £1.05 in today's parlance) and many did – including Paris Singer and Henry Edmunds. The magazine commented,

> *Side-slip is undoubtedly the greatest drawback in connection with modern motor cars, and affects every automobilist ... the importance of the trial cannot be overestimated. In order to stimulate clever inventors to give close attention to the prevention of side-slip, it is necessary that there should be a handsome reward held out in connection with the trial.*

A committee was subsequently set up to arrange for the trial under the chairmanship of Sir John Thornycroft and among its members was Charles Rolls. It took time to get the trial organised. It was originally scheduled for November 1903: then March 1904, but the event was further delayed for lack of a suitable test track. A date could be set once the Clement Talbot company offered the use of their track, which was nearing completion adjacent to their works in Ladbroke Grove, London. Entries were invited and, when the list closed on 29 February 1904, sixteen companies had registered, including Parsons – of which more later. The Automobile Club Journal then published details on 17 March 1904 stating that the trials would encompass endurance tests of 1000 miles, each car carrying an official observer. Sideslip and brake trials would follow, the intent being to demonstrate the durability of the anti-skid devices before testing their effectivity. The tests were to be made on a greasy wood surface – firstly a series of 90° zigzags over a set course at 15-20 mph and then brake tests at the same speed.

Edmunds and the Parsons Non-Skid Company

We come now to yet another string in Edmunds' bow. The sewing machine magnate, Isaac Merritt Singer (1811-1875), produced no fewer than twenty-three children and he chose to name them after their place of birth as he journeyed around the globe. One was Paris Eugene Singer who is remembered as a pioneer motorist and in that Isidora Duncan was at one time his mistress. Shortly after the turn of the century, having a belief in the future of battery-powered electric cars, he established the City & Suburban Electric Carriage Company. At that time great interest was being shown in electric town cars.

By 1902 Claude Johnson felt he needed a fresh challenge. Over his five years at the helm he had grown membership of the Automobile Club to 2000, prompting

---

[25] *Lord Northcliffe – and the early years of Rolls-Royce* by Hugh Driver, Historical Series No 27, published by the Rolls-Royce Enthusiasts' Club, 1998.

a move from Whitehall Court to Cambridge House – the previous home of The Duke of Clarence – at 119 Piccadilly. His impending resignation was recorded in *The Car Illustrated* at the end of 1902, and in June 1903 he joined Singer at City & Suburban. He did not stay long: maybe because of having overrated the prospects of electrical propulsion, which was constrained by battery capacity, or maybe because he found Rolls' offer to join him in C S Rolls & Company more interesting. For whatever personal reasons, Johnson joined Rolls late in 1903 at just the time Rolls acquired the Brook Street showroom.

Among Singer and Johnson's employees in 1903 was a young engineer, Harry Parsons, from Beechdale Road on Brixton Hill. He had been a member of the Polytechnic Bicycle Club and had experienced slipping while racing on wet grass. He had found a way of improving adhesion greatly by lacing whipcord around his rims and tyres. It was but a small step to his patenting a chain device to achieve a similar effect on motor cars: it was the first such device to be made, and led him to establish the Parsons Non-Skid Company Ltd. The company's first board meeting was held on 10 February 1903 at its registered office, 2 Queen Anne's Gate, Westminster. Singer was a director, and the chairman was Henry Edmunds. Indeed, 2 Queen Anne's Gate was W T Glover's London office. Parsons' business address was given as c/o The City & Suburban Electric Carriage Co, 157A Manor Street, London, and he continued to use it until 1917 – long after City & Suburban had ceased trading. The first board meeting was informed that orders had been received for 66 pairs of non-skid devices, and that 48 had already been delivered. Enquiries had been received from Belgium, France, Germany and the USA. Edmunds negotiated overseas contracts and patents, and patent applications had been lodged in Hungary, Italy and Switzerland.

The first Royce car becomes a guinea pig

When the Parsons board met on Tuesday 22 March 1904 it was for the thirteenth time. Paris Singer had resigned and sold his shares, which apparently caused no surprises, and William Crampton was elected to replace Singer on the board. The most urgent agenda item was the finding of a car on which the Parsons chains could be demonstrated on the imminent side-slip trials, and this task fell to Crampton. Why that should have presented a problem is difficult to see, but Crampton failed and at some time shortly after the board met, the task landed in Edmunds' lap – and the trials were due to begin in little more than a couple of weeks' time on Monday 18 April. The easy solution would seem to have been to use one of his own cars. Rhoda and Antrona had already demonstrated their reliability over 40,000 miles by the end of 1903. Antrona, at least, had pneumatic tyres and had been used to test the non-skid device. But Edmunds did not choose the low risk solution. At some point in time, either just before or shortly after the first Royce prototype made its maiden journey on 1 April, Edmunds either asked for, or Royce offered, the loan of the car for the trials.

Considering that the Royce would have accumulated less than a fortnight's running as a complete car (the engine had undergone countless hours of bench testing in the stable yard) this demonstrated a great deal of confidence on behalf of both Edmunds and Royce. It perhaps also reflects Edmunds' determination to get the car to London and ensure that Rolls heard about it from other motorists, if not saw it or even drove it. The plan would not delay the car's development programme: the sideslip trial would ensure that, and Royce would be left to complete the second car. It all seemed very logical and it does not appear that Edmunds saw the demonstration of the Parsons device as being put at risk. He had, we might recall, the confidence to take delivery of Antrona part way through an ambitious motoring holiday.

At some time in the first fortnight of April the first Royce car had been relieved of its formal registration number, N-414, and been given the trade plate N-MR-6. Either by rail, or perhaps less likely by road, it was sent to London. There it joined the other participating cars in the Automobile Club garage at Down Street, Piccadilly.[26] These included an Argyll, a Lanchester, two Panhards, a Parsifal and two Wolseleys.

The Sideslip Trials

The cars set out from the garage on the 18th and headed off down Piccadilly, each being despatched by the Automobile Club's technical secretary, Basil H Joy (it had taken three men to replace Claude Johnson in the secretary's role). The Royce left shortly after 9.30am and was the third car to leave, bearing competitor number 14 on the first leg. Happily a photographer from *The Motor* captured the event (Fig 106). The photograph is far from clear enough to be completely certain about its occupants, although its registration is legible. One deduces that Edmunds is at the wheel. The man sitting behind him is clearly his chauffeur, William Goody, and, between them, they were among the most experienced in the country at long distance driving. Contemporary records tell us that the car also carried Massac Buist as Automobile Club observer and a journalist from the *Morning Post*, although he was not named. Buist is sitting in the front seat with what must either be his exam paper or, more likely, the day's route map. Massac Buist was not only a member of the Club but a journalist who first became a personal friend of Charles Rolls when they were fellow undergraduates at Cambride.[27] Years later he wrote *Rolls-Royce Memories*, in which he recorded:-

---

[26] *The Godfather of Rolls-Royce. The life and times of Henry Edmunds, MICE, MIEE, Science and Technology's forgotten pioneer* by Paul Tritton, published by Academy Books in 1993.

[27] In the 1960s I received a call from Cdr 'Wally' Tuck RN (Retd) who was responsible for the aero engine collection at the Science Museum. He told me the museum had received a call from an old gentleman who was in hospital and claimed to have parts of the aircraft in which Rolls died at Bournemouth in 1910. Wally wanted to know whether I could shed any light on the potential validity of the claim. I asked who it was who had contacted the museum and was told he had an odd name – something like Massac Buist. I told Wally, *"Believe him: he was a long-term close friend of Rolls"*. I later found out that Massac Buist died in 1966.

I consider myself peculiarly favoured to have ridden on it on the 18th of that month (April) ... it did all its work with a splendid ease, and had no use for 'followers', whether hansom cabs or cars.

The man from *The Morning Post* was equally complimentary in his reporting of the experience:

It is the first car to be built by the well-known Manchester firm of electrical engineers and as it comes newly from the workshop it is pleasant to be able to record its excellent running, whether on the level or in negotiating long and steep hills, with four passengers, on the second of three forward speeds. The engine is at all times very flexible and it picks up splendidly after ascending trying gradients and on encountering less stiff ones.

A fair compliment, although it does not mention Royce Ltd. One would hardly expect it to: it was the non-skid devices which were on trial, not the cars.

Some 850 miles were aggregated over a series of day long runs. Day one saw the cars drive to Margate in Kent and back, a total of 145½ miles. The second day involved driving to Marlborough in Wiltshire and back. On the Wednesday the cars drove twice by way of Slough to Beaconsfield and back, in large part over slippery tramlines. Then on Thursday 21 April they set off on a three-day journey to the Midlands. An incident did occur on the Royce when the car was due to leave Birmingham for Nottingham. The differential had suffered damage, and despite assurances that repair would not take long, the Motoring Illustrated passenger recorded that the incident delayed departure by some ten hours. The official circuitous route of 116 miles had to be forgotten and a direct route taken by way of Tamworth and Long Eaton – 53 miles in all excluding incidents and excursions. However, on arrival in Nottingham at one in the morning, they were surprised to find that several cars which had set out that morning had still not shown up. On the Saturday the cars were driven back to London and on the Sunday, as was the wont in that era, the Lord's day was respected.

Road tests continued again on Monday 25 April and daily through until the Thursday when judges examined the surviving devices. Every night the cars spent in London they were made secure in the Locomobile company's garage in Sussex Place, Bayswater, where they could be locked up, presumably to ensure that no remedial work took place on the equipment under test. We have no evidence to prove any assumption but, as Paul Tritton has pointed out, it seems inconceivable that Rolls, as a member of the trial's organising committee, did not see the Royce. Edmunds' intent may even have led to Rolls having examined the car closely or even driven it. While neither recorded that such events took place, one has to ask, why would they?

On Friday 29 April the entrants gathered at Stag Hill, Potters Bar in north London for the last tests before the ordeal of the skid track. The cars were freewheeled down the hill with and without their non-skid devices to measure the losses caused by rolling resistance when they were fitted. The Royce recorded 380 feet without and a creditable 364 feet with the Parsons chains fitted.

"Can you come to Manchester …?"

Returning now to *Reminiscences of a Pioneer*, episode XIV, Edmunds recorded that he received a letter on that same day – 29 April 1904 – as follows:-

> *Dear Edmunds, - Can you come to Manchester any time next week?*
> *Yours truly*
> *(Sgd) CHAS S ROLLS*

The bait had been taken. To continue to quote from the episode we read the often-quoted passage:-

> *Mr Rolls accompanied me to Manchester, to which I was then a frequent visitor, as I had to look after several business concerns there and held a traders' ticket between London and Manchester. I well remember the conversation I had in the dining-car of the train with Mr Rolls, who said it was his ambition to have a motor car connected with his name so that in the future it might be a household word, just as much as 'Broadwood' or 'Steinway' in connection with pianos; or 'Chubbs' in connection with safes. I am sure neither of us at that time could foresee the wonderful development of the car which resulted from my introduction of these two gentlemen to each other.*
>
> *I remember we went to the Great Central Hotel at Manchester and lunched together. I think both men took to each other at first sight and they eagerly discussed the prospects and requirements of the automobile industry which was still in its early infancy. Mr Rolls then went to see for himself the Royce car; and after considerable discussions and negotiations on both sides it was decided to form a separate concern in which the name of Rolls was conjoined with that of Royce forming the compound which is held in the highest regard today. Eventually they opened their works at Derby. I recollect the gathering of people there and the lunch which was given, where there were many complimentary and prophetic speeches and all expressed their hopes and good wishes for the new organisation: and I had the flattering experience of being alluded to as 'The Godfather of the Rolls-Royce Company'.*

A number of observations have to be made about this account. Firstly, Edmunds gave no date, and we will turn to Paul Tritton's detailed work on the day of the meeting shortly. Secondly, Edmunds refers to the 'Great Central Hotel'. Harold Nockolds picked up on that when he wrote the original *Magic of a Name* and many other authors repeated the error. There never was a Great Central Hotel in Manchester. Surviving Cooke Street employees all told me in the 1960s that the meeting took place at the Midland Hotel: George Clegg was adamant about that, and pointed out that the Midland was adjacent to Central Station (now the G-MEX sporting and exhibition centre) (Fig 107). He suggested that this association, plus the fact that the Midland Hotel was then Manchester's newest – it opened its doors on 5 September 1903 – and greatest might have led Edmunds to inadvertently mistile the venue. Sir Max Pemberton[28] includes Edmunds' account and the allusion to the Great Central Hotel, but then immediately refers to the meeting having taken place at the Midland Hotel: he must have spotted the error, but chose not to comment upon it. And from whom did Pemberton learn the truth? The most likely answer is from the man whose biography he was writing: Sir Henry himself. The third point is that the words *'after considerable discussions and negotiations on both sides it was decided to form a separate concern in which the name of Rolls was conjoined with that of Royce ...'* are perfectly correct, but this is an extremely condensed summation of events which extended through to 15 March 1906, when Rolls-Royce Limited was registered as a company.

Let us now turn to Paul's analysis of the meeting.[29] He points out that Rolls' letter to Edmunds asking about *'next week'* was dated 29 April – a Friday. It might have reached Edmunds' nearby London home on the same day – or at latest with the rapidity of the Royal Mail in London then, early on the following day, Saturday 30th. In either case there would hardly have been time to arrange their journey to Manchester for Monday 2 May. The last day of that week, Saturday 7 May, can be ruled out because Rolls was ballooning at Crystal Palace and, on less firm grounds, Friday 6 May, as Rolls could not have got back from Manchester in time to prepare for his flight on the following day. If this logic holds good, then Tuesday 3, Wednesday 4 or Thursday 5 May must have been the date of the meeting, assuming, of course – and we have no proof – that the journey was not postponed. One would have thought there might have been some slight mention if it had.

The date of the meeting

The final element of evidence was gleaned by Royce's long-term friend, Neville Minchin, and is to be found in his charming book *Under My Bonnet*.[30] Minchin

---

[28] *The Life of Sir Henry Royce,* by Sir Max Pemberton, published by Selwyn & Blount, 1933.
[29] Paul Tritton initially researched the meeting for the Rolls-Royce Motors Journal but then expanded his researches to produce *The Godfather of Rolls-Royce. The life and times of Henry Edmunds, MICE, MIEE, Science and Technology's forgotten pioneer* by Paul Tritton, published by Academy Books in 1993.
[30] *Under My Bonnet* by G R N Minchin, originally published by G T Foulis in 1950.

became a personal friend of Royce in the 1920s through his professional involvement in the manufacture of car batteries. Alexander Graham Bell, of telephone fame, was one of his great uncles but, more to the point, Minchin had joined the ailing Peto and Radford battery makers and, before the First World War, had turned the business around and risen to be joint Managing Director. He subsequently worked to consolidate the industry across his working lifetime. Here the name Pritchett and Gold occurs again. We will recall that Royce had made the motor for their electric car, and many a motorist will remember their later trade name Dagenite. Chloride Ltd, which produced the Exide brand, also featured and, by 1939, Minchin chaired the combined organisation. By that time he was also chairman of Franco-Britannic Automobiles, Rolls-Royce's French motor car arm.[31]

Minchin was among the first to take an interest in the early days of Rolls-Royce and it was a subject he explored at length with Royce. Were it not for Royce having reminisced on so many occasions to his young designers, and Minchin's pursuit of accounts of what happened, it would not have been possible to reconstruct events in the way we can. Among the first to benefit was Sir Max Pemberton.

During the Second World War Minchin lived in London and a fire at his home led him to rent a house in 1945 in Knightsbridge, which transpired to belong to the Rolls family estate. By then the sole member of the family still surviving[32] was Charles Rolls' sister, Lady Shelley-Rolls, who lived nearby at the family's townhouse, South Lodge, Rutland Gate, Knightsbridge, until the end of her life. Minchin had many conversations with Lady Shelley-Rolls during which she would recall her late brother's exploits – not least their shared motoring and ballooning adventures. She also showed him her brother's papers and photographs. Again, Minchin followed his interest in the early days of Rolls and Royce, and he recorded much of what he learned from Lady Shelley-Rolls, as well as from Royce, in his book.

It has sometimes been suggested that Lady Shelley-Rolls gave us the date of her brother meeting Royce as 4 May. It is not quite so simple as that. Minchin devotes most of a chapter to her reminiscences, but the passage of importance to us appears in a later chapter on Royce, much of which is derived from conversations with him:-

"You must see this car, Charlie", said Edmunds, "and then you might change your views!" Some time later, finding that Rolls had done nothing about it, Edmunds took the law into his own hands. Two days later he went to Rolls and said, "Charlie, you and I are going to Manchester on Wednesday to see Mr Royce and his car. All is arranged and accommodation is reserved".

---

[31] Among the staff of Franco-Britannic was Royce's nephew, Errol Punt.
[32] Charles was killed when his aircraft crashed at Southbourne outside Bournemouth in July 1910. His father died in September 1912. His older brother, Henry Allan Rolls, died in June 1916, followed by the oldest, John Maclean Rolls (second Lord Llangattock). He died of wounds in the First World War in November 1916 and is buried at Boulogne Eastern War Graves Cemetery. His mother died in April 1923, but Eleanor Georgiana, Lady Shelley-Rolls remained at South Lodge until she died in September 1961 (the actual year and month in which the author began the Rolls-Royce Museum Project).

Minchin makes frequent use of quotes in inverted commas to simplify the telling of a story and the reader will quickly conclude that they are rarely verbatim. While the above story might have come from Royce, it is far more likely to have been based on the recall of Lady Shelley-Rolls. Let us examine it:-

* *"You must see this car, Charlie"*

That was beyond question Edmunds' intent, although one would expect from the formality of their written correspondence that use of 'Charlie' was somewhat unlikely. Its use could, however, indicate that the source was indeed Lady Shelley-Rolls: her family's diaries disclose that he was known at home as 'Charlie'.

* *"and then you might change your views"*

This is used to refer to Rolls' belief that no English-made car was good enough – quoted in the preceding paragraph. True, or the teller may have failed to understand that, as heard, the views held concerned Rolls' dislike of two-cylinder cars.

* *Some time later, finding that Rolls had done nothing about it, Edmunds took the law into his own hands.*

True, for long enough Rolls had done nothing about it and, equally true, Edmunds made the arrangements. The only missing ingredient is that Rolls had asked Edmunds if they might go to Manchester in the following week – so Edmunds actions were in response to this.

* *Two days later he went to Rolls and said "Charlie, you and I are going to Manchester on Wednesday to see Mr Royce and his car. All is arranged and accommodation is reserved"*

This is interesting. The teller was unaware that Rolls had written on the Friday. Assuming Edmunds received the letter on the following day, the earliest he could have made arrangements and told Rolls, whilst respecting the Sabbath, was Monday 2 May – TWO DAYS after receiving Rolls' commitment to journey. It adds credibility to Minchin's recording of events: why should he have invented the two days – and that suggests in turn that we should believe the allusion to Wednesday was no mere invention. As Paul Tritton deduced, the meeting must have taken place on the Tuesday, Wednesday or Thursday and, bearing in mind that Edmunds would not have broken the Sabbath for matters of business, and could, therefore, not have informed Rolls of arrangements until the Monday, Tuesday would have been short notice. A guess would have left Wednesday or Thursday as logical – and Minchin communicates a memory of Wednesday. That was 4 May 1904 and, for want of any shred of evidence to the contrary, we must take that as the pivotal day from which Rolls-Royce was to spring. Accommodation can be taken to refer to seat reservations: there has never been the suggestion that Rolls and Edmunds did anything but return to London after the meeting. The oft-used yet unproven story that Rolls went straight to Johnson's flat on return to London and that he got him out of bed to tell him what he had found supports the same-day return.

The journey to Manchester

Paul builds his scenario of likely events on the day Rolls met Royce on the basis that the date was indeed Wednesday 4 May. Four railway companies provided services to Manchester then, and as Edmunds lived in London yet spent much of his working life in Manchester he will have been familiar with the options. Indeed, he records that he held a trader's ticket in *Reminiscences* and one might assume he had taken this with the company which offered the most convenient service. Among the options were:-

* Great Central

    A train departing Marylebone at 8.45am and arriving in Manchester at London Road Station (renamed Piccadilly in 1960) at 1.32pm and at Central Station at 2.00pm. Hardly a timely arrival for a luncheon appointment.

* Midland Railway

    There were options: from St Pancras the 8.30am Manchester Liverpool and Leeds Express, which arrived at Manchester Central at 12.50pm and then Manchester Victoria at 1.00pm. While convenient, it did not advertise dining-car facilities and their journeying in one is clearly recalled in Reminiscences. A later option entailed a 10.00am departure, but this did not arrive at Manchester Central until 1.30pm: too late for lunch, and that is why the train did have a luncheon car.

* Great Northern Railway

    No likely train was on offer. The one which arrived at an appropriate hour at Manchester Central did so at 12.13pm, but that entailed a 7.15am departure from King's Cross and no dining facilities were advertised with this train.

The earlier service from Euston departed at 7.10am and was slow. It arrived at London Road, Manchester, at 12.05pm. As with the GNR's comparable service, there was no dining car. Their later option, however, Paul identified as almost inevitably the one Edmunds chose. It left at the seemly hour of 8.30am and breakfast was served in a dining car as the train headed north out of London. It was a Liverpool train, but one carriage was detached on arrival at Crewe at 11.39, and taken on to Manchester, pulled by a locomotive embellished with blue, white and vermilion stripes, the colours of the L&NWR. On arrival at London Road Station at 12.30pm, less than a mile separated the visitors from the Midland Hotel. A hansom cab could easily have covered the journey along Whitworth Street and Oxford Street in time to arrive by 12.45pm – certainly in time to dine at 1.00pm.

As to the day, despite Manchester's reputation for heavy drizzle, they would have been greeted by calm, dry weather and by occasional glimpses of the sun. For Royce, of course, the journey was significantly easier. (Fig 107)

The historic luncheon

The next question is: Where at the Midland – at the time of writing known as 'The Crowne Plaza, Manchester – The Midland' – did they dine? There were then, as now, options. There was the Trafford Restaurant, which served Table d'Hôte from 12.00 until 3.00pm. The French Restaurant served both lunch and dinner, both prix fixe and à la carte, and possibly by then the German restaurant, which seems only to have functioned in the evenings. There was also a Ladies' Tea Room on the terrace, which served lunch and, it is believed, private dining rooms, as well as a banqueting hall. These can, beyond all reasonable doubt, be set aside when compared with the Grill Room which, over its few short months of existence, had established itself as the 'in' place to eat for Manchester's business community. It served *'breakfast, dinner and supper'* when the hotel opened, according to the *Manchester Guardian* at the time. It might be added that all the Midland's restaurants had a reputation for serving fine foods and, a full century later, the excellence of cuisine remains. The Grill Room (Fig 108) lay immediately adjacent to the main entrance on the right as one entered the lobby. It remains a restaurant to this day, although over the years it has served since as the Garden Café, the (rather incongruous) Butty Bar, and now the franchised Nico Central.

What did they eat? We don't know, and no menus from 1904 exist to indicate what their options might have been. Rolls was 'faddy', and Royce unused to eating unless pressed to do so. There were stories years ago that they chose the hors d'oeuvres because they were free. One hopes, if this was so, that Edmunds, as host, ordered and paid for a square meal for himself!

Viewing the Royce car

When Ray Tootall painted the meeting of Rolls and Royce he was guided by me and I have to admit I got it wrong. I had overlooked the fact that Edmunds was quite clear in *Reminiscences* that they viewed the Royce car after lunch. Had they started by looking at the car, both Rolls and Royce being blessed with 'long range' stomachs, Edmunds could well have found himself going hungry. And he would not only be aware of that, but of the danger his guests would get carried away with the nuts and bolts rather than discuss the prospects of working together. The setting for the painting was undoubtedly right and great pains were taken to show the terracotta tiling of the Carriage Court as it originally was. My next mistake lay in failing to realise that the final element of the Sideslip Trials did not take place until Saturday 7 May. As it happened, the 'skid pan' trials were not held at Clement Talbot's Ladbroke Grove track, but at the Locomobile Garage Riding School. There, according to *The Car Illustrated*, a section of cement floor had been covered with Thames mud, and coated by a layer of soft soap. It was admirably described thus '*The result was to form a surface that was villainous in its excess of sliminess, and seldom would anything so vile be encountered on the road*'. Paul's account concludes by telling us that, when results were announced some two weeks later, the Parsons Non-Skid device had been placed second to the Empereur, and for that it was awarded the Silver Medal and £100.

The missed point was that the first Royce car (N-MR-6 at the time) completed the rolling resistance tests at Stag Hill on Friday 29 April and, there being no evidence to the contrary, must be assumed to have remained under quarantine in London for the mud tests on Saturday 7 May. If correct, it would not have been back in Manchester until at least Sunday 8 May: Rolls must have been shown the second car which would have been completed in time and which initially wore the registration borrowed from the first – N-414. We should have seen a crimson car rather than a dark green one, wearing this latter number, but we could perhaps cheat a little by suggesting that, rather than portraying Edmunds introducing Rolls to Royce, we have Rolls congratulating Royce on what he had achieved. Ray modified his painting for us in January 2004. The car is now crimson and wears the number N-414. We have not, however, altered the title of the painting.

Confessions are not over yet, for in the original version of this book I stated that the location on which the painting was based, the grandiose vaulted Carriage Court, was a feature which had now disappeared. There can be little doubt that this was where Rolls was shown the car. The error, shared with Paul Tritton (Fig 109), was to believe that the feature had been demolished because of its interference with traffic flow. We now know that the feature in question on the station side of the hotel was not the Carriage Court. That was, in fact, the main entrance on Peter Street and internal to the building's main structure. It remains as the main entrance to the Midland to this day (Fig 181), although guests pass through it today on foot rather than in cabs or motor cars, and it is right beside what was the Grill Room. It gave me great joy to note that the left-hand archway still bears the shadow of an erstwhile brass plate reading 'IN' and the right-hand archway a shadow reading 'OUT'. It is indeed an historic site, and the error is one I am more than pleased to correct. Today it includes a stylised modern terracotta piece of artwork depicting the meeting.

Shared wavelength

That leaves just two aspects of the meeting to consider: firstly, what did they say, and how did they relate to one another, and secondly, did they take the car out on a run?

The many accounts of the meeting and of Rolls' enthusiasm for the little Royce make good reading but there is no clear evidence to suggest that these are anything more than the exercise of their authors' imaginations. What we can accept is Edmunds' own account,

> *I think both men took to each other at first sight and they eagerly discussed the prospects and requirements of the automobile industry which was still in its early infancy ...*

Edmunds went to America shortly after introducing Rolls to Royce and was there through May, June and July, returning at the beginning of August. It would seem likely that Rolls and Royce would have met – possibly on several occasions – between 4 May and 8 August. Then there is a further passage in Edmunds' narrative:-

> *I have also a letter from Mr Royce dated the 8th of August, 1904 –*

> *Dear Mr Edmunds – With reference to Mr Rolls taking our manufactures, he has at present in his possession an agreement we have got out on these lines, and with reference to his suggestion that you should be named as umpire, I should be most happy to agree to this, as I know your anxiety would be for everything to be quite fair on each side.*
> *I must thank you for your introduction, which is promising well, and I think we ought to be of great service to each other.*
> *Yours faithfully*
> *(Sgd) F H Royce*

The only other 'known' in the early equation which lay behind the emergence of the Rolls-Royce motor car was that the formal agreement between Royce Ltd and the Hon C S Rolls did not get signed until 23 December 1904. I recorded in the original version of this book that *'no copy of that document is known to survive'*.

Stories have been told of visits to Cooke Street or even a test run extending as far afield as Crewe, but there is no credible evidence that either took place. It took Edmunds and Rolls four hours to get from Euston to Manchester and it will not have taken less to get back: it is unlikely that they caught a return train much later than 4.00 or perhaps 5.00pm, and one can quite see the discussions from 1.00pm, when they will have sat to dine, and departing the Midland Hotel having filled the hours available. The least one might hope is that Royce performed the courtesy of driving them back to London Road Station for their train.

Of all the unproven stories the one which appeals to me is that which John Oldham wrote[33]:-

> *(Rolls) returned to London full of enthusiasm and went straight to CJ's flat to tell him about his trip to Manchester, saying, "I have found the greatest engineer in the world ..." Claude Johnson was as enthusiastic as his partner when he, too, had inspected the 10 hp car and met its designer; so it was quickly arranged that the firm of C S Rolls & Co would have the sole selling rights of the marque, one of the conditions being that the car would be sold under the name Rolls-Royce.*

The charm of this would be – if it is true, and it might be – that Claude Johnson, his first wife and small daughter Elizabeth had shortly before moved from their first home in a flat near Olympia to 120 St James' Court on Buckingham Gate. Now a hotel, it then comprised elegant flats for nobility, gentry and businessmen who found such accommodation more to their liking than retaining townhouses. St James' Court still has its terracotta friese in its courtyard – purportedly the longest in Britain, if not Europe – and the fountain gifted by Queen Victoria. We know that when the young Elizabeth contracted meningitis – from which she was fortunate enough to ultimately recover – Johnson had straw put down on the road outside to deaden the noise of horses' hooves and the wheels of passing traffic. The road can only have been Buckingham Gate itself, and that tells us that the Johnsons' flat overlooked it. The interesting point is that the headquarters of Rolls-Royce plc are directly opposite St James' Court at No 65. In his many years as Chairman of Rolls-Royce, Sir Ralph Robins' office overlooked St James' Court and Claude Johnson's old flat. All but a century separated those words, *"I have found the greatest engineer in the world"*, from the living proof that Rolls might have got it right on day one. Even if the story is apocryphal, the achievements and stature of Rolls-Royce today are realities.

---

[33] *The Hyphen in Rolls-Royce – the story of Claude Johnson,* by Wilton J Oldham, published by G T Foulis in 1967 (I was much involved in the writing of this book and thought up the title for it). Bill Morton included a similar story in his book, but referred to *'the greatest motor engineer in the world'.*

So what happened between that luncheon at the Midland Hotel and the formality of the agreement of 23 December 1904. And … one further change: since writing this book in 1982 we have found the original copperplate agreement which bears that date.

Fig 106: The first Royce car in Piccadilly on the Sideslip Trials in April 1904. There is no proof that Rolls saw it before his train journey to Manchester on 4 May 1904, but all experts concur that it is highly likely that he had found an opportunity, not least bearing in mind Edmunds' involvement in the Sideslip Trials as well as in bringing about the meeting. The car has its first body. *(National Motor Museum)*

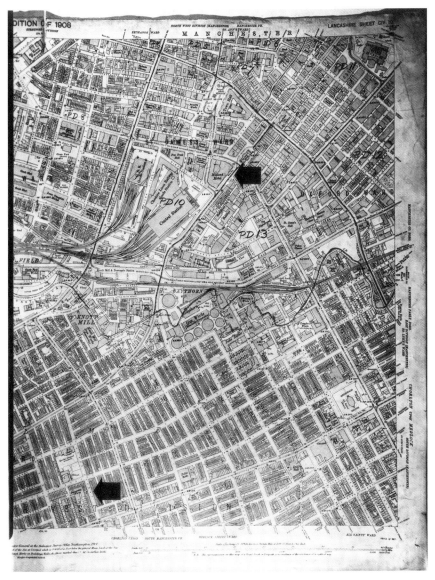

Fig 107: The 1908 map of Manchester, showing the locations of Cooke Street and the Midland Hotel. *(Manchester City Library)*

Fig 108: The Grill Room of the Midland Hotel, in which Royce, Rolls and Edmunds lunched together on first meeting. The Midland had opened its doors on 5 September 1903. This area, adjacent to what was then the Carriage Court, is now the Nico Central restaurant.

(Manchester City Library)

Fig 109: The extension over the rear entrance adjacent to Central Station, which was wrongly assumed to have been the Carriage Court. It was demolished long ago.

(Courtesy Midland Hotel)

198

CHAPTER TWELVE

From first meeting to launch

The three Royce prototypes

In this chapter we will explore what happened with the three Royce cars and the development work carried out on them, and then try to trace the stages in the launch of the Rolls-Royce marque.

The story of the three Royce cars is anything but simple, and it is little wonder that it took so long to make sense of the changes in both coachwork and registration numbers used on them.[34] Let us outline each in simple terms and then look at the technical problems they displayed.

We have noted that the first Royce, chassis 15196, was taken on its first outing by Royce on 1 April 1904. It was soon handed to the reluctant Claremont in the hope that he would run up development mileage while Royce concentrated on building the second. That plan had to change when the Sideslip Trials entered the equation. Soon after the Trials finished on 7 May the car returned to Cooke Street where its coachwork – a green painted rear entrance tonneau by John Roberts – was replaced by almost identical coachwork of lighter colour and unknown make. The Roberts body was put on the third Royce chassis. The car was then sent to Rolls who used it through until the end of the year. From around June until September 1904 it carried the registration N-MR-8. Later in the year the second body was replaced by a Barker two-seat Park phaeton, which it retained from around November 1904 until May 1905. For the Paris Salon it carried one of C S Rolls & Co plates, A-8093, and thereafter M-612, which had been used on the Rolls-Royce two-cylinder ten at the Salon. Once Rolls had Rolls-Royce demonstrators, the first Royce returned to Manchester, where it had its original Roberts body refitted around May 1905. Royce used it as his personal car, with the registration M-612 (a Knutsford number) until he bought the two-cylinder Rolls-Royce, chassis 20167, in December 1907. Harry Cumley told us in 1982 that his father, Tom, used to collect Royce from home and bring him in to the factory. This entailed setting out at 5.00am as 'the old man' started at 6.00am. He often did not return home until 10.00pm, making a very long day for Tom. 15196 then became a runabout, giving service in Derby. In all, it had four bodies (Figs 98, 106, 110, 111, 112, 113 and 141).

The second prototype – 15881 – had its engine tested and tuned between 23 March and 7 April 1904, whereafter it was installed in its chassis. The photographs, which Edmunds sent to Rolls on 26 March, were of the first chassis but, to get further pictures for Rolls, Miss Irwin (or Unwin) had to photograph the engine and components of 15881 as the first car was fully assembled. The second chassis

---

[34] The definitive study is that of Tom Clarke in *The Edwardian Rolls-Royce*, published by John Fasal in 1994.

again received rear entrance tonneau coachwork of unknown make, but it is recorded as being painted crimson. The car was completed in April and received the registration N-414, which had been taken from the first car when N-MR-6 was attached for the Sideslip Trials. This car did go to Claremont, and seems to have been used as something of a guinea pig: today we would call it a test vehicle. A free-wheel device was added to the gearbox, if not to make gear changing easier at least to make errors of judgement less audible. Claremont accumulated many miles of development running, although his lack of faith was such that he always briefed a hansom cab to follow his intended route. 'Failures to proceed', to use the Rolls-Royce jargon, were not infrequent, but when Joe Capel was sent to the rescue he always took a can of fuel. More often than not, the tank had run dry. Claremont, although dour, must have had some sense of humour for he had a plate attached to the dashboard. On its ivory face were engraved the words, *'If the car breaks down, please do not ask a lot of silly questions'*. Harry Cumley said his father told him about it, and the Derby Repair department were amused by the plate when the car was sent to them for servicing in later years by W T Glover & Company.

Compared with the first and third prototypes the history of the second was simple. It only ever had the one body and two registration numbers, but therein lies a bit of a puzzle. From 4 April 1906 it was re-registered as M-1137 on the basis that it was at Endsleigh, Legh Road, Knutsford. Claremont separated from his wife Edith around 1906, although she remained at that address until 1914. He had established a relationship with Clara McKnight in 1899 and had used Throstle Nest House at Old Trafford, at first as a weekday home because of its proximity to work: it was, in effect, the Glover guesthouse, to the running cost of which he and other directors contributed. But, for whatever reason, he used both addresses from time to time. It is possible Edith had use of the car. On 6 August 1909, however, it was given to W T Glover & Co Ltd and was used by their Contracts Manager, W T Anderson (Fig 114 and 115). It gave many good years of service but was ultimately dismantled, the engine and gearbox being donated to the Royce Laboratory of Manchester Technical College in 1921.

The third prototype remained a mystery for many years and, at one stage, a car with Royce-type radiator registered as P200 (Fig 116) was thought possibly to be it. In the first edition of this book I suggested that it had been the third Royce prototype which, it was thought, might – with a fresh bonnet and radiator – have become the first Rolls-Royce: the latter was nearer the mark yet still not true, as we shall see. The reason for the obscurity of 15880? was that it wore its older brother's clothes. The first and most interesting thing about the car lies in a recall of Royce himself, writing to Claude Johnson in 1923:-

... we could rely upon our third engine starting up and taking to the road within the hour of completion, which it did without having previously smelt petrol ...

This was a remarkable rate of progress, showing that the extensive bench testing of the first two engines made it unnecessary to test the third. In later years, such practice was not accepted. Every 40/50 hp 'Silver Ghost' engine, for instance, was run in for hours on clean-burning coal gas from the mains and then each was tested on dynamometer first and then on road test in the chassis.

When built, 15880 was given the green John Roberts rear entrance tonneau from 15196 – the first Royce – and the number N-MR-6 from the second, 15881. That was in May 1904. In September the body was removed and replaced by the second body from the first Royce, although it was now darker in colour. It was given the trade plate N-MR-7 in place of N-MR-6 and was used for a time by Royce. The better part of a century later his adopted niece, Violet – by then Mrs Maynard, correctly recalled it by its nickname, 'Mister Seven' (Fig 117).

Between March 1905 and 1923 the third Royce bore a different body – yet again a rear entrance tonneau, possibly by Barker, and painted red. From 26 September 1904 it had been registered in Royce's name with the now-familiar Knutsford number M-612, and one has to wonder which registration it carried while M-612 was in use on the Rolls-Royce two-cylinder for the Paris Salon: doubtless an N-MR-plate. Perhaps because he had got the first car back from Rolls, Royce sold the car to Charles Henry Benton of Knutsford on 12 April 1905. It then took the registration M-795. Some time between then and 1909 Rolls-Royce bought the third prototype back and gave it back the number M-612, which had previously been used on the first Royce and the Paris Salon Rolls-Royce. Perhaps that signalled the end of 15196.

The body just described was modified to a two-seater truck for Works use some time before 1914 and it continued in use (Figs 118 and 119) until 1923, when – as M-612 – it was broken up. The registration number for years led historians to presume that this was the first of the three cars.

It is no wonder the cars were so difficult to differentiate. With N-MR-6 it boils down almost to differences in the way the front number plates were attached to the chassis.

Development problems

Let us now look in broad terms at the problems that were found with these cars and at how they were addressed. These fell into several categories – engine overheating, oiling of sparking plugs, simplicity of carburation, crankshaft bowing, braking and chassis rigidity:

* Overheating

The first car was not fitted with a cooling fan, although a mounting face was provided for one. Part of the overheating problem arose from having the cylinder too close together such that there was inadequate cooling between them. A first stage towards a cure was to put a fan on the second car, and to introduce a modified cylinder block. That was not enough, so the third car was also given a different type of radiator. In place of the honeycomb structure on the first and second cars, the third used a secondary surface structure like modern cars. Instead of lots of tubes exposed to the water outside and cooling air inside, the secondary surface design recognises that it needs much more metal in contact with the air than it does in contact with the water to dissipate the heat. It therefore has vertical tubes full of water surrounded by their copperplates through which they pass – really fins, like many motorcycle engines. This design was used well into the era of the 40/50 hp 'Silver Ghost', but for some reason – possibly structural longevity – a reversion was made to honeycomb years later.

* Oiling of sparking plugs

This seems to have gone away as the cooling problems were mastered. It is quite possible that it related to distortion of the cylinder bores caused by the hot region between the cylinders. That would have caused ovality of the bores and a misfit with the pistons.

* Carburation

It is easy to forget that many cars of the era had automatic inlet valves – that is to say that the suction caused by the movement of the piston caused them to open and draw in a mixture of air and petrol. Such valves and their springs tended to have quite a narrow range of running speed. Hence, what we now call changing gear was often referred to as changing speed and we still talk about four-speed or five-speed gearboxes – not four or five gear gearboxes. That was because the gear determined the road speed. Royce arranged for mechanical opening of the inlet valves (although still flat-faced as automatic valves had been) and this potentially allowed a wider rev range to call upon through use of the accelerator pedal. The cars also, of course, had governor control – what we now call cruise control – and this was a standard feature throughout Royce's lifetime. The problem was that proprietary carburettors of the day only gave optimum performance at a particular operating condition. You could use the accelerator but then had to trim the carburettor controls to achieve optimum economy, response and performance. Such was the Longuemare carburettor fitted to all three prototypes but, as early as when writing the specification for Rolls, Royce described his intended *'extra air valve carburettor'.*[35] This would release the driver from having to constantly adjust two levers, although mixture strength adjustment would still be provided for the driver.

* Crankshaft bowing

It was observed early on when running the Royce engines on test that the nose of the crankshaft could run a little out of focus, showing that it was bending between its front and rear bearings – in fact in the web between the two big end bearings. The cure for this was to introduce a third main bearing halfway between the other two (Fig 120), but this involved lengthening the crankcase, and that was a major undertaking which took until the first Rolls-Royce to introduce. We will return to that, because it allowed a further opportunity to be taken.

* Braking

As mentioned earlier, the Royce car was originally designed with external contracting band brakes operated by the handbrake on the rear axle – the foot brake worked on the transmission. The first and second Royces had these but at some stage in its development the third car saw the introduction of the drum brake with internal expanding lining. This was more progressive in the way it worked as the natural tendency was to prevent grabbing whereas the external design was more prone to developing a servo tendency – putting itself on harder than you intended – and that in the days of 'sideslip' was not a desirable feature.

* Chassis rigidity

The first Royce chassis was put together as a rectangular frame: it had little to prevent its becoming a parallelogram. From the second chassis onwards, stays were introduced at 45° across the insides of the rear corners of the chassis to overcome the possibility. There is no suggestion that the first chassis had encountered a problem: it was probably just a matter of a commonsense addition.[36]

---

[35] Essentially, it was like an SU except in that the dashpot allowed air to bypass the throat with the fuel needle in it rather than alter the size of the throat and position of the needle simultaneously. Some say Royce had thought of the SU but did what he did because he could not machine sufficiently accurately to centre the needle in the jet. Either way, the thing which mattered was that the carburettor made its own changes. All the driver need worry about was the accelerator pedal. The 'extra air valve' carburettor was, again, used on all Rolls-Royce cars throughout Royce's lifetime. Derby-built Bentleys, however, actually used SUs when introduced in 1933.

[36] In 1913, however, a 40/50 hp 'Silver Ghost' suffered an accident which did cause the parallelogram effect. A modification was introduced consisting normally of two tubes mounted at 45° between the chassis frame and the front cross-member. These were fitted – free of charge – worldwide on certain series of chassis – including Henry Ford's 40/50 hp – and are clearly visible in front of the radiator on photographs.

Before exploring the outcome of the meeting of Rolls and Royce it would be well to cover the lengthening of the two-cylinder engine and development of the Royce carburettor. All early engines, incidentally, had cylinder capacities of 1.8-litre per block of two: 3.75" bore (95 mm) x 5" (127 mm) stroke. In 1905 the two-litre block would be introduced with bore increased to nearly 4" (100 mm). Royce had established these dimensions by taking the average of what other leading manufacturers were using. It might be added that Royce was not only early in moving from fractions of an inch to decimals, but also an early supporter of the metric system. It was to be some sixty years, however, before Rolls-Royce produced its first metric engine, the Adour. The delay was not one of logic but of market expectation. According to the Mayfair magazine for January 1919, Royce supported a complete change to metric – including a monetary system based on 100 cents to the unit.

There was inevitably some delay between the build of the third Royce engine in May and the testing of the first production series engine in August because of the extensive changes required to introduce the centre main bearing on the crankshaft: new crankshaft forgings, new aluminium crankcase upper and lower halves and new camshafts for a start. The distance between the push rods, which operated the valves, was also increased from 4" to 4.75", and this allowed for a new cast iron cylinder block with a cooling passage between the individual cylinders. The result was a much more rigid crankshaft location and reduction of cooling and oiling problems. There remained the matter of getting the Royce carburettor to work.

A test log record dated 21 August refers to the engine for chassis 20151, which was to be delivered as a Rolls-Royce, thus *'The Royce carburettor was used on this engine and various kinds of jet spindle were tried'*: it was signed by Tommy Haldenby.[37] A further entry dated 14 September relates to the engine for 20150 which, as all production chassis, would be sold as a Rolls-Royce. It records, *'First run with new carburettor as designed'*. This time the entry bore the signature of Eric Platford and comment that Royce had passed the engine off as satisfactory two days earlier: the engine had been installed on 13 August. Problems arose, however, when the engine for 20152 went to test and a log entry on 27 September shows that *'back to back'* testing was done, comparing the Royce with the Longuemare carburettor. Similar testing was done on the engine for 20153 when it was shown that the Royce carburettor gave as good fuel efficiency as the Longuemare *'worked by hand so as to give best mixture'*.

Through the process of experiment and a continuous series of minor alterations to settings the refinement of the two-cylinder engine and its running were improved. It is interesting to note that, when Rolls-Royce Motor Cars Ltd asked P & A Wood to thoroughly overhaul their two-cylinder 10hp, chassis 20165, registration SU 13, in the 1990s, Andy Wood found himself going through the same process. He concluded that the more time he spent on the engine's test running the better he

---

[37] *A history of Rolls-Royce Motor Cars 1903-1907* by C W Morton, published by G T Foulis, 1964.

could get it to perform. He felt he was treading in the footsteps of Royce, Platford and Haldenby – except in one matter. Andy had trouble with valve springs and found a solution not available at Cooke Street. The spring that really worked was the inner of the two used on each valve in the Merlin aero engine of the Second World War era. I sometimes wonder if Crewe fully appreciated the heroic effort Andy put into getting SU 13 right: I cannot believe that effort was fully reflected in invoicing the work.

The name Rolls-Royce

Shortly after he introduced Rolls to Royce on 4 May 1904, Edmunds departed for America and, as we have noted, he was there through much of May, June and July. By the time he returned, Rolls and Royce had been in communication with each other over the way forward. Royce Ltd had put together a first attempt at an agreement and Rolls had suggested that Edmunds act as umpire as formalities were brought to a conclusion. We can surmise that – however expressed in the draft – the intent was to produce a range of motor cars which met the technical requirements of Rolls, which would be sold exclusively through C S Rolls & Co and which would bear the name Rolls-Royce. Meanwhile, there being mutual agreement and trust, the two concerns would get on with that intent: the formality of the agreement could wait. It did.

From the point of view of Royce Ltd, Rolls offered an established name in the motoring world, with ready access to the key markets of the nobility and gentry. He also offered repair services and facilities in the London area. Thomas Nadin *(Na)* recalled sixty years later that news of Rolls' intent to handle sales led at Cooke Street to *"a certain feeling of exultation among us and work on the improvement of many details was pressed forward eagerly"*. He continued, *"but it seems strange when one looks back how little we knew of the hard road which lay ahead before we had a car which was comparatively free of the many faults and problems which extended experience on the road made obvious to us later"*.

From Rolls' point of view the benefits were superficially less obvious. Edmunds had written to Royce, as we have noted, on 26 March 1904 stating of Rolls that *'... several other houses are now in negotiation with him wishing to do the whole or part of his work ...'*. That could have been a ploy lacking in substance, but history records the following:-

May 1904	On the day Rolls visited Manchester his business manager, Johnson, concluded an agency agreement for an electric town car, on which Rolls subsequently wrote off his losses.
November 1904	New Orleans and an agency for part of the Minerva range were signed up.

December 1904	The Royce Ltd and Hon C S Rolls agreement of 23rd effectively consolidated the Rolls-Royce name and product range.
May 1905	Agreement with Dufaux in Switzerland. Apart from an unsuccessful racing car, this led to nothing.
July 1905	Agreement with the Swiss CIEM company over a chassis which was used for the 'Rolls bus'. One was built, but again the intent came to no more.

Rolls was indeed active in other directions, and continued to be so on accessories for a while even after Rolls-Royce was registered as a limited liability company in March 1906. One has to ask, therefore, why Royce was special to Rolls. We have already seen clues. Rolls wanted a car which was British and the equal of others. None of his other agencies was. Edmunds remarked that they seemed to take to each other instantly, and – if true – the story about telling Johnson he had found 'the greatest motor engineer in the world' would point us towards the answer. Some months later, however, two Rolls-Royce four-cylinder twenty horsepowers were entered in the first-ever Isle of Man Tourist Trophy race. Rolls drove one and suffered a gearbox failure, but the other, in the hands of Percy ('Vere!') Northey, not yet an employee of C S Rolls & Co, but later known as *PN*, recorded a highly creditable second place.

The race took place on 14 September and, some time later, on 3 November 1905, Rolls arranged a dinner at the Trocadero to celebrate the victory. After the meal he delivered a speech which served not only to congratulate Royce on the car and Northey for his driving but also to announce a new model. We will take the first part of the speech which, although perhaps not devoid of the salesman's spin, gives us the reason for Rolls' enthusiasm for Royce and his work:-

I would like to say a few words of introduction as it were to Mr Royce – I say introduction, for although you have frequently heard his name in connection with the excellent motor-car manufactured by him, and with which I have the honour to be associated, yet the greater part of those present in this room have never before had the opportunity of making his actual acquaintance; indeed, there are but few who know him, for Mr Royce is of a very retiring disposition. He is one of those unassuming hard-working men who devote their lives to the study and solution of difficult and mechanical problems, and to whom indirectly are due the general advancement of civilisation and the high position which Great Britain holds at the present time in the engineering world.

You may ask yourselves how it was that I came to be associated with Mr Royce and Mr Royce with me. Well, for a considerable number of years I had been actively engaged in the sale of foreign cars, and the reason for this was that I wanted to be able to recommend and sell the best cars in the world, irrespective of origin, and the cars I sold were, I believe, the best that could be got at that time, but somehow I always had a sort of feeling that I should prefer to be selling English, instead of foreign goods. In addition I could distinctly notice a growing desire on the part of my clients to purchase English-made cars; yet I was disinclined to embark in a factory and manufacture myself, firstly on account of my own incompetence and inexperience in such matters, and secondly on account of the enormous risks involved, and at the same time I could not come across any English-made car that I really liked. Although I had numerous offers of sole concessions and sole agencies and so forth, on terms which represented a far higher rate of profit than I was working for with my foreign cars, yet the majority of British manufacturers at that time all seemed to suffer from the same thing, what I might call sheer pigheadedness, that is to say they had a deep-rooted objection to copying the foreigner who had had many years' more experience. Being intimately acquainted with the best foreign practice and having followed pretty closely the gradual evolution of the motor-car and the improvement and perfection of every detail by the French specialists whose names are household words, it used to annoy me considerably to see the average English motor-car builder bringing out for example as a wonderful new improvement a device which anyone who had followed the movement closely enough knew had been tried and discarded in France perhaps five years previously. Many manufacturers thus went over ground which they could have saved had they chosen to take advantage of the foreigners' experience; and this together with bad finance have undoubtedly been the chief causes of the backwardness of British automobile manufacturers during the earlier years of the movement.

Eventually, however, I was fortunate enough to make the acquaintance of Mr Royce, and in him I found the man I had been looking for for years.

Mr Royce, whose firm – a firm of long standing, much respected and of the highest repute in the engineering world – have been renowned for their electrical cranes, dynamos, electromotors, and various kinds of mechanical work down to scientific instruments requiring the utmost precision and the very highest quality of workmanship.

Well, Mr Royce, like myself, always had a hankering after the designing and making of mechanical carriages, and not long after we met each other arrangements were made whereby he commenced the manufacture of various types to suit my special requirements, and I won't say he has suited me in quantity, for we could have sold double and treble the number, and I see no

207

chance of getting satisfaction in this respect for a considerable time to come, but in quality and other respects he has more than fulfilled my requirements. In addition to carrying out the general ideas and designs that come from my side – that is from my able colleague, Mr Claude Johnson, and myself – his extraordinary genius – for Mr Royce is no ordinary man but a man of exceptional ingenuity and power of overcoming difficulties – his extraordinary genius has enabled him to effect clever improvements in general and in detail which have been possessed in no other make of car.

The result is the vehicle which you now know under the joint name of Mr Royce and myself, and which I think I may go as far as to say has now to be reckoned amongst the first rank of automobile manufacturers in the world, having established for itself in a very brief period an honest reputation for silence, simplicity and high quality. This success has been due in no small measure to the fact that Mr Royce is an unprejudiced man, and though possessing originality to the very highest degree he is not too proud to acknowledge the valuable work and experience of our friends across the Channel and to benefit thereby. This, I think you will agree, is a very unusual thing to find in a British engineer, and it has enabled us to start on even grounds with the foreigner and level with him, for I venture to say that no engineer, however able he may be, could possibly set to work and design a motor car with anything but failure awaiting him, unless he is thoroughly well acquainted with, and is prepared to benefit by, the corresponding work that has been done by his Continental rivals, for otherwise he must waste years covering old and useless ground which has been traversed and abandoned by others, and he will thus be following along always two or three years behind them – if you understand what I mean – instead of being on a level with them.

You will thus understand the reason why we have always been anxious to make it clear that although it is a new car the Rolls-Royce is not an experiment, for we have not started off by thinking we knew more about it than anyone else, but we started with the full knowledge of what we were doing and, what is even more important, what other people were doing and had done; and the car has thus embodied all such modern improvements as we knew had been proved to be right, and the only real improvements we wished at first to devote our attention to were in the direction of simplifying and standardising the number of working parts, and silencing and balancing the engine. In regard to the extraordinary silence of the Rolls-Royce, many of our rivals content themselves by telling people we do this by shutting up the exhaust at the expense of power. Well, it would take too long to explain to you how it is done, but I can only assure you this is not the case; if it were we should never be able to get the hill-climbing power we do out of the Rolls-Royce; we should never be able to climb to such hills as Hindhead,

Guilford High Street, Hog's Back, and the Richmond Park test hill of 1 in 7.8
on the top speed with a standard gear of 33 miles per hour.

With regard to the noticeable absence of vibration on our cars, well, I
suppose there is no one who has devoted closer or more careful study to the
important question of balancing than Mr Royce, and this is what accounts
for it. Indeed, it seems to me no one actually in the automobile business
has really attacked and gone properly into this matter from a theoretical
point of view, for correct balancing of internal combustion engines is one of
those things that cannot be attained properly by practice without the use of
theory.

It is hardly incumbent on me to say more about the merits or otherwise
of the Rolls-Royce, if indeed as much as I have already said; suffice it to
say that in consequence of the utter impossibility of coping with the demand
there has been for the cars this year, and the fact that in some types we are
already quoting September 1906 as the earliest date we can possibly deliver,
arrangements are rapidly being made to extend and also to still further
equip our present works with more of the latest automatic machinery. I might
mention, however, that the present works already possess some of the most
perfect gear cutting machinery in the world, and to this fact together with
the system of supervision and general organisation of the works, are due in
a great measure the silence and sweet running of the gearing and general
mechanism of the Rolls-Royce car. (continues)[38]

This is a very long passage to quote, but it does more than highlight Rolls'
reasons for committing his business future to Royce and his team. It shows how
astute Rolls was for a twenty-eight year old and that he was almost visionary in
setting out the fundamentals of an engineering ethos that remains to this day: base
new products on proven technology, adding such advanced technology as is judged
necessary and deliverable. Royce was inventive and held many patents, but he
believed in starting from firm foundations, improving on current practice, and
creating something new – such as his carburettor – only when it was needed. The
factor which comes out most strongly is Rolls' strength of opposition to what is
now known as 'NIH' – 'not invented here'. For many years, both in the 1930s and
perhaps too in the 1950s, individual designers at Rolls-Royce had a little too much
freedom and found expensively different ways of doing the same thing on their
engine. Even more recently, I recall Sir Ralph Robins expressing his views in the
strongest terms against a propensity to commit expensive resources to developing
special steels, for instance, which differed from industry standards for no strong
reason.

---

[38] During the course of this speech Rolls presented Royce with a cigar box in gratitude for the
performance of the TT car. During the proof-reading of the typescript for this book I was told that the
cigar box remains with the family.

So how quickly did signs of the future name Rolls-Royce emerge after the first meeting? At Cooke Street, drawing 4801 must have been produced either before or during August 1904. It was entitled *Rolls-Royce 10 hp standard car type no 2* ('Standard' referred to production specification and 'type no 2' – or 'type A' – referred to the two-cylinder model). Rolls, on the other hand, was reported on 17 September in the Motoring Illustrated as having taken part in an event near Colchester: he had stated that he was using a Rolls-Royce: it can only have been the first Royce prototype, but it is the name that concerns us.

The first Rolls-Royce cars, and their radiators

Although there were inferences, we now know it to be fact that the first two Rolls-Royce cars to be delivered both had radiators like the prototype Royce cars. Harry Fleck (1883-1968) joined C S Rolls & Co on 18 August 1904 and claimed memory (at a very impressionable stage in his career, one might add) of the first two Rolls-Royce two-cylinder cars having Royce radiators. They were, however, to latest specification with three bearing crankshaft (Fig 120), better cooling passages, secondary surface radiators, Royce carburettors and drum brakes. Unlike the first Royce cars both had sloping bonnet tops. We have already noted their chassis numbers, 20150 and 20151. The latter was the first Rolls-Royce to be delivered, and went to Paris Singer in August 1904. 20150 was a bit of a mystery in that we cannot be sure of its first customer. It seems to have been a Mr Amos, possibly in Lancashire, and, despite its engine being tested in September 1904 and installed in its chassis on the 13th, there is no evidence as to when it was sold. A possible answer is that the sale was directly between Royce Ltd and the customer rather than through C S Rolls & Co.

Correspondence remains in which C S Rolls & Co offers commission to Royce Ltd on Rolls-Royce cars sold by Royce Ltd – on their behalf. What we do know is that 20150 was fitted with Barker coachwork and bore the registration P200. It appeared in the first edition of this book (Fig 116) with Percy Northey at the wheel. The picture was taken by Royce Ltd, possibly in Blake Street, and is thought to date from late 1905 or early 1906 when it was returned by its original owner. If indeed it was Amos, he had been in dispute with Royce Ltd between December 1905 and May 1906. I recall the oldest practising solicitor in Lancashire, as he described himself, writing to me in the 1960s. He was then around ninety and had found among his files papers on a claim he had handled for an early Rolls-Royce owner against the Company. I must look his letter up when time permits.

From chassis 20152 the classic Rolls-Royce radiator appears. Initially it had no badge and we now know[39] that the oval plaque bearing the words *'The Rolls Royce Radiator'* (no hyphen!) (Fig 121) was first used in February 1905 on the

---

[39] In the first edition of this book I wrongly believed that the oval badge appeared at the same time as the classical radiator.

six-cylinder 30 horsepower, chassis number 24274. We will come to the subsequent classic radiator badge in Chapter Fourteen. When I joined the Company there were two views on the origins of the radiator. One was that it was inspired by Johnson in order to create a brand image based on the classic Greek elegance of the Parthenon in Athens. If that had been so, however, one would have thought he would have been careful to emphasise it in the first-ever Rolls-Royce catalogue produced in January 1905. That publication does not even show the classic shape. The other view was that Royce made the change himself for reasons of simple logic. A third possibility was later raised by Bird and Hallows:[40] a similar classical shape had been used by Blackburn & Co on a car called the Norfolk. This Cleckheaton-based firm had received very large orders late in 1903 for looms for South America and this had led them to abandon their car project. One or two car workers had been made redundant and had joined Royce Ltd. The authors dismiss the tale as improbable. The story as I was told it was that Royce thought about what the header tank had to do. Hot water came in from the engine in the middle of the header tank. Some went down the nearest radiator tubes, leaving a bit less to go down those on either side of them and so on until, at either side of the header tank, there was little left to feed down the tubes to cool. It was logical, then, to reduce the volume of the header tank between its centre and its two extremes. Result? The classical shape created itself, and it would have saved weight as well as the use of unnecessary material. A further development of this thought process might have been that a header tank does need some air space to allow for expansion. With the original shape, driving on a severely cambered road might have seen tubes on the uphill side of the radiator starved of hot water: cooling would have been impaired. With the classical shape this would not happen unless the header tank was in sore need of a top-up. The logic is difficult to escape and, indeed Lord Hives *(Hs)* wrote in 1959 that, '*Royce created the radiator but came to hate it*'. Why? Well, from an origin based on engineering logic it came to be the visual feature which identified a car as a Rolls-Royce. That was fine, up to a point, but it constrained styling and was not helpful when road speeds began to rise and aerodynamics began to take on an importance. Years later, the last Rolls-Royce car built at Crewe, the Silver Seraph, reduced it to a vestigial token. It took courage and ingenuity – not least with all the European safety regulations – for BMW, and in particular Karl-Heinz Kalbfell, Director of 'Project Rolls-Royce', and the car's Chief Designer, Ian Cameron, to reinstate it so boldly on the Rolls-Royce Phantom launched in 2003. The first car to have the classic radiator, meanwhile, 20152, was delivered to its owner, Joseph Blamires of Huddersfield in April 1905.

The Rolls-Royce motor car is revealed

What Rolls and Royce set out to do was simple enough in terms of logic – to create a range of cars of two, three, four and six cylinders in-line, using common

[40] *The Rolls-Royce Motor Car* by Anthony Bird and Ian Hallows, published by B T Batsford in 1964.

pistons, bearings, connecting rods, valves and springs. The four could use two cylinder blocks from the two, and the six three of them. That left only the three-cylinder, much favoured by Rolls, as the odd one out in that it had to be configured around three newly-designed single bore cylinder blocks. To deliver these cars was something else. The prototypes had been built by classic experimental techniques – virtual 'one-off' knife and fork methods with fast-make back-up. Such techniques are expensive, and for production purposes cost must be removed in the longer run by spending money on tooling – jigs and fixtures – in the shorter term. 'Productionising' includes specifying condition of supply – for instance, ordering crankshaft forgings which do not have huge unwanted quantities of metal on them which needs machining off. The whole production approach reduces machining times and, therefore, cost. It also reduces lead time – the time between launching a part onto the shops and getting it into stores as a finished component. Lastly, and equally importantly, there is far less potential for error, which is the frequent cause of scrap. Today's jargon would refer to 'process control aimed at ensuring conformance to specification'.

All this would have been task enough for just the two-cylinder ten horsepower but, in terms of engines alone, new crankshafts, crankcase upper and lower halves and camshafts were required for the three-, four- and six-cylinder engines and new cylinder blocks for the three. Then there were the matters of chassis frames, which differed, gearboxes, radiators and axles. And the timescale? C S Rolls & Co had set themselves the task of making a major launch appearance at the Paris Salon early in December 1904.

The pace at Cooke Street became pressured. R D Spinney was recruited to ease the overload on the Drawing Office and he was given the task of incorporating Tommy Nadin's detail designs into the General Arrangement of the model that differed – the three-cylinder fifteen – under Royce's guidance. Royce oversaw all aspects of the process – design, procurement, manufacturing, assembly and test. It was small wonder that Nadin's recall was of Royce becoming so exhausted that he was often absent, even though others drove him to and from work, *"Progress was punctuated by the indisposition, due to overwork, at more or less regular intervals of Mr Royce. His absence for a few days would allow the tension in both the Drawing Office and the Works to ease but with an accompanying loss of a sense of direction"*. But the load did not fall on Cooke Street alone. C S Rolls & Co had to seek exhibition space, order coachwork for the chassis to be displayed – and that entailed close co-ordination to ensure it would fit on the chassis – design the stand and have it built as well as brief staff and arrange shipping.

The Paris Salon took place between 9 and 25 December 1904 and was the seventh such event – a reflection of the lead France had established over Britain. The first Royce was there as a demonstrator, temporarily carrying one of Rolls' registrations, as was the Rolls-Royce two-cylinder ten, chassis number 20154, temporarily using the registration M-612. Both cars were driven from Lillie Hall to

Paris. Alongside 20154 on stand 31 appeared further Rolls-Royce exhibits which had been freighted out there – three-cylinder fifteen 24273 without coachwork and with its chassis incomplete, a four-cylinder twenty, 24264, with an exquisite body yet possibly without an engine, and an as yet incomplete six-cylinder thirty engine destined for chassis 24274 (Fig 122).

At the end of the Salon de L'Automobile, the Salon Commissioners awarded the Rolls-Royce exhibit their Special Diploma and medal (now in the Science Museum) *'for the Elegance and Comfort of the Rolls-Royce Cars'*. Much positive comment appeared in the British motoring journals and the national dailies reported favourably too. Among the many comments was that in *The Autocar* dated 24 December 1904, and which had the following to say:

We are interested to hear that the new British car, the Rolls-Royce, which made its first bow to the world in the Paris show has not been shown there in vain. Up till Tuesday last, 27 cars were positively ordered and deposits paid. This is certainly an excellent start for a new car but we are not surprised, as our short run on the two-cylinder 10 hp a few days since proved to us how great must have been the care exercised in the building of the car to attain such results.

No wonder it took from early August until 23 December 1904 to finalise the agreement between Royce Ltd and the Hon C S Rolls and sign it. Before revealing its contents for the first time in nearly a century, let us explore Cooke Street.

Fig 110: The first Royce car being demonstrated on manoeuvres at Folkestone. Rolls, in the uniform of the Motor Volunteer Corps, is at the wheel. At his side is HRH The Duke of Connaught, Inspector General of Forces from 1904 until 1907, and at the starting handle is one of the C S Rolls & Co's apprentices, J T C Moore-Brabazon, later to become Lord Brabazon of Tara. The photograph was taken on 5 August 1904 and shows the car with its second body. At that time it carried the registration N-MR-8.

Fig 111: The first Royce prototype, chassis 15196, carrying its third coachwork and the registration M612. Sir James C Percy is seen pumping up the tyre while testing the car in Ireland. The photograph was loaned by his son, Lt Cdr D Percy of the Royal Canadian Navy, when stationed at Naval HQ in Ottawa after the war. Sir James was motoring correspondent of the long defunct *Irish Motor News* and a friend of Claude Johnson, and later also of Henry Royce. This car, in all, carried four different bodies and at various times the registrations N-414, N-MR-6, N-MR-8, A-8093 and M612. Tom Clarke believes the location to be *en route* to Brighton rather than in Ireland.

214

Fig 112: The first Royce car in the open stable yard where its engine had earlier been bench tested. Blake Street lies beyond the wooden gates. The photograph was taken in April or May 1904 and the driver is thought to be either G T Richards or Shipley, designers who worked under A J Adams.

Fig 113: The first Royce with the Hallam family at Brabyns Park, Marple near Manchester in the summer of 1905. The car has its fourth body, in fact, its original rear entrance tonneau by Roberts refitted in 1905. 'Billy' Hallam served in the war and lost an arm. Later he ran Derby Car Repair as Captain Hallam *(Hm)*.

Fig 114: The second Royce car when used by Mr Anderson, Contracts Manager of W T Glover. By then it bore the registration M1137. Ultimately the car was sold to Professor Stoney of Manchester University who later scrapped the chassis but saved the engine and gearbox, which are preserved in Manchester's Museum of Science & Industry.

Fig 115: The second Royce while with Glovers. W T Anderson is at the wheel. The photograph was taken in 1910 at Charleshead near Macclesfield.

Fig 116: The very first Rolls-Royce chassis, number 20150. The original customer appears to have been a Mr Amos of Lancashire. Its engine was tested on 14 September 1904 and the chassis was fitted with Barker rear entrance tonneau. Claremont Haynes records noted a dispute with a Mr Amos from December 1905 to May 1906, which might have referred to this car. The photograph was taken at Cooke Street, possibly after its being returned to the Company in 1905.

Fig 117: Minnie Royce and a friend, Mrs Smith, on the third Royce on the brick road at the Royce's home, Brae Cottage, Legh Road, Knutsford. It led to the rockery built to stop the De Dion Quad. In her last years the Royce's adopted niece, Violent Maynard (née Punt), still recalled N-MR-7 – correctly – as 'Mister Seven'.

Fig 118: The third Royce at the end of her days at carrying mail to and from the post office in Derby. The photograph was taken in No 2 Yard at Nightingale Road. The corner of the Commercial Block is visible beyond what is now part of No 1 Shop. Preparations are being made on the right to build the Technical Block, and that dates the picture to 1919.

Fig 119: Another photograph taken at the same time as 118. The location of the windows and doors are still visible at the time of writing. The number M612 led historians to believe this was the first Royce in past years, but it was the third. The 40/50 hp is chassis No 2011.

Fig 120: Two-cylinder 10 hp Rolls-Royce engine lower half. The photograph clearly shows the three main bearings of the crankshaft.

Fig 121: The original badge fixed to the radiator of Rolls-Royce cars. The first cars with the 'classic' radiator, however, had no badge. Note the lack of a hyphen between Rolls and Royce.

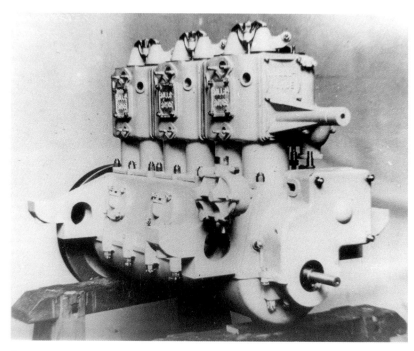

Fig 122: The incomplete six-cylinder 30 hp engine shown at the Paris Salon in December 1904.

CHAPTER THIRTEEN

The Cooke Street factory

A return in our imaginations to the factory of long ago

Please join me. We will pay a visit to Cooke Street and make a brief tour of the factory in our imagination. The plan found by Derek Gration served to allow reconstruction of the layout of the three floors (Figs 123 and 124) and these provide a map which we can follow. The names and locations of various activities were added for me on sketches of the factory, as they remembered it, in the 1960s by remaining Cooke Street employees – Tom Broome, Jimmy Chadwick, George Clegg, Tommy Nadin and Ben Pope.

The entrances to the factory were from Cooke Street and Blake Street. One suspects that only the senior people entered at 1A Cooke Street and climbed the staircase to the offices. All other employees entered under De Looze's eagle eye and clocked on at No 3. No pictures remain of the front portions of the ground floor and their use was not devoted to any significant activities, so let us begin at the front door.

Entering the registered office door at 1A we find that it leads immediately onto a staircase of sixteen steps, each edged in brass and covered in rubber on the treads – or that is how it was when the meticulous valuation was carried out in 1884. At the head of the staircase (Fig 124) Sergeant Jack Bennett,[41] the Commissionaire, greets us. We are directed to begin by turning right along the short landing past Sanderson's office and then to follow the corridor to the left. The more junior staff enter and leave the office by way of the staircase on the left. On the right is the stairway to the electrical drawing office above and, beyond it, looking back over our right shoulder, the general office seemingly crammed with dutiful souls diligently working in rows at long benches. For all the world the scene has the appearance of something from one of Dickens' novels.[42] We may catch sight of a lady with a neat

---

[41] In 1996 the Managing Director of the Corps of Commissionaires, C J Salt, checked on Sgt Bennett and concluded that he might have been Sergeant Ralph Bennett, late of the 90th Foot (2nd Battalion) The Cameronians. He joined the Corps on 25 July 1905 and was given the shoulder number of Bm 177. He left the Corps on 22 February 1919. Our only pictures of Sgt Bennett date to Derby days, the latest being taken in 1912. Whilst the Corps identified their Sergeant Bennett as 'Ralph' and employees recall a 'Jack', this is not too uncommon in the history of Rolls-Royce: individuals have often been known by first names which do not appear on their birth certificate.

[42] Such offices were not unknown at Derby when I joined. One, which dealt with employee records at Gresham Road, comprised a very long table with silent figures crouched at work on either side, presided over by a giant figure who dominated one end of the table. He would expound, to the detriment of the work rate, on the beneficial effects on the moral standing of young men to be gained from blowing an instrument in a brass band. On more than one occasion, I found myself dealing with this gentleman at the behest of the Financial Director and, I must say, he gave me every help – once he found that I had played in the 'second horns' of a brass band!

quarter plate camera. She shares an office in this area: Miss Irwin (or Unwin), who takes all the photographs of the Company's products and premises.

Continuing, we pass the typing pool and filing office on the left and the print room and Mr Watkins' office. He is responsible for site contract work. We are now at the door of the office shared by Mr Royce and Mr Claremont and their secretaries: no pretentious desks or furnishing here. And, ahead, we can look down the staircase onto the factory floor. Before descending, we will look at the remainder of activities on the first floor. Turning right past the partners' office, we walk down a long corridor. On the right is the office of Mr De Looze and his staff. Among them is the young Ben Pope, who served later in Derby, as did most of his colleagues. His son John, known as 'Jumbo', retired from the Rolls-Royce Small Engines Division at Leavesden in the year this book was first published. Then the corridor becomes lighter, the windows of the left offering a view across the roof of the woodworking and pattern shop to the brazing shop where Mr Smithson's team are making parts such as radiator header tanks. Although we cannot see in, we know that Mr Croston and Mr Cheetham below have their people making teak battery boxes, boxes for trembler coils, rims for steering wheels and some floorboards. Finally, we pass the car design office on our right and enter Billy Ellis' instrument room. We knew we would find Florrie Austin there but, among others, we can see George Clegg assembling carburettors.[43]

Retracing our steps we walk back to the big staircase and descend into the old pre-1888 main shop. Standing against its northern wall (Fig 125) we can see a two- or three-cylinder car. Beyond, the crankcase of a four is visible, and to the right the chassis of a six-cylinder thirty horsepower lies between us and the stairs we have just descended. The partition of Mr Royce and Mr Claremont's shared office can be seen upstairs. Engine build took place exactly where we are standing and in the background we can see George Bagnall's[44] marking-out table.

Let us now walk through into the major extension, which had been approved in October 1895 to allow the erection of cranes. No contemporary picture survives giving a general view so we will have to transpose ourselves in time to the 1930s when another electrical engineering concern called Triangle had the factory. The shop can be best seen by crossing the floor (Fig 127) and climbing the staircase to the gallery, which was originally designed into the building to help in the erection of cranes. We do have a contemporary picture of the tool room (Fig 130), and among the machine tools is a small second-hand Rivett lathe which Royce will, many years later, have sent from Derby to his personal workshop at West Wittering.

---

[43] Both came to Derby, George being retained to the age of seventy as an Inspector in No 2 Shop (PC03) because of his brilliance as a mathematician. Florrie became responsible for all personnel issues for female employees on the shop floor, and was awarded the MBE.

[44] Bagnall was later among the team who established Rolls-Royce car production at Springfield, Massachusetts, USA. He remained in the States when Springfield closed. The last evidence we have of him is a letter in Lord Hives' files dating to the outbreak of the Second World War in 1939 offering Rolls-Royce whatever assistance he could.

Here we meet the foreman, Bill Reilly, and his right-hand man, James Archer. We also meet Alf Mathews, Rowland Marshall, Ernie Cowgill, Harry Angel and an apprentice, W E 'Billy' Smith, who had joined the Company in 1901 at the age of fourteen. When he retired from the tool room in Derby he had served 57 years and even then his son Eric was working there. That was in 1959, the year the author joined.

We also meet Arthur Wormald (*Wor*). Arthur is standing on the right, and later in Derby will become Works Manager and a Director of Rolls-Royce. He was to become one of the most important individuals in the period in Derby up to the mid 1930s. Born in Yorkshire in 1873 he began work as a 'half timer' at the age of eleven with the Lancashire and Yorkshire Railway in Leeds at half a crown a week (12½p), on a lorry which collected goods for the railway. At thirteen he joined the local firm of John and H McLaren building traction engines, and it was there that he served his time. By the age of nineteen he was chargehand of the cylinder bench. At the age of twenty-two he unwittingly followed in the footsteps of Royce, joining Greenwood and Batley as a die sinker working on single shot Martini Henry rifles being built for Japan. From there he moved to the repair of Merryweather steam trams in Dewsbury in 1899 and then in 1901 he went to Manchester. He worked in the tool room of the Linotype Company and, a year later, joined Westinghouse in their tool room. The story used to be told that he met an old Cooke Street acquaintance when out of work, having been dismissed from Westinghouse for union activities, and the acquaintance asked why he didn't apply to Royce Ltd. He did, and heeded the warning that, when the 'old man' asked if he was a member of 'the club' (union) he should say no. This was in 1904. When Royce was pressured to work away from Derby in 1911/12 and leave management of the factory to others, Wormald rose to fill this role. Having first-hand knowledge of the shop floor and unions led him to set up the Works Committee, which has stood Rolls-Royce in Derby in good stead ever since. He was awarded the OBE, the same as Royce, in 1919. His health failed in 1936 whereupon he retired, dying soon afterwards. Roy Fedden was considered as a replacement but the head of Experimental, Ernest Hives (*Hs*), was subsequently appointed General Manager in 1936. On hearing the news of Wormald's death, Maurice Olley (*Oy*) wrote to Hives on 20 January 1937, '*The news about Wor was a shock, even though one had expected it. I have always admired the Machiavellian skill with which he steered a course through and around unions, strikes, fires, directors and assorted acts of God, even though it does not seem to me that is a way to run a factory. I know so little about such things – probably it was more necessary than I realised.*'

If we now look down from the crane gallery (Fig 128), across the 1895 crane factory floor and through the brick pillars – all that remained when the wall was knocked out during the extension process – to the point where we had stood a little while earlier (Fig 125), we can see the area where Jimmy Roscoe, T Hyde and Eddie McGarry used to assemble axles.

Walking to the other end of the gallery we can look down again (Fig 129). The big doors lead into Blake Street and it was from just this side of the doors that Royce set out on his first journey in his prototype car on 1 April 1904.

Descending to a point directly below where this picture was taken, and moving back in time – not to 1904 but to 1906 (Fig 126) we find Albert Wheatman machining a crankshaft for the 30 hp six-cylinder model Rolls-Royce on his Darling and Sellars lathe. The 30 hp proved to be a technical nightmare and presented Royce with one of the biggest challenges of his lifetime. The crankshaft Albert is machining is of what proved to be the successful '3+3' type, of which more in a later chapter. Although not visible, he is surrounded by other lathes – mainly centre lathes and one or two other types of machine tools, including Gisholt machines. The area in which these machines stood, and Albert is seen, are visible, along with the crane gallery above, in a photograph taken in Triangle days (Fig 127).

Let us now take a walk out of the factory and into Blake Street. Turning round, and again leaping to the 1930s we can look back at the factory (Fig 131). This was the starting point on the road which led to fame for Rolls-Royce. The factory gates are clearly visible. To the left were some of the earliest premises rented by F H Royce & Company and just before the overhead walkway on the right one can see the gateway to the open stable yard (Figs 94, 102, 103, 112 and 135). It was there that the Decauville was stripped, the first Royce engine – and its successors – were tested, and the Royce cars often garaged.

Sergeant Bennett shares a few confidences

Before leaving, let us retrace our steps by way of the Monitor Shop (Fig 132), where we will find Jimmy Broom and his colleagues, to Sergeant Bennett, and see what observations he can make on the culture of the factory. He has not been there all that long so some of what he tells us will have been passed on to him by his predecessor, Schofield. The hours are long and hard, but life at Cooke Street is not without its camaraderie and fun, and among the workforce are many fascinating characters – some erudite and others distinctly individual. Most are Manchester men born and bred, and proud of it. Others come from farther afield – Wormald, for instance, from Leeds.

Let us continue to learn of these men and women from a detached viewpoint, looking down on the factory through the medium of Mick Watts' reconstructions (Figs 133 and 134). These were drawn to scale from photographs taken across the years, from 1903 to 1965, and using the ground plan from the insurance files.

Sergeant Bennett talks freely about some, with reticence about others and with some awe about Mr Claremont (*EAC*) and Mr Royce (*R*). He confides that Mr De Looze (*D*) places his trust, for personal transport, in his bicycle. Every week he is called for and Mr De Looze presents him with a small roll of tools with which he is expected to maintain his bicycle. His work complete, the Sergeant returns the spanners, only to face the slightly humiliating experience of having to wait until all tools have been checked as present and correct. The seniority of Mr De Looze is such that one dare not say anything. On the other hand, some recompense comes from the way Mr Royce ribs him. When he does, it's Mr De Looze who daren't answer back. Mr De Looze likes using bits of Latin, and that is fair game for Mr Royce. One day Mr De Looze talked about 'quid pro quo'. I don't know what that means, but Mr Royce immediately told him, "*You look after the pro quos – it's the quids I'm interested in*".

Down on the factory floor, he tells us, there are some real characters from pranksters like young Ernie Wooler to people like Joe Penny who earns his living as a miller but who could have done so singing in the music halls. And he's not alone in that. Many put on a good turn giving recitals, singing or playing musical instruments (Fig 136). Then there are people like George Clegg who could recite any of Shakespeare's works to order and cap that off by speaking French with no hesitation. It's a great collection of individuals – including a few beer swillers – more than a couple of hundred of them in all.

What of Mr Claremont? He's strict and a bit of a tartar, but he knows what he's doing. If you do a good job he's fair with you, but if you get up to any tricks it's as like as not he'll catch you out. He doesn't spend all that much time here these days because he runs Glovers too. Some say that's a good thing, especially after the way he gave Mr Royce so little support when he first tried to build a decent motor car. I've been in the Army and I know his type: typical Officer whose made it on his ability and not because he was born to nobility. If anything, they treated us more as 'other rank' than the sons of dukes and lords.

We have to raise the question: how do the workforce view Mr Royce? Bennett starts diffidently. Well, he's a big man – over six foot and you know he's around even if you can't see him. He's got that thing called 'presence'. He's got piercing blue eyes and people tend to avoid looking straight back at him because it isn't always a good thing having what you might call his undivided attention. He doesn't look from side to side – he moves his whole head, and that's because, some of the old hands say, he damaged his eye muscles years ago when he worked a lot with arc lamps. But what he looks at he sees. He's got eyes like an eagle! And when he talks to you he's very clear, but it's a bit odd. You'd expect a big man like him to have a booming voice but it's a bit – well – almost squeaky. Bennett loses a little of his diffidence and opens up. He is held in awe, we learn. He works all hours of day and night, and expects us to do the same. Nothing is ever good enough for him but, to be fair, there is no job in the factory that he can't do better than any of us. He doesn't even stop to eat. Mr De Looze sends young lads around with glasses of milk for him and it's usually cold before he realises they're there. I've even heard say that early on Saturday mornings those two young apprentices on the car job go down to the corner shop for a loaf of bread and some eggs. When they get back they cook the eggs down in the factory and make sure Mr Royce joins them. One day they even got a half hour lecture on how eggs should be cooked. And they're only paid five bob a week. Meanness? No: he just gets so absorbed by what he's doing. He'll spend hours, for instance, heat treating bits of metal, wrapping them in a cloth and putting them in a vice, only to smash them with a hammer! I've heard say he does the same with engines. He sits in the stable round on Blake Street for hours on end, just looking at things like what they call the valves while they're running. I was told just the other day that 'the old man' – what everyone calls him behind his back – took little Jimmy Chadwick out on a run to his home in Knutsford not long ago. He grows peaches, you know. He's a very good gardener, and he gave one to Jimmy. He asked Jimmy, "*Do you know what they cost?*", but Jimmy hadn't heard right. "*Yes sir, peaches*". "*No*", says the 'old man', "*How much they cost. They're half a crown each in the market*". Without thinking Jimmy says, "*I'd rather have the half crown*" and gets himself told off, "*Jimmy! You cheeky monkey!*" But then the 'old man' really cares about youngsters.

I'll tell you something else. It isn't only youngsters the 'old man' has a soft spot for. Last winter he was in one day and noticed one of the old unskilled blokes looking really sad. So he asked him what the trouble was. The man's missus had died. They'd been married a tidy long time and what hurt was that he couldn't afford to give her a decent Christian burial. He looked the 'old man' in the face and said tearfully that she deserved better than a pauper's grave. The 'old man' asked how much it would cost to lay her to rest properly, then told him to go to Mr De Looze and say Mr Royce wanted him to be loaned the sum, repayable in instalments over a year. He added – and then come back to me with the piece of paper. Well, Mr De Looze wrote out an official document with so much a week for a year, and handed out the money from the cashbox in his safe. The labourer returned to the 'old man', who looked at the piece of paper, got out a pencil and, leaning on something handy, wrote on it and handed it back. What the labourer saw was that the 12 months had been crossed out and six months written in its place, initialled 'FHR'. The 'old man' had paid half the cost of paying proper respect to the departed life's partner. That's the way he is, deep down.

He isn't easy to work with though. He can work himself into a lather. When he's in a good mood he puffs a pipe. He has a favourite he bought locally – a little curved thing they call a Meerschaum – and the stuff he usually smokes is called Log Cabin. Of course, he never drinks here, but the odd one who knows him well enough tells that he likes a good pint of beer from time to time, but he wouldn't say thank you for a whisky or a gin or anything like that. He sometimes even sings a bit of Gilbert & Sullivan around the works, which some people reckon he got to like when he did the lighting of theatres in Liverpool. When he isn't, we all have to keep our heads down in the hope he won't pick on us. One wrong move or one word in the wrong place and you're out on the pavement, although you probably get your job back when he's cooled off. You can tell the signs of trouble – he has his trouser bottoms hitched up high when he's on the warpath. Sometimes he asks,

"Where the hell's so-and-so?" even though he'd sacked them that morning. And swear! He could have been a professional soldier.

There was one day when he was carrying on and I've heard tell of some swear words he used that even I didn't know. Then he sees what he'd missed – some of the women and the odd young lass could hear what he was on with. Well, he doesn't usually use any bad language when the women are about and, when he saw them he got even more het up. He starts bawling at the foreman for not warning him and then he realised what he was doing. He stopped and just fell about laughing at himself. The lads breathed a sigh of relief … they just hoped the lasses didn't go home and ask their dads what some of those words meant!

One of the things that makes everyone respect him is the way he insists on things being right. It wasn't long ago he got a sledge hammer to a couple of his precious castings for new cylinder blocks because they weren't thick enough all the way round. One day he even gave young Wooler one of his new gaiters to cut a leather washer out of because he couldn't find a good enough bit elsewhere. If you get things wrong, it's one thing not taking enough metal off. You'll hear about that. But if you've taken too much off you can get sacked … only, like I've said, he usually wants to know where you've gone a bit later. And he's just as hard on himself. I was told some time back by young Cooper how the 'old man' wanted three castings made in this aluminium stuff he's started using. When the first two were poured a load of liquid metal and air bubbles shot out, so he told Cooper, *"Try the next one"* and then, as an afterthought said, *"I suppose this third bxxxxr is going to blow up!"* It nearly did, so it was what they say 'back to the drawing board'. No criticism of the lads in the foundry. He knew it was his job to fix.

I know one day, a year or more ago, some of the lads were in a cold sweat. Mr Royce went down near the new heat treatment furnace and Archer was hardening some little cogs for a bicycle hub gear, a bit of jarvo he was doing with some of his mates. Bill Reilly had designed this thing when he was foreman of the tool room. Albert Underwood turned what they call the structural components and Ron Marshall cut the gears on a milling machine. Reilly had moved on and Archer had become the foreman. Everyone was worried in case the 'old man' looked in the furnace – but he didn't. Archer[45] collected the royalties and went to Raleigh in Nottingham, but I heard tell Raleigh pulled a fast one somewhere over this Sturmey Archer gear. It's as well this all happened some time ago: if I'd known I suppose I'd have had to tell on them. All in all, though, there is hardly a man or woman in this factory who wouldn't walk to hell and back with the 'old man'. His standards are almost like those of a religion, and there are more than a few around here who've said they know we are making history.

The foregoing is, of course, fictitious in terms of the way in which the scenario is presented as the comments of Sergeant Bennett. But the content is factual. It is

---

[45] Archer's son, Len, became a renowned Rolls-Royce car tester in later years and was a key figure in the Second World War in the factory which overhauled Merlin aero engines in India.

based on the many memories of those who worked at Cooke Street, related later to Bill Morton and later still to myself and others. Jimmy Chadwick himself told me the story of the peaches and he recalled Bill Reilly designing what became known as the Sturmey Archer gear. It did start life at Cooke Street and Len Archer's dad did collect royalties when Raleigh took it up.

If this chapter appears contrived I ask the reader's forgiveness. It seemed the only way to revisit the long-gone Cooke Street factory and get a feel for what it must have been like to work there.

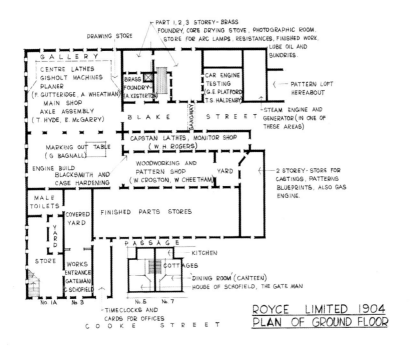

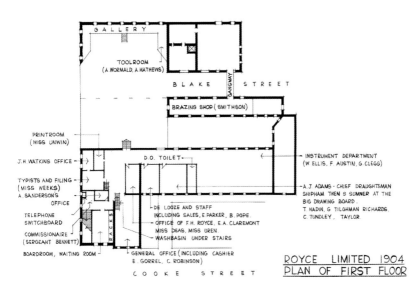

Fig 123/ 124: Reconstructed plans showing activity locations and names of some of those involved. Redrawn by Michael Watts for clarity from the plans in the Cooke Street insurance files. Identification of activities and who worked in which area had earlier come from the last Cooke Street employees.

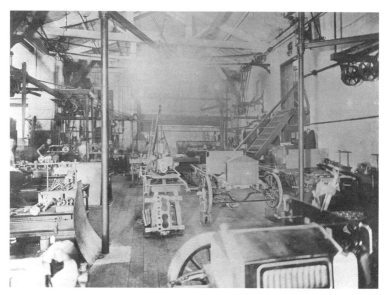

Fig 125: The original factory as rented in 1888 as it was when employed as the fitting shop or erection bay for the early cars. The staircase on the right leads to the offices. Above the doorway is a Royce electric bell and, through it, Royce's office is just visible.

Fig 126: Albert Wheatman machining the successful 3+3 30hp six-cylinder crankshaft on his Darling and Sellars lathe in 1906. On the bench are crankshafts for the two-, three- and four-cylinder cars. This apparently routine photograph conceals a saga of its own. The first six-cylinder crankshafts broke and presented Royce with one of the biggest challenges of his life. It is masterfully recorded in Tom C Clarke's Rolls-Royce Heritage Trust Technical Series No 6, *Royce and the vibration damper.*

Fig 127: The 1896 extension photographed in Triangle days. The roof supports carry brackets for travelling overhead crane rails. In earlier times a staircase gave access to the gallery half way along its length where the heavier railing supports are visible. Albert Wheatman machined crankshafts in the area beneath the gallery.

Fig 128: The 1896 extension at Cooke Street as it appeared in the days of the Triangle engineering company between the wars. Across the floor and beyond the pillars is the erection bay shown in Fig 125.

231

Fig 129: A further view in Triangle days, again taken from the crane erecting gallery, and showing the main factory doors into Blake Street. It was from just inside these doors that the first Royce motor car started on its historic first journey.

Fig 130: The tool room in early car days. It was situated on the crane gallery. Arthur Wormald is standing on the extreme right. He became Works Manager of Rolls-Royce in Derby, being awarded the OBE for his work in the First World War, and was later made a Director of the Company. He died in 1936. Like Royce, he worked as a young man at Greenwood and Batley in Leeds for a period. Seated in front of Wormald is an apprentice, W E 'Billy' Smith. He joined Royce Ltd in 1901 at the age of 14 and served 57 years in the tool room at Cooke Street and at Nightingale Road before retiring at the end of 1958.

Fig 131: The Blake Street entrance to the factory as it appeared when the Triangle company occupied the premises. It had changed little. On the right, just before the covered overhead walkway, is the entrance to the stable yard where the first Royce petrol engine was tested in 1903. All car engines appear to have been tested there subsequently for reasons of safety. It was in this yard that Ernie Wooler remembered sketching the Decauville as Royce and Ernie Mills took it apart. The doors into the main shop lie behind the parked van and, to the left,is the Royce Ltd Transport Department, which comprised a horse and cart, a van and a barrow.

Fig 132: The monitor shop – capstan lathes, as they are called today. Jimmy Broom is posing for the photograph while a number of colleagues look on with interest. From right to left, they are, firstly, Ike Turner according to one source (Ernie 'Charlie Chaplin' Taylor according to Ted Foulds), Henry Watkins, the foreman, W Gradwell (looking like the boss!) and Joe Chiswell immediately to his left. The individuals either side of Jimmy have not been identified, but the lathes were recalled as the first No 4 Herberts. Jimmy Broom retired in Derby in November 1953. 233

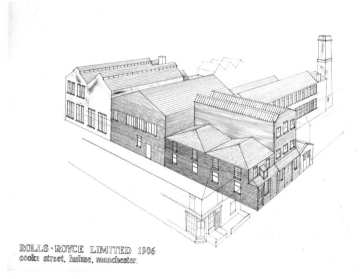

ROLLS-ROYCE LIMITED 1906
cooke street, hulme, manchester.

Fig 133: Isometric view of the Cooke Street factory as it was in the days of the early cars. This drawing was created with great attention to accuracy of detail by Michael Watts of the Rolls-Royce Architects Department in Derby in 1982. He based his work on all existing photographs, both contemporary and later, and on the plan from the insurance file. Cooke Street borders the right-hand side of the factory.

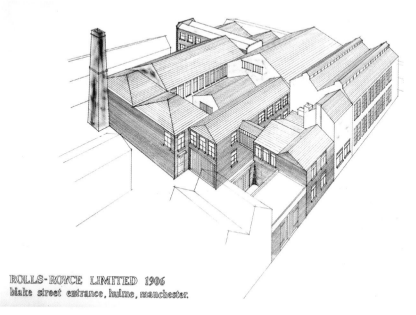

ROLLS-ROYCE LIMITED 1906
blake street entrance, hulme, manchester.

Fig 134: The second of Michael Watts' isometric views of the factory, showing the Blake Street aspect. Blake Street ended just short of the covered overhead walkway.

234

Fig 135: A further view of the first Royce car taken in the open stable yard – or is it? Meticulous research by Tom Clarke has shown it to be the third Royce, chassis 15880, when fitted with the Roberts body from the first Royce, chassis 15196. The picture was taken in the spring of 1904 and shows it as the first car to bear N-MR-6 before this was transferred to the first Royce, previously N-414. At that point the second Royce took the number N-414 from the first.

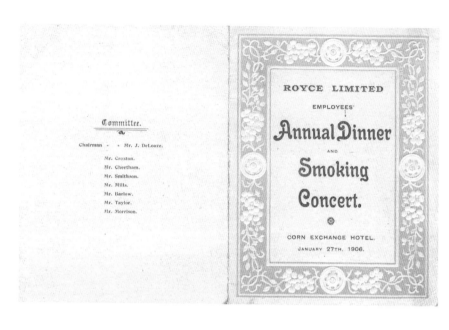

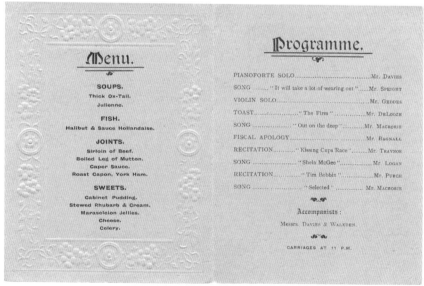

Fig 136: Menu and programme for the Royce Ltd Annual Dinner and Smoking Concert, 27 January 1906. Top: front and rear of card. Bottom: centre pages.

CHAPTER FOURTEEN

The Rolls-Royce motor car makes its debut

Brought before the British public

We have already noted that the name 'Rolls-Royce' was in use at Cooke Street by, if not before, August 1904 and that the first car to bear that name was delivered by C S Rolls & Company in the same month. Public exposure, however, had to wait until Cooke Street had managed to translate intent into reality and turn out examples of the new range of cars.

What was achieved for the Paris Salon was remarkable and that was followed by the Rolls-Royce name being placed before the British public at the Olympia Show in London between 10 and 18 February 1905. On show (Fig 137) were the completed ten horsepower, chassis 20154, and the fifteen horsepower, 24273, still incomplete but with a body fitted. Both had been shown in Paris. A thirty horsepower, the engine for which had been shown in Paris, was also on display, incomplete mechanically but with body fitted. For the first time, however, a complete twenty horsepower was at the show as a demonstrator, 24263. It was the first of many Rolls-Royce cars to bear a name, in this case 'Grey Ghost' (Fig 138). It has to be added that, while C S Rolls & Co majored on the Rolls-Royce, Minerva and New Orleans were also featured. The Rolls-Royce name appeared again at Olympia in November 1905, and on this occasion two additional models were to be featured, both powered by a new V-8 engine – but we will come to that in due course. Another event had served to put the name Rolls-Royce on the map in the meantime. A small sales brochure was also produced entitled *The New All-British Motor-Car*, with the entwined RR and the address of C S Rolls & Co on its cover (Fig 139). This dated to January 1905. When I joined the Rolls-Royce Public Relations department in 1961 this booklet had been replicated, ostensibly using the original plates which were alleged to have been found in the basement of Conduit Street (and having later rescued several treasures from its dusty floors, I will not dismiss the story!). It was unfortunate that nothing on these replicas indicated that they were: many copies were given away and latter day owners think they have something special. I can tell the difference, but it requires a practiced eye.

The pamphlet emphasises C S Rolls & Co (Fig 140) and its management very strongly, yet mention of Royce Ltd is very much in lower case, far more emphasis being placed on '*honest British workmanship*'. Royce and his team, in fact, attract less coverage than Rolls' clientele, and here one should add that the patrons listed – including Rolls' father – were, in the main, customers for other than Rolls-Royce cars at that date. A last interesting point is that the models illustrated in both the brochure and the advertisements of the day make no real effort to emphasise the unique shape of the Rolls-Royce radiator. From this one might deduce that Conduit Street had yet to recognise what a pearl Royce had inadvertently given them.

The formula of Royce's engineering, coupled with Rolls' appreciation of market needs, and his ready access to the wealthy and landed minorities who could afford such luxuries, was one that had every chance of success (Fig 141). Add to that Claude Johnson's (Fig 142) brilliant flair for publicity, based on a deep-rooted faith in the cars, then success became inevitable. However, there was another potential market outlet. While the first Rolls-Royce, 20151, was sold by C S Rolls & Co to Paris Singer, 20150 might have been sold as a Rolls-Royce by Royce Ltd.

On 5 December 1904, clearly recognising that opportunity, Rolls wrote to Royce Ltd, thus:-

Dear Sirs
    Would you be prepared to take up the sale of ROLLS-ROYCE cars at your other branches, and provide them with cars for show purposes, say one for each depot? You to hand to us when sold the difference between the cost price of the chassis to us and our trade price for the same.
    Yours truly
    pp C S Rolls & Co
    Chas S Rolls

A nice try: C S Rolls & Co would have gained their mark-up without earning it, and Royce Ltd would have received no extra benefit for their efforts.

The reply, addressed to C S Rolls & Co at Lillie Hall rather than 28 Brook Street (Conduit Street still lay a few weeks ahead in time) was as follows:-

*   7 Dec 1904*
Dear Sirs
    We are much obliged for your kind letter of the 5th inst ref R/O with regard to sale of 'Rolls-Royce' cars at our other branches, and we are afraid it is not possible to send cars to our agents as they have neither premises suitable for storing them nor any knowledge sufficient to sell them. They are, however, keenly alive to the desirability of obtaining orders and we propose whenever they advise us of a sound enquiry or interest being taken in such goods, to instruct them to follow the matter up. It would be as well if we were to come to an understanding as to what commission you would pay them for any sales effected. We should be glad if you would forward us at once a number of catalogues, illustrations and specifications which you are having printed that we may assist you as far as we possibly can in obtaining orders.
    Yours faithfully
    John De Looze

The above indicates that Cooke Street was fully in the picture concerning the imminent sales brochure we have discussed above: the reply came on 8 December

Dear Sirs

In reply to your letter D 7/12 re your branches, we would give our maximum commission of 10%.

We will forward specifications and catalogues to you as soon as possible.

pp C S Rolls & Co
C S Rolls

De Looze presses his point, writing on 16 January 1905:-

Dear Sirs

We are much obliged for your letter of the 14th inst ref R/O.[46]

We are content if you wish that the commission be only paid to our agents or representatives. We will assist you as far as we can in introducing business, but of course we can give no undertaking to render services in such direction either for ourselves or our agents or representatives.

We suggest for your consideration that it would be better to allow us a commission as well as our agents and representatives, since it would enable us to got to much more trouble and expense than would otherwise be the case. For instance, we are contemplating even now the employment of a salesman for the purpose of interviewing potential buyers, and his services should be distinctly valuable to you, but if we are only to have the profit (if any) from the sale of chassis to you there is not much inducement to us to go to considerable trouble and expense.

We leave you to decide, as to whether you will pay us a commission apart from our agents and representatives.

……… (etc) ………
Yours faithfully
John De Looze

In this we can detect a seasoned hand in terms of commercial dealings, and he had not finished yet. Rolls replied on 18 January:-

Dear Sirs
Re your commission

In reply to your letter D 16/1, would it meet your requirements if we gave you a commission of 5% for orders received by us from persons who have been previous clients of yours, who are not in communication with us, and on

---

[46] We do not have this letter.

*which no other commission is payable by us to your agents; no commission
to be payable for simply showing cars, giving information to casual callers
or clients sent by us.*
.... (etc) ....
Yours faithfully
pp C S Rolls & Co
Chas S Rolls

De Looze now looks back to Royce's market vision as it had been prior to
meeting Rolls. On 20 January he wrote:-

Dear Sirs
Re commission
*Your letter of the 18th inst to hand, ref R/O. We have always looked upon
our circle of friends and clients as the chief source from which we should
receive orders for cars, and this would not appear to be covered at all by
your suggestion. We think our agents and representatives should receive the
commission you have promised of 10%, and we at least 5% on all the orders
we may introduce, or solicit in the first case.*
Yours faithfully
John De Looze

The deal is now crystalising in Royce Ltd's favour:-

Jan 21st 1905
Dear Sirs
Re commission
*In reply to yours D 20/1, we will agree to give you 5% commission on
any of your friends you may introduce who may order cars from us at retail
prices, provided that they have not been in communication with us. Such
commission to be payable when the transaction had been completed and the
car paid for.*
Trusting this will be satisfactory
We are
Yours faithfully
pp C S Rolls & Co
Chas S Rolls

Still De Looze is not satisfied. Writing for the first time to 14/15 Conduit Street,
he presses a little harder:

240

Dear Sirs
Re commission
    Your letter of the 21st inst to hand, ref R/O. It is very difficult to define the exact conditions upon which you will pay us a commission. We will rest contented for the time with your assurance, which we feel you have given us, of our receiving 5% (five per cent) on orders which we introduce. You do not say anything with regard to the 10% for our agents and representatives and we shall be glad to know if you agree to the amount mentioned in our letter of the 20th inst to you on this subject. Please reply, as we should like to advise them as to what they may expect.
    Yours faithfully
    John De Looze

Rolls replies on 27 January:-

Dear Sirs
Re commission
    In reply to yours D 26/1, we agree to give your regularly appointed agents 10% commission on cars sold by them at our retail price, and upon which we have no other commission to pay. Such commission to be payable when we have received the full purchase price of the car.
    Yours truly
    pp C S Rolls & Co
        Chas S Rolls

Still De Looze comes back, writing on 3 February:-

Gentlemen,
Re commission
    Your letter ref R/O, Jan 27th to hand, for which please accept our thanks. In order to thoroughly understand this matter and to concentrate the discussion which has taken place in our letters of the past few weeks, and to enable us to communicate with our Agents on the point, we understand the matter to be settled between us as follows:
    (a) You will pay us a commission of 5% (five per cent) on the nett amounts as and when received by you from all sales of Rolls-Royce cars negotiated by you to persons whom we have introduced to you.
    (b) You will pay to us a commission of 10 (ten) per cent on the nett amount as and when received by you from all sales of Rolls-Royce cars negotiated by you to persons whom our agents or representatives have introduced.
    Kindly let us have your acceptance promptly, that we may advise our Agents without delay.
    Yours faithfully
    John De Looze

On 4 February 1905 Rolls accepted both stipulations, adding only '*In each case the orders must be placed by persons who have not previously communicated with us and are not on our books*'.

This might seem to have been an inordinately lengthy coverage of the correspondence, but there are a few fundamental points to be taken from it. The most important is that De Looze was, if somewhat entrepreneurial, very conscious of the fact that, if two organisations are to work together successfully, they must be absolutely clear on their relationship. Perhaps the greatest domestic competitor to Rolls-Royce was Napier. The chassis were made by the long-established D Napier & Son, by then under the third generation Montague Napier, and marketed through the agency of Selwyn Francis Edge. While there was a relationship between Rolls and Royce which transcended commercial considerations, that between Napier and Edge was not so deep. Over the years Napier's profits fell at the same time Edge's increased. The end result became inevitable. Despite the personal relationship, the fortunes of Royce Ltd and C S Rolls & Co on cars might have gone the same way had the interface not been removed in 1906, and that event will introduce Arthur Harry Briggs to our story.

The other points are, firstly, De Looze seems to have secured agreement to 5% on the finished price of the cars, so Royce Ltd would have received profit on the coachwork and fittings provided by C S Rolls & Co – on top of that percentage on the chassis, after marking up in price by Rolls. The final point regarding business achieved through Royce Ltd's agents is that the 10% was to be paid to Royce Ltd. How much of that was to be passed on to the agents was presumably for De Looze to decide!

The legal agreement between Royce Limited and the Honourable C S Rolls, dated 23 December 1904

In the earlier manuscript of this book I commented that when Rolls-Royce Limited was registered in 1906 another company was registered on the same day, namely Rolls-Royce Distributing Limited (Fig 143), and C S Rolls & Co were the sole agents for this company. (Actually, comparing the Certificates of Registration (Figs 1 and 143) discloses a difference of one day). I wrote further that it would be '*a fair guess*' that the agreement of December 1904 led to the formation of a paper company called Rolls-Royce Distributing. Its purpose, like the 1906 limited liability company, would have been to act as a marriage bond between Royce Ltd and C S Rolls & Co, ensuring that the car output, but no other products, of the former were sold exclusively through the latter. It would not have limited Rolls to selling only Rolls-Royces, however.

I pursued this assumption over many years and, ultimately, Bill Boldison, Assistant Company Secretary of Rolls-Royce plc, made time to do some deep digging for me at the end of 1987. He handed me a file in which were inserted all the documents he could find relevant to C S Rolls & Co, covering the crucial years 1903 to 1907. Among them were several legal documents in immaculate copperplate. As I perused the file my eyes fell upon one which bore the date 23 December 1904. I have to admit my heart skipped a beat and – yes – it was entitled *Royce Limited and the Honble C S Rolls – Agreement* (Appendix III). I had in my hands a priceless piece of history.

A detailed examination of its contents brings no surprises and one suspects that it is much the document drafted to Rolls while Edmunds was away in America in the early summer of 1904. We have noted before that the relationship between Rolls and Royce from the day they met was one of mutual admiration and trust, so they got on with what they intended. The agreement is between Royce Ltd and the Hon Charles Stewart Rolls of South Lodge, Rutland Gate – his parents' London home. So it rested with him rather than with C S Rolls & Co which, not being of limited liability, did not have the same status in law. Had the agreement been between C S Rolls and Royce Ltd one can be sure that De Looze would have chased it, nitpicked it, and got it signed within weeks, if not days. As it was, 23 December to my reckoning was the Friday before Christmas in 1904. The beautiful copperplate document, which extends to twelve sides, includes the date '*One thousand nine hundred and four*'. Both within and on the title page the '*23 December*' is added. I do wonder whether Rolls signed simply to avoid the need to rewrite the document '*One thousand nine hundred and five*'. It is clearly a statement by Royce Ltd for the acceptance of C S Rolls: it is signed by him and witnessed by Claude Johnson but includes no signature of an official of Royce Ltd. Let us explore its contents.

There is a preamble which includes:-

... the Company has recently commenced or is about to commence as a department of its business the manufacture of Chassis and intends in particular to manufacture four types of Chassis according to specifications and as shown and further described by drawings now being prepared by the Company which types of Chassis are respectively hereinafter referred to as type No 2 type No 3 type No 4 and type No 6 and whereas the said Charles Stewart Rolls is a dealer in Chassis or Motor Cars and the parties hereto are desirous of entering into arrangements such as herein contained now the parties hereto agree as follows:-

I will try to crystallise the twenty-five clauses which follow, and comment on them as appropriate in brackets.

1. The company was to prepare Specifications and General Arrangement drawings showing each model for Rolls' approval: the No 2 type forthwith' and the other types within a calendar month of the date of the agreement. (All substantially achieved long before. The Spec

243

of the No 2 was almost exactly Royce's document sent by Edmunds to tempt Rolls to Manchester eight months earlier. That for the thirty horsepower was the last. The Specification for that was dated 20 January 1905 and the chassis drawing '*Rolls-Royce No 6 type chassis*'. Royce signed both off on 1 February 1905, a little outside the 'calendar month' stipulation. Happily both survive with the Sir Henry Royce Memorial Foundation.)

2. Rolls had four days in which to respond to each Spec – in writing, saying whether he agreed with it or not. (He obviously had: long ago).

3. If Rolls agreed in writing Royce Ltd would manufacture and deliver a chassis: for type No 2 within two calendar months. (The first had already been sold and delivered four months earlier). And '*as to the types if the engine thereof, the form of which is not yet finally determined, be multiplied on the basis of the engine now determined upon for type No 2 within 4 calendar months .., but if the engine shall not be multiplied as aforesaid within such time – not being more than 6 calendar months - ... as the Company may deem necessary*'. (This recognises that the four and six, as multiples of the two-cylinder, would be easier than the three).

4. Gave Rolls the right to road test each specimen chassis, and to take them to pieces. He had 30 days in which to approve or otherwise. In the latter event he '*must return ... having previously put together in a proper and workmanlike manner any of the same which he may have taken to pieces, the cost of return carriage being paid by the parties equally*'.

5. If Rolls disapproved of either the Specification of any or all of the four types, or any or all of the specimen chassis, '*this agreement shall have no further operation*' as to the type or types disapproved. (No allowance is included for discussion and agreement on changes). If approved, the Agreement would continue with regard to the chassis so approved '*until the expiration of one year*' from the date Rolls approved. It was then renewable for a year, subject to no notice of termination being given by either party no less than four calendar months prior to the expiry of twelve months since approval. If Royce Ltd withdrew on any model they would not be free to sell other than to Rolls for a period of one year. If they did, they would pay Rolls 10% commission on the purchase price. The agreement was to continue in force for three years, with escalation clauses applying to the third.

6. Royce Ltd agreed to sell and deliver to Rolls – who would purchase, chassis as approved, on the following terms:-

    - type No 2 at one per calendar month
    - type No 3 at one per calendar month
    - type No 4 at three every two calendar months
    - type No 6 at three every two calendar months

    priced at

    - type No 2 - £215
    - type No 3 - £255
    - type No 4 - £347
    - type No 6 - £387

    Deliveries could be up to 75 days late without penalty, chassis to be delivered to Rolls properly packed at no extra cost: Rolls was to return the packing materials.

7. Royce Ltd could, during the life of the agreement, make any other models submitted to and approved by Rolls.

8. Rolls would provide a suitable office, showroom and garage, either at Lillie Hall and Brook Street or elsewhere conveniently situated in London. He was also charged as follows '*and shall put up and maintain upon such premises in manner to be reasonably approved by the company (ie Royce Ltd) an announcement* (sign) *as follows:* '*Rolls Royce Motor Cars*' (no hyphen!) *but nothing herein shall prevent him from also putting up announcements relating to other Cars dealt in by him*'.

9. All chassis were to be road tested for at least 50 miles before delivery to Rolls such that they were '*ready for the road*'. They were to be put right by Royce Ltd if not.

10. This section relates to material held at Cooke Street to support modification campaigns. In addition to 14 sets for No 4 heavy, 15 for No 4 light, 17 for No 6 short and 14 for No 6 long, an amendment (which cannot date until some nine months later) covers 13 sets for No 8 (the yet-to-be launched V-8).

11. Allows for Rolls to recover costs on modification campaigns.

12. Constrained Royce Ltd from selling any chassis produced surplus to Rolls' requirements, but allowed Royce Ltd to sell any he had ordered

but not taken up. It was stipulated that such sales could not be to a dealer in motor cars.

13. Rolls would receive 5% commission on cars sold by, as in 12, Royce Ltd. (Perhaps the start point for all the correspondence with De Looze).

14. Rolls was not to use the name Royce in association with any other cars.

15. (Emphasis is the author's) 'ALL CHASSIS MANUFACTURED BY THE COMPANY OF A TYPE APPROVED UNDER THIS AGREEMENTSHALL (SO LONG AS THIS AGREEMENT REMAINS IN OPERATION) BE SOLD' [whether sold by Rolls or by the Company – ie Royce Ltd] ' UNDER THE NAME ROLLS ROYCE CARS [again, no hyphen] AND SHALL BE SO DESCRIBED IN ALL LETTERS INVOICES AND ADVERTISEMENTS'. Rolls was not to use the name Royce nor Royce Ltd the name Rolls in other manner.

16. Deals with defective parts.

17. Spares to be charged as:

    -    if made by Royce Ltd – net prime cost of material + 15% plus net prime cost of labour + 150% taken together and subject to an increment of 10% profit
    -    if supplied but not made by Royce Ltd, net cost + 5%.

18. Royce Ltd would pay Rolls 5% of sums received by him for repairs to cars *'known as Rolls Royce Cars'*.

19. Deals with default of payment or bankruptcy of either party.

20. Limited liability: if Rolls converted his business into, or sold it to, a limited company, the company would assume his rights and liabilities (there had been thoughts in 1904 of converting Rolls' company into C S Rolls & Co Ltd, but it did not happen).

21. Neither party was to assign rights, privileges or liabilities without the agreement of the other.

22. Protects Rolls from any responsibilities in the event of Royce Ltd having infringed patents.

23. Simply states that any differences should be dealt with in line with the Arbitration Act, 1889.

24. Allowed Royce Ltd to supply cars for the use of its Directors and Officers, not exceeding six in number. They were to remain Company property.

25. (Emphasis is again the author's) ' THIS AGREEMENT SHALL NOT BE VARIED OR TAKEN TO BE VARIED BY ANY CORRESPONDENCE BETWEEN THE PARTIES UNLESS IN SUCH CORRESPONDENCE THIS AGREEMENT IS SPECIALLY REFERRED TO AND EXPRESSLY VARIED'

Signed	Chas S Rolls
Witnessed	C Johnson
120 St James Court	
Buckingham Gate	
London SW	

So, these are the facts we have been forced to assume for almost one hundred years. The only surprise is the lack of a hyphen in Rolls-Royce, and that was certainly in use at the time Rolls signed. Like much of the content, it is suggestive of the original document dating to around August 1904. It seems that it took Rolls four months to sign it! One might also observe that De Looze and Rolls took little notice of the final clause, 25, when corresponding about commission. I have to add that, now we know that the agreement had a three-year life from some point in the autumn of 1904, I can drop any search for a Rolls-Royce Distributing company. The bond between manufacturer and retailer rested in the 23 December 1904 agreement. It allowed Rolls to place an annual order for 1905, then another for 1906 and finally for 1907, and indeed he did. Unless something were done, there would be no formal basis on which Rolls could order beyond that. It is here that Rolls-Royce Distributing Limited provided the answer. The company belonged wholly to Rolls and established an ongoing bond with the manufacturer, until it became Rolls-Royce Limited through the hiving off of Royce Ltd's Cooke Street chassis operations. But this is to anticipate events which lay well ahead still in time: it was then that the December 1904 Agreement had to change. As we now know, it was replaced by Rolls-Royce Distributing Ltd.

On Friday and Saturday 3 and 4 March 1905 a meeting took place at Cooke Street to discuss C S Rolls & Co's order for 1905 and hopes for 1906. Royce, Claremont and De Looze were there for Royce Ltd, and Rolls and Johnson for C S Rolls & Co. On Monday 6 March both parties wrote expressing their recall of agreements reached to the other. From De Looze's letter one learns:-

A. *That the agreement dated Dec 23rd/04 shall be taken as varied in that it shall be considered as dated from the 1st inst so that the sample chassis shall be due for delivery by September 1st next.*

B. *That you kindly, apart from the agreement, order chassis at prices and in order of despatch etc as hereunder mentioned.*

What follows may be summated. All chassis prices were as per the 23 December 1904 agreement except the two-cylinder No 2 Type, which were sold to Rolls at £208 – a reduction on the £215 in the agreement.

No 2 Type

(Interestingly chassis 20150 does not feature in any of the correspondence indicating its direct sale by Royce Ltd).

- The first five, 20151-20155, had already been delivered.
- Six to nine, 20156-20159, were on order.
- Ten to twelve, 20160-20162, were ordered on 3 March at the meeting.

No 3 Type

- The first five were on order, 23924, 24272, 24273, 26330 and 26331,
- The sixth was ordered on 3 March.

No 4 Type

- The first, 24263, was on the road.
- The second to the sixth, 24264, 26351, 26352, 26353 and 26354, were on order.
- The seventh to tenth, 26350, 26355, 26356 and 23925, were ordered on 3 March.

No 6 Type

- The first, second and fourth, 24274, 24275 and 23927, were already on order.
- The third, and fifth to ninth, 26370 and 26371 to 26375, were ordered on 3 March.

248

The internal memo sent by C S Rolls & Co to Royce Ltd on 6 March contains additional points. Royce had expressed the hope that the first three-cylinder engine – and the six-cylinder engine – would be running on bench test by Monday March 13th. It also stated:-

Messrs Rolls agreed that the manufacture of the 1905 Cars should be proceeded with without their waiting for trial cars or subjecting the trial cars to the month's trial contemplated under the contract.

It continues – and this shows the mutual confidence which existed:-

This agreement was made on the understanding that Messrs Royce would not proceed with the manufacture of Cars until they were thoroughly satisfied that the Cars in their design and manufacture would prove satisfactory to the purchasers, and would be Cars which would not be discreditable to the firms of Rolls and Royce.

Further points include:-

That Messrs Royce should at once take into consideration the question of providing two Cars which should be suitable to compete in the race for the Tourist Trophy of 1905.

These were to be delivered to Messrs Rolls no later than 1st of August.

Type No 4. Messrs Royce have undertaken to proceed at once with the preparation of a design for Type No 4 for 1906 in which the engine is to be under the seat.

1906 Clutch
Messrs Royce undertook to at once consider substitution of a plate clutch for cone clutch in the 1906 models

Further reference is made to plate clutches in the 1907 order but, in fact, the cone clutch remained standard from the two-cylinder 'ten' right through to the end of the era of the 40/50 hp which followed. The last were made in Derby in 1927.

There follows an expression of concern over losses that were being sustained in 1905 due to Royce Ltd being unable to deliver sufficient cars. A subsequent memo on 8 March 1905 stresses a specific shortage:-

We are hoping to hear from you as to whether you can supply us with
a skeleton Chassis of Types 3 and 6 on which we can display bodies in our
Show-rooms.

Our position at the present time is really almost ridiculous as regards
these Types, in as much as although we are advertising them we cannot show
Callers any example whatever of these Types and we, therefore, hope you
will see your way to help us out of this difficulty.

Yours faithfully
C S Rolls & Co
C Johnson, Joint Manager

The four models

So far in this chapter I have attempted to reveal how Rolls and Royce worked together to launch the four initial models. Much has been written on these in the past[47] and it would serve little purpose to repeat what is already well known. Let us see if we can indulge in some broad observations and look for any lessons they might contain.

We know the Royce prototypes enthused Rolls because of the way they were engineered, although his sights were really on three or four cylinders. Going for six was then a bit adventurous. The Dutch Spyker had pioneered the concept and Napier was already active with a six. The motoring world, in general, still tended to the view that four was enough and thought that six simply added to the cost and the number of bits that could go wrong. One might assume, therefore, that Rolls pressed for the six partly because he could appreciate the effect on smoothness of having smaller angles between the firing impulses: he had begun to see that with the three-cylinder French cars, and partly because he had his eyes on S F Edge.

Edge had been the London manager of the Dunlop Tyre Company and a successful motor- racing driver before proposing to his old boss at Dunlop, Harvey Du Cros, that they set up a motor car agency. They did – together – as The Motor Vehicle Company in Regent Street, London, undertaking to accept all the cars Napier could make in addition to having the idea of taking agencies for one or two French makes. This was some years before Rolls met Royce, for the first batch of six Napiers were to be delivered, complete with coachwork by Mulliners of Northampton, but unpainted, by 31 March 1900. Since then the Napier-Edge partnership had gone from strength to strength and it was inevitable that Rolls should have seen that alliance as his benchmark.

---

[47] For the story of the engineering of the models, their problems and their development the key work remains *A History of Rolls-Royce Motor Cars, 1903-1907* by C W Morton, published by G T Foulis, 1964.

The most thorough historical analysis of each individual car and its owners appears in *The Edwardian Rolls-Royce* by John Fasal and Bryan Goodman in the early section by Tom Clarke entitled *Before the 40/50 hp – 1903-1907*. Published by John Fasal, 1994.

Engines in those days turned slowly, their maximum normal revs being not that much greater than the tickover of today's engines – say 1100 rpm compared with 800 or so. For that reason the individual impulses of the cylinders firing could be felt at low speeds and the solution lay in having more cylinders such that they overlapped. As a tyre expert, Edge was well aware too of the effect of firing impulses on tyre wear, and even on getting tyres to move on their rims: too much movement and the valve would fail. Edge had thus suggested such a design to Napier around the beginning of 1903. Napier had a fundamental belief in simplicity but yielded, producing his first six-cylinder prototype chassis before the summer was out. The new engine seemed to give all that was hoped – smoothness and silence – and a reduced need for gear changing, so Edge announced his new six-cylinder model to the motoring world at a dinner given at the Trocadero on 16 October 1903. By February 1904 he had a demonstrator. *The Autocar* wrote that '*The car was on its way before we knew it: it just melted into speed*' and by 1905 a 90 hp Napier six had covered the flying mile at Daytona Beach at 104.65 mph. It was a world record at the time. If C S Rolls & Co were to be among the elite, Rolls must have felt that having a six was an essential ingredient.

The original idea of having common pistons, connecting rods, bearings, valves, springs and (excepting the three) common cylinder blocks, was excellent in itself. It was revisited in the late 1930s by R W Harvey-Bailey (*By*) and W A Robotham (*Rm*) when the Rationalised B Range of four-, six- and eight-cylinder petrol engines was launched. These not only relaunched the Rolls-Royce and Bentley cars after the Second World War, but also powered the wheeled – and some tracked – combat vehicles of the British Army in the 1950s and later. The problem with the range in 1904 was that it started from the wrong point. For such a range to work, we now know that one should start with a crankshaft stiff enough for a 'six' and then shorten it. To have started with one barely adequate for two cylinders led to the crank for the 'six' looking like a bent hairpin, and it was early days in terms of understanding crankshafts. There was another problem; for all the logic of his approach, Royce was on a learner curve in terms of what extensive road use did to a car. He knew it, and that is why the Visiting Inspector service was established, firstly to ensure that owners were satisfied and that their chauffeurs took proper care of the cars, and secondly to report to Cooke Street on problems such as wear or vibration. Launching the 'three', 'four' and 'six' took time, as we shall see, and, when one adds essential change brought about by hard experience to Royce's natural propensity to think of a better way of doing something, the theoretical advantage of commonality was soon lost. The cars were good – very good by the standards of the day – but the whole philosophy sooner or later needed thinking through afresh.

The two-cylinder ten led the way, with the first car going to Paris Singer in the autumn of 1904. Seventeen were built altogether out of an intended nineteen, and the last was not delivered until December 1907. It went to Royce himself, shortly before he moved home to Quarndon, Derby.

The four-cylinder twenty followed, employing effectively two cylinder blocks of the ten – except in that the cylinder blocks and pistons were soon increased to a bore of 100 mm. The first 'twenty' to be completed was 'Grey Ghost' (Fig 138) in February 1905, placing its launch about on a par with the two-cylinder cars with the same classic radiator. Twenty of the 'Heavy' model were built and twenty of the 'Light', making a total of forty in all through a period ending when the last was delivered in May 1907.

The three-cylinder, whilst being Rolls' original hope, took longer to engineer than the 'four' or 'six' because it could not be made from multiples of the two. Instead it required three separate cylinders. That delayed delivery of the first example until late in 1905. The first 'four' had been delivered nearly a year earlier and even the first 'six' had beaten it. That had reached its owner in June 1905. In short, it had missed the boat. The norm by the time it appeared was four cylinders, and it was a commercial failure. Only six were sold. That does not mean that it was not a competent car. Andy Wood, who has driven all of this early range, comments favourably on its smoothness and compares it with the 'six' rather than the 'four'. Years ago, Bill Morton allowed me to drive the surviving three-cylinder and I too was impressed by both the engine and gear changing on the governor.

The 'six' incorporated three two-cylinder blocks and became almost as successful as the 'four'. Much publicity was required to establish the case for the extra cylinders and this Edge and Rolls achieved without cost through writing many 'Dear Sir' letters to motoring journals: one paid for advertisements, but not for publication of readers' letters. In addition, Johnson took up a challenge which had been laid at Edge's door in which a 30 hp 'six' competed with a four-cylinder Martini. The agreed trial became known as the 'Battle of the Cylinders' (Fig 144). The 'six' won albeit by a comparatively narrow margin. As noted, the first thirty horsepower 'six' was delivered to its owner in June 1905. Nineteen short chassis versions were sold, together with 18 long, making a total of 37 by the time the last was delivered in March 1907. It was a smooth and flexible car, but not blessed with the agility and turn of speed of the 'twenty'. Part of the reason was the forward positioning of the engine in a manner that placed weight over the front axle, and which resulted in heavy steering.

So, in all, 106 of these early cars were delivered and the first to be discontinued – or so it would seem – was the 30 horsepower 'six'. We shall shortly learn that this was not so. The chassis would continue, but with a brand new engine. It is illuminating to comb through the list of customers who bought the early Rolls-Royce cars. There were two Lords, both motoring peers, Montagu and Rolls' father, Llangattock. There were two Ladies, six 'Honourables' – including Rolls himself – and Mrs Assheton Harbord, who was at least a fellow motorist and balloonist friend of Rolls. She did much to help him present himself properly and, I have always suspected, rather more than that besides! There were also two 'Sirs', one of which was Oswald Mosley: the father of the late leader for the British

Union of Fascists party. Among other customers were seven Colonels and Majors, and two Captains who might equally have been Army or Navy. There were also four doctors although, strictly, one does not count. That was Dr Warre, Headmaster of Eton. Rolls persuaded fellow old boys to subscribe to the gift of a 15 hp on his retirement.

Among this early range of cars, one model in particular brought great credit to the marque, and that was the 'twenty'. Arthur Harry Briggs of Bradford in Yorkshire had taken delivery of the first chassis, 24264, on 27 May 1905: it had been the show car at the Paris Salon some months earlier, albeit then mechanically incomplete. Why, when the coachwork Briggs accepted on ordering the car in January 1905 was that shown in Paris, it took so long to complete is not obvious. It might have been because 24264 was the first chassis to be given blocks and pistons of 100 mm bore in place of the previous standard, 95 mm. Records show that Briggs took delivery personally at Cooke Street, the balance due being paid to Royce Ltd.

Development of a lighter version of the 'twenty' began at some time shortly before Briggs took delivery of his 'heavy twenty', as it came to be known. It seems that it was Briggs' idea and it led to Rolls entering two of this model in the first-ever Tourist Trophy race, which was due to take place on the Isle of Man in the September. March to September was not a big window, but it was achieved. Percy W Northey drove 26357, wearing the race number 22, and Rolls 26358, again owned by him, as number 1. Rolls suffered a gearbox failure, which he attempted to attribute to sabotage of the nature he claimed was not unknown in Continental road races. Some, however, have attributed the incident to Rolls' propensity to clutchless gear changes. To be fair, however, these cars had the new four-speed boxes with overdrive top, and Eric Platford had already suffered a failure on one of these cars on test before the event. Northey, however, covered the 208.5 miles round the mountainous circuit at an average speed of 33.75 mph. He took a highly creditable second place to an Arrol-Johnson (Figs 145 and 146), and both he and the car featured in C S Rolls & Co's second 1905 catalogue.

In 1906 this success was improved upon. Again the drivers were Rolls and Northey as respective drivers of new 'light twenties', Rolls on 26350B wearing race number 4 and Northey on 40523 wearing the number 5. This time it was Northey's gearbox which broke – but during the Scottish Trials, not on the Isle of Man – and the failure, on 14 June, was ascribed to Glaswegian garage mechanics. In the race, however, it was the failure of a front spring which put Northey out of the race and occasioned the telegram '*Spring broken, heart broken!*' (Fig 147). Rolls faired much better. He won the race on 27 September (Fig 148) at an average speed of 39.5 mph, and a fuel consumption better than 25 miles per gallon. The special carburettor George Clegg had built had been shown capable of giving up to 28 mpg – and this out of a four-litre engine under race conditions.

De Looze was on the Island and kept Cooke Street informed by telegram. At 1.10pm Rolls, with Platford riding as mechanic, crossed the finishing line to a tumultuous welcome – 27 minutes ahead of the next man. It even caused De Looze to slap his colleagues on their backs – a clear loss of decorum! Shortly afterwards he sent his final telegram to Royce, who opened it, read it and walked to the top of the stairs outside his office (Fig 125). Below him, his 'family', as he was wont to call them, some 200 to 300 souls, gathered. In a voice heavily tinged with emotion he read it out. In modern parlance the factory 'went ballistic': hammering and banging on everything that would raise din. One employee had come prepared, and attempted to make his contribution heard, blowing his cornet from which came the tune *Hail the conquering hero comes*. 'Pa' Royce was then picked up, carried down the steps and off out into Cooke Street. In due course a degree of composure returned, whereupon Royce gave an unprecedented order. He told the whole workforce to take the rest of the day off – with pay! It really was as important a success as that; shortly afterwards C S Rolls & Co advertised '*The premier and champion Tourist Cars of the world: Rolls-Royce*' (Fig 149). And there were other noteworthy achievements with 20 horsepower Rolls-Royces too, again with Rolls at the wheel.[48]

If the successes of 1905 and 1906 really were attributable to Briggs, there were to be even greater reasons for Rolls and Royce to be grateful to him, both in 1905 and in the closing days of 1906.

The Rolls-Royce monogram

We have alluded to the early appearance of the name 'Rolls-Royce, with or without the hyphen. That was registered – with the hyphen – as a trademark in 1907. We have referred to the intertwined Rs. They were in existence from at least September 1904 at which date they can be seen on the hub caps in photographs of 10hp 20152, the first chassis to have the 'classic' radiator shape.

We have also noted that the first radiators were unbadged and that the oval plate appeared on the radiator in February 1905, bearing the inscription *The Rolls Royce Radiator* (Fig 121) without hyphen. The one remaining item to record is the appearance of the radiator badge in the form we know it today. That happened around November 1905 although, for a year or so, they were fixed in place by six small pins or rivets. From some point early in 1907 they were soldered in place and the lettering of the names Rolls and Royce changed quite markedly in style.

As to how the monogram came into being, there are no clear answers.[49] In the 1960s a letter fell on my desk claiming that a relative of the writer, a Miss Beatrice T Eccles, had designed it in response to a public competition. A number of Cooke Street employees, I believe, claimed that the basic design arose from a sketch by

---

[48] *Rolls of Rolls-Royce,* by Lord Montagu, published by Cassell & Co Ltd, in 1966.
   Rolls – man of speed by Lawrence Meynell, published by the Bodley Head in the 1953.
[49] The subject is explored in articles entitled *Who designed the Rolls-Royce badge?* by Tom Clarke, Rolls-Royce Heritage Trust *Archive* magazine numbers 57 and 58, and *Flying Lady* June/Feb 2000.

Royce during an early meeting with Rolls. Others, including Tom Broome, believed a lady tracer had won an internal competition and Bill Morton quoted a prize of two guineas - £2-10p in today's parlance, but more than a week's wages for a skilled man then. A tracer named Miss McLaren has been mentioned. Professionals have also been considered as possible originators, among them the Czech Peter Paul Hubner and Eric Gill who later inscribed Royce's mantelpiece at West Wittering. We simply do not know. The 'Flying Lady', of course, did not follow until 1911 at which point its creator, Charles Sykes, registered the design as 'The Spirit of Speed': not Ecstasy. Inlay of the badge was, of course, still in red enamel.

A fifth and sixth model

As if creating four models was not enough, Rolls and Johnson decided that a model was needed to counter the electric carriages then in vogue for town use. They were smooth, silent, free of vibration, smell and smoke, but their one drawback was their limited range before batteries had to be recharged. What C S Rolls & Co had in mind was to ask Royce to remove that limitation by designing an engine which would match the positive attributes of the electric car, and this Rolls did around 3 March 1905. It needed one further attribute, namely that the engine would have to be hidden to emulate an electric town carriage. Hence the request was for a 20 hp variant 'in which the engine is to be under the seat'.

Royce came up with an engine of eight cylinders with the objective of smoothing the firing impulses even further and he saw that further smoothing could be achieved by using low gearing. As to the engine, he chose a very shallow angle V-8 of 120° (the norm now is 90°) to keep height down, and further reduced height compared with the other models by using side inlet as well as side exhaust valves. He chose a bore and stroke of 83 mm (3¼") and, to minimise smoke and smell, discarded the total loss drip feed lubrication used on the other models in favour of a recirculatory pressure feed.

The side valve feature proved a success, not least in its quietness but also because of the ease with which a valve could be reseated or changed. So too did pressure lubrication which became a standard feature of all later Rolls-Royce engines.

As time progressed two models emerged – one the 'Landaulet par Excellence' to compete with electric carriages (Fig 150) and the other a variant of the 'twenty' with a very low bonnet line. It was to be sold as the 'Legalimit', in that it would not exceed the speed limit of 20 mph (Fig 151). That might sound ingenious but, as all Rolls-Royce cars had governor control as well as an accelerator pedal, this was easily achieved through adjusting the effect of a governor on the carburettor.

In the second section of Chapter Twelve, I quoted from Rolls' speech at the dinner he arranged to celebrate Northey's TT success on 3 November 1905 at the Trocadero. The portion quoted was that which revealed his respect for Royce, but there was more. It was to be the launch of the new models:

... there are two entirely new types in particular which I might say constitute a marked departure in the history of automobile construction. The first is a novel form of convertible town carriage possessing in a manner never hitherto accomplished the great advantages of the electric brougham combined with long range and speed capacity of the petrol car.

No one will deny that electricity is the ideal motive power for purely town or city work where the owner does not require to take occasional drives into the country. The limited range of use, however, to which the electric carriage can be put, and the expense of maintenance, charging, etc have put it out of the question for all except those who can either afford to keep a petrol car or who never require to go outside London.

Many attempts have been made to combine the sweet running and luxury of the electric carriage with the independence of the petrol car, but none of them can be said to have succeeded, and for the following reasons which constitute the drawbacks of the ordinary petrol laudaulette:-

1. An engine of the usual four cylinder type giving a series of powerful impulses causing shock and vibration.

2. Smoke and smell through faulty combustion and crude lubrication, which have called forth much disapproval of the petrol landaulet amongst persons accustomed to the electric carriage.

3. The situation of the engine and bonnet in front of the cars renders them too long for street traffic and for storage in small coach houses.

4. Transmission often by chains causing a disagreeable rattling.

5. Transmission through gear wheels which hum when running, and cause a grating noise and shock to the occupants when the changing of gear is effected (often clumsily) by the driver.

In the spring of this year we decided to attack this important problem, and I will just enumerate the conditions we laid down as to the design and construction of the car and then I will leave it to Mr Royce when he replies to his toast to explain how he has fulfilled them.

Firstly – The appearance and dimensions of this car must closely resemble the best electric carriages in use in London.

Secondly – The engine must be situated <u>not</u> in front of the dashboard under a bonnet, <u>nor</u> under the driver's seat, but must be somewhere under the driver's floorboard so as to render the car short and easy to manoeuvre, and at the same time the engine will be entirely insulated from the occupants of the car.

Thirdly – The engine must have a perfectly even turning motion and be entirely free from shock and vibration.

Fourthly – The motion of the car must be absolutely silent.

Fifthly – The car must be free from the objectionable noise of chains which also interfere with a proper side entrance.

Sixthly – There must be little or no changing of speeds.

And lastly, the exhaust must be smokeless and odourless.

These conditions have been fulfilled in such a manner that I believe we have produced the first petrol-driven carriage to possess the smoothness of running, silence and other advantages of the electric carriage.

All these parameters it achieved, yet in others it failed. George Clegg recalled the V-8 as having "*no noise, no smoke, no smell, but alas no speed*". It had been anticipated that the engine would give 20 hp at 1100 rpm but only 18 were achieved. Installed, its gear ratio gave 26 mph per 1000 engine rpm in top: 770 rpm at 20 mph, at which point it would have given much less than 18 hp. In comparison the 'light twenty' was geared to give 54 mph per 1000 engine rpm in its overdrive fourth gear (in the highest of the three optional ratios).

Why the power was so low is not on record, but it may have related to the 120° angle of the blocks and the flat crankshaft: fine for racing cars, but not the ideal arrangement for smooth running. Royce may have limited power to avoid roughness. In terms of performance it did not compete with the four-cylinder 'twenty' and on test runs its fuel consumption of some 16 miles per gallon hardly compared with the 25-plus that Rolls was to achieve in due course in the 1906 TT. Only one car was delivered – a Legalimit – to Sir Alfred Harmsworth, and that was retrieved but resold. Quite apart from lack of performance, the advancement of petrol-driven cars had really sounded the death knell of the vehicle with which the V-8 intended to compete – the electric carriage.

So what became of the examples that had been built? There appear to have been three, if memories relayed by Tom Cumley to his son Harry were correct. Eric Platford, Joe Capel and Tom Cumley used these, one at least with a box body, to visit customers on the Inspection Scheme introduced early in 1906. Joe Capel and Tom Cumley each had crashes as a result of serious skids. One, however, Tom Haldenby remembered as remaining in use for several years. One of the Maddocks brothers, John, recalled before his death in 1957, that a V-8 was still in the factory at Nightingale Road, Derby, in 1912. Remaining chassis were made good use of, becoming the platforms for the last of the two-cylinder 'tens'.

At best, the exercise allows Rolls-Royce to claim one of the first V-8 engines ever, but the reality was that it was a diversion when the resource could least be spared and money spent on which there was little return.

The best six-cylinder car in the world?

In one of his letters to me, Maurice Olley wrote in May 1965:

... RR chassis had been built with 2, 3, 4, 6 and V-8 cylinders ... The V-8 was of course the old 'flat crank' type.

Of these the only type which should have been smooth, since it was in secondary balance, was the line 6.

So, when it was necessary to settle down to building one type only, for the sake of making some money, R decided on the 6. This took courage ... since the public opinion and technical press everywhere, and particularly in Britain, were solidly, and loudly, convinced that 4 cylinders were plenty, and 6 were pure swank. (After all, if a locomotive needed only 2, what was a motor car doing with 6?).

Unfortunately, the line 6, which should have been smooth, was actually, at the higher road speeds, quite rough!

The above, and what followed in the letter, was learned directly from Royce's reminiscing over the years when Olley was one of his principal design assistants. The roughness turned out to be a disaster waiting to happen, when the fundamental problem with any in-line six-cylinder crankshaft exposed itself: torsional vibration at one of the several natural frequencies of the shaft being energised by the impulses caused by the firing of the cylinders. It did not only affect Royce. Edge experienced it on Napier sixes, having one crankshaft break on the Continent on an L48 engine (and others later). Various attempts were made to overcome the problem at Napier. One involved fitting a lower compression piston on number six cylinder. Another was to increase crankshaft journal diameter. Additionally, progressive reductions in overall compression ratio were tried – but the problem did not go away. Edge attempted to turn the problem to advantage by describing the audible vibration as '*power rattle*'. The Mercedes 75 and Hotchkiss 60 hp suffered alike, their vibrations being described as '*octaves of chatter from the quivering crankshaft*'. For all the problems, Edge was not deterred from describing the six-cylinder Napier as '*The best car in the world*'.

It was against this benchmark that the Rolls-Royce had to compete. The six-cylinder 'thirty' was the only chassis in the range capable of carrying the larger more luxurious styles of coachwork and, for this reason, as well as for the logic of overlapping power strokes, Royce was inevitably inclined to see in it the future of the marque. This would have been especially true when he found that the flat crank V-8 offered no advantage over the 'six'. Royce having created his 'six', it was now up to Rolls and Johnson to prove its place among its competitors.

Much positive press coverage was obtained in the autumn of 1905,[50] including

---

[50] *A history of Rolls-Royce Motor Cars 1903-1907* by C W Morton, published by G T Foulis, 1964.

that on an observed run in top gear only from London to Salisbury. Any ground gained by that, however, was regained when Edge's cousin drove an equivalent 30 hp six-cylinder Napier from Brighton to Edinburgh, under Automobile Club observation, in top gear. The battle was on, although in this case Edge and Rolls were both espousing the same cause, namely the superiority of the 'six'. C S Rolls & Co became bold, advertising in *The Autocar* on 25 November 1905, '*When you see a six-cylinder car but cannot hear its engine or gear, you may be certain it is a ROLLS-ROYCE ... Silent as a Ghost – Powerful as a Lion – Trustworthy as Time*' and then in comparatively small print, '*The best car in the world*'.

Then began the correspondence in the motoring press in which Captain H H P Deasy (later to be associated with J D Siddeley in what was to evolve as the Armstrong Siddeley marque)[51] espoused the four-cylinder's case in the form of the Swiss car in which he dealt, the Martini, against the 'six'. His challenge was aimed at Edge and the Napier, but it was Claude Johnson who took up and modified the challenge. Much open correspondence ensued, raising the whole issue of 'four' versus 'six' to a level of contention matched only through the medium of television in recent popular motoring series. One can imagine the feeling of crisis at both Cooke Street and Conduit Street when more than one six-cylinder 'thirty' broke its crankshaft. The first failure was on chassis 26355 when Royce had it out on road test on 11 January 1906. That was alarming in itself, but could be kept quiet: it might, in any case, have been due to an invisible material defect such as a slag inclusion. Four days later the crankshaft broke on 23927 – the first 'thirty' numerically, which had left Cooke Street on 12 July 1905. As if that were not bad enough the crankshaft failed on 26375 a month later on 20 February. Had news leaked it might have done serious damage to the reputation of Rolls-Royce. Had Royce not found a solution, however, the incidents might have brought about the demise of the marque, then little more than one year old.

When I joined Rolls-Royce, a driving philosophy among its development engineering teams working on aero engines such as the Avon, Dart, Conway and Tyne was a belief in the adage '*There is no such thing as an isolated failure. Today's isolated failure heralds tomorrow's epidemic*'. That philosophy had much to do with the Company's success in the days before super computers and modelling eliminated much of the guessology from the design process. Royce's own adage '*There is no sure way of knowing anything except by experiment*' still reigned supreme and, whilst its origins dated back to electrical engineering days, the broken six-cylinder crankshafts brought intense focus to the process. Today, it should be added, the power of semi-conductor technology and computing have lifted the whole process of design and its verification through development testing to levels we in our younger days – let alone Royce – could never have dreamed possible.

---

[51] *Armstrong Siddeley – the Parkside story 1896-1939* by Ray Cook, RRHT Historical Series No 11.

In his own delightfully simplified way, Maurice Olley continued in his May 1965 letter to me:-

Here, R said, he drew on his knowledge of gas engines. Tangye and Crossley both built horizontal single-cylinder gas engines of the open crank type, with twin flywheels, one of which carried a flat belt, which drove a crowned pulley on a dc generator. And occasionally one of these at its governed speed would 'feel rough'. If this roughness were ignored, sooner or later there would be a beautiful helical break through the crank pin. So to forestall this the makers would change the weight of one of the flywheels, by trial, until the engine felt smooth.

The obvious thing on the 6 therefore was to fit a flywheel on the front of the crankshaft, and, as things were done in those days, this was rigged up overnight. A steel rim was improvised and bolted to a hardwood hub turned up in the pattern shop. Early next morning, with its new front flywheel, the engine was smooth! Then, to make the job good, a bronze hub keyed to the crankshaft was substituted for the hardwood. It was a complete failure! The engine was rougher than ever. The hardwood hub was put back and the engine run continually at its normally rough speed, until finally the hub started to smoke! Thus the slipper flywheel virtually designed itself. The split rim with the friction linings against the two faces on the hub, and the bolts with compression springs, formed the logical final form of the device and was an immediate success.

Olley was not alone in handing this account down to us. Bill Morton learned from both Olley and Tommy Nadin, who was a designer at the time the failures occurred. Whilst a lesser man might have panicked, Royce set out immediately in pursuit of a solution. Nadin recalled that Royce discussed the failures and his memory of an experience with a single-cylinder Tangye gas engine which, to him, seemed to have a parallel. The Tangye engine, after a short period of service, broke its crankshaft. It had twin flywheels having a power take-off from one side and he knew that the answer had been found through experiments with flywheels of various sizes on the non-drive end: therefore, it was on these lines that his experiments were now conducted, on the front flywheel of the 30-six. The story as Nadin told it[52] continues in parallel with Olley's account, the distance piece in wood being made by Walter Cheetham, the patternmaker.

Sadly, Bill Morton did not have any contemporary evidence to prove Olley's account or to corroborate the memories of Nadin when his book was published in 1964. Bird and Hallows[53] published the first edition of their classic *The Rolls-Royce Motor Car* in the same year as Bill and they pooh-poohed the idea that Royce had originated the 'slipper flywheel' torsional damper. As far as they were concerned, the

[52] p311, *A History of Rolls-Royce Motor Cars 1903-1907* by C W Morton, published by G T Foulis, 1964.
[53] *The Rolls-Royce Motor Car* by Anthony Bird and Ian Hallows, published by B T Batsford Ltd in 1964.

achievement of damping was down to Fred Lanchester. Communications between Bird and Hallows on the one hand and Morton on the other left the latter feeling his integrity had been not only challenged but thrown into doubt. Bill carried the scar to the end of his life. So what did Bird and Hallows have to say?

> *A slight degree of mystery attaches to the genesis of the crankshaft damper, at least as far as Rolls-Royce is concerned. In 'Rolls-Royce Memories'[54] Massac Buist wrote of the 30 hp six-cylinder cars:*
>
> > *'Of course crankshaft vibration was a fault which, though it was generally deemed inevitable, had only to be pondered by Mr Royce for him to consider it unpardonable. After sleepless nights and several attempts each of which resulted in disappointment he evolved the 'slipper flywheel' which was actually standardised on the 30 hp 6-cylinder cars which were issued to the public as far back as 1906 ...... This is put on record because some four years later a master patent was granted for a much-discussed crankshaft vibration damper; whereas Mr Royce had found out that remedy and applied it as a routine part of his factory programme without ever troubling to patent the idea'.*
>
> *The patent to which Massac Buist refers was granted to Dr Frederick Lanchester in 1910 covering the damper he had designed the year before in his capacity as consultant to the Daimler Company who were experiencing a great deal of crankshaft trouble with their newly introduced series of 6-cylinder models. Different varieties of this device were then fitted to Daimler engines and to Lanchester's own 6-cylinder models. With all possible respect to Massac Buist and his 'Rolls-Royce Memories' it appears that his own memory, or information, must be at fault, for the 'slipper flywheel' was NOT standardised on the 30 hp models although many were the subject of experiments aimed at curing torsional vibration ...*

Bird and Hallows continued:

> *On closer view, however, it seems that certain discrepancies have yet to be explained, because, without further evidence, it is impossible to reconcile the details of C W Morton's account with the known dates of the grant of the Lanchester patent and the fitting of the 'slipper flywheels' to Rolls-Royce engines. Also, Dr Lanchester's only surviving brother, George, who was in close collaboration with him at the time, states quite categorically that there were no negotiations between Lanchester and Royce. All of which proves, if proof were needed, that even after a mere fifty years the exact historical truth is difficult to ascertain in default of reliable contemporary written evidence.*

---

[54] *Rolls-Royce Memories* by H Massac Buist, published privately in 1926.

Unfortunately Massac Buist's statement that the 30 hp cars were fitted with the 'slipper flywheel' has gained wide credence, together with his statement (about the 30 hp) 'Moreover, in these cars no crankshaft broke in service', which is misleading as it conceals the fact that some broke on test.

Such was the general understanding of events until Tom Clarke, the most meticulous of researchers on the early days of Rolls-Royce, determined that he would search for the contemporary evidence Morton had lacked and, in so doing, add substance to the shadow Bird and Hallows had cast.

As so often happens, Tom found that the truth lay somewhere among a labyrinth of assumptions and assertions: it was not the damper which overcame the crankshaft failures. Royce had taken a series of measures with the six-cylinder 'thirty' – firstly to reduce timing gear noise, then to overcome the mechanical failures and, finally, to address timing gear noise again. It was this last stage of the process which was particularly interesting because – yes – Royce did discover the slipper flywheel principle – and he did fit them to many of the 30 hp six-cylinder cars. Tom succeeded brilliantly and proved Royce's primacy over Lanchester conclusively. I would recommend the account of his work to all with an interest in engineering and its history.[55] As a touch of courtesy, he dedicated his book to C W 'Bill' Morton (1907-1989).

The first detailed analysis of the problems Royce encountered in moving up from four to six cylinders was written for us by Donald Bastow, who had been a member of Royce's personal design staff in the early 1930s.[56] Don indicated that the logic of moving from two cylinders to four (creating a '2+2' crankshaft layout) was extended for the 'six' by adding a further two (creating a '2+2+2' configuration). That was Royce's starting point, and there were two ways of doing so: one could be achieved without balance weights to counteract the mass of the pistons and connecting rods – the other with balance weights. He initially chose the option without: a conscious decision bearing in mind that such weights were already a part of the reason for the smoothness of the production two-cylinder 'tens' (Fig 152) and three-cylinder 'fifteens'.

The first engine, completed in March 1905, was configured as described but, in search of refinement, Royce tried the alternative 2+2+2 option – with and without balance weights during the later part of the year. He clearly found that the crankshafts were 'lively' in that they vibrated torsionally, and this caused a chattering noise in the timing gears which drove the camshaft.

By December 1905 he had settled on the balanced option. But the balance weights made the natural torsional frequency of the crankshaft occur lower down

---

[55] *Royce and the vibration damper* by Tom C Clarke, RRHT Technical Series No 6, published in 2003. The book contains an extensive explanation of the phenomenon of vibration and its manifestation in motor car crankshafts by Ken Lea, former Director and Chief Engineer (Power Train) of Rolls-Royce Motor Cars Ltd at Crewe.

[56] *Henry Royce – mechanic* by Donald Bastow, RRHT Historical Series No 12, published in 1989.

than the lighter unbalanced shaft – so he added a front flywheel weighing 27 lb to damp the vibration and quieten the gear noise. In this respect it worked, but the flywheel brought with it two real problems. Firstly, it constrained the shaft in terms of its natural tendency to vibrate – and that increased stress levels in the shaft, and secondly it was a huge mass to add to the end of the thin shaft so far away from its front bearing. Whether through bending or torsional loads or both, the failures followed.

A first move was to change to the 2+2+2 crankshaft configuration without balance weights, thus increasing the natural frequency of the crankshaft such that the firing of the cylinders caused less excitation within the engine's running range. At the same time the front flywheel was lightened to 17 lb then 14 lb. It was in April 1906, however, that Royce introduced the changes which overcame the breakages. Firstly, he abandoned the 'rationalised' crankshaft bearing diameter of 1.5", and substituted a new crankshaft with 1.75" diameter journals. Immediately, interchangeability was sacrificed but what was gained was a much stiffer crankshaft which was not only more difficult to deflect torsionally but also had a natural frequency further away from the running range. He further made a fundamental change from the 2+2+2 to using two three-cylinder crankshafts, back-to-back as a configuration: the 3+3 has since become the universal standard. He also introduced a modern type of connecting rod: a further departure from standard components. In doing all this, Royce's aim was to stop the breakages, and in that he succeeded. There is no certainty that he anticipated the reduced level of vibration.

A next major change, which took place soon after June 1906, was to abandon the established practice of carrying the crankshaft assembly in bearings forming part of the crankcase lower half and incorporate the seven main bearings in the crankcase upper half (Fig 153). It was a major change, incorporated in the four-cylinder 'twenty' as well, and it had the effects of stiffening the whole carrying structure in which the crankshaft ran as well as shortening the stress paths. At the same time a light front flywheel was added and connecting rods brought even more in line with what we would now see as universal practice.

Royce's third initiative looked into the mass of the main flywheel itself – part of which, of course, was the clutch assembly. Progressively lightening it reduced the degree to which it constrained the crankshaft in its natural tendency to vibrate, and this reduced the levels of stress caused by the restraining action.

The final element of sophistication in the smoothness and silence of the 'six' involved concentrating on reducing timing gear noise. It was towards the end of 1906 that Royce observed the charring of the wooden distance piece. From what that taught him, he designed and incorporated the 'slipper flywheel' torsional damper: the first chassis to incorporate it, 60535, was passed off test on 3 November. It was – almost – the complete answer to roughness and gear chatter: 'almost' because, in 1909, Royce added a further device – the 'spring drive' to the timing gears. At that time the 40/50 hp engine required no slipper flywheel but increasing demand for higher power led to its re-introduction in the spring of 1911: with the 'spring drive' incorporated in its hub. And there was more to come in terms of Royce's process of continuous improvement – but that belongs to the story of the 40/50 hp car that succeeded the 'thirty'. The odd aspects of this whole saga are, firstly, the widely held assumption that the slipper flywheel prevented the breakages – and, secondly, that Royce did not patent the device. It should be added that neither Nadin nor Olley inferred that the damper directly prevented breakages.

There are perhaps three concluding observations which arise from this saga. The first is that Royce triumphed over adversity on a number of occasions in his lifetime, but few equalled his response to the broken crankshafts. This was particularly so when one considers his other commitments at the time: hiving off car work from Royce Ltd to establish Rolls-Royce Limited in March 1906 and, as Managing Director, preparing for the new company's first public share flotation in December 1906. And that was not all. He had launched a new engine and begun the search for a future home for Rolls-Royce.

The second observation concerns Dr Lanchester and his patent. As the towering intellectual he was, Lanchester derived his solution from a consideration of principles and logic. Royce, on the other hand, found his solution through the process of experimentation and observation. It would seem that much of what drove Lanchester to his truculent stance over Royce's claim of primacy was psychological: the unacceptability of the thought that a lesser intellectual (as he thought) than himself might have beaten him to a solution. In a way it revives memories of the miner's safety lamp which bears the name Davy, after Sir Humphry, rather than that of George Stephenson who had reached the same design concept from a more pragmatic start point. However, in the case of Lanchester, his damper was not as effective as Royce's. Again I return to Maurice Olley's letter of May 1965:-

> *Fred Lanchester's patent was for something quite different, for a multiple plate arrangement which had the theoretical advantage of no static friction, since it depended on pure fluid damping. Unfortunately, it could not work until fluids which did not vary in viscosity with temperature were available, and these only appeared with the silicones thirty years later. But Lanchester's patent claims were wide and covered the RR slipper flywheel ...*

Who, some readers might ask, was Olley to comment thus on Dr Lanchester? Between being with A G Elliott *(E)*, one of the two designers to work with Royce on his first aero engine, the Eagle, in 1914-1915 and launching the Chevrolet Corvette, Olley became one of the greatest automobile engineers in the world. He was respected in America and Europe alike – by Dr Lanchester among many others – and he was revered by the many engineers who worked for and with him. When Ernest Hives *(Hs)* became General Manager of Rolls-Royce his first choice for Chief Engineer – Chassis Division, when he split car and aero work in 1937, was

Olley. He had earlier worked with Hives on torsional problems in the crankshaft of the Eagle and, in early 1917, it was he who added to his own design for the propeller reduction gear the design of a multi-plate friction damper. Without it, Alcock and Brown would not have been able to make their epic non-stop crossing of the Atlantic by air some two years later. Maurice Olley's greatest contribution to the modern motor car was, however, in its ride and handling.[57]

The third point was that, if the six-cylinder engine was to be a key choice (the work Royce did on the four suggests that the focus had not yet hardened to a single model) on which the Rolls-Royce car was to build its future reputation, Royce realised that circumstances had led him into a blind alley. He had learned a lot from the early range of cars – what worked; what did not – what lasted; what gave trouble with time – the importance of accessibility for maintenance and how a 'second generation' electrical system could be better protected from adverse weather. If the Rolls-Royce really was to be the best, all of this experience had to be built into a new engine optimised on six cylinders to replace the one he had. Initially, it could fit into the existing chassis but it needed more power to counter the continuous tendency of coachbuilders to put ever heavier bodies on them. Thoughts began to turn to such an engine early in 1906, and we will return to that in due course.

A legitimate parentage

From the outset the name Rolls-Royce was applied to a range of cars and used in advertising them, but it was essentially ephemeral. There was no Rolls-Royce company – limited in liability or otherwise – and the only legal declaration of the name lay in the agreement of 23 December 1904: and, at that, without the hyphen. Add the fact that the agreement covered a three-year period only and one realises that the Rolls-Royce marque lacked both substance and permanence – and these in an era when pedigree mattered.

There was a further problem: the capacity of Cooke Street was limited in terms of creating a viable business in Rolls-Royce cars, even if it had stuck to one model and not sought to perfect it. If one does some simple sums using the chassis prices charged to C S Rolls & Co by Royce Ltd, as shown in the 23 December 1904 agreement, and multiplies these by the numbers produced one has:-

17	two-cylinder cars	at £215	=	£3,655
6	three-cylinder cars	at £255	=	£1,530
40	four-cylinder cars	at £347	=	£13,880
37	six-cylinder cars	at £387	=	£14,319
				£33,384

[57] *Chassis Design – Principles and Analysis, based on previously unpublished technical notes by Maurice Olley,* compiled and edited by William F Milliken and Douglas L Milliken, published by the Society of Automotive Engineers International in 2002.

Although delivered between the autumn of 1904 and 1907, the above are essentially C S Rolls & Co's 1905 and 1906 orders on Royce Ltd. One also has to recall all the development work entailed, the three-cylinder being late to market, the ill-fated V-8 cars, redesign work on the four- and six-cylinder cars and what must have been classed as warranty work in replacing broken crankshafts. There would also have been raw materials, bought-out work such as crankshaft forgings, chassis frames and bonnets, rent and rates on Cooke Street, heating (including furnaces) and power to drive the machine tools. Add wages and salaries for a workforce of some 300 souls! Skilled men earned some £1.50 per week: then there were the management and staff, a large number of unskilled workers and few apprentices. Even if the average pay were £1 per week, times 300 adds to £300 per week or £15,000 per annum. Over two years or more these costs would not have been met by car sales alone of £33,384. It takes little skill as an accountant to recognise that, good though these early cars were, the process of launching them and developing them must have placed a burden on Royce Ltd during this period of traumatic recession in their traditional markets. And, at that, C S Rolls & Co were soon expressing concern at the cost of the two-cylinder 'ten'![58] Claremont had had forebodings: Royce had seen the need to do something different, yet in the end both had shown the courage to take the risk. To an unknown degree, a saving grace must have lain in the fact that work at Cooke Street continued to include work for the traditional products of Trafford Park. There is one final possibility namely that the workforce of 300 included Trafford Park. If one takes Bill Morton's number, a suggested 200 at Cooke Street, the numbers begin to look a lot more tenable – but no employment records remain to test the point.

If Rolls were to be believed when he introduced Royce at the dinner at the Trocadero, his greatest concern was with regard to output. Doubtless the salesman's tongue was at work when he said, *"... I won't say he has suited me in quantity, for we could have sold double and treble the number, and I see no chance of getting satisfaction in this respect for a considerable time to come ...".* More credible perhaps as an indicator was his statement, *"... in some types we are already quoting September 1906 as the earliest date we can possibly deliver ...".* And the speech was being made on 3 November 1905. If sales were to be increased there were two factors to be considered – firstly the manufacturing capacity of the factory and secondly the focus on what it sought to produce. In that regard, the initial vision of a rationalised range had been good. It had followed Royce's standardised 'off the shelf' component approach to special purpose crane building but, as we know, it would fail to be achieved through having started from the wrong point – the two-cylinder – and from the learning process inherent in entering a new industry.

We have noted earlier the name Arthur Harry Briggs as the customer for the first

---

[58] Following the meeting over 1905 and 1906 orders at Cooke Street, C S Rolls & Co wrote to Royce Ltd on Monday 6 March 1905 thus, *'Type No 2 - Unless price of the chassis can be considerably reduced Messrs Rolls will not give any further orders for Type No 2 for 1906'.*

four-cylinder 'twenty', and as the man who suggested to Rolls that he enter such a car in the forthcoming 1905 TT on the Isle of Man. That must have been before March 1905 – for Royce Ltd agreed with C S Rolls & Co to provide two such cars at a meeting at the very beginning of that month. If one refers back to the first general history of Rolls-Royce,[59] Nockolds wrote:-

> *It was left to the enthusiastic Mr Briggs to take the next step. This astute Yorkshireman had seen his belief in the 20 hp Rolls-Royce triumphantly vindicated in the TT Race, and he saw clearly the great potentialities of a closer combination of the two firms. He completed the job in the spring of 1906, and on 16th March a new company known as Rolls-Royce, Ltd was formally registered at Somerset House ...*

At the early stage when Nockolds wrote he did brilliantly in the author's view in establishing a general framework of events. It is no wonder, however, that the huge amount of research undertaken since has sharpened our understanding of the detail. He continued:-

> *By this move, the firm of C S Rolls and Company ceased to exist as a separate entity, but only the motor-car side of its business was ceded by Royce, Ltd, which continued in operation as manufacturers of electrical equipment until it was wound up soon after its founder's death in 1933.*

We now know that Rolls-Royce Limited was registered on 15 March – not 16. We also know that C S Rolls & Co was not directly affected by that event. It was not absorbed until Rolls-Royce Limited could afford to take on its assets, and that had to await the first public share flotation in December 1906. Even then Rolls was recompensed in shares – not from subscribed cash, a point stressed in the Prospectus. And Royce Ltd was taken over by Morris of Loughborough in 1932[60] – a month or two before Royce died. None of this detail detracts from Nockolds' two key points – firstly that Briggs proposed the establishment of a Rolls-Royce company with a view to integrating the interests of both Royce Ltd and C S Rolls & Co in the marque, and secondly that the proposal followed Northey's success in the first TT, which had taken place on 14 September 1905. That date, or one shortly afterwards, is interesting because it would seem the right time horizon to have initiated the processes which would ultimately bring about a single Rolls-Royce company.

Before looking at what we know of events between the 1905 TT and Rolls-Royce Limited being registered in March 1906 a brief diversion might be in order to introduce Briggs more fully. Arthur Harry Briggs was born in Bradford

---

[59] *Magic of a Name*, by Harold Nockolds, published by G T Foulis between 1938 and 1961.
[60] The Memorandum of Association and Articles of Association of the company as acquired were signed on 15 November 1932 and the new company was registered on 21 November 1932.

on 11 October 1863, the only son of the mill owner Edward Briggs (1841-1898). Edward Briggs and his brother, Moses, had been taken into the firm of J Briggs & Co of which their father, John, had been a co-founder. Their initial business was the Holme Top cloth mill in Bradford, but in 1868 a new mill, Briggella, was added at Little Horton, Bradford. The 'ella' referred to material produced for umbrellas, which was the leading product. The mill operates to this day as Briggella, albeit no longer under family control. A H Briggs married Emma Sutcliffe (b 20 August 1864) and the couple lived initially at 5 Cecil Avenue, Horton, Bradford. They had one son, Arthur Edward. After the death of his grandfather, John, and father, Edward, A H Briggs took charge of Briggs mills, moving at some stage to Cambridge House, Horton Lane, Bradford. Later he moved to an address which was to be familiar during many of his years as a Director of Rolls-Royce, Tyringham, in Duchy Road, Harrogate.

Briggs was a practical man of whom it was said that he could strip and rebuild motor cars. He certainly set time aside in his life from managing the business to pursue other interests. He was a keen motorist and he had an interest in scientific aspects of aviation. More locally he was involved with the Bradford Conservative Club and he served as a magistrate from 1913. He was also committed to his local rugby club, for which he played into the early 1880s. Indeed, the Briggs family owned its grounds at Park Avenue. Around 1895 he became involved in the club's management, and caused considerable enmity among the 'die-hards' when he changed the game to soccer in the hope of generating money, which rugby did not.

Briggs died at his final home, The Manor, at Cottingley near Bingley on 31 March 1920. In his honour De Looze had the Rolls-Royce Limited Annual Report for the year 1919 framed in black when printed on 22 April 1920. On being questioned, he pointed out that this was to mark the passing of a man *"without whom there would be no Rolls-Royce company"* – but that referred to an event which had taken place in December 1906. A final point of interest is that Briggs' grandson, Eric, became a racing motorcyclist and rode in TT races before the Second World War. In 1947, on the Isle of Man mountain course, he became the first rider to win three races in one year, on each occasion on a Norton. In 1948 he rode for the Norton works team and raced for the last time in 1951, finishing seventh in the senior race. Thereafter he took his motoring pleasure in driving a Bentley – in all probability a Continental.

In outlining events hereafter I must take care not to trespass too deeply into the content of my next book, *The formation of Rolls-Royce Limited – and the move to Derby.* However, referring to my draft manuscript I read the following text:

> *It was in November of 1905 that Briggs made the further suggestion to Rolls and Johnson that it would facilitate production if the two firms of C S Rolls & Co and Royce Ltd were to form a single company. Both saw the advantages immediately, and so too did Royce when the idea was put to him.*

The draft dates back a long time – to 1983 – and I must look afresh into what made me use those words when I presented my lecture of the above title. I may have had credible sources or may have quoted on the basis of a previous author's licence. I do not rule November out. Certainly Briggs' proposal post-dated 14 September and, if it was made as late as November, it must have been early in the month, as I shall now explain.

Among the papers and legal documents passed to me by Bill Boldison were many papers concerning the formation of Rolls-Royce Limited, and these included invoices sent by the solicitors Claremont Haynes to De Looze at the newly registered Rolls-Royce Limited. One long list of charges dated April 1906 includes:-

22 November 1905
-                   Instructions for Memorandum of Association
-                   Drawing (I assume drawing up) Memorandum of Association, and
-                   Drawing Articles of Association

25 November 1905
-                   Instructions for contract for sale Royce Ltd with Rolls-Royce Ltd
-                   Instructions for contract Rolls-Royce Ltd with Rolls-Royce Distributing Ltd

8 December 1905
-                   Agreement Royce Ltd and Rolls-Royce Manufacturing Ltd
-                   Agreement Rolls-Royce Ltd and Rolls-Royce Distributing Ltd

The former of the two agreements still exists in the file incidentally.

So the whole plan was under way before November was through, both in hiving off part of Royce Ltd to become Rolls-Royce Limited and in getting C S Rolls & Company alongside. One has to recall that this company had little legal status. As early as 17 October 1904 Rolls had announced in the *Automotor Journal* that he intended converting C S Rolls & Co into a limited liability company with Claude Johnson as a Director, but that did not happen. As late as July 1906 – after Rolls-Royce Limited had been registered – Johnson still signed himself off on C S Rolls & Co correspondence as 'Joint Manager'. So a business entity of legal status had to be established with which Rolls-Royce Ltd could entreat once it had come into being. This entity was Rolls-Royce Distributing Ltd: it was registered on 16 March 1906 (Fig 143) and was wholly owned by the Hon C S Rolls.

To the outside world an early clue as to what might come to pass was provided when C S Rolls & Co made a statement in *Autocar* late in November to the effect that they would, in future, concentrate their entire effort on promoting the Rolls-Royce car (all orders in hand for the 1906 Minerva models would be taken over by Minerva Motors Ltd). That seemed straightforward enough, yet in Rolls' mind that singularity did not yet extend to commercial vehicles or to motoring accessories, although he did stress his intent around this time to deal only in British accessories. In the same month an article appeared in *Motor Transport*, with illustrations, describing the new 'Rolls' commercial vehicles in 30 cwt and 4 ton forms – the latter suitable for omnibus use. The chassis were built in Switzerland by CIEM but were renamed for the British market. Such a bus was actually on trial in December 1905 between Edgeware Road and the Law Courts. It was run by the Associated Omnibus Company yet wore C S Rolls & Co trade plates.

If one thinks back to the 23 December 1904 agreement, it is clearly in the form of an offer by Royce Ltd, which – for want of C S Rolls & Co being of legal status – was to be accepted by the Hon C S Rolls personally. It follows that, in the process of forming a single company, the lead body would be the portion of Royce Ltd at Cooke Street which was to be hived off as Rolls-Royce Limited. C S Rolls & Co and, in certain issues demanding a legal entity, Rolls-Royce Distributing Limited would be absorbed into Rolls-Royce Limited once it had been established and had proved its ability to raise capital on the money markets to pay for agreed expansion. Their acquisition, as noted, was to be accomplished in shares: not cash.

Pondering a little further, whether motor car manufacture was or was not covered by Royce Ltd's Memorandum of Association, the option of treating car work as the 'Rolls-Royce Division' of Royce Ltd would not have worked. Royce Ltd was, in the main, an electrical engineering company suffering like its competitors from deep recession. There was no way Royce Ltd could have made a successful appeal for investment capital through the stock exchanges in such circumstances. A new and separate company unconnected with electrical engineering had to be established, and this became Rolls-Royce Ltd, motor car manufacturer. This then had chance of success in raising money but, as my next book will show, that would prove difficult enough.

One can perhaps understand how, as part of this process, one finds occasional mention of the Cooke Street operation which was to be hived off as the Rolls-Royce Manufacturing company – especially when it was necessary to distinguish it clearly from Rolls' intended privately owned Rolls-Royce Distributing company.

Registration of Rolls-Royce Limited – effectively to the benefit of Royce Ltd – took place, as we have noted, on 15 March 1906 (Fig 1), almost in parallel with that of Rolls-Royce Distributing Limited (Fig 143) on behalf of the Hon C S Rolls on 16 March. A day later, a letter was written:-

17th March 1906

To Messrs Rolls-Royce Ltd
Dear Sirs
 We have authorised Messrs C S Rolls & Co to act as our General Agents in the carrying out of our Contract with you and all other dealings with you, and we will be bound by all obligations incurred by them and all instructions issued by them.
 Yours truly
 pp Rolls-Royce Distributing Ltd
  Chas S Rolls
  Director

and this confirms that Rolls-Royce Distributing Ltd was essentially a legal device rather than a trading organisation.

Once registered in March, what still lay ahead was the flotation of Rolls-Royce Ltd – on the Birmingham Stock Exchange in December 1906. That sought to finance a significant increase in manufacturing capacity, either by extending Cooke Street or by renting or building a factory elsewhere on the one hand, and through the purchase of a limited number of high specification machine tools on the other. Such machines – Joe Penny's Becker Branard milling machine being one – were needed to dramatically reduce the time and cost of making certain key components. The revenue generated through increasing output would in part be needed to service the shares which were to be given to Rolls in settlement for the absorption of C S Rolls & Co's assets and to Rolls-Royce Distributing Ltd.

The Prospectus was issued late in a year which had seen extensive flotations of motor manufacturing companies and subscriptions fell far short of the minimum a day before the flotation was due to close. De Looze sought Claremont's permission and took a train to Harrogate, where he made a personal appeal to Briggs who, it should be added, had recently been elected a Director of Rolls-Royce Ltd. Briggs responded positively, enabling De Looze to telegram Cooke Street that he had a cheque which would save the flotation. Had Briggs not responded, one is forced to conclude that the company, then a mere nine months old, might have ceased to exist. The strain of this, together with that of resolving the broken crankshaft problem, must have told on Royce for the mantle of responsibility fell on him on both counts. A further major load fell on him throughout 1906 (and that will be the subject of Chapter 15). Between March and December he was Managing Director of Rolls-Royce. Thereafter the task was split between Rolls as Technical Managing Director and Johnson as Commercial Managing Director: Royce became Engineer in Chief.

The outcome of the flotation, however, was that only some half of what had been sought was raised. That had the effect of extending time horizons to enable the key objectives to be financed, in part from the capital raised and in part from revenue.

271

This process became most noticeable once Derby had been selected – from many options examined – as the Company's future home. The move to Nightingale Road, initially into part of No 1 Shop (Product Centre 01) and Car Test (the Medical Centre) began in the autumn of 1907. Thereafter, as money allowed, walls were knocked out and extra bays added to both buildings. Then further buildings were erected before the final vacation of Cooke Street as the lease ended in June 1910. Last to move were the Blacksmiths' Shop and certain staff. As it happens, the landlord, Shorland Ball, would have been supportive of his tenant's problems: he had ordered a three-cylinder 'fifteen', chassis number 23924, although he did not take delivery: it went to the retiring head of Rolls' old school, Eton. Interestingly, correspondence was interchanged between Royce Ltd and C S Rolls & Co early in March 1905 in which Royce Ltd held that Shorland Ball's should be the first three-cylinder to be delivered and C S Rolls & Co stated that the first delivery should be of 24273 ordered by a Mr Thomson of Darwen. This does support a view that Royce Ltd was active in selling Rolls-Royce cars from an early date.

Such was the shortage of money that the Board decided it could not afford the services of an architect to design the Derby shops. All the architectural work and a most detailed specification of materials to be used – including their sources – was produced by Royce himself. Handysides of Derby simply followed his directions. Even then, it was 1912 by the time the Company could afford to build the Commercial Block for all office functions – and, by then, illness had taken Royce permanently away from Derby. A less obvious impact was on the Company's ability to afford enough good machine tools. For years many machines were only able to produce the quality of component they did through the sheer skill and experience of their operators and, even then, items such as cylinder block faces were often hand-scraped. It was really with the two World Wars, which brought Government support for aero engine production, that many of the machine tools were provided which the Company had lacked. The undoubted quality of the end product was, as Alec Harvey-Bailey once described it, due to *"the air one breathed"* in the factory. It took Ernest Hives to lead the process of change. His adage, *"Give a man a file and the only thing he will produce is scrap"* really reflected a commitment to capital investment rather than a lack of faith in the workforce.

Let us just walk through the final stages in the creation of an integrated Rolls-Royce company as Rolls' interests came to be absorbed.

On 19 March 1906, at the first Board meeting of Rolls-Royce Limited – attended by Claremont, Royce, Rolls and Johnson – Claremont was elected to the chair. Item 19 of the minutes reads, *'That the agreement between this Company and Rolls-Royce Distributing Ltd be approved, that Mr F H Royce do sign the same on behalf of the Company and that the same be forthwith carried into effect'*. That formalised the paper bridgehead.

Months later the Chartered Accountants J & A W Sully of Queen Victoria Street, London, submitted an invoice to C S Rolls & Co dated 24 January 1907. It covered services provided between 6 October and 31 December 1906. A key item was for the preparation of accounts of C S Rolls & Co for the six months ending 31 October 1906, and certifying the Balance Sheet as of that date. We still have those accounts. The significance of 31 October arises from a decision taken at the Rolls-Royce Limited Board meeting on 19 April 1906:-

(b)   That the financial year of this Company be so fixed that the Accounts shall be closed at October 31st in each year.

On 11 December 1906 the Board of Rolls-Royce Limited met (in fact the only persons present were Claremont, Royce and De Looze). Among resolutions passed was:-

(8)   That the contract produced to purchase Mr Rolls' business for £14,434 payable in Preferred Ordinary Shares and £12,000 payable in Ordinary Shares and the business of the Rolls-Royce Distributing Company Ltd for £1,000 payable in Ordinary Shares be executed and carried into effect.

Item (7) had approved the Prospectus inviting subscriptions for 100,000 Preferred Ordinary Shares, and (9) *'that Mr A H Briggs be elected a director'.* The Prospectus stressed, as earlier indicated, that neither Royce Ltd nor the Hon C S Rolls would receive cash. Both had been recompensed in shares for the property which was to be handed over to the new company.

So the date of the purchase was 11 December 1906. Its effective date, however, was to be the earlier date of 31 October when C S Rolls & Co accounts had been certified. Furthermore, the sale was to be completed by 31 January 1907. One can assume that this was achieved for, on 17 January, Claremont Haynes wrote to De Looze at Rolls-Royce Ltd as follows:-

Dear Sirs
The stamp duty on the C S Rolls purchase contract has been assessed at £86-5-0 [£86.25 today].
We are today paying this so that amount may be added to our list of payments delivered.
Yours faithfully ....

Happily the contract, or Agreement as it is entitled, has come to light once more. Dated 11 December 1906, it is between The Hon C S Rolls of 14 and 15 Conduit Street, Rolls-Royce Distributing Limited, for which the same address is given, and Rolls-Royce Limited. It bears out what was assumed earlier in this script, namely that C S Rolls & Co had no legal status so its sole owner is cited. In that, it differed from the distributing company, which was of limited liability. Although wholly owned by Rolls, it appears in its own right in the Agreement.

The 'C S Rolls purchase' referred to by Claremont Haynes over stamp duty refers to his relevant assets collectively – C S Rolls & Co and Rolls-Royce Distributing Ltd.

As might be anticipated, the Agreement contains many words yet few surprises. Its clauses are as follows in outline:-

1.　Rolls agrees to sell and Rolls-Royce Limited ('the Company') agree to purchase (assets of C S Rolls & Co)

　　1.1　The Leasehold property described.

　　1.2　'All and Singular the stock in trade moveable machinery and all other goods and chattels passing by delivery of and connected with the said business of Mr Rolls'.

　　1.3　The goodwill including benefits of all contracts and of all patent rights relating to said business.

　　1.4　The surplus (if any) remaining of the book debts … (but not to include any shares held by Mr Rolls either in the Company or in the Distributing Company).

2.　The Distributing Company agrees to sell and Rolls-Royce Limited agrees to purchase 'the whole of the undertaking and assets of the Distributing Company other than and except its uncalled capital if any and the shares in the Company belonging to the Distributing Company …'

3.　The consideration for the sale by Mr Rolls to the Company shall be

-	as to 1.1 :	nil
-	as to 1.2 :	£14,434
-	as to 1.3 :	£12,000
-	as to 1.4 :	nil

4.　The two sums, jointly £26,434, to be discharged by issue to Mr Rolls of shares as earlier noted.

5.　The considerations for the sale by the Distributing Company to the Company shall be £1,000, discharged as earlier noted by shares issued to the Distributing Company (not to Rolls).

274

6. Rolls was to assign the leases to the Company.

7. The Company would act as agents for and on behalf of Mr Rolls in pursuing book and other debts and in discharging liabilities.

8. Covers a similar undertaking with respect to the Distributing Company.

9. The effective date of the Agreement to be 31 October 1906.

10. The sales of Rolls' assets in C S Rolls & Co and of the Distributing Company to the Company were to be effected by 31 January 1907.

11. The Company would pay all costs of Rolls and of the Distributing Company in bringing the intent to fruition.

12. The Agreement would only be effective if the Company share flotation proved successful and, if within four calendar months of the date of the Agreement, the capital pledged was actually supplied.

13. Until completion of the sales, Mr Rolls and the Distributing Company 'shall carry on their respective businesses properly and effectively in the same manner as heretofore'.

A schedule defines the properties leased at Conduit Street, Lillie Hall and elsewhere at Lillie Bridge Mews.Signatories were to be:-

* C S Rolls on his own behalf.

* Walter M Mason, who had been appointed to sign on behalf of the Distributing Company on that day.

* and De Looze for 'the Company' – that is, for Rolls-Royce Ltd.

On 21 March 1907, Mason was asked to take the necessary steps to have Rolls-Royce Distributing Ltd wound up. One assumes that the delay was occasioned by awaiting the subscribed money's arrival by way of the various brokers. Finally, on 11 May 1907, Notice attesting the winding up of Rolls-Royce Distributing Ltd was drawn up for placement in the *London Gazette*. On the same day the Agreement was registered with the Companies Registration Office and allotted the serial number 45211.

It had been a very long road and much hard work had been entailed in bringing Briggs' suggestion to fruition. The Rolls-Royce car was now designed, built, marketed and supported in customers' hands by a single Rolls-Royce parent company. Effectively two balance sheets had been reduced to one, and the chance of problems such as those encountered by Napier and Edge eliminated. One big issue remained: how should production be better focussed?

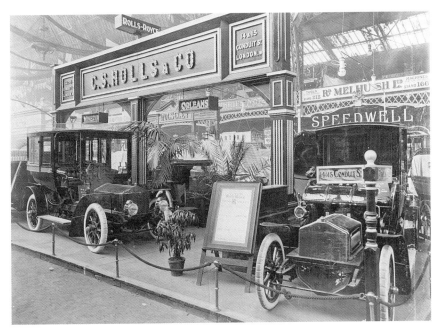

Fig 137: C S Rolls & Co's stand at Olympia in February 1905: Rolls-Royce cars brought before the British public for the first time.

Fig 138: The first four-cylinder 20 to be completed, 24263. It was the first Rolls-Royce to bear a name, Grey Ghost. Platford and Macready are seen reconnoitring the Isle of Man prior to the 1905 TT.

1905.

THE NEW

ALL-BRITISH

MOTOR-CAR.

C. S. ROLLS & CO.,

14 & 15, CONDUIT STREET,
REGENT STREET,
LONDON, W.

Fig 139: The cover of C S Rolls & Co's booklet advertising the Rolls-Royce range of motor cars, dated January 1905. At some time in the early 1950s this was unfortunately reproduced as a Rolls-Royce 'giveaway'. The story was still told in 1961 when the author joined the Public Relations Department that the original plates had been found in the basement of Conduit Street.

C. S. ROLLS & Co.

Head Offices & Show-rooms:

14 & 15, Conduit St., Regent St., London, W.

Telegrams: "Rolhead, London."
Telephones: 1497 Gerrard, and 1498 Gerrard.

Branch Office and Show-room:

28, BROOK ST., BOND ST., LONDON, W.

Telegrams: "Rollicking, London."
Telephone: 2326 Gerrard.

Repair Shops and Garage:

LILLIE HALL, SEAGRAVE RD., FULHAM, S.W.
(Adjoining West Brompton Station.)

Telegrams: "Sideslip, London."
Telephones { 1692 Kensington.
{ 104 Kensington.

WORKS: MANCHESTER.

PERSONAL ATTEN-TION TO CLIENTS.

The MANAGEMENT of C. S. ROLLS & Co. is in the hands of

THE HONOURABLE
CHARLES S. ROLLS,
M.A.

—— AND ——

Mr. CLAUDE JOHNSON,

who, at their Head Offices in Conduit Street, will at all times be pleased to PERSONALLY INTERVIEW Clients as to their requirements.

See pages 18 and 19.

2

THE ROLLS-ROYCE CAR.

C. S. ROLLS & CO. have had practical experience for many years past with all the leading makes of cars. Until recently they have specialized in Panhard cars, which in their opinion, were among the best and most reliable on the market.

In consequence of the number of enquiries received by C. S. ROLLS & CO., and the constant pressure brought to bear upon them to produce in this country a motor vehicle of the VERY HIGHEST GRADE, which will compare favourably with the best Continental makes, they have after much experiment perfected and placed upon the market

AN ALL-BRITISH CAR.

In its design has been incorporated what experience has proved to be the best features in the leading types of cars, and to these have been added notable and most valuable improvements.

The vehicle which C. S. ROLLS & CO. now place before the public has been declared by experts to mark the MOST NOTABLE ADVANCE that has been made of late years in the brief history of Automobilism.

WORKS.

The car is manufactured exclusively for C. S. ROLLS & CO. by Messrs. Royce, Ltd., of Hulme, Manchester, established in the year 1884, a firm of the highest standing in the engineering world.

HONEST BRITISH WORKMANSHIP.
SOUND MATERIAL. BEST FINISH.

3

SOME OF C. S. ROLLS =& CO.'S PATRONS.=

H.R.H. THE CROWN PRINCE OF ROUMANIA
H.S.H. PRINCE D'ARENBERG.
H.S.H. PRINCESS BLUCHER.
H.S.H. PRINCE POTENZIANI.
HIS GRACE THE DUKE OF SUTHERLAND.
  (President Automobile Club).
HIS GRACE THE DUKE OF MANCHESTER.
MAJOR-GENERAL THE EARL OF DUNDONALD, C.B
THE RT. HON. THE EARL OF VERULAM.
THE RT. HON. THE VISCOUNT CLIFDEN.
THE RT. HON. LORD RAGLAN.
  (Governor of the Isle of Man).
THE RT. HON. LORD SUFFIELD, P.C., K.C.B.
THE RT. HON. LORD BRASSEY, K.C.B.
THE RT. HON. LORD DUNSANY.
THE RT. HON. LORD LLANGATTOCK.
THE LORD WILLOUGHBY DE ERESBY, M.P.
THE LORD DALMENY.
THE BARON DE ZUYLEN.
  (President of the Automobile Club de France).
THE RT. HON. SIR FRANCIS JEUNE, P.C., K.C.B.
  (President Probate Division).
THE HON. SIR SWINFEN EADY.
  (Judge of the High Court).
SIR DAVID SALOMONS, BART.
SIR JAMES BLYTH, BART.
SIR THOMAS LIPTON, BART.
ETC., ETC.   JAN., 1905.

20

Fig 140: Inside pages from the booklet which give great emphasis to C S Rolls & Co yet dismiss Royce Ltd with the simple statement *'Works: Manchester'*. *'Honest British Workmanship'* seems more important than the name of Royce Ltd. The booklet boasts the names of some of C S Rolls & Co's clients. In 1905 they were an essential ingredient of marketing motor cars, shotguns, jewellery or fly fishing rods. Note that Rolls did not hesitate to include his father – also that the clients had not actually bought Rolls-Royce cars!

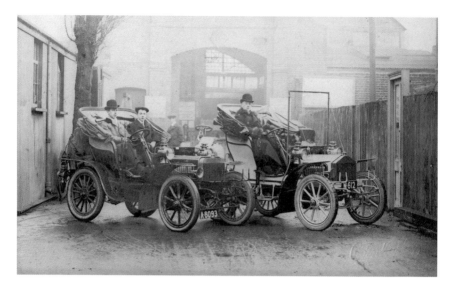

Fig 141: The first Royce two-cylinder prototype, chassis 15196, and the fourth Rolls-Royce two-cylinder, chassis 20154, at Lillie Hall in December 1904. Both were driven to Paris, where they were displayed at the Salon in that month, the route taking them to Southampton and Le Havre. Both are Barker park phaetons but note the further confusion in registration numbers. The first Royce is temporarily displaying a London number supplied by C S Rolls & Co, A8093 while the Rolls-Royce wears the familiar number M612. Harry Fleck is the passenger in the Royce and C Vivian Moore is in the driver's seat of the Rolls-Royce. His father, C Harrington Moore, was the founder of the Automobile Club. 20154 still exists.

(Photograph Tom Clarke)

Fig 142: Claude Goodman Johnson *(CJ)*, who probably did more than anyone to establish the motor car in Britain. He was founder secretary of today's RAC and pivotal to the reputation Rolls-Royce came to enjoy in the years ahead. His memorial stone at the Derby Works, composed by Rudyard Kipling, records: *"He had the imagination to foresee and the energy to meet the needs of his country both on land and in the air, and his ideals were reflected in all his work".*

Fig 143: Certificate of Incorporation of Rolls-Royce Distributing Limited, which was wholly owned by the Hon C S Rolls until wound up when C S Rolls & Co was absorbed into Rolls-Royce Limited in 1907.

282

Fig 144: The 30 hp six, 60528. Johnson is at the wheel and Rolls is seated behind. Also on board are two RAC observers. The car is about to set off on 7 June 1906 for the non-stop London to Glasgow run, followed by the Scottish Reliability Trials between 13 and 16 June, popularly known as 'the Battle of the Cylinders'.

Fig 145: Percy Northey on his way to finishing second in the 1905 TT.

Fig 146: Percy-'Vere' Northey *(PN)* with the 20 hp car, chassis 26357, in which he had just finished second in the first Isle of Man Tourist Trophy race in 1905. Rolls sits disconsolate in the rear seat having endured a gearbox failure with Durlacher while Johnson looks on. The photograph was taken in the marshalling field after the race. The winner, an Arrol-Johnson, is just visible on the right.

Fig 147: Percy Northey dejected in the 1906 TT, *'Spring broken – heart broken'*.

Fig 148: Rolls winning the 1906 Isle of Man TT. Riding as his mechanic in the Light Twenty, chassis 26350B, is Eric Platford *(EP)*. Despite its four-litre engine capacity it did better than 25 miles per gallon in the race.

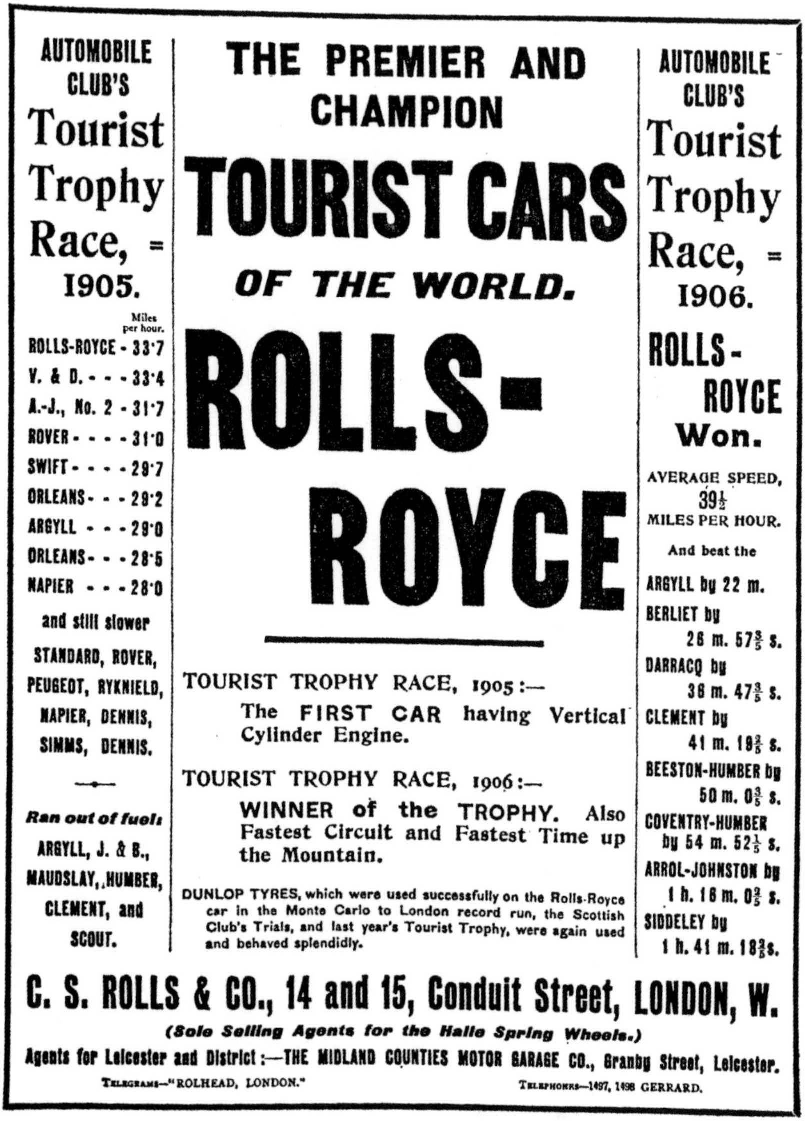

AUTOMOBILE CLUB'S Tourist Trophy Race, = 1905.

ROLLS-ROYCE	Miles per hour. 33·7
V. & D.	33·4
A.-J., No. 2	31·7
ROVER	31·0
SWIFT	29·7
ORLEANS	29·2
ARGYLL	29·0
ORLEANS	28·5
NAPIER	28·0

and still slower STANDARD, ROVER, PEUGEOT, RYKNIELD, NAPIER, DENNIS, SIMMS, DENNIS.

Ran out of fuel: ARGYLL, J. & B., MAUDSLAY, HUMBER, CLEMENT, and SCOUT.

THE PREMIER AND CHAMPION

TOURIST CARS

OF THE WORLD.

ROLLS-ROYCE

TOURIST TROPHY RACE, 1905:—
The FIRST CAR having Vertical Cylinder Engine.

TOURIST TROPHY RACE, 1906:—
WINNER of the TROPHY. Also Fastest Circuit and Fastest Time up the Mountain.

DUNLOP TYRES, which were used successfully on the Rolls-Royce car in the Monte Carlo to London record run, the Scottish Club's Trials, and last year's Tourist Trophy, were again used and behaved splendidly.

AUTOMOBILE CLUB'S Tourist Trophy Race, = 1906.

ROLLS-ROYCE Won.

AVERAGE SPEED, 39½ MILES PER HOUR.

And beat the
ARGYLL by 22 m.
BERLIET by 26 m. 57⅗ s.
DARRACQ by 36 m. 47⅗ s.
CLEMENT by 41 m. 19⅗ s.
BEESTON-HUMBER by 50 m. 0⅗ s.
COVENTRY-HUMBER by 54 m. 52⅕ s.
ARROL-JOHNSTON by 1 h. 16 m. 0⅗ s.
SIDDELEY by 1 h. 41 m. 18⅗ s.

C. S. ROLLS & CO., 14 and 15, Conduit Street, LONDON, W.

(Sole Selling Agents for the Halle Spring Wheels.)

Agents for Leicester and District:—THE MIDLAND COUNTIES MOTOR GARAGE CO., Granby Street, Leicester.

TELEGRAMS—"ROLHEAD, LONDON." TELEPHONES—1497, 1498 GERRARD.

Fig 149: C S Rolls & Co capitalised on Rolls' 1906 TT victory.

THE R.-R. "LANDAULET PAR EXCELLENCE."

Fig 150: The short-lived V-8-engined car. There were two models, the Legalimit and Landaulet par Excellence. This is the latter, its engine fitting neatly below the driver's feet.

Fig 151: The one and only V-8 Legalimit 40518 with Claude Johnson at the wheel.

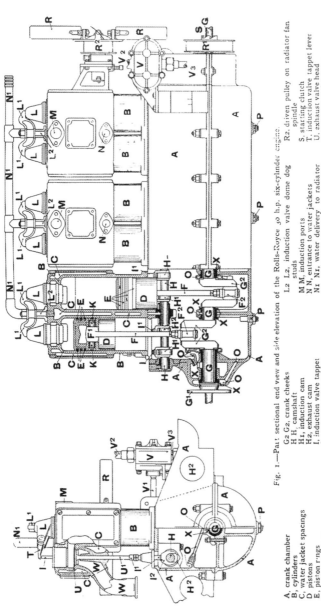

Fig. 1.—Part sectional end view and side elevation of the Rolls-Royce 30 h.p. six-cylinder engine.

A, crank chamber
B, cylinders
C, water jacket spacings
D, pistons
E, piston rings
F, connecting rods
F1, little end bearing
F2, big end bearing
G, crankshaft
G1, flange for attachment of flywheel

G2 G2, crank cheeks
H H, camshaft
H1, induction cam
H2, exhaust cam
I, induction valve tappet
I1, exhaust valve tappet
I2, guide fork of exhaust valve tappet
K, gudgeon pin
L L, induction valve domes
L1 L1, induction valve dome dogs

L2 L2, induction valve dome dog studs
M M, induction ports
N N, entrance to water jackets
N1 N1, water delivery to radiator tank
O, oil cups and leads
P P, oil drain plugs to crank chamber
R R, vanes of radiator fan
R1, driving belt pulley for fan

R2, driven pulley on radiator fan spindle
S, starting clutch
T, induction valve tappet lever spindle
U1, exhaust valve head
U1, exhaust valve stem
V, water circulating pump
V1, pump spindle
V2, delivery pipe
V3, suction pipe
W, exhaust pipe
X, crankshaft bearings

Fig 152: General Arrangement drawing of the 30 hp six-cylinder engine, showing the crankshaft supported by bearings in the sump casing. This is how the engine was originally built.

288

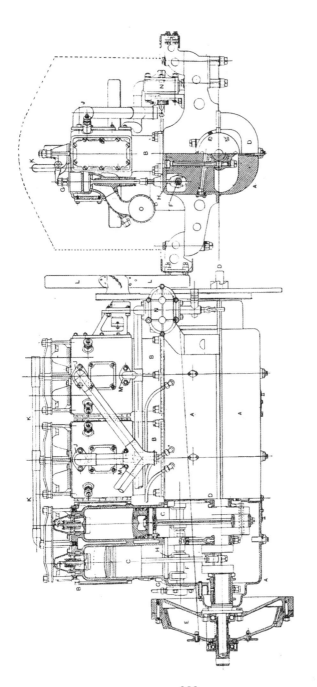

Fig 153: Modification of the 30 hp engine to carry a larger diameter '3+3' crankshaft in the upper half of the crankcase. Note also the front flywheel to dampen torsional vibrations of the crankshaft. Royce was one of the first to design an in-line six-cylinder engine and, like Napier, found himself battling with their inherent torsional vibration problems. He overcame these on the 30 hp engine but decided that experience allowed him to launch a far superior engine as an alternative.

CHAPTER FIFTEEN

"The best thing I have ever done"

The process of learning

As we have noted, the delivery of the original range of cars in two, three, four and six cylinder forms had involved many trials and tribulations during which Royce had learned a great deal. His first chance to design a 'clean sheet' engine came when C S Rolls & Co asked for an additional model on 3 March 1905 '*in which the engine is to be under the seat*'. He chose the wide angle V-8 configuration to achieve this and we have noted that formal launch came at the dinner at the Trocadero on 3 November of that year. By 21 November a car was available for trial at the Olympia Show (17-27 November 1905) and, on 2 December, *Autocar* took a test drive.

Whilst the engine (Fig 154) was very soon dropped, it did introduce several features reflecting Royce's experience. New were:-

* Crankshaft and camshafts having 'their bearings complete in the top half of the crankcase so that the bottom half … may be removed without disturbing the mechanism'.

* Pressure lubrication in place of drip feed, the oil being recirculated by a gear pump. It fed both crankshaft and camshaft bearings.

* Tappet levers between the camshaft and the tappets to avoid any side loads being applied to the tappets.

* Vertical inlet as well as exhaust valves with removable screw threaded caps for easy access. Provision was made in these caps for two sets of ignition plugs if required. It should be noted that the earlier cars had overhead inlet valves which, apart from attendant distortion problems, required daily lubrication of both valves and rocker gear to keep them quiet. In the case of the six-cylinder this required the application of oil at thirty individual points.

Other features perpetuated earlier practice. The water pump (Fig 104), again a gear pump of similar design to the oil pump, was exactly the same on all models from two to eight cylinders. It was not quiet, even new, as its bronze spindles ran in a bronze casing lubricated solely by water. Over eighteen months of use they could become noisy. On the two cylinder it tended to overcool the engine. On the three, four and eight it was about right, but on the six it was inadequate. The rear cylinder block tended to overheat.

The end for the V-8 and beginning of the new six-cylinder engine

The sidelining of the V-8 programme was swift. The one car delivered – to Lord Northcliffe – was retrieved and a statement by C S Rolls & Co in *Automotor Journal* reported on 1 February 1906 that one of these cars was to be used on the new Inspection Scheme. So any thoughts of the V-8 offering potential to match the six-cylinder were set aside. Royce knew, anyway, as Maurice Olley remarked, that the 'Line six' was the right configuration to attain smoothness. And it was on exactly this time horizon – 11 January 1906 – that the first six-cylinder crankshaft broke.

Royce knew it was imperative that he understand and overcome the shortcomings in this regard on the six-cylinder 'thirty': but, at some point quite early in the year, he must have decided that he should focus all he had learnt on a 'clean sheet' engine to succeed the 'thirty'. It could, initially at least, power an almost identical chassis, the opportunity simply being taken to make it a little longer: that would allow it to accommodate more opulent coachwork at the same time as making more generous space for the engine. The other thing he had to think about (then and on every model thereafter) was how to increase power to keep apace with the ever-heavier creations of the coachbuilders. We do not know when the process began. Perhaps if dated drawings of early 'U' prefixed parts could be found we would know: those we have for N schemes, Le Canadel schemes and detail drawings – D, E, F, G and K – all date from around 1911 and later.

What is clear is that Royce had decided on six cylinders and that he was rapidly learning about the problems inherent in six-cylinder crankshafts. Until he had mastered the problems on those, he could not begin. We noted earlier that the breakages were cured by three concurrent changes. These were, firstly, moving from '2+2+2' to a mirror image '3+3' design: secondly, increasing the bearing diameter from 1.5" to 1.75" to make the crankshaft stiffer and, thirdly, carrying the crankshaft in the upper half of the crankcase – a move away from normal industry practice.

So the key was the crankshaft. The earliest recall of the new engine to come to us from Cooke Street lies in a memory from George Clegg. One day he stopped to have a word with his friend Eddie McGarry who machined all cylinder bores on his Bullard vertical borer. McGarry was machining a block with three bores – not two (Fig 155), and Clegg remarked on it: there were, he was told, two blocks to be bored. Clegg recalled this as being in the summer of 1906. That must have been about right. In terms of written evidence a surviving memo from Johnson to Rolls dated 24 July 1906 is interesting for more than one reason:-

It is difficult to say whether Rolls-Royce can reduce the price to us of the 6-cylinder car. They do not altogether welcome an order for 6-cylinder cars only because they look upon the 6-cylinder car as being the least profitable car to them. I do not think it is at all likely they can see their way to reduce the price to us at present, which is as follows:-

Chassis without tyres £397

*Extra for bigger engine and steering
rod behind the axle .... £ 42   for the first 50 then £30*

Plate clutch .... £ 9   for the first 50 then £8

Longer frame .... £ 4-16   for the first 50 then £3

£452-16s

say, £453 without tyres

We sell the existing chassis including 135 m/m Samson or non-slipping metal device on back wheels and 120 m/m on the front, for £840.

The tyres cost us roughly .... £ 49-3-4

*The selling price of the chassis without
tyres is £790-16-8*

and the gross profit is £337-16-8

May we definitely fix the price of the new chassis, whether 100 ins or 115 ins behind the Dash, at £950 including 135 m/m non-slipping metal and rubber tyres on the back, and 120 m/m on the front?

Mr Royce anticipates that the new 6-cylinder engine will give 40 H-P at 1200 revs and we might quite well sell it as 40/50 H-P. The chassis having new engines would not be delivered to us before the end of February, and at first only at the rate of one per week.

CJ

The first point is that Johnson expresses concern that Cooke Street might not welcome an order for six-cylinder cars only. This appears to reflect Johnson's thought process which led, in March 1908, to the 'One Car Policy'. The second is that the arrival of Royce's new engine was seen as no more than a substitution for the existing 30 hp engine. The third is how little more the new engine was to cost. The last – and it is important – is in the final paragraph … *'we might quite well sell it as 40/50 H-P'*. So that is where the term '40/50' came from. It was to remain for the 'Silver Ghost', New Phantom, Phantom II and Phantom III through until the outbreak of the Second World War in 1939. An observation rather than a point is that the process of 'learner curve' was understood, with prices reducing after the first fifty units.

The specification of the new 40/50 hp engine

The key to the new engine, as I have indicated, was the crankshaft. It was of the '3+3' design, and massive in proportion when compared with its predecessors. Main and big end bearings had all been increased in diameter to 2.25", and the crankshaft was carried in its seven bearings in the upper half of the crankcase. Such a stiff crankshaft meant that no slipper flywheel damper was required.[61] Bearings were all pressure-lubricated – main, big end and even little end in the style of the V-8. Instead of three blocks of two cylinders, two blocks of three were designed to match the 3+3 crankshaft, and this made room at the centre main location for a massive bearing (Fig 156). It equalled the front and rear mains in length, which was important in that the centre main probably takes the highest load of all. (On the Schneider Trophy R engine in 1931 the load on the centre main bearing rose to nine tons at full power).

Capacity was increased from six litres to 7.036 but Royce knew that long piston strokes excited vibration in crankshafts, so he reduced the stroke from five inches to four and a half. To gain the increase he sought in capacity he moved from four to four and a half inch bores. With the cast iron pistons of the day that, together with the 2.25" crankshaft journals, allowed an increase in speed from around 1000 rpm to 1500.

Sources of potential noise were addressed. Pressure lubrication of the little ends made a contribution. Dispensing with the overhead inlet valves did too. Instead, valve gear followed V-8 practice: both inlets and exhausts were vertical and accessible through screw-threaded brass caps in the tops of the cylinder blocks (Fig 157). That eliminated the noise that had been experienced with push rods and rockers. Johnson later demonstrated that a valve could be replaced in less than three minutes: not a frequent necessity, although every chassis carried at least one valve complete with spring in its tool kit. More to the point, it made the regrinding of valve seats much easier, and this was a reasonably routine need at that time on

---

[61] It became necessary again in 1911 as the power of the 40/50 hp was progressively increased.

293

all cars. The 40/50 also used the roller cam follower levers introduced on the V-8. A further advance lay in the design of the water circulation pump. Unlike all its predecessors, it was not a 'positive displacement' type. Instead it had a double-sided shrouded impeller so that, whilst its capacity to pump was more than adequate at low engine speeds, it did not find itself circulating too much coolant when running fast. Whilst still running 'bronze on bronze' bearings these were now equipped with lubricators and there was a friction device in the drive to allow for pump seizure – whether through freezing or what. A final major contribution to the all but totally silent running of the 40/50 came from a complex exhaust system comprising large exhaust manifolds, a first and a second silencer. These contained little in the way of baffles to constrain the flow of exhaust gases yet performed their task admirably.

Royce had learned a lot about servicing too. The engine oil system and side valves dispensed with the need to continually adjust drip feeds to each bearing and to apply the oil can to thirty points each day on the inlet valves alone. A small valve in the rear of the crankshaft made sure that the clutch was automatically lubricated every time the pedal was depressed and after it was found that pistons could suffer through lack of lubrication Royce introduced the 'extra oil valve'. This ensured that, when you put your foot down more than about two-thirds of the accelerator pedal's travel, a poppet valve automatically opened to squirt engine oil directly at the pressure-loaded sides of each piston, through pipes in the cylinder block walls.

Another improvement over the 'thirty' lay in the ease with which the fan belt could be tightened. The fan was mounted on the front cylinder block by way of a cast iron bracket in which was a circular bore of some 2.25" diameter. The fan was mounted on a spindle with two ball bearings in an aluminium housing of 2.25" external diameter, but this was so arranged that the spindle was off-centre in the housing. Thus, turning the aluminium housing in its mounting bracket caused the fan spindle to rise or fall relative to the crankshaft pulley which drove the fan belt. A simple pinch bolt on the bracket locked the aluminium housing at the point desired to tension the fan belt.

Electrical ignition was also carried a whole step further forward. Indeed, in later years, A G Elliott (E) said that when he joined Rolls-Royce from Napier, it was the most advanced system he had ever seen. All earlier Rolls-Royce cars had used a trembler coil to produce high-tension sparks. These had been supplied to the required sparking plugs as needed through a distributor in which a wiping contact closed circuit through contact pads set in a non-conducting rotor (Fig 104). Each plug received several sparks but the rubbing of the wiping contact damaged the non-conducting vulcanite area between one pad and the next. The system worked well, but after every month or two the distributor needed expert attention to ensure that the timing of the sparks remained as intended. For the 40/50 Royce initially retained the trembler coil but to that he added what, to all intents and purposes, later evolved into the 'world standard' until the age of electronics. This arrangement employed a cam wheel which opened and closed a set of points to make or break the circuit. Readers will be familiar with the practice of the points being opened on the low tension circuit thus causing the generation of a spark on the high tension winding of the ignition coil through what is known as 'back EMF'. These early cars, however, still employed a trembler coil, so the points caused continuous sparking when they closed to complete the circuit. Royce's arrangement ensured that the sparks were only generated when the rotor arm was already aligned with the lead to the appropriate cylinder. Initially the distributor used a carbon brush to complete the circuit with each cylinder in turn.

This system was a great improvement but was to become even better with the later introduction of the high tension coil. Ultimately the electrodes on the rotor arm and on all six cylinder pick up points were made in platinum, as were the ignition points. The rotor arm did not touch the six points: there was a 0.004" gap, adjustable through individual collets. From the outset the whole contact maker and distributor unit was combined with an 'advance and retard' linkage (although Royce preferred the Anglo Saxon 'early and late'), sat on top of the governor control and that, in turn, above the oil pump assembly: it was a superb piece of engineering (Fig 158).

Although not of Rolls-Royce make, German magneto ignition was just coming into use. It had been an optional extra on the six-cylinder 'thirty' but its fitment, beneath the front passenger's floorboards, had resulted in problems with water and mud from the road. Apart from occasional unwanted excitement in the wet, it was poorly situated in terms of servicing. Initially magneto ignition was to have been an option on the 40/50 hp but it did not take long to become standard. Simms-Bosch units were used. Magnetos cause mechanical 'chatter' through their drives so Royce incorporated a small version of his 'slipper flywheel' on the driveshaft: it was really too small to function consistently and was soon superseded by a friction brake to achieve the same end. The magneto was mounted in an easily accessible location beside the engine. Instructions for early 40/50s with both systems specified that the 'Battery' system be used for starting but the 'Magneto' once running. This had a simple logic. Cars had no dynamos in those days so use of the trembler coil system slowly flattened the battery. The magneto system generated its own electrical energy, and needed no battery. A knob in the centre of the steering wheel gave the driver ignition off, Battery, Magneto and Battery, and Magneto only options.

A further little touch in the way of reducing the task of servicing was to provide a system which made it unnecessary to lift the bonnet to check the engine oil level and top it up. A lever on the chassis frame connected to a tap on the sump. Operating the lever opened the tap and, if no oil dripped onto the road, one knew that the sump no longer contained enough oil to cover the internal standpipe. An oil tank was mounted on the outside of the chassis frame for such an eventuality and it was connected to the sump by a pipe. The oil tank was pressurised with a tyre pump when it was filled so that, if the engine needed more oil, the operation of the tap on the tank allowed the air pressure to force oil into the sump. Once the tell tale sign of dripping oil was observed, both taps were shut: the sump was at its full level. Of course, Royce foresaw the consequences of dirt blocking the sump drain: he added a shield to the tap to protect the drain from road dirt.

Precautions were also taken to overcome the stresses transmitted to the engine crankcase by flexing of the chassis on bad roads. It was a problem which had been evident on the six-cylinder 'thirty'. The 40/50 engine was anchored firmly to the chassis at its rear, through massive aluminium feet and large nickel steel bolts. The front, however, was mounted in a way that maintained the engine's alignment yet isolated it from any deflections of the chassis. The device was a Royce patent, applied for on 7 December 1906 and formally accepted on 14 November 1907[62].

The foregoing describes the engine. The chassis, as already indicated, was – with one exception – the same as that of its predecessor, and that exception was with regard to its length. It differed both in wheelbase and distance behind the dash in both short and long versions:

	Six-cylinder 'thirty'	40/50 hp
Short chassis		
Wheelbase	112"	135.5"
Dash to rear of frame	96"	100"
Long chassis		
Wheelbase	118"	143.5"
Dash to rear of frame	106"	115"

In essence, the 40/50 hp had some two-foot greater wheelbase yet offered little greater platform in its short form and only nine inches in the long: initially. Inevitably, once he was satisfied with the engine, Royce would turn his attention to refining the chassis. He did – and the process continued for not far short of twenty years.

Commitment to the 40/50 hp

One might assume from Johnson's note to Rolls that his understanding of Royce's new engine was, at best, sketchy when he wrote in late July 1906. I wonder. The note was between the two joint managers of C S Rolls & Co and the time was

---

[62] The system employed two 'L' shaped steel brackets. The toe of each was secured to the chassis frame by loose fitting fore and aft bolts. The heel of each bracket was attached to the crankcase by a loose fitting fore and aft bolt and the tops of each 'L' were separated by a tie rod across the front of the engine, again with loose fore and aft bolts. The device provided a parallelogram action, which preserved alignment of engine and gearbox yet isolated the crankcase from any distorting loads.

approaching for them to place their 1907 order – the third under the three-year agreement of 23 December 1904. Such was the closeness of working of all parties concerned that the order appears to have been drafted at Cooke Street: the paper bears a manufacturer's code R.R.387 22.3.06. Perhaps that should not surprise us. Rolls and Johnson were by now both Directors of the new Rolls-Royce Ltd and what they could ask, wearing their C S Rolls & Co hats, depended completely on what Rolls-Royce could deliver: and that was ultimately down to its Managing Director – Royce. The draft order was certainly approved by Royce in person on Rolls-Royce Ltd's behalf on 18 August and then subsequently modified and approved by Johnson in its final form acting for C S Rolls & Co on 23 August 1906. One paragraph was deleted from the draft, both by Royce's pencil and Johnson's red pen. It read, "*If required by us supply and fix a plate clutch at a further extra charge of £9 (nine pounds) per chassis*". It is possible that Rolls and Johnson had developed an aversion to the leather-lined conical clutches used on the earlier range and, equally, that their concern had been the result of customers failing to lubricate them. The 40/50 hp retained the cone clutch and it is possible that Royce's scheme for automatic lubrication answered that problem, thus making a change to plate clutch unnecessary. The finalised document, on outdated C S Rolls & Co to Royce Ltd memo paper, the 'Royce, Ltd,' being overtyped 'Rolls-Royce Ltd' extends to eight pages in all, including delivery schedules. It is too long to repeat in full, but let us examine its key contents:-

Dear Sirs,   *Sept 5th 1906*

Re   1907 Order

The following constitutes our order for 1907:-

50 No 6 Type chassis (1907 type) at £397 (three hundred and ninety seven pounds) each, similar to those already supplied and known as 1906 type with the following exceptions, viz:-

(1)   Make provision for an extra set of ignition plugs the engines having side by side valves. Where ignition plugs are not required by us you will use untapped plugs over the valves. Where they are required, they will be dealt with under clause 10 of this order.

(2)   Increase the diameter of cylinders from 4" x 5" to 4½" x 4½" so that the engine may be rated at about 40 H-P at 1200 revs instead of 30 H-P at 1000 revs.

(3)   Increase the diameter of the crank shaft so as to permit of the engine running at 1500 revs per minute without excessive vibration.

(4)   Increase the length of the bearings on the crank shaft by about 40%.

(5)   Substitute ball bearings on the front axles.

(6)   Arrange the steering rod behind the axle.

(7)   Provide the following:-

   (a)   A special means to facilitate the removal of valve springs, and
   (b)   An accessible and easy adjustment of the fan belt, and
   (c)   An adequate water cooling system, also
   (d)   lubrication of engine thro' crank shaft, or by some similar method.

For all the above items an extra inclusive charge to be made to us of £42 (Forty-two pounds) each chassis.

(8)   Supply 115" frames (21 in number) at a further extra charge of £4-16-0 (Four pounds sixteen shilling) per chassis.

(9)   Brass plate as heretofore the steering columns, change speed levers, brake levers, and quadrants of all chassis at a further extra charge of £2-8-0 (Two pounds eight shillings) per chassis.

(10)   If required by us supply and fix magneto ignition with an efficient drive for magneto at an extra charge to be hereafter determined.

If no further alterations are made from the type as now settled, you will supply any future chassis with the alterations referred to above, and reduce the above extra prices by the following amounts after the delivery of the first fifty chassis referred to above –

Clauses				
1 to 7		*inclusive at*	*£12.0.0*	*per chassis*
8 only		"	*£1.16.0*	*do.*
10 only		"	*£1.0.0*	*do.*

instead of the charges referred to in the said clauses.

Thus far the order covers all chassis to be added to those already on order. Every one of them is a 40/50 hp and the detail shows us not only that C S Rolls & Co appreciated what Royce intended to deliver, but also that there was an understanding of why the changes would be of benefit. Much of the rest of the order concerns late delivery. It includes:-

In the event of your failing to deliver by October 31st 1906 the whole of the 1906 order, we undertake to accept delivery of the balance as set out in the schedule attached hereto, and the five No 2 type known as Nos 20163, 20164, 20165, 20166 and 20167, still to be delivered as soon as you are able to deliver them.

It is understood that on completion of the 1906 type No 4 and 6 chassis above mentioned, you will then only supply us with No 6 1907 type.

There is also a 'carry over' clause for any late delivery of 1907 orders into 1908. Finally:-

We recognise that each year's order should be of the value of £28000 (Twenty-eight thousand pounds) and we undertake to increase the present order to this value as soon as you are able to show us that you can deliver chassis to that value.

Wherever the terms of this order are a variation of the agreement made between Rolls-Royce Ltd and Rolls-Royce Distributing Ltd dated the 27th day of March 1906, we agree that the said agreement shall be varied to such extent.

Yours faithfully
pp C S ROLLS & CO
Chas S Rolls

The above is interesting in that it seems the partner firms had agreed in 1906 to Cooke Street aiming for an output to the value of £28,000 pa, and that the figure was not as yet achievable. Also passing reference is made to Rolls-Royce Distributing Ltd: its days were already numbered.

The intended schedule of delivery dates is also interesting. It refers first to 1906 deliveries, with four six-cylinder 30 hps heading the list. Numbers five to eight are the 40/50 hp cars required for the Olympia Show and Paris Salon:-

5	60539	115"	for delivery	Sept 26th
6	60541	115"	" "	October 3rd
7	60540	100"	" "	October 10th
	Running chassis			
8	60542	100"	" "	October 17th
	Show chassis			

Of the above, short though the lead time was, 60539 did not pose too great a problem. It was the chassis shown at Olympia with the monstrous Barker coachwork which so offended its designer Montague Grahame-White. It did not have a 40/50 hp engine under the bonnet so the key task was to supply a chassis of greater length and wheelbase than the long 'thirty'. The others presented a major challenge. Rolls, for instance, had hoped to take a 40/50 to New York at the end of the year but that proved unachievable. 60541 may have missed its target. It was fitted with a Barker landaulette body from the V-8, 80500, and became the London trials car early in 1907. It was beaten by 60540 which was the first 40/50 hp to be completed and served as the running demonstrator, as noted in the order, for Olympia and the Paris Salon. 60542 was polished and shown at Olympia as a bare chassis with its sump removed and a mirror placed below the engine so that its internal workings could be seen (Fig 159).

Surprisingly, three V-8s follow as 9, 10 and 11: chassis 80502, 80503 and 80501, scheduled for delivery on 20, 24 and 27 October 1906. It is difficult to believe that these were actually built. 12 to 17 are all four-cylinder 'twenties' and 18 to 25 six-cylinder 'thirties'. All these were part of the 1906 order, and the latest delivery was scheduled for 26 January 1907: a much happier situation than was seen on deliveries in 1905. The list then states, "*Delivery of 1907 chassis commence here, proper*" (ie 40/50 hps) and 26 through to 36 – a break recorded as "*Whitsuntide Holidays*" – cover chassis 60544 to 60554 in strictly numerical order. The delivery dates span 9 March to 17 May. So there was a significant gap of some seventeen weeks between the last of the show chassis and the first true production 40/50s in 1907. And somewhere in the scheduling process, the potential chassis number 60543 got lost. That number was never listed as an intent.

All that fell between the discovery of a cure for the failures of 30 hp crankshafts and the delivery of a running 40/50 hp chassis before the middle of October suggests a frantic workload on Royce and his team. And, as has already been mentioned, this came on top of the launch of Rolls-Royce Ltd and in parallel with planning its flotation and the absorption of Rolls' companies. The load on Royce must have been prodigious and, did he but know it, he was soon to be asked not only to find a new home for the Company but also to design a new factory. No lesser man would have survived the load, with or without days of absence. Yet, for all this, he had immense confidence in his new engine: he said of it that it was "*The best thing I have ever done*". And that from a man who was always modest about his achievements.

Debut of the 40/50 hp

The 40/50 hp made its debut at the Olympia Motor Show as had been planned. The show took place between 15 and 24 November 1906 and C S Rolls & Co was allotted Stand 68. Their exhibit was headed by a huge illuminated intertwined RR logo, and the words *six-cylinder* took equal prominence to *Rolls-Royce*. Four cars were shown: the winning 1906 four-cylinder 'twenty', which Rolls had driven in the TT – 26350B, a six-cylinder 'thirty', 60537 (after all, existing stocks had to be sold off) and two 40/50 hps. One was the polished chassis with which 'Little Jimmy' Chadwick and Ernie Wooler had helped (Fig 159), 60542, with the mirror under the sump. The other was 60539 with its Barker-built body based on the design of Montague Grahame-White (Fig 160). Unfortunately, Johnson had agreed with Barker on a number of changes without consulting the designer, and these had the effect in Grahame-White's eyes of spoiling the elegance of his intent. The designer commented: "*... the body, on completion of the modifications, bore only a poor resemblance to the exterior lines and interior layout originally planned. Not only had the available body space been shortened but the height of the body increased nine inches to accommodate passengers wearing tall hats, on instructions received from Claude Johnson, although I had not been requested to design a glorified mute-carrying hearse!*"

The first Press comment on the 40/50 hp appeared in *The Times* on 19 November, and was quite acidic in part, although not with regard to Rolls-Royce. It started with a reference to the success of the Rolls-Royce six-cylinder over the four-cylinder Martini in the '*Battle of the Cylinders*' and continued:-

> *It stands to reason that the houses, notably Napier and C S Rolls & Co, which have been longest engaged on six-cylinders and since the latter succeeded when Napier failed in making a match with the Martini and in winning that match in a fashion leaving no room for doubt, it is legitimately entitled to the prior place ..... Now the visitor who uses his eyes will see that in the Rolls-Royce the six cylinders are arranged in two groups of three and that in most, perhaps all, of the others this arrangement is not traceable.*
>
> *Mr Royce, whose arrangement this is, is a singularly earnest and thoughtful engineer, who takes no step without good reason and the reasonable probability is that the Rolls-Royce is the best of the six-cylinder cars ...*

The comment about Napier is actually a 'dig' at Edge, whose advocacy of the six-cylinder almost caused that term and the name of Napier to be synonymous. So unrelenting was he that it caused J T C Moore-Brabazon – some two years earlier an employee of C S Rolls & Co, but later to become Lord Brabazon of Tara – to write to *The Autocar* early in 1907:-

... I wonder if it has ever occurred to your readers what a masterly mind the head of a well-known English firm has for advertising. Formerly one had only to write to the papers about the weather, when a reply invariably came the next week, bringing in a certain make of English car, curiously enough signed by this remarkable man. .....

The Times coverage is interesting in that its praise of the Rolls-Royce performance in the *'Battle of the Cylinders'* is given in ignorance of the problems which beset Royce on crankshaft failures. It is equally interesting that the reporter observed the cure, and its uniqueness to Royce, without being aware of the problem which had brought it about: the 3+3 crankshaft layout.

A few weeks later, on 15 December, *The Autocar* published a detailed description of the 40/50 hp engine. It was prefaced by the following:-

Anything which appertains to automobile mechanism which issues from the works at Manchester under the direction of that finished and talented engineer Mr F H Royce is certain to attract the immediate attention of the motoring world ...

Something of a hiatus followed between the Olympia Show and there being demonstrator cars available for the Press to experience the 40/50 hp in action. Between November 1906 and March 1907 other things had added to the problems of building the first production chassis: Rolls-Royce had been floated, and not without problems as we noted earlier, on the Birmingham Stock Exchange, and the Executive Directors, Rolls, Royce and Johnson in particular had been away from base exploring locations for a new home for the Company.

By the end of March, however, Johnson was able to place an advert in *The Autocar* (Figs 161 and 162) which claimed the 40/50 hp to be *'The best six-cylinder car in the world'* ... *'the most graceful, the most silent, the most flexible, the most attractive, the most reliable, the most smooth running'*. Some claim! But it added, *'You are invited to take a trial run to prove the above'*. And *The Autocar* did. Under the heading *'The new 40/50 Rolls-Royce'* it wrote in its 20 April edition:-

The new six-cylinder 40/50 hp Rolls-Royce has made its appearance in London and Mr Claude Johnson was good enough to afford us a slight taste of its quality just in time for a brief notice. The running of this car at slow speeds on the direct third is the smoothest thing we have ever experienced, while for silence the motor beneath the bonnet might be a silent sewing machine ... at 1,000 rev/min the speeds are 14, 22, 38 and 47, the highest is a geared fourth. A little trial run up a certain well-known test hill, which has an average gradient of 1 in 11 for 850 feet with 72 feet of 1 in 7.8 showed this superb car to be able to take this rise at a speed of 26.1 mph. The car is delightfully sprung and the steering is so arranged that upon taking pressure off the steering wheel the car runs on in a straight line.

The allusion to a silent sewing machine almost coincided time-wise with Paris Singer declining to join the Board of Rolls-Royce Ltd. Further testing was done on a 40/50 hp with *The Autocar* to explore the relative merits of battery and magneto ignition. Writing following a run from London to Bexhill and back the magazine commented – not on the ignition – but as follows:

At whatever speed this car is being driven on its direct third there is no engine as far as sensation goes, nor are one's auditory nerves troubled, driving or standing, by a fuller sound than emanates from an eight-day clock! There is no realization of driving propulsion: the feeling as the passenger sits either at the front or back of the vehicle is one of being wafted through the landscape. ...... The car only left the works on the Saturday previous to the occasion in question and the run above chronicled was merely a part of its testing drive. It has been named the 'SILVER GHOST' – 'Silver' because the metal parts are to be silver-plated and the body finished in aluminium paint, and 'Ghost' by reason of its extraordinary silence and stealthiness. (Figure 163)

Only in the final paragraph does the writer return to the comparison of the ignition systems, and then he finds them almost impossible to differentiate. What an endorsement for the new model: it was inadvertently to inspire two things. One is the near century-old joke about having to do something to quieten the clock. The other was to be that single word 'waft'. When BMW set up their team in London to begin the process which led to the launch of their Phantom in January 2003, they devoted a great deal of effort to trying to get inside the mind of Royce, such that they could follow in his footsteps in evolving a specification. That word caught their imagination and they coined the term 'waftability'. The subtleties which defined a Rolls-Royce are not easy to turn into words yet this one comes close to the essence of the matter. Late in the car's first year Andy Wood of P & A Wood kindly allowed me to drive their Phantom demonstrator over a two-day period and I can confirm: it has waftability!

Johnson's 'One Car' Policy

The 40/50 hp was soon to prove that it was indeed outstanding through the high profile 15,000-mile run. Chassis 60551, The 'Silver Ghost', was used for this, and the Press soon began to call all 40/50s 'Silver Ghosts' – a name Rolls-Royce only accepted retrospectively for the 40/50 hp when it was eventually succeeded by the New Phantom in 1925. Meanwhile many other 40/50s bore individual names of their own.

Having created such a superb motor car one might have thought Royce would have wished to standardise it and devote all his energies to making it better. Most manufacturing engineers – and Royce was gifted when it came to that – would have seen the benefits to profitability offered by larger batches of fewer parts in terms of queues, set-up times and learner curve. But that was not what he set out to do initially. Rolls had rightly been very fond of the 'light twenty' and had entered one for the 1907 TT. Having won in 1906 he was entitled to have worn race number one, and he was very disappointed when he had to withdraw, the reason given being that Rolls-Royce was too occupied with the 40/50 hp. Royce's thinking seems to have run a little later but in parallel. From his crane days he had developed his ability to adapt ranges of standard component to differing individual situations and this he had attempted to do with the early range of cars – and he was clear that the two cylinder start point had cheated him of his objective.

Now he had the 40/50 hp, however, he had an engine which would withstand redesigning in four cylinder form. He proposed such a car, its engine being of four and a half inch bore and stroke, like the 40/50 hp, and of 32 hp, which was all but a direct linear scale-down of 50 hp. It was Johnson who thought otherwise. Whether he saw the logic of sticking to a single model for reasons of production or because, in a market which was then limited to those of means, he knew the Rolls-Royce was on the point of proving that it was 'the best car in the world' we can only surmise. One has to add that one suspects the latter. We have already noted that Johnson seemed to be thinking in terms of the new six-cylinder as the sole model as early as the summer of 1906, and the 1907 order was based wholly on the 40/50 hp.

During 1907 Royce's thoughts turned to the new four-cylinder but, at a Board meeting on 13 December, Johnson – by then Commercial Managing Director of Rolls-Royce – spoke for the first time against proceeding with such a car. He subsequently wrote on the subject and his letter was considered by the Board on 7 March 1908. The letter concluded with the words that it would be more profitable to stick to the one model, "*the best 6-cylinder car in the world*". When the Board next met on 13 March Johnson's letter was discussed at length, after which it was resolved no new model would be introduced. He had won his 'One Car Policy'.

The legend begins

The achievements of the 40/50 hp 'Silver Ghost' do not belong within the confines of this book. A further volume, *The formation of Rolls-Royce Limited – and the move to Derby*, is in partly drafted form. That will explore the background of Rolls and Johnson in more detail, of C S Rolls & Co and the exploits of racing and demonstrating the Rolls-Royce marque. It will explore the launch of Rolls-Royce Limited and its separation from Royce Limited, the mistimed appeal to the Stock Market and absorption of Rolls-Royce Distributing Ltd and C S Rolls & Co.

It will examine all the locations considered for the new factory, the near-move to Leicester and ultimate choice of Derby (Fig 164). Finally, it will indicate ways in which the 40/50 hp was developed over ensuing years.

All who have studied the history of Rolls-Royce will know that the 15,000-mile run of the 'Silver Ghost' in 1907 consolidated the reputation of the Company – then little more than one-year old – as the makers of the best car in the world. It was the beginning of a legend which was to extend to 1925 in Derby – and a year later in Springfield, Massachusetts, USA. It covered many series of 40/50s, each offering technical advances, which will be recalled as such types as the 'London to Edinburgh', the 'Colonial' and the 'Alpine Eagle'. It served as transport for the nobility and gentry of many lands, the Maharajahs of India, Henry Ford and even Lenin. And it went to war as the Rolls-Royce Armoured Car – the invention of the Royal Naval Air Service. These cars passed to the Army: Lawrence of Arabia was one of their most skilled users and greatest admirers. And then, between the wars, they served with the Royal Air Force in the Middle East, and finally passed back to the Army again, protecting airstrips behind the front line as late as the battle of El Alamein. The very last 'Silver Ghosts' were built as late as 1927, as armoured cars, to fulfil an order from ARCOS, the Russian trade delegation. And it achieved more. It was to the 40/50 engine's technology base that Royce turned when the nation's need brought him to design his first aero engine in 1914, the Eagle.

Fig 154: The V-8 was of 120° angle rather than today's 90°, and had a 'flat' crankshaft. Many of the advances it contained were designed into the 40/50 hp engine.

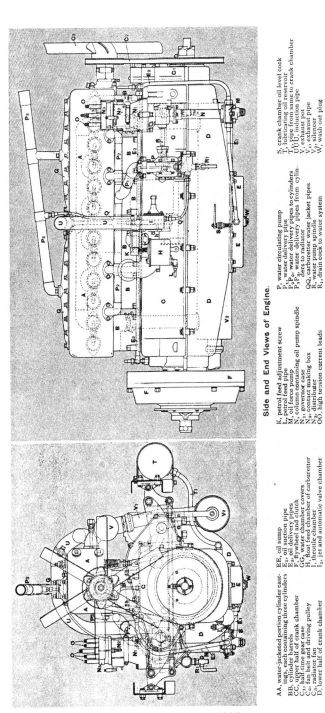

Side and End Views of Engine.

AA, water-jacketed portion cylinder castings, each containing three cylinders
BB, cylinder barrels
CC, upper half of crank chamber
C_1, half-time gear case
C_2, fan belt and driving pulley
C_3, radiator fan
D, lower half of crank chamber

EE, oil sump
E_1, oil suction pipe
E_2, oil delivery pipes
F, flywheel and clutch
GG, water chamber covers
H, float feed chamber of carburetter
I, throttle chamber
I_1, jet and automatic valve chamber

K, petrol feed adjustment screw
L, petrol feed pipe
M, oil force pump
N, column containing oil pump spindle
N_1, governor case
N_2, contact making box
N_3, distributer
OO, high tension current leads

P, water circulating pump
P_1, water delivery pipe
P_2P_2, water delivery pipes to cylinders
P_3P_3, water delivery pipes from cylinders to radiator
Q, carburetter
QQ, water jacket pipes
R_1, water pump spindle
R_1, drain cock to water system

S, crank chamber oil level cock
T, lubricating oil reservoir
T_1, pipe from same to crank chamber
UUU, induction pipe
V_1, exhaust pot
V_1, exhaust pipe
V_2, silencer
W, wash out plug

Fig 155: A very early drawing of a 40/50 hp engine. It was reproduced by *The Autocar*, December 15, 1906, in an article entitled *The new 40-50 HP Rolls-Royce engine.*

307

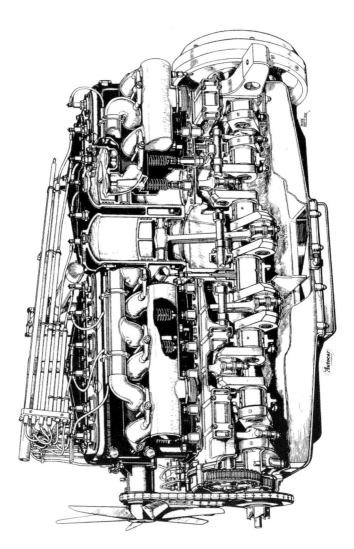

Fig 156: Cutaway drawing of an early 40/50 hp engine. Note the massive crankshaft with large centre main bearing facilitated by grouping the cylinders in threes instead of pairs. The crankshaft was pressure-lubricated. This engine consolidated all that Royce had learnt over the previous four years and, as the power behind the Silver Ghost, remained in production until 1925 in Derby – 1926 at Springfield, Massachusetts.

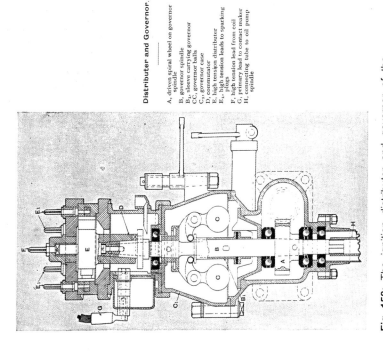

Distributer and Governor.

A, driven spiral wheel on governor spindle
B, governor spindle
B_1, sleeve carrying governor
CC, governor balls
C_1, governor case
D, commutator
E, high tension distributor
E_1, high tension leads to sparking plugs
F, high tension lead from coil
G, primary lead to contact maker
H, connecting tube to oil pump spindle

Fig 158: The ignition distributor and governor of the 40/50 hp engine – an elegant design. From *The Autocar,* December 15, 1906.

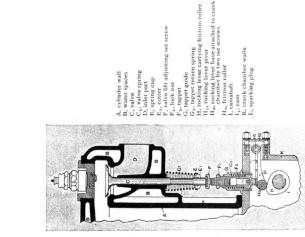

Section through Inlet Valve.

A, cylinder wall
B, water spaces
C, valve
C_1, valve spring
D, inlet port
E, spring cup
E_1, valve lift adjusting set screw
F, cotter
F_1, lock nut
F_2, tappet
G, tappet guide
G_1, tappet return spring
H, rocking lever carrying friction roller
H_1, rocking lever pivot
H_2, rocking lever base attached to crank chamber by two set screws
H_3, friction roller
I, camshaft
I_1, cam
K, crank chamber walls
L, sparking plug

Fig 157: Illustration of a valve from the 40/50 hp engine: inlet and exhaust were identical. Unscrewing the brass cap above containing the sparking plug afforded excellent access. Note the side lever which protected the tappet from the imposition of side loads by the camshaft. From *The Autocar,* December 15, 1906.

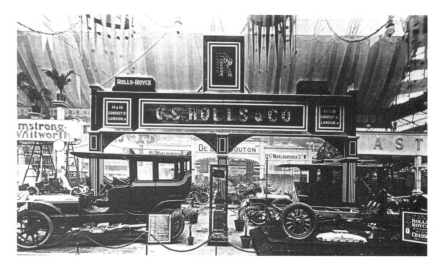

Fig 159: C S Rolls & Co stand number 68, Olympia Motor Show, November 1906 – debut of the new six-cylinder 40/50 hp. To the right is the bare hand-polished chassis. The sump has been removed and lies alongside the mirror which gave the public a view of the inner workings of the engine. The 40/50 hp beyond features in Fig 160.

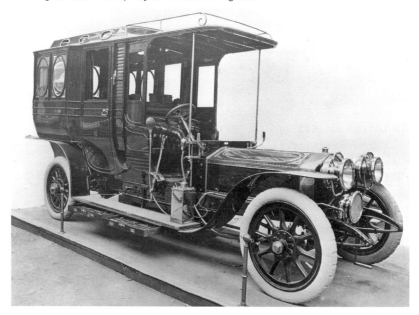

Fig 160: The first 40/50 hp Rolls-Royce. Chassis 60539 was exhibited at Olympia in November 1906, its bonnet remaining closed to hide the fact that it either had no engine or that the engine was incomplete. Coachwork was by Barker – a Pullman limousine. It had been based on a design by Montague Grahame-White, the changes introduced greatly upsetting the designer.

Fig 161: Rolls and Johnson had boundless confidence in Royce and his engineering at all times. The 40/50 hp was new and, although yet unproven, they knew they had a world beater: after all, Royce had told them it was *"the best thing I have ever done"*.

311

THE AUTOCAR. ADVERTISEMENTS. APRIL 20TH, 1907. 15

ROLLS ROYCE

THE BEST SIX-CYLINDER CAR IN THE WORLD?

A FEW REASONS WHY THE ROLLS-ROYCE IS THE BEST SIX-CYLINDER CAR IN THE WORLD.

Because of its

(1) Flexibility.
(2) Lightness and cheapness in tyres.
(3) Reliability.
(4) Silence.
(5) Efficiency and cheapness in upkeep.
(6) Safety—brakes, steering gear, etc.
(7) Ease of manipulation, lightness of steering, clutch operation, etc.

A private owner of a R.R. writes:

"I may say my car is a perfect dream. It is so reliable that I have done away with my carriages and horses."

The original of this letter and many other letters from private owners of Rolls Royce cars may be seen at

ROLLS-ROYCE, Ltd.,

14 & 15, CONDUIT STREET, LONDON, W.

Telegrams: "Rolhead, London." Telephones: 1497 / 1498 Gerrard.

AGENTS for LEICESTER, NOTTINGHAM, RUTLAND, AND DERBYSHIRE	The Midland Counties Motor Garage Co., Granby Street, Leices.
AGENTS for NORTH RIDING OF YORKSHIRE AND DURHAM	The Cleveland Car Co., Cleveland Bridge Works, Darlington.
AGENTS, FRANCE	La Société Anonyme "L'Eclaire," 59, Rue la Boëtié, Paris.
AGENTS, UNITED STATES of AMERICA	The Rolls-Royce Import Co., Broadway New York.
AGENTS, OTTAWA (CANADA) and DISTRICT	Messrs. Ketchum & Co., corner of Bank St. and Sparks St., Ottawa.

Fig 162: A viable alternative to the horse.

Fig 163: The Silver Ghost, chassis 60551, registration number AX 201, was the twelfth of the new model. Finished in silver she was a sales demonstration car and in 1907 established a record of 15,000 miles non-stop. The cost of refurbishing her to original 'as new' condition following this run was £2 2s 7d.

Fig 164: The new Derby factory in the course of being built in 1907. Although extended, these buildings remain in use into the 21st century.

CHAPTER SIXTEEN

Lingering traces of the pioneering days

One hundred years have now passed since Henry Edmunds introduced Rolls to Royce and it would seem fitting to conclude with a review of the traces which remain and how, in so many cases, they have passed irretrievably into the realms of history. Happily that has not been the universal fate imposed by the passing years and we can still see and touch examples of both the products and everyday items of the Cooke Street era.

Henry Edmunds – Godfather of Rolls-Royce

Before seeing what happened to the Cooke Street factory, let us ask what became of Henry Edmunds? As was so often the case in his life, he did not receive the benefit he might from performing the introduction at the Midland Hotel. Writing of his bringing Rolls and Royce together in his *Reminiscences of a Pioneer*, he recorded:-

> *My interest, however, did not extend any further beyond the fact that as a shareholder of Royce, Ltd, I received some slight benefit from the formation of the new concern.*

As regards his subsequent life story, that is to be found in Paul Tritton's treatise. There are many quirks to fate, however, and in August 1995 I had the real pleasure of dining with his granddaughter, Mrs Muriel Pritchard (Fig 165) while visiting my aunt Gwyneth in Belfast. It transpired that Muriel and her late husband, Professor Jack Pritchard, had been close friends of my aunt and my late uncle, Professor Estyn Evans, and that her children had almost grown-up with my cousins. Corresponding with her son, Dr Michael Pritchard, recently, he told me of another coincidence. His mother-in-law was the niece of 'Little Jimmy' Chadwick!

If that could be described as a turn up for the books, then another was the recent rediscovery of the Henry Edmunds Trophy (Fig 166). Presented to the Automobile Club in 1903, it ceased to be put up for competition when war broke out in 1914. The trophy went missing and it was not until 1996 that a member of the Midland Automobile Club discovered it in the back of his garage. The Club made it available to the Sir Henry Royce Memorial Foundation and it is now awarded annually for the most important contribution during the previous year to a sport involving mechanical assistance. One suspects that Henry Edmunds would have approved of the first three recipients: Damon Hill – Formula 1 World Champion (1997), Sqn Ldr Andy Green – the Fastest Man on Earth (1998), and Ken Moss – the Fastest

Blind Man on Earth (1999). He might even have taken some satisfaction from the fact that the first supersonic car in the world was powered by Rolls-Royce.

The last days of Cooke Street

Turning to the bricks and mortar, let us now examine what became of the Cooke Street factory.

The last picture of the registered office door, initially of the Royce electrical companies and then of Rolls-Royce Limited, was taken by 'Old Ben' Brown on a nostalgic return trip to Manchester early in the Second World War (Fig 167). Shortly afterwards a German bomb hit the Cooke Street office block, leaving only the workshops standing. At one stage an engineering company named Triangle occupied the factory but ultimately it was used as a crockery warehouse by a company called Levisons. Before final demolition loomed in 1965 a number of photographs were taken – some on the fiftieth anniversary celebrations in 1954 and others later by the author's old friend and colleague, David Tod, who worked for the Rolls-Royce Motor Car Division in the 1960s (Figs 168, 169 and 170). Finally, in 1965, the bulldozers removed all trace of our ancestral home, but not before George Clegg, Bill Morton, Jack Titley – the Rolls-Royce Staff Photographer – and I had paid homage to the sad remains. We viewed the factory from where the corner shop had stood (Fig 171). We walked round to the Blake Street side (Figs 172 and 173) and finally into the factory (Fig 174). It was a sad and sordid sight. The winter sun melted the frost on the roof and the cold droplets were the only sound to break the silence as they hit the floor. Broken crockery (Fig 175) lay everywhere and in the dejection of its last days we found it hard to conjure up any image in our minds of those vibrant early years. All four of us retreated to a chip shop, the tiled walls of which had once been white and uncracked. It offered us warmth and a soggy sustenance, but George seemed to be the only one among us with any spirit left. The visit remains vivid in my memory, and it hardly seems possible that nearly forty years have passed since. I particularly recall that Bill made sure he did not appear in the pictures – he had pinched the day off: more a reflection on his bosses than on his commitment to Rolls-Royce. And, while we were there, we visited Manchester Southern Cemetery to pay homage at the grave of Sir John Alcock, pilot of the transatlantic Vimy.

Weeks before our visit I asked a friend in Manchester to try to find nameplates on both Cooke Street and Blake Street for preservation. All that were left were modern painted ones, and these were rescued. Years later it transpired that the old nameplates had already been removed: they are now preserved in the Royce Room at the Hunt House.

Later that year one of the nearby tower blocks was named Royce Court in memory of Rolls-Royce's Manchester days. The opening ceremony was accompanied by the unveiling of a plaque in the presence of some of the last of the Cooke Street team (Fig 176 and 178). They were Tom Broome, George Clegg, 'Little Jimmy' Chadwick and Ben Pope. I was privileged to be there and, more so to have been given the honour of writing the words on the plaque (Fig 177). There were – at the time I originally wrote this book – only two other visible pieces of evidence of the Company's presence in Manchester. One was a further plaque. It hung in the Midland Hotel which, to this day, takes pride in the fact that it was there that Rolls met Royce. The other was the engine and gearbox from the second Royce prototype (Fig 179) – parts of the very car Royce showed to Rolls at the Midland Hotel on the day they met. They are preserved at the Manchester Museum of Science and Industry.

Time has moved on. The initial ghastly high-rise redevelopment of the area – typical of the 1960s yet showing even then the assumption of authority that it knew best what would be good for the inhabitants – has given way to a more enlightened wave of redevelopment. A number of buildings, albeit few in all, remain which Claremont and Royce would remember and a lot that they would not. In all, it once more feels like a place where people can live but, among the tower blocks of the 1960s, Royce Court still stands. I paid a return visit in 2003 and found that the plaque had gone, although its backing board remains. Hulme, however, has not forgotten its heritage. Vestiges of the rather unfortunate redefinition of the area in the 1950s and 1960s remain, including the Sir Henry Royce pub. However, its earlier layout has in part at least been restored. A green sward (Fig 180) now covers the approximate area which lay between Cooke Street and Blake Street, and earlier days are perpetuated with road names such as Royce Road, Claremont Road and Rolls Crescent. There is also a pub called the Platford. Furthermore, street name plates incorporate the name Royce.

The Midland Hotel, Manchester

By far and away the most important visible reminder of the Company's earliest days in Manchester is the Midland Hotel, which celebrated its centenary on 5 September 2003. From its earliest days, the Midland became a focal point and a clear choice of venue for Edmunds to introduce Rolls to Royce. It remains an institution to this day, regarded with fondness by customers and staff alike over the intervening years. The plaque which recorded the meeting has unfortunately been lost during a period of extensive refurbishment: it warrants replacement. Although elements of the hotel's interior have evolved over the years, the three who met there on 4 May 1904 would instantly recognise The Midland from outside and doubtless marvel that its terracotta work showed no signs of the passage of a hundred years. The twin arches of the Carriage Court remain exactly as they were (Fig 181), although it is now the main pedestrian entrance to the hotel. Its terracotta tiling has gone, but they would recognise the general shape of the entrance and also the restaurant in which they ate – now the Nico Central. They might even be touched that their meeting should have been commemorated by a new terracotta feature in the entrance, although they might take issue over its historical accuracy! (Fig 182)

Remaining products of F H Royce & Co Ltd and Royce Ltd

Royce Ltd continued to trade at Trafford Park long after Rolls-Royce had moved to Derby. Then, in November 1932, the firm was acquired by Herbert Morris of Loughborough and soon afterwards operations were moved to that town. There has been a tendency to assume that Royce Ltd ceased to trade around 1936. It therefore came as a surprise to learn from Morris' in the course of preparing the original script that the last Royce crane was not built until 16 November 1964. The customer was a firm called Brooks Thomas & Co Ltd. Most of the late cranes were for paper pulp mills, and were of the overhead variety. Their last Manchester employee died in 1981 and, more amazingly, Royce Ltd still exists, as a subsidiary company. It was reactivated on 25 October 2002 for the selling of cranes on the US market. Product support continues and Morris' still have lists of spares.

And what of the early products? An electric motor (Fig 183), made by F H Royce & Co Ltd, was discovered in a shoemaker's shop in 1963 when the Southern Electricity Board was standardising voltages in the Southampton area. It had been used by the shoemaker to drive a finishing machine every day of his working life. His father had used it before him, having purchased it second-hand shortly after the turn of the century. And in all that time the only attention it had received was an occasional drop of oil and one new set of brushes. It is now in the possession of a local electrical engineering museum, the Wedgewood Electrical Collection, Southern Electricity, at the Old Power Station, Bargates near Christchurch in Dorset. An almost identical, but larger, example has since been found and is on display at the Sir Henry Royce Memorial Foundation.

The electric lighting installed under the contract by Royce Ltd at Ulverston continued to give good service until 1955, when it was deemed prudent to replace the original wiring. Its ultimate rescue by Philip Hall of the Sir Henry Royce Memorial Foundation in 2002 is recorded in the chapter on Royce Limited. The whole file on the Penny Bridge Hall installation has been with Rolls-Royce in Derby for more years than can be remembered and it is now in the custody of the Rolls-Royce Heritage Trust.

A Royce electric capstan served many years in Derby at St Mary's Wharf (Fig 184). It was rescued in the late 1970s by Keith Kidger of the Rolls-Royce Enthusiasts' Club, with a little help from the Rolls-Royce millwrights. The Company's apprentices at Mickleover then cleaned it to a presentable standard for the Sir Henry Royce Memorial Foundation. The capstan originally hauled railway trucks of grain at Warwicks' Brewery on Fox Street. That was in 1912. Then from 1928 until the 1960s it was used by Derby Co-op at their St Mary's Wharf warehouse. It is now on show at the Hunt House, Paulerspury, having been restored once more to working order through the good offices of the late Dr Harry Watson.

Many of the cranes are still in service today. Taking the Derby area alone, until 1979, British Rail – as it then was – had one dating to about 1906 which could be seen in their yard over the high fence on Litchurch Lane, which links Osmaston and London Roads. I took Don Bastow to see it one day when he was writing his book *Henry Royce – mechanic*. It was no longer visible, so we called on the offices. There we learned that it was a six-ton gantry crane but had been used to lift far greater loads. When lifting twelve tons one day they said it had been "*creaking a bit*", so they decided it had served its purpose and, as it no longer owed them anything, they had set about it with oxyacetylene torches. British Rail took no persuading to donate it to the Sir Henry Royce Memorial Foundation: all that remained was to persuade the Rolls-Royce millwrights – yet again – to mount a rescue squad and move the remnants to Paulerspury.

Fletcher and Stewart, the sugar refinery equipment manufacturers – also on Litchurch Lane, used at least one Royce crane until they ceased trading. More remained in use at International Combustion in Derby in the years before they were to become part of Rolls-Royce following the takeover of their owners, Northern Engineering Industries Ltd, in 1989.

But one does not have to look that far afield. A Royce travelling crane still continues in use (Fig 185) at the time of writing this second edition at the Rolls-Royce Nightingale Road factory. Originally installed in the Iron Foundry, it was moved to the Steel Stores alongside Central Stores at the Hawthorne Street entrance before the Second World War. Perhaps the most tangible evidence of its many years' service are its war wounds, for it bears the scars in the form of shrapnel damage (Fig 186) caused by the lone German raider which bombed the Works on the morning of Monday 27 July 1942.[63] Only one of the bombs hit the factory, others falling on Davenport Road just outside the factory gates. Among those permanently injured was 'Little Jimmy' Chadwick's wife.

Relics of Cooke Street

One machine tool survives from Cooke Street, that little American-made Rivett lathe from the Tool Room. As already noted, Royce had it in his workshop at Elmstead, West Wittering (Fig 187). When he died it was brought back to Derby with the vice he had used. At one point in time after the Second World War it was sold off, along with other dated machine tools, but it was subsequently bought back. The lathe, the vice and Royce's vernier calliper were all in the Apprentice Training School at Sandown Road when I went through machine training there in 1959. Some time around the receivership in 1971, the vernier calliper (Fig 188) went missing and it has not been seen since. Happily the lathe and vice survived

---

[63] *The bombing of Rolls-Royce at Derby in two World Wars* by Kirk, Felix and Bartnik, published by the Rolls-Royce Heritage Trust, Historical Series No 32, 2002.

the turmoil of that era and continued to be used by apprentices when the training school moved to Mickleover. Then, in 1983, we celebrated the 75th anniversary of the formal opening of the Derby Works by Lord Montagu on 9 July 1908. His son, today's Lord Montagu, unveiled a plaque to commemorate the event 75 years later, to the day, by Royce's fireplace and, for that occasion, the lathe and vice were placed beside the plaque in No 1 Shop (Product Centre 01). They remained there in the custody of the Rolls-Royce Heritage Trust, Derby & Hucknall Branch, until the opening of the Company's new Learning and Development Centre a mile or so away. There they form part of the Trust's prestigious Heritage Exhibition (Fig 189). Also in the Trust's care are a Royce electric motor and F H Royce & Co Ltd switchgear, previously held at the Mickleover apprentice training school (Fig 190).

A final fitment from Cooke Street to survive is the factory 'master' clock. It is believed to be the one beside which De Looze stood every morning as the workforce arrived to start their day's toil. Its dial carries the wording 'F H Royce & Co Ltd' and the date 1898. It continued as the Works master clock in Derby well into the 1950s, if not later, at Nightingale Road. Then, along with the lathe, it moved to Mickleover where it again kept good time on the upstairs landing. On the closure of Mickleover in the late 1990s, the clock was given to the Trust for safekeeping and, in 2003, it was mounted on the wall at the Trust's 12 Shop premises where, once more, it displays the time of day (Fig 191).

Cars built at Cooke Street

Of all the cars Rolls-Royce has ever made more than half are believed to be still on the road. Among them are a number which bear no reference to Derby, Springfield, Crewe or indeed Westhampnett: they were built at Cooke Street. Of the 106 cars built before the 40/50 hp ('Silver Ghost') appeared no less than nine are still known to exist, and parts of others do as well.

The oldest Rolls-Royce known is the two-cylinder 'ten', chassis number 20154. Its engine was tested in November 1904 and it was the car exhibited by C S Rolls & Co at the Paris Salon. Wearing the borrowed registration M-612, it was driven to Paris with the first Royce prototype. 20154 survived in 'modernised' form in the hands of Percy C Binns of Harrogate, who owned the car from 1920 till 1950 (Fig 192). It was then acquired by Oliver Langton of Leeds. He not only restored it but was a frequent participant in events. In 1977, 20154, which had borne the registration U-44 since 1920, passed to Tom Love who still owns her. Years ago Tom took me out on U-44 through his native Perth one day in Scotland (Fig 193). She remains with him, but in Northern Ireland now.

Until recently there were two other known two-cylinder 'tens'. The older of the two was 20162, which was delivered to C S Rolls & Co for stock late in 1905. Many of Rolls' cars were registered in Monmouth with numbers prefixed 'AX', and this was the first Rolls-Royce to be so treated. AX-148 has ever since borne the same registration. Her first owner was Paris Singer but, from 1930 to 1935, she belonged to Sir John Prestige. It was while he owned AX-148 that the trip was made to West Wittering. Amateur film was made of the day's outing, with shots of Sir Henry and Nurse Aubin admiring the car and climbing aboard (Fig 194). The film is the best 'movie' record of him to survive. In 1935, Rolls-Royce acquired AX-148 from Sir John and presented her to the Science Museum, which remains her owner (Fig 195). For the centenary year AX-148 will be in Manchester.

The third two-cylinder 'ten', 20165, was delivered to Dr Sidney J Gammell of Bielside in Scotland in 1907, and was used by him in his medical practice until he bought a 40/50 hp in 1920. He was so appreciative of SU-13, as 20165 has always been registered, that he gave her back to Rolls-Royce when he received his 40/50 hp (Fig 196). For some years SU-13 greeted visitors in the main VIP entrance at Nightingale Road but, at some stage in the Second World War, she was pushed into the yard of No 6 Shop. According to Bill Morton, it was the protests of USAAF pilots attending Merlin engine courses in Derby which led to her being put back under cover again – and he should have known: he was a Senior Instructor at the Engine School at the time. After the war, SU-13 was sent to Crewe when car production was recommenced and she is still there although now, of course, the property of Bentley Motors Ltd (Fig 197).

The big surprise came one day a year or two ago when Peter Baines, General Secretary of the Rolls-Royce Enthusiasts' Club, received a call asking him for help in identifying a car. He said its radiator looked like a Rolls-Royce but it didn't have a badge on it. He added that there were traces of solder where one might have been. Peter told the caller he would need the chassis number. The caller looked, and rang back: he could not find it. So Peter proffered advice on where one might be found on the engine. Some time later the caller rang again: "*20159*", he said. "*No*", said Peter, "*that's impossible. That would be a two-cylinder 'ten'*". "*Oh yes!*", came back the voice, "*It's only got two cylinders*". The caller further described the car. He said that part-way down the steering column it had a thing like a drum with levers on it. At this stage, Peter began to believe that what he was hearing added up: it was the description of a two-cylinder 'ten'. This 1905 car, the engine of which was tested on 31 May, originally bore the registration P-2037 (oddly close to the designation of Rolls-Royce's rival to the RB211-535 engine on the Boeing 757). It was delivered new to Julian Whittington in Surrey and had last been heard of in Yorkshire in 1914. I later spoke to the owner, who told me of its rediscovery in a condemned barn in the southern counties. As purchased the car was complete bar one headlamp which, it turned out, had been used as an outside light on a house. The light has been retrieved and, apparently, although paintwork is dull and the leatherwork hard and dry, there is only one small patch of corrosion on one wing. Otherwise the car is reported to be complete and original.

There is only one known three-cylinder 'fifteen', although parts of another have been claimed to exist. 26330 survived because Adam McGregor Dick of Kilmarnock hid it away in the Dick Institute there rather than scrap it. His father had owned the car from 1908 until 1921. She then belonged to Adam, who put her in the Institute in 1933, and she remained there until 1957 (Fig 198) when Bill Morton took on the restoration. He and two apprentices – Paul Gleave and Barry New – painstakingly rebuilt 26330 (Fig 199) and Bill let me drive her. Barry New, incidentally, retired from Rolls-Royce North America Inc in the last year or two, having meanwhile become an American citizen and the recipient of an OBE for services to Anglo American business relationships. Before his death in the 1980s Adam Dick gave the three-cylinder to the Royal Scottish Automobile Club, which has since found itself in financial difficulties. Andy Wood is currently caring for the car at P & A Wood, and the Rolls-Royce Enthusiasts' Club is trying to ensure that work is funded to secure her long-term roadworthiness. Bill Morton would not have been happy to see the way in which 26330 went off colour whilst in the museum at Doune.

The four-cylinder 'twenty' is better represented. The oldest survivor is 26350, which formed a part of C S Rolls & Co's first order on Cooke Street dated 3 March 1905. She was the first production 'Light 20' and spent many years from January 1906 until 1945 in either Knutsford or Manchester, ultimately being laid up in the garage of Royce's old home, Brae Cottage, Knutsford. Royce's nephew, Erroll Punt, learned of its existence in 1945 and went with Stanley E Sears to see it. Sears recorded elsewhere how nervously he waited for formal confirmation of sale from the tenant, Richard Davies (Fig 200), who had become a heavy drinker and died shortly after selling the car to him. Sears undertook an extensive restoration of 26350, which entailed using some components from a further four-cylinder 'twenty' – 40520 (Fig 201). The car remained with Sears until 1983, when it passed to James C Leake of Oklahoma. Happily she returned to Britain in 1987 and to the ownership of John Kennedy, Honorary Secretary of The 20-Ghost Club. John drives her in a manner which demonstrates just how spirited a car the 'twenty' was.

40509 is the only 'heavy twenty' to survive. She spent her early years in Australia – 1907 until 1947. Thereafter she moved to Chicago, then Toronto, then New York, and Reno, Nevada, before returning to Britain in 1987 (Fig 202). She now resides in Manchester but is rarely seen compared with 26350.

The third four-cylinder is 'light twenty' 40520. Her engine was tested on 22 March 1906, so the car was largely completed by Royce Ltd before Rolls-Royce was registered as a company on 15 March. Stanley Sears acquired 40520 in 1939 but she passed to Tom Love in 1983. Today 40520 resides alongside 20154, the oldest Rolls-Royce in the world, with Tom in Northern Ireland.

One six-cylinder 'thirty' remains and, again, the late Stanley Sears was the leading figure in bringing an early Rolls-Royce back from the brink of oblivion.

26355 was a 'short thirty' and her engine was tested on 11 January 1906. After being owned by a number of individuals in England she was exported to Australia in the 1920s and, in 1939, was acquired by a farmer in South Australia. Her remains were recovered in 1956 (Fig 203) and, two years later, Stanley Sears acquired the remnants and shipped them back to Britain. Phenomenal effort led to 26355 becoming roadworthy again and the author recalls the occasion when Sears brought her to Derby (Fig 204). XAP 1, as she was re-registered … 'ex Australian parts', as Stanley suggested it indicated, … was placed in the Welfare Hall and, to allow the hub nuts to get through the doors, the steel doorframe had a notch sawn out of it. Since Stanley Sears parted with the car in 1977, she has resided with owners in Switzerland, the UK, Oklahoma and Florida. In recent months she has been with P & A Wood and, at the time of writing, remains in the UK pending shipment to her latest owner in the Middle East (Fig 205).

Some ten 40/50 hp cars built at Cooke Street remain, the earliest being 60547 which was one of the first 'production' chassis, tested in March 1907. The most famous of them all, 60551, 'The Silver Ghost' herself (Fig 206), registration AX 201, was acquired back by Rolls-Royce in 1948 and remains the property of Crewe to this day, albeit now as Bentley Motors Ltd. Perhaps the most original and untouched of all early survivors, however, is 60577 which, even in her early days, was known as 'the auld lady'. She now belongs to Graham Mead, not far distant from Derby.

The people who worked at Cooke Street

It is inevitable that no-one survives who can talk at first-hand of Cooke Street days, yet many remain who remember those who did. Among them is Frank Shaw, Chairman of the Sir Henry Royce Memorial Foundation, whose father worked there long before Frank himself joined the staff in Derby. Many sons and daughters followed in their parents' footsteps, as will have become apparent from reading this book. Then came the grandchildren and, today, great grandchildren. When I joined Rolls-Royce in 1959 the application forms sought details of any relatives who already worked, or had worked, for the Company. Such practice would be seen as discriminatory now, yet succeeding generations do seek to join the Company on the basis of merit alone. Earlier in this chapter I referred to quirks of fate. After completing this script my wife and I were invited to join our daughter for dinner to celebrate her husband's birthday. Our son-in-law is Martin Roden, and his parents joined us for the meal. Some days earlier Tom Clarke had suggested I include his listing of all known Cooke Street employees as a tribute to their memory. I had done this and noted a 'Roden' had been listed. Martin's father, John, had worked for Rolls-Royce so I asked him if his grandfather had been at Cooke Street. He did not know, as he had limited knowledge of his family history. What he did know was that his grandfather as well as father had worked for Rolls-Royce in Derby. Both had been Henry Rodens. He also knew that his grandfather had joined Rolls-Royce from Bolton, where he had been a machinery setter in the mills. On returning home I checked Tom's listing: H Roden. So, beyond reasonable doubt, my son-in-law is the great grandson of a Cooke Street employee.

The achievements of the Cooke Street team were outstanding under Royce's leadership. They called him 'pa' behind his back yet when, years later, the employees made a gift to him when he received his Baronetcy, he wrote in thanks, adding beneath his signature *"sometimes known as father"*. He didn't miss much! Among the employees were saints and sinners alike and, if they had one fault, it was that they stuck tightly together on moving to Derby. As the workforce grew, the dwindling core of Cooke Street men and women were sometimes viewed as clannish. It is my personal belief that this would have been far less so were it not for the episode of Rolls-Royce of America Inc when the 'Silver Ghost' and later the New Phantom were produced in Springfield. Many of the very best people Rolls-Royce had were posted there including Maurice Olley – who postdated Cooke Street – plus leading figures from Cooke Street such as George Bagnall. In truth, they were those whose power or intellect might have challenged Wormald's iron grip on all but the design and experimental teams at Nightingale Road. And, with few exceptions – Gilbert Humpston and Bob Moon's fathers being among them – they weren't absorbed back when car production ceased at Springfield. It would be fair to add, though, that the depression affected Britain as well as America and the early 1930s was the period when Rolls-Royce was held to stand for 'rush 'em and rest 'em' due to the practice of temporary lay-offs.

Of course, a number of the drawings, ledgers, memos, formal letters, original photographs and legal agreements on which Cooke Street worked and which would have been familiar to the Drawing Office, De Looze's team or Watkins' contracting team survive. They tend to be in the safekeeping of the Rolls-Royce Heritage Trust or Sir Henry Royce Memorial Foundation, and many have been source documents in writing this book.

One or two smaller documents remain which reflect on the social activities. One is the menu and programme for Royce Limited's annual employees' dinner and smoking concern (Fig 136) held at the Corn Exchange Hotel on 27 January 1906, some six weeks before Rolls-Royce Limited was registered. Perhaps unexpectedly, bearing in mind his rather dour traits, we note that De Looze was not only Chairman of the dinner committee but also the proposer of the toast, *"The Firm"*. Other members of his committee had names which will now be familiar to the reader, all accorded the prefix 'Mr': Croston, Cheetham, Smithson, Mills, Barlow, Taylor and Morrison. And a final touch, indicative of a sense of occasion and self-esteem, is *"carriages at 11pm"*. One suspects that, even in the case of De Looze, this might have indicated a contrivance of two wheels with pedals.

A poignant reminder of the 'old man' himself is his favourite pipe (Fig 207). We have remarked that Royce enjoyed a good pint of beer occasionally, but few people are aware that he also enjoyed smoking. He normally confined himself to a pipe, and his favourite 'charge' was Log Cabin tobacco. He still smoked when he moved to Derby but he was advised to give up after his first major illness in 1911. One could assume that the advisor was Dr Campbell Thomson. Rather than throw his best Manchester-made meerschaum pipe away, he gave it to Tommy Nadin who cared for it until around 1963. When the memorial window to Sir Henry Royce was unveiled at Westminster Abbey he handed the pipe to William Tait Gill *(WG)*, the Financial Director of Rolls-Royce Limited, during the Service. On returning to Derby, 'Willie' Gill handed the pipe over to me, then the Company's Corporate Historical & Information Officer, and it has remained in my safekeeping ever since, latterly with the Rolls-Royce Heritage Trust.

So what of Royce, his lieutenant in Derby – Wormald – and the latter's 'band of brothers'? This volume is hardly the right place to detail Royce's end in 1933. We have already noted that only two people attended his funeral at Golders Green. His ashes were left to Nurse Aubin, who subsequently agreed with officials in Derby that the resting place he would most have liked would be among the workforce on the shop floor. So it was that his ashes were placed, below a bronze bust created by William Macmillan, RA, in one of the bays of No 1 Shop. The bay was tiled and roped off, and the only person allowed to cross the rope was Ted Fould's mother, who kept the area pristine. As the 1930s progressed, the Marble Hall was created as a true VIP entrance to the Main Works. Tommy Haldenby had a section halfway along the Commercial Block removed and the Marble Hall added around 1938. Royce's bust was placed in its right-hand alcove, and one of Rolls was commissioned to match it for the left. The ashes remained on their own for a while until Ernest Hives *(Hs)*, then General Manager, called on one of his leading engineers, Dr Frederick Llewellyn Smith *(LS)*, to get them moved. Years later, when he came to retire as Director responsible for the Motor Car and Oil Engine Divisions, Llewellyn Smith recalled his embarrassment, *"I didn't know whether to call for a Minister or the millwrights!"* The ashes were moved, and now repose inside the village church at Alwalton, where he was born.

One wonders whether Wormald had a feeling that all was not well with his health when he called all the surviving Cooke Street employees who had transferred to Derby for a group photograph in his garden at Sunnymede in Littleover in 1935 (Fig 208). He was very strict in that some, like Frank Shaw's father, were invited to the occasion yet not allowed to pose for the photograph because they had broken their service between leaving Hulme and joining again at Derby. Three individuals were missing on the day, but photographs of them were taken and stuck on the right-hand side of the group. This is evident on an original which reposes in my office. It was recovered in 2003 from an outbuilding of a house which had belonged to a member of the Wormald family. Wormald retired on 15 October 1936. Weeks later he died.

Unpopular though it might have proved, Olley's letter to Hives quoted earlier provided a pretty accurate epitaph. However, he might have set about his task, he was undoubtedly a loyal and effective servant of Rolls-Royce.

From then on the numbers inevitably began to dwindle. De Looze himself (Fig 209) retired after fifty highly effective years' service in 1943 yet many remained to serve in the postwar era. Among them were Jimmy Broom (Fig 210) and Joe Capel (Fig 211) who had been out on the road driving one of the V-8s in the inspection of customers' cars. Joe's grandson, David, served in parallel with me and remains active with the Rolls-Royce Heritage Trust. When I joined the Company in 1959, however, few Cooke Street veterans remained and they had all long since retired. Ernie Wooler sometimes visited us from Florida, but far more frequent visitors were Tom Broome, 'Little Jimmy' Chadwick – who still lived round the corner at Davenport Road, George Clegg and Ben Pope. Tom and Ben remained in Derby whereas George and his wife had returned to their native land at Grundy Street in the suburbs of Manchester.

In the end the last to survive was Tom Broome. He attended the ceremony to mark the 75th anniversary of the formal opening of the Derby Works on 9 July 1983 (Fig 212) and that was probably his last 'public appearance'. Some time later his son, Derek, moved him from his home at Horwood Avenue in Derby to a nursing home near Northampton, where he could better keep an eye on him, grandson Toby having decided to leave Rolls-Royce in Derby. Tom survived to the age of 99 and in his last years was known to say, *"There's only me and Mike Evans remember what Cooke Street was like"*. Well, I didn't, but I took it as an enormous compliment. I attended his funeral and somehow had a strange yet powerful feeling that the 'old man' was there to mark the passing of the last of his team. This might sound like invention: it is, in fact, a confession, and one I find hard to admit.

As a world leader in providing power both under the sea and on it, on land and in the air, Rolls-Royce is everything the Memorandum of Association set out to achieve in March 1906. Today, a single Trent 800 engine gives well over ten times the power of every Rolls-Royce car built at Cooke Street added together, yet the Company will always owe a debt to those early employees. They knew they were making history and it was a beginning. More than that, it was a sure foundation for the first one hundred years, and it will prove to be equally so for the next.

Fig 165: Muriel Pritchard, granddaughter of Henry Edmunds, with the author at his aunt's home in Belfast in 1995. *(Author's collection)*

Fig 166: The Edmunds Trophy, now in the hands of the Sir Henry Royce Memorial Foundation. *(Photograph: Philip Hall, Sir Henry Royce Memorial Foundation)*

Fig 167: The last photograph of the doorway of 1A Cooke Street. It was taken by 'Old' Ben Brown on a nostalgic return to Manchester during the Second World War. Shortly afterwards a bomb destroyed all the front office block. Ben joined 'Royces' at Cooke Street as an apprentice in 1901 at the age of 14. He left at 17 because he could not live on six shillings per week, but he rejoined Rolls-Royce as one of the first to sign on in Derby, having cycled from Manchester. He worked permanently on nights until he retired in 1953 with 51 years' service.

Fig 168: Cooke Street from the corner shop after the Second World War. The buildings at 1A and 3 had been bombed in the war.

(Photograph: David Tod)

Fig 169: The first extension built by F H Royce & Co Ltd. The upstairs housed the drawing office and, beyond, that of De Looze and his staff. Toilets were situated between the drawing office and Billy Ellis' instrument department to the right. Their drains remained visible. *(Photograph: David Tod)*

Fig 170: The Blake Street entrance before demolition of the area began.
(Photograph: David Tod)

Fig 171: The Cooke Street factory being viewed by George Clegg shortly before it was demolished in 1965. George is standing roughly where the corner shop had been. The corrugated building occupies the area of the original offices at 1A Cooke Street.To the left is the 1896 extension, in the centre foreground the 1880s workshop and beyond the prefab is De Looze's office.

Fig 172: George Clegg reminiscing with the author at Cooke Street. Between them can be seen De Looze's office and beyond the 1880s fitting shop and, to its right, the two bay roof of the 1896 extension. Nearer, on the right, is the brass foundry and the gates leading to the Blake Street factory entrance. The open stable yard, then flattened, lay to the right-hand side of the boilerhouse.

Fig 173: Looking across the area once occupied by the stable yard and the boilerhouse with its whitened previously interior walls at the remains of the Cooke Street factory in 1965. The gates mark the Blake Street entrance to the factory.

Fig 174: The desolate remains, Cooke Street, Manchester in the winter of 1965. This view from the gallery clearly shows the 1896 extension and, beyond, the earlier premises. To the left are the main factory doors into Blake Street, a part of which belonged to the factory and was protected by the exterior gates shown in Fig 173.

Fig 175: In the cold of winter, the only sound to break the silence was that of droplets of water hitting the floor as the weak sunlight thawed the frost on the factory roof. It was hard to conjure up any image among the darkness and desolation of that vibrant culture which, some sixty years earlier, had created one of the greatest names in the history of engineering.

Fig 176: The unveiling of a plaque at a block of flats close to where Cooke Street had been. At this ceremony, which took place on 15 December 1965, were – left to right – Tom Broome, George Clegg, Alderman Bernard S Langton, Lord Mayor of Manchester, Dr F Llewellyn-Smith *(LS)* Executive Director responsible for the Rolls-Royce Motor Car Division, 'Little' Jimmy Chadwick, Ben Pope and Jimmy's brother.

Fig 177: The author viewing the plaque at Royce Court, which he had been given the honour to word. The plaque has since gone.

Fig 178: After the unveiling at Royce Court. From left to right: George Clegg, Tom Broome, Jimmy Chadwick and Ben Pope with The Silver Ghost, 40/50 hp, chassis 60551.

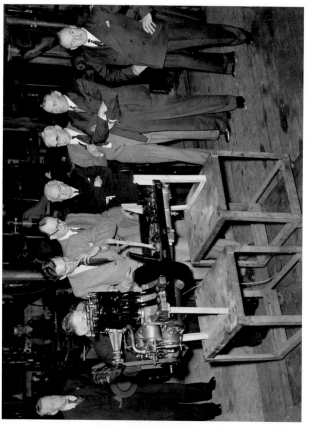

Fig 179: On the fiftieth anniversary of the meeting of Rolls and Royce in May 1954, the engine and gearbox of the second Royce prototype, which had been used by Claremont, were taken back to the Cooke Street factory where this photograph was taken. Behind the engine is Fred Bates (ex-Cooke Street), then Raymond Baxter from the BBC. Next is T S Haldenby (*Hy*) who tested the engine in 1904 with the late Eric Platford (*EP*). Beside him is A G Elliott (*E*), who had been Royce's principal design assistant from about 1912 to 1931. By 1954 he was Deputy Chairman of Rolls-Royce. Next is H I F Evernden (*Ev*) who had been on Royce's personal design staff and retired as Chief Engineer of the Motor Car Division. At his side is R N Dorey (*Dor*) who had worked on the R engine in Experi and run Hucknall Flight Test in World War II. By 1954 he was a Director and General Manager of the Motor Car Division. Lastly R F Messervey (*Msy*) who had been involved in persuading Avro to put four Merlin engines in the Manchester bomber, thus creating the Lancaster. He had recently retired as Manager of the Company's London Repair Dept.

Fig 180: The green sward at Hulme. Cooke Street and Blake Street would have run parallel, the former to the left and latter to the right. The factory stood roughly where the tree-covered knoll is now. Behind the camera is Stretford Road and set in the near foreground are 'timelines' for the area. The second image refers to Rolls-Royce. *(Author's collection)*

335

Fig 181: The 'in' and 'out' arches of the Carriage Court of the Midland Hotel. Today they form the main pedestrian entrance.   *(Author's collection)*

Fig 182: A modern depiction of the partnership of Royce and Rolls forms a major feature in the old Carriage Court at the Midland Hotel.

(Author's collection)

Fig 183: A small electric motor made by F H Royce & Co Ltd. It was still in use in 1963 in a shoemaker's shop when the Southern Electricity Board came across it during a campaign to standardise voltage.

Fig 184: A Royce Ltd electric capstan being recovered from the Co-op warehouses at St Mary's Wharf in Derby, 1979. Rescue work is seen being carried out by the late Keith Kidger of the Rolls-Royce Enthusiasts' Club. The capstan is now at the Sir Henry Royce Memorial Foundation's premises at Paulerspury, and is once again in working order.

337

Fig 185: The Royce crane still in use in the Rolls-Royce works at Nightingale Road, Derby, in 2003.

Fig 186: War damage. The Royce crane was damaged by shrapnel when a lone German raider bombed the Rolls-Royce works at Nightingale Road in the Second World War.

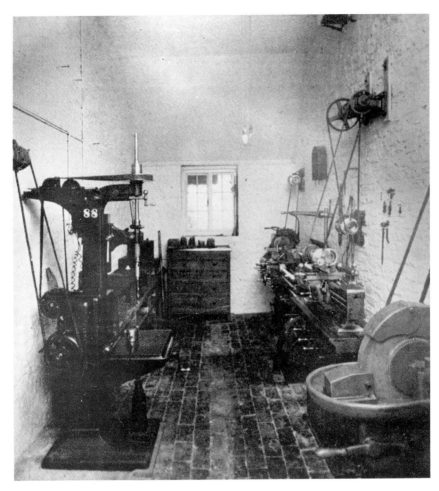

Fig 187: The Rivett lathe is visible on the right in this photograph of Royce's workshop at Elmstead, West Wittering.

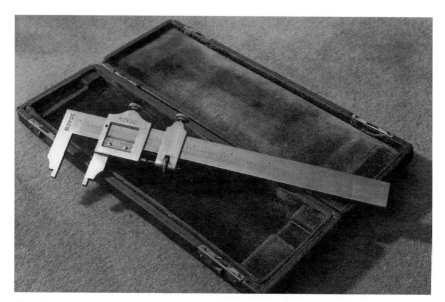

Fig 188: Royce Vernier calliper held to have been Henry Royce's personal instrument. In the author's early days with the Company it was on display at the Sandown Road training school. It has not been since 1971.

Fig 189: Royce's Rivett lathe now on display in the RRHT Heritage exhibition at the Learning & Development Centre at Sinfin in Derby.

Fig 190: Products of F H Royce & Co Ltd and Royce Ltd preserved by the RRHT.

Fig 191: The Cooke Street master clock now in the safekeeping of the RRHT.

Fig 192: Percy Binns at the wheel of 20154 (U-44) while in his possession. Oliver Langton acquired it from Binns and undertook the renovation. To be historically correct, the radiator should bear no badge.

Fig 193: The oldest Rolls-Royce car in the world, 1904, chassis 20154. It was rescued in much modified form in 1920 by Percy C Binns of Leeds and Harrogate. Between 1950 and 1977 it was restored and used by Oliver Langton of Leeds and then acquired by Tom Love then of Perth, Scotland, who kindly took the author out in it after it came into his possession. At the wheel is the author's wife. Tom now has 20154 in Ireland. *(Author's collection)*

Fig 194: 20162 (AX 148) reunited with Sir Henry Royce at Elmstead, West Wittering in 1931. Sir Henry is at the wheel and beside him is Neville Minchin.

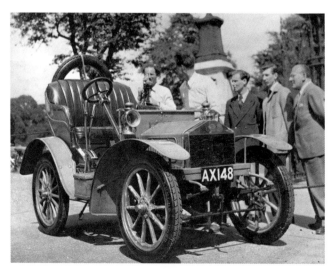

Fig 195: The third of the four remaining two-cylinder cars, chassis number 20162, dates to 1905. Sent to C S Rolls & Co as stock it received the Monmouth registration number AX 148, which it carries to this day: Rolls used many AX registration numbers. It was sold in 1906 to Paris E Singer, son of the sewing machine magnate. By 1930 it belonged to Sir John Prestige and it was from his London home that it was taken to West Wittering for Sir Henry Royce to examine and take a ride in. Rolls-Royce acquired 20162 in 1935 and donated it to the Science Museum in London.

344

Fig 196: 20165 (SU 13) at Nightingale Road shortly after being given to Rolls-Royce by its grateful owner, Dr Sidney Gammell, in 1920.

Fig 197: One of the four remaining two-cylinder 10 hp Rolls-Royce cars. 20165 was originally delivered to Dr Sidney J Gammell, a Scottish doctor from Bielside early in 1907. After some 100,000 miles good service he donated it to Rolls-Royce in 1920 when he took delivery of a 40/50 hp Silver Ghost. It remained with Rolls-Royce at Derby and Crewe until VW acquired Crewe. It is still at Crewe, but now belongs to Bentley. From new, 20165 has borne the same registration, SU 13. It is shown here shortly after the Second World War with Harry Fleck, one of C S Rolls' demonstration drivers, at the wheel.

Fig 198: 26330, the only known three-cylinder '15' being removed from the Dick Institute in Kilmarnock in 1957.

Fig 199: The one remaining three-cylinder 15 hp Rolls-Royce car, chassis number 26330, built in 1905. It was meticulously restored by Bill Morton, then the author's apprentice tutor, who was brave enough to insist that he drove it one evening on the public highway. Bill is at the wheel. Next to him is 'Little 'Jimmy Chadwick who worked on the early cars at Cooke Street.The third occupant of the car is Adam McGregor Dick, who saved the car from destruction over a period of many years prior to its restoration.

Fig 200: This four-cylinder 'Light Twenty' (26350) was effectively inherited by R G Davies when he purchased Royce's old home, Brae Cottage at Knutsford from T A Stuttard in 1938. Errol Punt came to hear of it and arranged to see it with Stanley Sears in 1945. Sears waited on tenterhooks while Reg Davies decided whether to sell. He died in 1946 shortly after selling the chassis to Sears.

Fig 201: The four-cylinder 'Light Twenty', 26350. The picture was taken at Prescott in 1953 with its restorer, Stanley Sears, at the wheel. This chassis was acquired from R G Davies who lived at Royce's old home, Brae Cottage, Knutsford after the Second World War. The chassis had been left at Brae Cottage by its previous owner, T A Stuttard, when he sold the house to Davies in 1938. It now belongs to John Kennedy of the 20 Ghost Club.

Fig 202: Another surviving four-cylinder 'twenty' (40509) photographed in Canada in the 1950s. It has since had two successive owners in America and four in Britain, moving to Manchester in 1990.

Fig 203: Retrieving the one remaining six-cylinder 'thirty' from a farm in Australia.

Fig 204: The one remaining six-cylinder 'thirty', 26355, visiting Derby on 10 September 1963 shortly after its mechanical restoration. Mr and Mrs Stanley Sears are in the car. Bill Morton is shaking hands with Mr Sears and looking on is Alec Harvey-Bailey. On the steps is Paul Gleave, ex-trainee, who together with Barry New had helped Bill rebuild the three-cylinder 15 hp.

Fig 205: A recent photograph taken at P & A Wood in Essex. A rare event - it shows, left to right, a two-, the three-, a four- and the six-cylinder models.

Fig 206: The Silver Ghost, chassis 60551, AX 201 on her most recent visit to the Marble Hall, Nightingale Road, Derby. David Preston, seen in the picture, and colleagues were driving her from John O'Groats to Land's End for a children's charity.

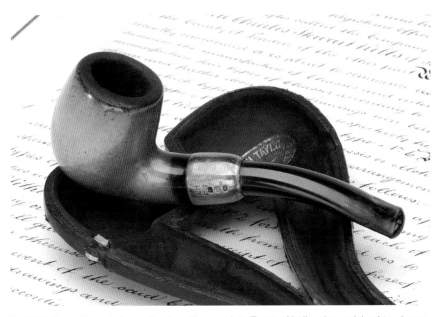

Fig 207: Henry Royce's favourite pipe. He gave it to Tommy Nadin when advised to give up smoking in 1911.

353

Fig 208: Cooke Street employees at Arthur Wormald's home, Sunnymede, in 1935. Although all serving ex-Cooke Street employees were invited, only those who had worked on cars at Cooke Street, and who had unbroken service, were allowed to sit for the picture. Frank Shaw, who was there, confirms the claim that they were clannish.

354

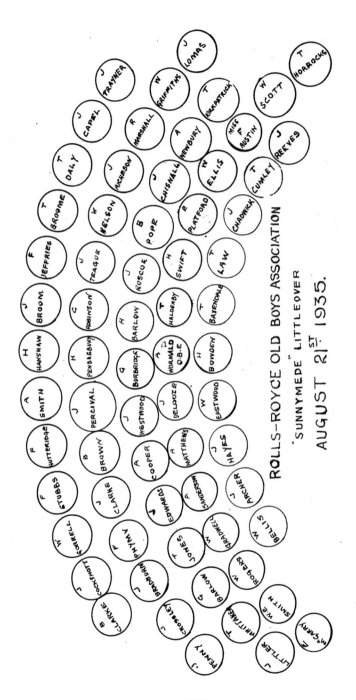

ROLLS-ROYCE OLD BOYS ASSOCIATION
"SUNNYMEDE" LITTLEOVER
AUGUST 21ST 1935.

Fig 209: John De Looze in the years before retirement in 1943. He was dour yet a committed and effective Company Secretary over fifty years.

Fig 210: 'Jimmy' Broom started at Cooke Street at the age of under 14 in 1899. When the picture was taken in the 1950s in Derby he was a turner on jigs and gauges. At the time he said, *"My daughter met her husband when they were working here and now he and my two granddaughters are here".* *(Photograph: COI)*

357

Fig 211: 'Joe' Capel started at Cooke Street in 1899. For a while he was personal mechanic to E A Claremont before he became involved with the visiting inspection service in which he travelled the country, surviving a skid which wrecked one of the V-8s. He elected to spend his later years in the Transport Department. When the picture was taken in the 1950s two of his sons worked for the Company. Later his grandson, David, did too, retiring in the 1990s. Joe retired in June 1953 after 54 years' service. He died in the autumn of 1955.

(Photograph: COI)

Fig 212: Tom Broome, a photograph taken on a return visit to No 1 shop, to mark the seventy-fifth anniversary of the official opening of the Rolls-Royce Derby factory by Lord Montagu's father on 9 July 1908. Tom was the last survivor of Cooke Street, living to the age of 99 and, like many others, his son Derek and then grandson Toby worked for Rolls-Royce. In his final days in a nursing home near Northampton, Tom used to tell callers, *"There's only me and Mike Evans remember what it was like at Cooke Street"*.

APPENDIX I
Sir Henry Royce
Great Northern Railway connections

Peterborough Works

Peterborough was a major traffic and operating centre on the GNR from the earliest days. As at other main centres, the locomotive shed was almost a miniature locomotive works and undertook much heavy maintenance work that would in more recent times have been handled by a central works. For many years there was, in fact, a Works Manager at Peterborough; Samuel Johnson (later Locomotive Superintendent of the Midland Railway at Derby) held this post in the early 1860s. This was not uncommon in the early days of railways. The GNR's principal works was at Doncaster, laid out in 1851 but not building any locomotives until 1868, but even so the tradition of carrying out intermediate if not general overhauls at the larger sheds persisted until the turn of the century if not later: Kings Cross shed carried out a complete rebuild on one of its locomotives as late as 1901. The reason was quite simple: it took anything from two to four months to carry out a general overhaul because standardisation was minimal and much of the work done with the most basic of tools. Doncaster had enough to do building new locomotives and overhauling the principal classes, so a lot of work was delegated to local centres. For this reason, although it did not actually build locomotives, Peterborough was, at the time Royce went there, effectively the second locomotive works of the GNR.

F Rouse

In the mid 1890s, he was District Locomotive Superintendent at Peterborough. As Peterborough provided the motive power for most of the principal expresses into and out of Kings Cross (to reduce the number of light engine movements in and out of Kings Cross shed over the congested approaches to the terminal) he was, in effect, if not in reality, in overall control of the southern end of the line. He reported directly to Patrick Stirling, the GNR's legendary Locomotive Superintendent (and son of the Rev Stirling of hot air engine fame).

It was to Rouse that on Wednesday 14 August 1895 Stirling sent one of the most famous of all internal railway memoranda, concerning anticipated competition with the West Coast Route to provide the fastest service to Aberdeen. Headed *"Very Important"*, it began with the following uncompromising statement: *"The L & N W Co have expressed their intention to reach Aberdeen before us. This, of course, we cannot permit ..."* and ended *"Put your men on their mettle!"* Stirling was not a 'good loser'! Neither, though, were the opposition, who scored a convincing victory. (ref *Railway Race to the North* by O S Nock, published by Ian Allan, 1958, p 98).

Locomotive rebuilds

Shortly before his retirement, Archibald Sturrock – Stirling's predecessor – ordered six large 2-2-2 locomotives, three from John Fowler & Co, Leeds, and three from the newly-formed Yorkshire Engine Company of Sheffield. The latter were, in fact, the very first order received by YE and carried works numbers 1-3; coincidentally, Alfred Sacré, a partner in the new firm, was a former GNR man from Peterborough. These were among the largest and most powerful express locomotives of their time and while under construction they were altered to 2-4-0s to improve adhesion.

Unfortunately, this introduced coupling rods no less than 9ft 7in long, by far the longest so far used on a British express locomotive, and in an age only just beginning to appreciate (and indeed to afford) the benefits of steel they were too long. Bent or thrown rods were a common problem in those days but these big 2-4-0s were worse than most. (ref *The story of the Steam Plough Works* by Michael R Lane, Northgate Publishing, 1980, pp 139/140).

Despite rapid advances in metallurgy and the widespread adoption of steel for motion work, it would be another 31 years before anyone used coupling rods of that length again!

Patrick Stirling had a horror of thrown or broken coupling rods; as a young man he had seen the result of a broken rod piercing the side of the firebox. Right to the end of his days (he died in office on 11 November 1895 at the age of 75) the fastest GNR expresses were hauled exclusively by 4-2-2 or 2-2-2 locomotives. It was hardly surprising, therefore, that between 1873 and 1878 the six troublesome 2-4-0s were rebuilt as 2-2-2s. Having been designed as such, the conversion was relatively simple. They were fitted with standard Stirling boilers in 1885-89 and withdrawn between 1898 and 1902. The details are as follows:

GNR No	Maker / No		Date delivered	Rebuilt 2-2-2	Withdrawn
264	JF	747	11/1866	10/1878	2/1900
265	JF	748	11/1866	11/1875	8/1901
266	JF	749	12/1866	12/1873	4/1899
267	YE	1	12/1866	2/1873	5/1902
268	YE	2	1/1867	3/1878	6/1901
269	YE	3	2/1867	3/1875	12/1898

Ref *British Locomotive Catalogue 1825-1923* by Bertram and David Baxter, Moorland Publishing, Volume 5B (1988) deals with the GNR.

Depending upon Royce's starting date at Peterborough, he may have worked on 264 or 268. The period taken to convert these locomotives suggests that it wasn't considered an urgent matter to be carried out at the next general overhaul. Presumably they were rebuilt as necessary, ie the next time the rods were damaged and the wheel quartering disturbed by a violent bout of slipping. As some, if not all, of them were stationed at Peterborough, they would naturally have been rebuilt there.

In later years, Royce seems to have had a horror of overloaded crank pins, this being the reason he would never entertain a radial engine. Might this be in part attributable to his earliest contact with the realities of rotating and reciprocating masses?

Rodney Weaver
RRHT Coventry Branch
25 February 1990

APPENDIX II
The description of the two-cylinder 10 hp car written by Henry Royce for Charles Rolls

SPECIFICATION OF "ROYCE" 10.H.P. PETROL MOTORCAR.

The Engineers' Car.

THE ENGINE is the twin cylinder type, 3¾" bore by 5" stroke, and is
capable of developing 12.B.H.P. on the brake when running at
a speed of about 1000 revolutions per minute. A very high
compression is used and very great economy of fuel is obtained.

THE CYLINDERS are cast complete in pairs, there being no internal joints
to maintain or leak. Cast iron of a very specially hard and
close grain is used to ensure a good wearing surface. The
design is such as to give the practical minimum of internal
surface to cool the gases; for this reason the inlet valves
are placed on top of the cylinders, which at the same time
provide excellent inspection openins to examine the condition
of lubrication and cleanliness of the cylinders and piston.

THE CRANKSHAFT is cut out of a solid forging of nickel steel, very hard
and tough, and is machined on all surfaces to ensure soundness.

THE BEARINGS are bushed with special bearing phosphor bronze, and duplex
oiling is provided to the main bearings by "ring" and "Splash"
and to the crank by "centrifugal" and "Splash"

THE CRANK CHAMBER is of aluminium and is in halves jointed horizontally,
the lower half carrying the complete bearing for the crankshaft,
very materially helping to ensure perfect lubrication, alignment
and repairs. An inspection door is provided to enable connecting
rods to be examined without dismantling.

THE CAMS and the half speed shafts and cams are machined from solid
forgings of steel and are afterwards carefully hardened. These
and the cut steel spur wheels driving them are completely enclosed
to ensure lubrication by "Splash" and to exclude dust.

THE CARBURETTER. is of the "Float" feed spray type, fitted with an automatic
valve for preventing the mixture becoming too rich when the suction
on the carburetter is great. It is provided with an efficient
(close fitting) hand throttle, to enable the gas to be shut off
(in such case as descending hills etc.) if required. There is
also provided a valve for modifying the richness of the gas. Both
of these are operated from the driver's seat.

THE CONTROL is extremely effective and is secured by the use of a very
sensitive and efficient centrifugal governor valve in the inlet
pipe. The governor is capable of controlling the engine at
any speed from about 500 to 1000 revs. - (equalling respectively
about 15 to 30 miles per hour, using top speed with normal gears)
and desired adjustment being made from the driver's seat.
Provision is also made for accelerating (by driver's foot lever)
to the utmost limit.

THE IGNITION is of the high tension type. Two accumulators each of about
1500 miles capacity are provided. These are coupled to the coil
and commutator through a two-way switch so that either can be
switched on instantly, and making it impossible to get both
incorrectly connected together.

THE COMMUTATOR is of the wipe pattern, the contacts being wide and substantial
and the brushes pressed on with long range springs which will give
practically constant pressure through great time.
A special contact is provided to ensure the commutator shaft being
properly earthed at all times, as we find the contact of well
lubricated bearings is not always satisfactory.
Coils are provided with tremblers of the high speed (Carpentier)
pattern, and the plugs are of the most reliable and substantial
proportions, (Standard thread 24 m/m diam. 1.5 m/m pitch)
An adaptor is sent in the tool box to enable the smaller plugs
(18 m/m diam.) sold in most large towns, to be used.

THE COOLER is of the Honeycombe Type, made of about 2000 thin metal tubes,
each separately throughly tinned and sweated together by immersion,
no corrosive soldering flux being used in the process. They are
carried on a substantial cast brass base and provision is made for
drawing off the water in frosty weather.

THE PUMP   consists of a pair of our bronze wheels on bronze shafts, running in a bronze casing. It is driven by one of the half speed shafts, through a flexible driver, therefore running at its very slow speed, (200 to 600 revs.) per minute.

THE TRANSMISSION CLUTCH   is of the internal cone type with leather and cast iron faces. It is of very large diameter with a wide face and the external part is made up of a heavy section of the flywheel, which ensures the friction surfaces remaining cool, even although imperfect manipulation the clutch might be made to slip considerably. The spring is of special pattern to give practically constant pressure through considerable range. No end pressure is exerted on any rubbing faces when the clutch is in working position. It is also self-contained so as to be exactly concentric. It is connected to the change speed gear box by universal joint.

THE CHANGE SPEED GEARS   are of the sliding gear type, having three speeds forward and one reverse, the direct drive being on the highest (i.e. third) speed. The normal gears are kept low so that the car will run up modern hills without changing from the top speed and a sufficient reduction is made when running on the second gear for the car to mount all but the steepest hills without further change being made. No expense has been spared to make all the parts from solid forgings of special tough steel which are afterwards case hardened. The journals are ground to exact standard dimensions after hardening. The bearings are made of phosphor bronze and are continuously lubricated by splash. Great care is taken that the aluminium gear case retains the lubricating oil.

THE SPEEDS   are three in number. The first, or slowest, enable the car to mount an incline of 1 in 5 (or 20%) without fear of pulling up the engine. The following gears are provided with the engine at 1000 revs. per minute:-

     1st. 7.5 miles per hour that is 12 Kilometers.

     2nd. 17   "   "   "   "   " 24   "

     3rd. 30   "   "   "   "   " 48   "

THE FOOT BRAKE is at the rear end of the gear case and acts upon the
differential gear.

The brake strap is lined with phosphor bronze and is effective
even when oiled.   This brake is <u>not</u> interlocked with the clutch,
and so the engine (with the gas turned off) can be simultaneously
used as an auxiliary brake when descending long and steep hills.

THE REAR AXLE is of particularly strong construction, the pinion of the bevel
gear being forged solid on its shaft.   It does <u>not</u> overhang its
bearing but has a well arranged bearing on each <u>side</u>, and the
construction is such as to ensure this shaft being exactly at right
angles and radial to the axle; the bevel wheel is turned from a solid
steel forging, and the teeth are planed on a machine producing the
highest possible degree of accuracy.

The differential gear is of the spur type; the wheel and pinions
being cut from nickel steel forgings, and these and the whole of the
above are enclosed in a substantial aluminium casing.

The revolving axles are high class nickel steel forgings, having
cut gears solid, therewith forming part of the differential gear, and
the outer ends are turned conical leaving solid keys upon which the
road wheel are fixed.   No loose keys are used in this construction.
The whole is so enclosed as to be oil retaining, self-lubricating,
and dust excluding.   Substantial tublar radius rods are provided to
keep the axle at right angles to the car, which avoid many of the
strains otherwise often imposed upon the central porition of the axles
on the springs.

The spring rests are free to revolve on the axle and the axle cannot
be turned (by the reaction of the bevel pinion) and the brake action
owing to the double rods forming a substantial and long lever, which
is supported by spring connection to the frame, thereby forming a somewhat elastive drive.

367

THE REAR HAND BRAKES, are of the internal double acting type having metal to metal surfaces, and are formed by expanding a band of metal within a drum which forms part of the driving wheel hub. Ample adjustment is provided to take up the wear, and being double acting the car is held equally well backwards as forwards. No material is used in the construction which will char and so reduce through heat the brake power. The bands are supported in such a way as to clear of the ring when the brake is off. They are also compensated to equalise.

THE WHEELS are of the Artillery pattern (wooden spokes) and are shod with very large tyres (considering the weight of the car), being 810 m/, (32") x 90 m/m (3½")

THE WEIGHT is about 12 cts. completed for the road.

APPENDIX III
Extracts from the formal agreement between C S Rolls and Royce Ltd
dated 23 December 1904

Dated 23rd Dec. 1904.

Royce Limited

—— and ——

The Hon.th C. S. Rolls

Agreement

21

Memorandum of Agreement made the

twenty[?] day of December One thousand nine hundred and four Between Royce Limited whose Registered Office is at Cooke Street Hulme Manchester (hereinafter called "the Company") of the one part and The Honourable Charles Stewart Rolls of South Lodge Rutland Gate in the County of London of the other part Whereas the Company has recently commenced or is about to commence as a department of its business the manufacture of Chassis and intends in particular to manufacture four types of Chassis according to specifications and as shown and further described by drawings now being prepared by the Company which types of Chassis are respectively hereinafter referred to as type N.º 2 type N.º 3 type N.º 4 and type N.º 6 And whereas the said Charles Stewart Rolls is a dealer in Chassis or Motor Cars and the parties hereto are desirous of entering into arrangements such as herein contained Now the parties hereto agree as follows:—

1. The Company will prepare and submit for the approval of the said Charles Stewart Rolls a Specification and a drawing or drawings showing the general arrangement in respect of each of the said four types of Chassis as to Type N.º 2 forthwith and as to the other three types within one calendar month from the date hereof.

2. Within four days after the receipt of the Specification and a drawing or drawings of any of such types the said Charles Stewart Rolls will give notice in writing to the Company stating whether he approves or otherwise of such specification and — drawing or drawings.

3. In the event of the said Charles Stewart Rolls approving of the drawing or drawings and specification of any of such types and giving notice accordingly the Company will manufacture and deliver to the said Charles Stewart Rolls a Chassis made in accordance with such specification and drawing or drawings as to Type N.º 2 within two calendar months after receipt of the notice of the approval aforesaid and as to the other types if the engine thereof (the form of which is not yet finally determined) be multiplied on the basis of the engine now determined upon for type N.º 2 within four calendar months from the receipt of such notice but if the engine shall not be multiplied as aforesaid within such time (not being more than six calendar months from the receipt of such notice) as the Company may deem necessary.

4. Forthwith after the receipt of any Chassis pursuant to the last paragraph the said Charles Stewart Rolls shall test the same on the road and may subsequently submit such Chassis to examination (for

1

The Schedule above referred to.

In the case of Chassis of Types N°. 2 and N°. 3 the due dates for delivery shall be as follows:-

The first Chassis of either such Type shall be deemed to have been delivered on the day when the same shall have been finally approved.

The subsequent Chassis of either such Type shall be severally due for delivery at intervals of one calendar month commencing from the date of the approval of the first Chassis of such type.

In the case of Chassis of Types N°. 4 and N°. 6 the due dates for delivery shall be as follows:-

The first Chassis of either such type shall be deemed to have been delivered on the day when the same shall have been finally approved.

The second and third Chassis of either such type shall be due for delivery 22 days and 44 days respectively after the date of the approval of the first Chassis of such type.

The fourth fifth and sixth Chassis of either such type shall be due for delivery 22 days 44 days and 66 days respectively after the due date for delivery of the third chassis of such type etc etc.

Claude Rolly

Witness.

C. Johnson
Claude Goodman Johnson
120 St James Court
Buckingham Gate
London S W

12.

APPENDIX IV
Employees at Cooke Street works, Manchester
Compiled by Tom Clarke and extended by the author

Notes:

- Many employees were at Cooke Street over short periods. At any one time for instance, the Drawing Office had little more than half the names listed.
- * denotes transfer to Derby

THE EARLIEST DAYS AT BLAKE STREET

F Henry Royce (1863-1933)	1884-1933	*
Ernest A Claremont (1863-1922)	1884-1922 Chairman	
Thomas Weston Searle (?-1904)	Probably freelance	
S Kendall	Paid for Sunday overtime in 1887	
T Mulcahy	Paid for Sunday overtime in 1887	
E Taylor	Paid for Sunday overtime in 1887	
(the above three may have been women – about six were employed)		
'Old Tom' Jones	c 1887 Ninth employee	*

EARLY 1890s

John De Looze	1893-1943 Company Secretary	*
Jimmy Whiteley	First turner	

LATE 1890s

William Thompson Anderson (1870-1957)	Joined in 1893 as a outside erector
D H Casson	Site contracting team
W Crowe	Worked on Penny Bridge contract
R D Hulley	Director: Royce Ltd
James P.Whitehead (1860-1932)	Director of Royce Ltd in 1894

MOTOR CAR ERA

Works Security

Sgt 'Jack' (? Ralph) Bennett	Commissionaire	*
G Schofield	Caretaker	

Print Room

Miss Unwin

Small office

J H Watkins	Site contracts manager: Royce Ltd

Small office

A Sanderson (1874-1960)	1903-	*

Typists office
Miss Weeks

General office

W Chiltern		*
J Davies	Clerk	
E Gorrell	Cashier	*
J Ritson		*
G Robinson	Cashier	*
Alfred E Hook	1891-? Bookkeeper	
Miss Outram (1877-?)	Nursing sister	*
Miss Towers		*

Directors office

Ernest A Claremont	Chairman	
F Henry Royce	Managing Director	*
Miss Gertrude W Blackley	Typist	
Miss Anne J Deas	Secretary to Royce	
Miss Irwin (? Uren)-		
(Unwin) (? both)	Photographer (apparently in or near this office)	

Company Secretary's office

John De Looze (1872-1953)	Company Secretary 1893-1943	*
W ('Bill') Johnson		
William Kenyon	Succeeded D as Company Secretary of Royce Ltd	
A Lomas		
Joe Lomas (?-1957)	1907	*
Mr Kilner		*
Ernest Parker (1888-?)	1903-1906 sales: then to William Arnold	
Ben Pope (1889-?)	1906-1955 sales	*
? W Sanderson		
S G Wheeler		*
Herbert Wooler (?-1903)	Previous commercial salesman (Ernie Wooler's father)	

Drawing office

A J Adams	Chief draughtsman in earliest car days	
Mr Arnold	Died of an ear infection	
Jimmy Bradburn	Assistant	*
Jack S Cockshott (? - after 1978)	1908-? m Maud Blomley: i/c tracers	*
Mr Faulknes (or Faulknet)		
T Stanley Mercer (1884-1972)	1908 Draughtsman	*
Miss McLaren	Tracer (designer of radiator badge?)	
Thomas Nadin (1885-1979)	Pre 1903-?	*
George Tilghman Richards (1883-1960)	1904-1906 Draughtsman	
Mr Shipley	Worked on General Arrangement board. Died young.	
Ralph Simpson	1907-1910 Shipley's replacement. To USA in 1910.	
R D Spinney		
S Sumner		
Mr Taylor	Moved from tool and fixture design onto 3-cyl 15 hp.	
George Tundley	Junior draughtsman	
W H Watson		*
Ernie Wooler (1888-1969)	1903-? Apprentice. Derby and USA	*

Woodworking and Pattern Shop

Walter Cheetham	Patternmaker	
W Croston	Died aged 30 before end of WWI	
Tony Pegg	1908-? Patternmaker	*

Brazing Shop

(W 'Billy' ?) Smithson

Instrument Department

W 'Billy' Ellis	Foreman	*
Florrie Austin (MBE) (1882-1964)	1896-1947 Forewoman in 1905	*
Mrs Lily Blake	1894-? Female supervisor	
George Clegg (1886-1972)	1906-1956 Carburettors	*
Henry Watkins	Coils	
Mr Bedding	? to Trafford Park	

Main Shops

George Bagnall	Shop general foreman Derby & Springfield	*
G Barlow		*
Harry Barlow (1887-?)	1906-?	*
Fred Bates	1905-1908 to Cockshoot	
T (Tom?) Baxendale	Succeeded at Rolls-Royce by his son Tom	*
W 'Mac' Bellis	Boring machines	*
Billy Blackshaw		*
H Brierley	1906-1914	*
Tom Broome (1890-1990)	1906-1955. Chief Planning Engineer in Derby. Last survivor of Cooke Street. Succeeded by son Derek and grandson Toby.	*
'Old Ben' Brown (1887-1957)	1901-1904: 1908-?	*
George Burbridge (1873-1953)	1905-1945	*
Joe Capel (1887-1955)	1899-1953 Succeeded by sons then grandson David	*
Joe Chisnall		*
'Bandy' Clarke (? J Clarke)		*
Bert Clarke	Setter	*

H Clarke		
A Cooper	(? Mechanic to Northey in 1906 TT)	*
H V Colton	1902-1906	
J Crossley		*
Tom Cumley	Succeeded by son Harry	*
T Daly		*
Mr Davis	First Works Manager in Derby	*
Bert Day (1885-?)		*
Walter Eastwood		*
J Edwards		*
Joe Entwhistle		*
Walter Ellis		
F Finn		
J H Geddes	1899-1908 Played the violin too	
Alf Golding	1906 Foreman	
W ('Billy') Gradwell	1906-?	*
Walter Griffiths		*
F Gutteridge	Foreman on lathes	*
W Hallam	Became Car Repair Manager in Derby	*
H Hanshaw		*
Jack Hayes		*
Tommy Horrocks		*
G Howarth	Went later to Australia	
Miss May Hyde		*
T Hyde		*
F Jeffries		*
Jack Johnson	Bearing scraper	
T Jones		*
T Kirkpatrick		*
Tommy Law		*
J Littler		*
R Marshall		*
Walter Marshall		
Eddie McGarry	Vertical borer – cylinder blocks	*
Ernie Mills	Foreman Chassis Build	*
A 'Tim' Newbury	Worked on Rolls-Royce	
	40 mm gun in WWII	*
Joe Penny	Miller – crankcases	*
Joe Percival		*
Bill Peskett	?-1945 Succeeded by son, Bill, head	
	of Plant & Equipment into the 1960s	
	and grandson Inspector, No 1 Shop	*

Ted Poole	Derby then Springfield	*
Jack Reeves	Became a foreman in Derby	*
F Robinson		
H (Henry?) Roden	(Fitter from Bolton. Son and grandson worked for Rolls-Royce ?)	*
Percy Rose	Became Director of Morris Commercial post 1922	
J (? Jimmy) Roscoe		*
Charles Scoltock (1888-after 1979)	1903-? Toolmaker	
W A (? 'Billy') Scott (1885-1959)	1907-?	*
Joe Shaw	Father of Frank Shaw, Chairman SHRMF	*
Arthur H Smith (1892-?)	1906-?	*
Fred Stubbs	1904-?	*
H J 'Harry' Swift	(? Cooke Street) Became Works Mgr in Derby	*
George Taylor (survived until after 1965)		
Jimmy Teague		*
James R Trayner	(? Father of Walter, Wks Mgr, Hucknall)	*
J Westwood		*
Albert Wheatman	Turner	
J Whittaker		
Tommy Whittaker		*
Mr Willis	Second apprentice of Rolls-Royce Ltd (after Ernie Wooler)	

Toolroom

J Aitchison		*
James Archer	Foreman: son Len worked in Derby	*
Harry Angel		
Ernie Cowgill		
Rowland Marshall	Miller	
Alf Matthews		*
Bill Reilly	Foreman	
W E 'Billy' Smith (1887-?)	1901-1959	*
Albert Underwood	Turner	
Arthur Wormald (1873-1936)	1904-1936 Works Mgr and Director in Derby	*

Brass Foundry

H 'Joe' Bowden		*
A Kesterton		*
W ('Bill') Nelson (1886-?)	1901-?	*

Hardening Shop

H Pendlebury	*

Car Testing

T S ('Tommy') Haldenby (1886-1965)	1900-? Became Chief Plant & Equipment Eng'r	*
G E ('Eric') Platford (1883-1938)	1900-1938 Became Chief Tester	*

Monitor Shop (Capstan lathes)

Jimmy Broom	Started in Transport Dept 1898- post WW2	*
Jimmy Chadwick (1886-1968)	1900-?	*
Joe Chiswell		
W ('Billy') Gladwell	Became foreman in Derby	*
W H ('Billy') Rogers (1872-1968)	1898-? Foreman	*
Ernie ('Charlie Chaplin') Taylor		
Ike Turner		

Finished Parts Stores

Jim Roney (?-1948)	Storekeeper
? Dave Mallen	
'Wiggy' Taylor (?-1953)	?-1945 Given Royce's chair

Names not aligned with location

From menu/programme card Royce Ltd Annual Dinner and Smoking Concert January 1906 (which may include Trafford Park employees)

Mr Davies	Played piano
Mr Speight	Sang
Mr Macrorie	Sang
Mr Logan	Sang
Mr Purch	Recital
Mr Walkden	Recital
Mr Morrison	Committee member
Mr Allen	
Horris G Bevan	Lived at 3 Cooke Street whilst leased to F H Royce & Co Ltd in 1891.Possibly employee.
R Collis	
Mr Cooper	Worked in a foundry at Cooke Street. Brass was cast there, iron at Trafford Park, but we do not know where aluminium was cast. Suspect Cooper worked in aluminium. He became a foreman on light alloy casting in Derby. His son, Ernest A Cooper, died in Littleover, Derby, in January 2004: he had not worked for Rolls-Royce.
John W Craven	Lived at 3 Cooke Street whilst leased to F H Royce & Co Ltd in 1891. Possibly employee.
John Dobson	Apprentice started 5th January 1901
George Hancock (1883-?)	1906 ? might this be 'Titch' Hancock, tester in charge of Chateauroux in the 1930s
Robert S Newton	1890s Apprentice electrical engineer
F Phyms	*
Herbert Grace Richardson	1891-1895 At least apprentice
Mr Storrar	Grandson Mick in No 2 Shop, Derby into the 1990s
Joseph Whiteley	Lived at 3 Cooke Street whilst leased to F H Royce & Co Ltd in 1891. Possibly employee.

The Historical Series is published as a joint initiative by the Rolls-Royce Heritage Trust and The Rolls-Royce Enthusiasts' Club.

Also published in the series:

No 1   *Rolls-Royce - the formative years 1906-1939*
            Alec Harvey-Bailey, RRHT 2nd edition 1983
No 2   *The Merlin in perspective - the combat years*
            Alec Harvey-Bailey, RRHT 4th edition 1995
No 3   *Rolls-Royce - the pursuit of excellence*
            Alec Harvey-Bailey and Mike Evans, SHRMF 1984
No 4   *In the beginning – the Manchester origins of Rolls-Royce*
            Michael H Evans, RRHT 2nd edition 2004
No 5   *Rolls-Royce – the Derby Bentleys*
            Alec Harvey-Bailey, SHRMF 1985
No 6   *The early days of Rolls-Royce - and the Montagu family*
            Lord Montagu of Beaulieu, RRHT 1986
No 7   *Rolls-Royce – Hives, the quiet tiger*
            Alec Harvey-Bailey, SHRMF 1985
No 8   *Rolls-Royce – Twenty to Wraith*
            Alec Harvey-Bailey, SHRMF 1986
No 9   *Rolls-Royce and the Mustang*
            David Birch, RRHT 1997
No 10   *From Gipsy to Gem with diversions, 1926-1986*
            Peter Stokes, RRHT 1987
No 11   *Armstrong Siddeley - the Parkside story, 1896-1939*
            Ray Cook, RRHT 1989
No 12   *Henry Royce – mechanic*
            Donald Bastow, RRHT 1989
No 14   *Rolls-Royce - the sons of Martha*
            Alec Harvey-Bailey, SHRMF 1989
No 15   *Olympus - the first forty years*
            Alan Baxter, RRHT 1990
No 16   *Rolls-Royce piston aero engines - a designer remembers*
            A A Rubbra, RRHT 1990
No 17   *Charlie Rolls – pioneer aviator*
            Gordon Bruce, RRHT 1990
No 18   *The Rolls-Royce Dart - pioneering turboprop*
            Roy Heathcote, RRHT 1992
No 19   *The Merlin 100 series - the ultimate military development*
            Alec Harvey-Bailey and Dave Piggott, RRHT 1993

383

The Technical Series is published by the Rolls-Royce Heritage Trust.

Also published in the series:

Books are available from:
Rolls-Royce Heritage Trust, Rolls-Royce plc, Moor Lane, PO Box 31, Derby DE24 8BJ